Across the Great Border Fault

Across the Great Border Fault

THE NATURALIST MYTH IN AMERICA

KEVIN DANN

Rutgers University Press
New Brunswick, New Jersey, and London

Copyrights and Permissions:

"To Elsie" by William Carlos Williams, from *Collected Poems: 1909–1939*, volume I. Copyright © 1938 by New Directions Publishing Corp. Reprinted with permission of New Directions Publishing Corp.

Material by Benton MacKaye cited with permission of Dartmouth College, Rauner Special Collections Library

Library of Congress Cataloging-in-Publication Data

Dann, Kevin T., 1956–
    Across the great border fault : the naturalist myth in America / Kevin Dann.
      p. cm.
    Includes bibliographical references (p.).
    ISBN 0-8135-2790-2
    1. Natural history—Philosophy. I. Title.

QH14.3 .D36 2000
508'.0973—dc21   99-053245

British Cataloging-in-Publication data for this book is available from the British Library

Manufactured in the United States of America

To Jack Focht of the Trailside Museum and Fred Paddock of the Rudolf Steiner Library, whose devotion to their institutions has helped so many enlarge their understanding of Nature and History

CONTENTS

PREFACE

In September 1989, when I entered the graduate program in history at Rutgers University, I quickly became aware that the historical profession was in the midst of an existential crisis. Francis Fukuyama's essay "The End of History" had appeared just a few months before; although it referred to contemporary political events, its title gave voice to a widely felt anxiety among historians. The apparent abandonment of the "noble dream" of historical objectivity and the simultaneous death of narrative seemed to shake historians' confidence in their ability to impart meaning to even the shallow strata of the recent past. At Rutgers, I worked under Calvin Luther Martin, a rogue historian of North American Indians whose primitivist romanticism captivated many students, including myself. Martin saw history as a trap from which we had to extricate ourselves, preferably via the adoption of the eternal return of a mythological worldview. Although his colleagues resisted going native with him, his stance was just one example of a widespread dissatisfaction with traditional forms of academic storytelling.

In May 1991, after finishing my graduate coursework, I took a three-day walk in the Ramapo Mountains. I started at a favorite waterfall that nearly exactly straddles the Ramapo Fault, the tectonic raison d'être for such fine mountain tramping so close to the New York metropolis. Having grown up nearby, I had been there perhaps a hundred times to bathe in a little pool at the top of the falls. I can conjure the sound of the water there, see the liverworts flanking the place where water tumbles into the pool. A big chestnut hulk, fallen no doubt before 1920, spanned the brook in 1991 exactly the way it had on my first visit twenty-five years before. Water-polished gneiss forms familiar handholds on either side of the pool. The outer branches of a witch hazel shrub hang over one side; I remember that it was here that I first noticed the yellow confetti flowers appearing so out-landishly in November.

But never had I glimpsed the iridescent cerulean streak of a skink's tail while visiting this pool. Indeed, in all my days of walking the Ramapos, I had never seen a five-lined skink (*Eumeces fasciatus*, known in the Hudson Highlands as the "blue-tailed lizard"). I was transfixed the same way I remember being paralyzed by the sight of a copperhead that I al-most stepped on the previous spring while walking the Suffern–Bear Moun-tain trail for three days through fog, wrapped in the dripping chartreuse of mid-May's emergent leaves. When I grabbed the skink, its brilliant blue tail came off in my hand, and away it went, leaving me with an uncannily animated extremity and an overwhelming feeling of nature's ingenuity. De-cades of Darwinian schooling kicked in, and my thoughts ran toward the evolutionary dance of predator and prey, to the contemplation of natural selection's artistry in devising such a spectacular trick as a sequined squirm-ing decoy tail.

Like the flood of four-leaf clovers that follows upon the finding of the first one, skinks soon began to show themselves to me everywhere in the Ramapos. Little *Eumeces* greeted me at every southwest-facing knob of gneiss I visited after that poolside encounter. Bright jewels on the rust-stained Precambrian outcrops, they became one more in a long inventory of expressions of the Ramapo landscape, but special, because they had stayed invisible for so many years. They took their place in a mental map designed by Darwin, or at least by Darwin's amanuenses as I knew them: Helena Curtis's college biology textbook, Stephen Jay Gould's marvelous essays in *Natural History*, Paul Shepard's reveries on how animals helped humans become human, Hugh Cott's intriguing *Adaptive Coloration in Ani-mals*. For my undergraduate thesis in natural history, I had compiled a cur-riculum on adaptive coloration, celebrating natural selection's crafting of the visible spectrum for purposes of advertisement and camouflage.

A very different suite of colors—the "subjective" chromatisms of synaesthetes—had led me earlier that same year from Wassily Kandinsky's theories of art to the bizarre writings of Rudolf Steiner. When I came across art historians' references to Kandinsky's interest in Steiner, the name was not completely foreign. In the mid-1970s, in Santa Cruz, California, some of our neighbors' children attended the local Waldorf School, a chapter of the institution originally founded by Steiner in Stuttgart, Germany, in 1919. My knowledge of Waldorf School philosophy was typically superficial. I knew that Waldorf students were not taught to read until their second teeth erupted and that they made their own textbooks. Rudolf Steiner I came to know as a Theosophical Society "occultist" who had fantastic theories of human and cosmic evolution, who founded a form of agriculture called "biodynamics," and who lectured widely in Europe on such arcane topics as the esoteric dimension of bees. Not that I had ever read anything by Steiner; I only came to do this in 1992 after realizing that I must go to the source rather than read what art historians had to say about him.

The intervening years have brought me around to realizing that Rudolf Steiner's spiritual science—anthroposophy—had been for most of my life as near to me as the skinks, and every bit as invisible. Every few weeks my mother would drive the family station wagon about twenty minutes north of my childhood home in Ramsey, New Jersey, to prowl the discount outlets of Route 59 in Spring Valley, New York. On occasion I would go along for some back-to-school bargain. On those quick trips north, we passed right by the little hamlet of Hungry Hollow, where in the summer of 1933 a group of anthroposophists brought forth a very different view of Nature and History than the one displayed on the signs of the Trailside Museum at Harriman State Park.

In 1960, when my mother first started loading us into the car for her Spring Valley shopping trips, Ehrenfried Pfeiffer was still working in his lab at Hungry Hollow, conducting the crystallization experiments that made visible the invisible etheric formative forces. On Sundays, he lectured about the twentieth-century reappearance of Christ in the etheric realm and its meaning for humanity. At the twenty-seventh annual Anthroposophical Summer Conference in 1960, Pfeiffer's lectures included "The American Folk Soul," "Founders of the American Republic," "The Mission of America," and "Emerson and His Time."

Yet all this was invisible to me. Growing up during the 1960s, enveloped by the Arcadian myth, I inherited a civic religion whose rites centered on camping, hiking, and nature study. I followed in the footsteps of the founders of the Trailside Museum, becoming an interpreter of the natural world to audiences craving contact with the nonhuman world. Working as an interpretive naturalist for several of conservation education organizations, I gave children and adults the same spectacles for observing Nature as I had been given: spectator consciousness, paired with the organizing principle of evolution by natural selection. Somehow, through all the years of confidently explaining Nature's ways as they appeared to the senses, I must have harbored a secret doubt about the limits of the sensory. Beyond the bounds of the visible, the audible, the tactile, might there be something else? And if so, what did this mean for a nature-study epistemology founded on just the senses?

I had to wait twenty-five years before my senses awakened to five-lined skinks on the Ramapo rocks, and an equal number of years to discover that there existed a way of knowing nature and history other than that born of materialism. This book is offered in the hope that others will not have to wait as long.

ACKNOWLEDGMENTS

Though for most of my life I have been living with many of the places, characters, and issues taken up in this book, the opportunity to write about them came through a two-year postdoctoral fellowship from the National Science Foundation (NSF). As a participant in an NSF-funded project entitled "Nature, History, and the Natural Histocial Sciences," I was introduced to the scholarship and conviviality of the American history of biology community. I owe particular thanks to my fellow travelers in the NSF project—Juan Ilerbaig, Gary Kroll, Karin Matchett, Maureen McCormick, and Jon Synder—and to project directors Gregg Mitman, John Beatty, and Jim Collins. I received additional invaluable financial support from a Mellon Fellowship at the American Philosophical Society Library.

From Central Park to the Sonoran Desert, the historical trail I followed was well blazed by the librarians and archivists of the following institutions: the American Museum of Natural History; the American Philosophical Society Library; the Arizona-Sonora Desert Museum; the Rauner Special Collections of Baker Library at Dartmouth College; the Countway Medical Library at Harvard University; the Rudolf Steiner Library; and the Special Collections at Rutgers University's Alexander Library. Many thanks to the staffs of these repositories for their cheerful and generous guidance, and to these institutions for permission to publish materials from their collections.

Jack Focht, director of the Trailside Museum, opened many a door for me, and patiently heard out my ruminations; the Highlands may never again have as keen a student and as devoted a lover as they have had in Jack. Linda Powell walked the overgrown woods and roads of Halifax with me, and frankly but graciously guided me through the labyrinth of the

Houvenkopf's history. Henry and Christy Barnes generously shared their knowledge of anthroposophy and of Christy's father and uncle—Percy and Benton MacKaye—with me. Sara Tjossem kindly read and critiqued many of the chapters in an early draft. Finally, thanks to Helen Hsu of Rutgers University Press for her faith in this mercurial manuscript, and to the RUP staff.

Across the Great Border Fault

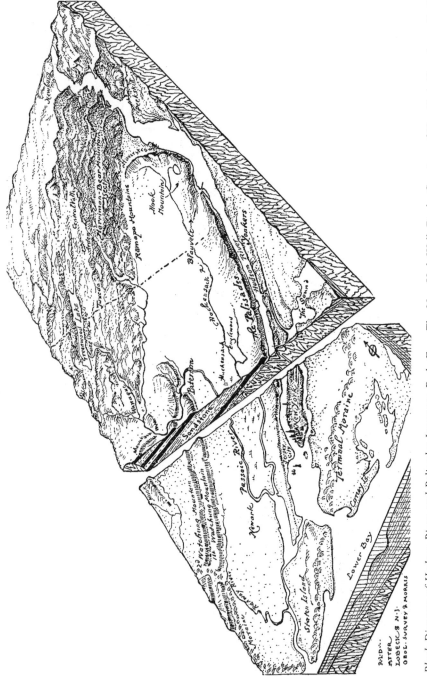

Block Diagram of Hudson River and Palisades Interstate Park. From The New York Walk Book. Courtesy of New York–New Jersey Trail Conference

Back to (Which) Nature?

Environmental History and the Arcadian Myth

"The Trouble with Wilderness; or Getting Back to the Wrong Nature," environmental historian William Cronon's 1994 essay, marked a turn in the scholarly literature exploring the human-land relationship in America. This literature takes a critical stance toward the long-held assumption among conservationists, nature writers, and many environmental historians that wilderness represents the highest good immanent in the physical world and that all declensions from wilderness are lapses from Eden. Cronon's essay appeared at a moment when scholars were intensively reexamining the myth of the frontier in American history, finding new and more inclusive narratives for understanding the five-centuries-long meeting of Europeans, and then Americans, with the native plants, animals, and peoples of North America. Only a decade before, at its birth, American environmental historical scholarship could fairly have been described as the academic wing of late-twentieth-century reform environmentalism, giving rhetorical support to the claims of environmental activists that Americans must find their way toward less exploitative relationships with the land that has so bounteously nurtured them.

Though still motivated by this desire for more benign forms of economic, social, and cultural production, environmental history has rapidly matured into a self-aware discipline that continually challenges its own limits. Mythic blind spots are identified almost as rapidly as they appear, as environmental history borrows and adapts insights from a wide range of disciplines. This self-realization is hardly limited to scholarly literature, finding its way into popular media catering to the wide audience of Americans seeking revitalized relationships with the natural world.[1]

Like environmental activists, environmental historians originally relied on the science of ecology to guide their narratives of how human culture has altered nature. Just ten years before his "Trouble with Wilderness" manifesto, which many environmentalists regarded as a dangerous capitulation to an ethos of "multiple use," Cronon had juxtaposed explorers' and colonists' accounts of the New England landscape with recent ecological literature, offering the scientific narrative of ecology as a transparent picture of what that landscape, *sans* human interference, was meant to look like. For Cronon and his fellow chroniclers of the human impact on the environment, ecological theories held a status not unlike that which Raymond Williams noted had long been enjoyed by nature: ecology described the essential constitution of the world, a sort of transcendent principle that could be counted upon to measure the degree of human folly in interfering with nature's essence. Environmental historians' recent escape from the myth of wilderness has been aided by a growing literature in the history of science, particularly works in the history of ecology. This distinctively American science, fledged a century ago at the moment of the "closing of the frontier," has come under scrutiny as a maker of its own myths in its pursuit of an objective picture of the "entangled bank" around us.[2]

At a certain moment during all of this self-examination, a few historians rediscovered a slim, smart, pathbreaking book that had been overlooked for nearly a quarter century. Working from an earlier awareness of a Jeffersonian agrarian myth within American history, Peter J. Schmitt, in *Back to Nature: The Arcadian Myth in Urban America* (1969), had neatly outlined the birth and development in postbellum America of a new "Arcadian" landscape of the imagination that deeply shaped twentieth-century attitudes toward nature. Borrowing the term less from its classical Roman associations than from nature writer John Burroughs, who in 1899 declared that "Arcadia" meant only a "scene of simple pleasure and untroubled quiet," Schmitt intuited the myth of Arcadia as both an idea and an actual place lying "somewhere on the urban fringe, easily accessible and mildly wild, the goal of a 'nature movement' led by teachers and preachers, bird-watchers, socialites, scout leaders, city-planners, and inarticulate commuters."[3] Schmitt convincingly demonstrated how the roots of this new Arcadian philosophy enjoining Americans to go "back to nature" grew entirely within late-nineteenth-century metropolitan culture, finding its most loyal adherents among urban moderns—writers, artists, clerics, social reformers, educators, and public intellectuals—longing for the premodern past. *Back to Nature* showed how Arcadianism, a philosophy once held passionately by a few metropolitans looking to transform America's physical and cultural landscape, became by the 1930s the reigning "style" of suburbia.

That style survives today. One need only walk into any Nature Company store, where "nature" is packaged as a therapeutic balm, to see the culmination of the historical process mapped by Schmitt for the early twentieth century. But the Arcadian myth lives on in certain arenas of scholarly endeavor as well as in popular consumer culture. Along with the myth of wilderness, the Arcadian myth forms the backdrop to the recent debates about social constructivism within writing on human-environment relations. Awareness of that myth can help to inform historical studies of landscape transformation, particularly in the "middle landscapes" of American parks and gardens, the physical expression of an ongoing twentieth-century quest for personal and social regeneration through the artful shaping of the physical and biological environment. In the last decade, the American "literature of place"—the principal vehicle of Arcadian mythmaking since the early-twentieth-century heyday of the "back to nature" movement—has stepped out of the myth and begun to explore more sympathetically the positive contributions that human beings have made to the diverse landscapes of America. The recent renaissance of regionalist study within the academy is another indication that Arcadianism has matured to the point where its call to go "back to nature" is being replaced with the invitation to go forward to a "second nature" cognizant of just how inescapably nature is as much a reflection of the human psyche as it is some transcendental Other capable of redeeming us.[4]

The Ramapo Mountains as a Middle Landscape

Although Schmitt's book—in its examination of nature study, school gardens, summer camps, the search for scenery in national parks, and the "new exploration" of the regional planning movement—gave a comprehensive overview of the sorts of places where the Arcadian myth was realized, it rarely focused in depth upon specific sites where the Arcadian myth translated into significant transformations of the American physical landscape. Perhaps nowhere in America was that transformation so actively and successfully pursued than in the Ramapo Mountains of southeastern New York State. On a satellite image of the New York metropolitan area, amid the patchwork of hues of reflected radiation, two nearly straight lines stand out in high relief. A north-south trending line at the mouth of the Hudson River marks the western shore of the island of Manhattan, the result of four centuries of riprapping and filling of the once irregular shoreline. Another, longer line slices from southeast to northwest, across northern New Jersey and southern New York State. North of that line, the crimson reflection of infrared radiation appears nearly unbroken; to the south, the gray, blue, and white areas are only infrequently dotted with red ones. The satellite image reveals that north of that line lies Arcadia—the crimson signifies healthy forest vegetation—and south of it lies Metropolis, the grays and whites denoting a landscape of asphalt, concrete, and denuded earth. If we were to drop earthward for a closer view, the boundary line between Arcadia and Metropolis would come into focus as most fundamentally a line of geological origin. The Ramapos, largely composed of Precambrian gneiss, are the front range of the Appalachian Mountains, rising up from the Ramapo Fault, the local name for a continent-long tectonic break once known as Logan's Line for the Canadian geologist who named it. To the east of this line, also called the Great Border Fault, lies the red sandstone bedrock and traprock ridges of the Newark Basin, a Triassic lowland that proved over the last four centuries a perfect terrain for the development of Manhattan's metropolitan hinterland.

From Bear Mountain on the Hudson, the Ramapos run southwest to a sharp end point wedged between the confluence of the Ramapo and Pompton Rivers, a short distance northwest of Paterson, New Jersey. The New York–New Jersey boundary, running perpendicular to the Ramapo Mountains, nearly bisects them. From end to end, the Ramapos present a fairly even wall—geologists and geographers occasionally refer to the mountain range as the Ramapo Rampart—the individual mountain summits differing by no more than a couple of hundred feet in elevation. The mountains have uniformly angled scarp faces that are turned toward the gentle lowlands of the Newark Basin. Until the end of the nineteenth century, the sharp rise in elevation marked by those fault scarp faces guaranteed that the Metropolis could spill only so far across the landscape. Eventually, however, the Arcadian impulse brought scores of Manhattanites and other metropolitans seeking regeneration in the region's forests.

Throughout the New York metropolitan area are scores of parks, parkways, zoos, public gardens, and other middle landscapes that owe their creation to the turn-of-the-century "back to nature" movement, but none approaches the scale and scope of Harriman State Park, which encompasses much of the northern Ramapo Mountains. Home to a vast walking trail system (one of the first in the nation), the original section of the Appalachian Trail, the nation's first nature trail and trailside museum, and extensive natural scientific field research in the early twentieth century, Harriman Park, on the eve of its one-hundredth anniversary, continues to serve as a major recreational outlet for seekers of Arcadian rejuvenation in the New York City region.

Arcadian Natural Science

The Arcadian landscapes created in the late nineteenth and early twentieth centuries were not solely playgrounds for city-weary metropolitans. With the rapid growth and development of the science of ecology after 1900, the protection of natural areas frequently had as its aim the preservation of biotic environments believed to be pristine enough to permit an understanding of undisturbed Nature. In 1917, two years after its founding, the Ecological Society of America (ESA) established a committee for the Preservation of Natural Conditions for Ecological Study. Professional ecologists in America were among the most vigorous advocates of natural-area preservation, and the ESA committee's work, culminating in the publication of *A Naturalist's Guide to the Americas* (1926)—a comprehensive description of areas suited to the conduct of natural scientific observation, experiment, and teaching—played a critical role in publicizing to ecologists and other scientists the features of already protected natural areas, as well as the need for future preservation efforts. One of the most active members of the ESA committee, Charles C. Adams, carried out fieldwork in Harriman Park shortly after its creation in 1909. Although there had been a tradition of New York–area naturalists working in the Ramapos and the rest of the Hudson Highlands, the creation of the park accelerated and expanded scientific work in the region.

The role of natural science in shaping the Arcadian myth is more implicit than explicit in Peter Schmitt's *Back to Nature*. Focusing as he does on literary rather than scientific narratives, Schmitt deals with individuals deeply involved in the popularization of science, even if, as in the case of the nature-study movement, these popularizers offered their knowledge as an alternative to professional science, which they considered insufficiently attuned to the moral education of young people. Behind most of the Arcadian rhetorical productions Schmitt examined—from sentimental natural history tales to nature-study manuals and even outdoor fiction—lies the authority of natural science. Indeed, the turn-of-the-century nature-faker debate, considered by Schmitt and more thoroughly examined by Ralph Lutts in *The Nature Fakers* (1990), marks the eclipse in natural science of the nineteenth-century faith in Protestant religion and its secular extensions as the arbiter of human relationships with nature.[5] Recent scholarship in the history of science has done much to temper an earlier "diffusionist" model of the popularization of science, and the case study examined here supports the view that professional science is as much generated *out of* popular culture as it is a voice of authority whose knowledge must be tailored to a passive public audience.[6] The activities of professional natural scientists within the Arcadian landscape of the Ramapo Mountains suggest that new insights may be gained from considering scientists' embrace of the Arcadian myth as well as their participation in the production of that myth.

While early-twentieth-century natural science in America was deeply involved in the wilderness myth that set human beings apart from nature, it was simultaneously, given its adoption of Darwin's theory of natural selection, extending its vision of nature to include human beings. This breaking down of the human/nonhuman divide was most conspicuous in the American eugenics movement. Scholarship in the history of eugenics has lately become so prolific that Philip Pauly, borrowing from Timothy Lenoir's description of "the Darwin industry," has called this outpouring the "eugenics industry."[7] Regions and themes overlooked by the pioneering works of the first two decades of the historical study of eugenics have now become the focus of scholarly attention.[8] The eugenics industry seems to have reached a watershed recently with the appearance of a number of review essays assessing the state of contemporary scholarship and suggesting new directions for historical research.[9]

Aside from Donald Pickens's *Eugenics and the Progressives*, historical studies of eugenics have paid little attention to the simultaneous rise of the conservation and eugenics movements during the Progressive era.[10] Given eugenicists' immersion in natural scientific thought about the human being as a product of natural selection, it is not surprising that many eugenicists—including scientific theorists, social architects, and the broad public who subscribed to eugenic ideas—were also conservationists. *Conservation* is a keyword of the Progressive era. It turns up prominently in the rhetoric of redwood forest preservers, sponsors of fitter-family contests and sterilization bills, and moral hygiene instructors, suggesting that the word may be a minor rosetta stone to understanding middle-class Protestant culture during the opening decades of the twentieth century. More than a few troop leaders who lectured their scouts about the need to "conserve" their semen also held campfire talks about natural-area protection and positive eugenics. Benjamin T. B. Hyde, Frank Lutz, and William Carr—key figures in the nature-study programs developed at Harriman Park—were all Boy Scout leaders, and each reflects a bit of this curious conjunction of conservationist values.

Beyond the mere chronological coincidence with conservationist ideals, there is a significant landscape dimension to the American eugenics movement that has been all but overlooked by the eugenics industry and by environmental historians and geographers chronicling twentieth-century landscape transformation in America.[11] This dimension is readily apparent in the early-twentieth-century transformation of the Ramapo Mountains from a working landscape of timber and charcoal production, iron mining and smelting, and subsistence hunting and fishing to a landscape of leisure for metropolitans seeking restoration of their city-frazzled neurasthenic selves. Eugenic rhetoric, backed by field studies of the mountain communities, played a significant role in effecting this transformation, as the Ramapos became the region most intensely studied by American eugenicists. For environmental historians, the discovery that the intensity of the eugenic fieldwork in the Ramapos owes its origin to two of the most important figures in the American eugenics movement—Mary Harriman and Charles Benedict Davenport—is perhaps less important than the implication that the myth of the rural feebleminded often intertwined with the Arcadian myth to produce Progressives' visions of landscapes of degeneration restored as landscapes of regeneration.

From naturalism to Naturalism

Eugenicists appear as archetypal villains in histories of the twentieth century, not only as the demonic criminals of Nazi *Rassenhygiene* but also as the authoritarian and coercive advocates and implementers of eugenic sterilization throughout the democratic United States. Our historical perspective makes Percy MacKaye's 1912 morality play *To-Morrow* (see chapter 4), with its central character paying homage to the plant breeder Luther Burbank, seem deeply amoral. We have lost sight of the fact that a great deal of the respect and admiration directed toward eugenics flowed from the respect and admiration that its principal proponents—frequently natural scientists—commanded in the early twentieth century. Men like David Starr Jordan, Henry Fairfield Osborn, Charles Davenport, and Madison Grant were naturalists before they were eugenicists, and the intimate relationship with Nature that the public believed they enjoyed lent credence to their pronouncements upon human nature. The notion that "a good naturalist can not be a bad man" was as widely current in the 1920s as it had been when the English artist-naturalist Thomas Bewick affirmed it in the 1820s.[12]

The word *naturalist* was just coming to have twin meanings in the American vernacular in the first two decades of the twentieth century. The traditional meaning of a professional or amateur engaged in field study of the natural world persisted, along with the concomitant perception of the naturalist's moral and practical prowess. But in the rapid professionalization of the natural historical sciences in the early 1900s, the term migrated away from the professionals and came to rest upon the amateurs.[13] Just as zoologists, ecologists, and other field-oriented natural scientists were finding the old moniker inadequate to encompass their diversifying professional practices, many educated Americans were embracing the term as a philosophical identity. When Thomas Henry Huxley in 1894 boasted of "a new Nature created by Science," he expressed a conviction widespread among educated moderns that post-Darwinian natural science offered a complete world picture, abolishing the need for any complementary supernatural apparatus.[14] As recently as the 1880s the term had been a pejorative used by Protestant clergy and other holdouts against Darwinian theory to label a wide range of scientific materialists, from T. H. Huxley and Ernst Haeckel to Joseph Ernest Renan and Hippolyte Taine. A generation later it was a badge of pride worn by all prominent Anglo-American intellectuals. By 1902, when "Naturalism" appeared as an entry in the *Encyclopedia Britannica*, it no longer bore any stigma of unbelief; rather, the onus of unbelief among naturalists rested with those resisters who clung to philosophies that permitted a supernatural realm. Throughout this book, I will use "Naturalism" when referring to the philosophical stance and "naturalism" for the professional practice of nature observation, that is, "natural history."[15]

"We are all naturalists now," triumphantly declared philosopher Roy Wood Sellars in *Evolutionary Naturalism* (1922). Whereas Henri Bergson (*Creative Evolution*, 1907) and Samuel Alexander (*Space, Time and Deity*, 1920), and later Conwy Lloyd Morgan (*Emergent Evolution*, 1923) and J. C. Smuts (*Holism and Evolution*, 1926), offered evolutionary philosophies that violated pure Naturalism, Sellars employed only categories that were derived from science's knowledge of the physical world. He resorted to no "emergents" or other supplementary principles devised by twentieth-century neovitalist thinkers. Despite his declaration of unanimity, Sellars felt that there was enough residual dissension among thinkers who venerated science to provide a metaphysical exposition of the new Naturalism. Sellars found his peers' "common naturalism is of a very vague and general sort . . . an admission of a direction more than a clearly formulated belief. It is less a philosophical system than a recognition of the impressive implications of the physical and biological sciences." Sellars wished to distinguish "crude Darwinism" and the "naïve" Naturalisms of Haeckel, Huxley, and Spencer from his generation's understanding that "while man is an animal he is not a brute."[16]

In the 1920s, the two meanings of "naturalist" converged. The naturalist studied natural things—plants, animals, and, in the post-Darwinian era, humans—and the Naturalist studied natural as opposed to spiritual things. This second, philosophical rather than methodological/professional meaning identified the Naturalist as one who regarded the natural causes identified by modern science as a sufficient explanation of the world and its phenomena. By 1920, very few who were naturalists in the first sense of the term were not also adherents of philosophical Naturalism. The "war between science and religion" was over—even if the 1925 Scopes trial suggested otherwise—the continuing divisions raging almost exclusively between scientific thinkers and fundamentalist Christians, not between fellow scientists and liberal Protestants. In 1920 America's most beloved naturalist, John Burroughs, published a work fully aware of the double entendre of his subtitle: *Accepting the Universe: Essays of a Naturalist*. Burroughs was conscious of both the semantic and the philosophical nuances of the word *Nature*. America's premier celebrant of Arcadia was a canny critic of the often incomplete nature of back-to-nature enthusiasts:

> The Nature that the poets sing and that nature writers exploit is far from being the whole story. When we think of Nature as meaning only birds and flowers and summer breezes and murmuring streams, we have only touched the hem of her garment. . . . In fact, are not all the qualities and attributes which we ascribe to Nature equally the creation of our own minds? The beauty, the sublimity, the power of Nature are experiences of the beholder. The drudge in the fields does not experience them, but the poet, the thinker, the seer, does.[17]

Not only Nature, but God, Burroughs argued, was a mirror of the human being: "We find God in Nature by projecting ourselves there; we find him in the course of history by reading our own ideals into human events; we find him in our daily lives by listening to the whisperings of our own inherited and acquired consciences, and by dwelling upon the fatality that rules our lives."[18] Burroughs shared with Sellars the pressing project to rationalize the new Naturalism, asking: "How shall we account for man on purely naturalistic grounds?" Less bound by philosophical rigor, and given more to poetic invention, Burroughs was content to allow his own "emergents" to coexist with his unabashed declaration of Naturalism. "It is not you and I that are immortal; it is Creative Energy, of which we are a part. . . . In us or through us the Primal Mind will have contemplated and enjoyed its own works and will continue to do so as long as human life endures on this planet." Along with coining new phrases to avoid the word *God,* Burroughs frequently employed Christian sacred terms to advance his Naturalistic secularism: "[The Primal Mind] will have achieved the miracle of the Incarnation, and have tasted the sweet and the bitter, the victories and the defeats of evolution. The legend of the birth and life of Jesus is but this ever-present naturalism written large with parable and miracle on the pages of our religious history. . . . Even the Christian theory of the vicarious atonement is not without its basis of naturalism." Compared with Christian dogma, Burroughs's Naturalism seemed an inviting and comforting "faith" for moderns: "Naturalism does not see two immeasurable realities, God and Nature, it sees only one, that all is Nature or all is God, just as you prefer."[19]

Horizon Lines

Most of the essays in *Accepting the Universe* had already reached wide audiences in popular periodicals before being collected as a resounding statement of a veteran naturalist's Naturalism. In book form, the essays progressed organically from a series of opening existential questions, through a confrontation with the horrors of Germany's militaristic embrace of Naturalism, to a suite of "Horizon Lines": the question of the origin of life; the problem of design and the issue of teleology in evolutionary science;[20] and the conundrum of free will. An ancient American sage in the youthful Roaring Twenties, the "Seer of Slabsides" even entertained the question of the soul's place in a Naturalist philosophy:

> Does it help us any to think of the soul, or consciousness, in terms of the imponderable bodies—light, electricity, radio-activity? Do all these wireless messages that go forth into the air, go on forever? Do these impulses reach the farthest stars, and still persist? Do our thoughts persist upon the ether? Here, in this room, here in this air that you may inclose with your two hands, are vibrating wireless messages from far and near, though we are not able to detect them. Here also the ether may be tremulous with the thoughts of our friends on the other side of the globe, yes, and with the thoughts of our friends who have ceased to live, as we know life. The ether of space may still be vibrating with the thoughts of Plato and Aristotle, of Moses and Solomon.[21]

By 1932, when novelist Upton Sinclair published *Mental Radio*, a report of his wife's experiments in telepathy, musings such as these were commonplace in America. Although the language of "soul" was outdated, the language of science and its technological application seemed completely capable of explaining the old imponderables.

Burroughs's cabin in the Catskills was awash in the same tides of simultaneous fascination with psychic phenomena and new communication technologies that swept the rest of America. In the 1910s and 1920s, nineteenth-century Spiritualism was transformed into a new ghost, draped in the language of science. Articles and books exploring "psycho-physical forces," telepathy, and "extra-sensory perception" (a term most widely popularized by a series of *Scientific American* articles in the late 1920s and early 1930s) chronicled modern science's confrontation with both old and new invisibles.[22] Burroughs did not shrink from incorporating these mysteries into his Naturalism: "Do we impress ourselves momentarily upon the ether around us, and is this what the mediums and the clairvoyants recover? Is the persistence of our thoughts upon the ether the secret of the mind-reader's art, and of all the marvelous things disclosed by psychic research?"[23]

Burroughs accepted the anomalies of psychic phenomena as easily as he accepted the rest of the universe, borrowing the age's most ubiquitous metaphor—energy—and wedding it to an archetypal image from nature: "There is enough that is verifiable in clairvoyance and mind-reading and mental healing to convince us that we are immersed in a world of subtle forces that ordinarily we are wot not of; that in some way a process of give and take between us and these things is constantly going on, and that our relation to them is at least one form or suggestion of our immortality. We are a part of the wave of energy that sweeps through the cosmos, as truly as the drops of the sea hold and convey the tidal impulse.[24] That Burroughs, America's consummate celebrator of the particular in nature and the naturalist who so ardently defended the "facts" of nature from trivialization by nature fakers, needed to grope for such a hackneyed metaphor to reconcile psychic phenomena with his Naturalism suggests how truly unconquered by modern science this realm remained.

New York in the first two decades of the century was a hotbed of popular occultisms that attempted to make sense of the violations of sensible science represented by clairvoyance, telepathy, and other psychic phenomena. Not everyone was content to dismiss these outright or explain them away through analogizing with the emergent technologies of radio and television. Theosophists, Spiritualists, and other occultists had their own systems of explanation and their own critiques of the sort of Naturalism offered by Burroughs and his scientific peers. Burroughs's rejection of these explanatory systems spoke for all who called themselves Naturalists: "Though a dreamer and an idealist, I am only interested in a natural explanation of things—an explanation that is in harmony with our experiences in this world. The so-called supernatural explanation does not interest me at all. We cannot grasp it and bring it to the test of reason and experience."[25] Burroughs and his fellow naturalists easily dismissed the occult philosophies because these had so little to offer in the way of descriptions of *this* world, despite their elaborate catalogues of fauna and flora from the beyond. Given natural science's spectacular power of investigation of nature

in the early twentieth century, it was difficult for any alternative epistemology to find acceptance among scientific thinkers.

Exotericizing the Esoteric: Rudolf Steiner's Occult Science

When it appeared in America in 1875, Theosophy claimed to be a
reconciliation of science and religion. A half century later, however, it had
yet to produce much knowledge that could be called scientific. Collabo-
rating with scientific bodies like the American Society for Psychical Research, Theosophists had sometimes submitted their paranormal productions
to experimental test, and this sort of laboratory investigation tentatively
mapped poorly understood psychic landscapes. "Field" knowledge of a
supersensible landscape lying behind physical nature was not forthcoming,
however. American popular occultism had no Audubon, Bartram, Thoreau, or
Burroughs, much less the growing cohort of professional field natural scientists that combed the American landscape in the early twentieth century.

Yet, throughout Europe and America, Theosophy and other occult systems exerted significant influence on modern art and literature, and even,
through theories of the "fourth dimension," seemed to find some purchase
with physicists and mathematicians. Such esoteric ideas, however, had no
impact on natural science.[26] Helena Blavatsky, who with journalist Henry
Olcott founded the Theosophical Society in New York in 1875, claimed to
base her inquiries on a "Divine Wisdom" at the foundation of all knowledge. Her works, built around an extended critique of Darwinian materialism, especially its denial of human beings' divine origin, are massive tours
de force of late-nineteenth-century natural historical science. Contemporary naturalists, however, would have found the experience of reading them
akin to visiting the American Museum of Natural History in a state of
hasheesh intoxication. Orthodox geological timetables alternate with charts
and descriptions of the Hyperborean, Lemurian, and Atlantean continents;
the narrative of humans' descent from the gods is interrupted by episodic
accounts of vertebrate evolution; dragons, serpents, and other monsters both
known and unknown from the fossil record are woven into the story, with
support from world mythology; and the latest literature on Paleolithic humans is cited alongside the Hebrew Bible, the Vedas, the Kabala, and the
Tibetan Book of the Dead.

If Blavatsky and Theosophy sought to bring order to the chaotic landscape of nineteenth-century Spiritualism, then Anthroposophy and its
founder, the Austrian philosopher, scientist, educator, artist, and clairvoyant visionary Rudolf Steiner, sought to order the newly exotericized landscape of once-secret knowledge offered by Theosophy. Steiner's earliest

works—*Nature and Our Ideals* (1880), *A Theory of Knowledge Based on Goethe's World Conception* (1888), *Truth and Knowledge* (1892), *The Philosophy of Spiritual Activity* (1894), *Conceptions of the World and of Life in the Nineteenth Century* (1900)—were written within the context of conventional European philosophy. But following the publication in 1901 of a series of lectures given at the Theosophical Library in Berlin (*Mysticism at the Dawn of the Modern Age*), Steiner made public over the next twenty-five years an unprecedented volume of previously esoteric knowledge.[27] Steiner's early writings and lectures, though largely devoted to bringing Christian esotericism and Eastern mysticism into a modern system of thought, ranged over an enormous breadth of topics. In 1904, the same year that Steiner published his exposition of human spiritual evolution in *Cosmic Memory*, he lectured on the history of hypnotism and spiritualism, mathematics, Greek and Germanic mythology, the Middle Ages, Freemasonry, and Tolstoy.

No matter the topic, Steiner offered all of his esoteric expositions as *science*, not as religion or mysticism. He caused great confusion among critics when he published essays or gave lectures in which he praised the contributions to Western thought of materialists like Darwin and Haeckel, for the unmistakable aim of his teachings was to overthrow the very Naturalism advanced by these thinkers. Naturalists either condemned Steiner or they ignored him, but they rarely read him. Those few who did found "anthroposophy," as he termed his philosophical system after 1911, defended his works as science throughout. An early example of this defense appears in *Occult Science: An Outline* (1909):

> Needless to say, for anyone who will admit as science only what is manifest to the senses and to the intellect that serves them, what is here named "Occult Science" can be no science. Such a man, however, if willing to understand his own position, should candidly admit that his categorical rejection of any kind of "Occult Science" springs not from reasoned insight but from an *ipse dixit,* due to his own individual feeling. To see that it is so, he need only reflect how sciences arise and what is their significance in human life. How a pursuit comes to be a science cannot in the nature of the case be ascertained from the subject matter to which it is devoted, but only by recognizing the mode of action of the human soul while engaged in scientific endeavor. . . . If one is used to employ this mode of activity only where sense-data are concerned, one easily slides into the idea that sense-data are the essential factor. . . . Occult Science seeks to free the scientific method and spirit of research, which in

its own domain holds fast to the sequence and relationship of sense-perceptible events, from this restricted application, while maintaining the same essential attitude and thought. Thus it would speak of the non-sensible in the same spirit in which Natural Science speaks of the sensible.[28]

Artists—a group of New York musicians, dancers, dramatists, poets, and painters—not scientists, originally brought Rudolf Steiner's anthroposophy to America in the 1910s, establishing the first anthroposophical community a few blocks from Carnegie Hall. In 1926 a group of these New Yorkers, looking for their own Arcadian retreat, established Threefold Farm in the township of Ramapo, New York, less than five miles from Harriman Park. Over the next thirty years, while the Naturalist remaking of the Ramapo landscape went on apace just over the Great Border Fault, the Threefold Farm anthroposophists shaped their own landscape of regeneration through biodynamic gardening, social initiatives, and educational activities. Sharing both the metropolitan outlook and the Arcadian enthusiasm of their Naturalist peers who so dramatically reshaped the Ramapo Mountain landscape, the Threefold Farm anthroposophists saw their efforts as an antidote to American Naturalism. The geographical juxtaposition of the Threefold Farm anthroposophical community with Harriman Park throws into high relief the Naturalist orientation of their fellow Arcadia-seeking metropolitan neighbors.

The Myth of Naturalism

The juxtaposition I create in this book—between the Arcadian activities of natural scientists, nature-study promoters, and eugenicists within Harriman Park and the anthroposophical activities of the Threefold Farm inhabitants—may seem unproductive as an analytical device. With the exception of playwright Percy MacKaye, there is virtually no interaction between the ideas and actors of the book's first and second parts. As a case study of the way the Arcadian myth operated in the hinterland of early-twentieth-century metropolitan New York, it can at best offer a very minor portrait, for the scope of the Arcadian thought and action centered on New York City in the 1920s and 1930s was nearly as richly variegated as the city's urban middle-class culture. The juxtaposition of histories, however, does serve to highlight an American myth as tenacious as the myth of Arcadia: the myth of Naturalism.

The "faith of a naturalist," once offered so gently and persuasively by John Burroughs to an American public seeking a substitute for an outworn Protestant creed, has long passed the point where conscious articulation of that faith is necessary. Within a generation Burroughs's Naturalism became the shared myth not only of the naturalists who planned nature trails, trailside museums, and other pedagogical devices to provide the proper epistemological spectacles for viewing Nature, but also of the many Americans who rarely or never went into the woods to become whole. When in 1994 Sharon Kingsland christened ecology as the "natural theology of the twentieth century," she did so in recognition of ecology's authority for a wide public concerned with environmental degradation.[29] Naturalism represents an even more pervasive natural theology, one particularly necessary to recognize because it is held most strongly by the very community that has helped Americans to understand the history of their relationship to the natural world. Despite its illumination of so many facets of America's environmental history, and despite its sensitivity to the dangers of social constructivism on one side and deconstructionism on the other, academic scholarship leaves unexplored its own foundational myth of Naturalism. Like the related disciplines of geography, environmental studies, history of science, and natural science itself, environmental history is deeply committed to a Naturalistic view of Nature and History. I do not set out to explore or understand that myth so much as to bring it into view.

In 1998 I attended a brown-bag discussion at the department of the history of science at the University of Minnesota, where a couple of dozen faculty and students met with University of Chicago historian and philosopher of science Robert J. Richards. At one point, echoing Roy Wood Sellars on Naturalism, Richards declared, "We are all neo-Darwinians now." When I objected to this unequivocal assumption of philosophical unanimity, Richards was aghast. His eyes swept around the table as he confidently restated his assumption: "Well, aren't we?" No one indicated dissent, and those assembled seemed a bit disconcerted that somehow a nonbeliever had managed to infiltrate their ranks. Within the academy, the Naturalist ranks are extremely close, and growing closer all the time. Scholarly discourse in America during this century about both Nature and History has progressively deepened the divide between Naturalists and their philosophical antagonists. A Great Border Fault runs down the center of twentieth-century epistemology, the Naturalists upon one side, the critics of Naturalism upon the other. To date, Naturalists seem to believe that their only antagonist is the creationist camp, fundamentalist holdouts against a scientific view of the natural world. The history of the Arcadian experiment at Threefold Farm, I believe, suggests otherwise. Perhaps this book can serve to awaken American historians to a new area of research and encourage fuller exploration of the limits of our own practices of knowledge.

PART I

CHAPTER 1

Arcadia and Metropolis

"Our Best Wild Up-and-Down-Country"

His hand moving across the paper like one of the nervous warblers flitting about among the unfurling, down-covered leaves of the wind-pruned chestnut oaks, Robert Latou Dickinson's pen went from left to right, reducing the impressive scene to the scale of his sketch tablet. His sparkling blue eyes swept back and forth, pulling in both the whole of the Highlands massif and its many parts. As he looked westward from Anthony's Nose in May 1923, there was Dunderberg on the south, the eastern terminus of the Ramapo Mountains, poking out into the Hudson across from Peekskill (artfully omitted from his sketch) and cradling in its lee the lovely marsh surrounding the old Iona Island arsenal. Just inland lay the still thriving hamlet of Doodletown. Carrying the horizon line across his canvas rolled Bald Mountain, Bockberg, the Timp, West Mountain, Black Mountain, Long Mountain, Turkey Mountain, the Popolopen Torne, and finally the Crown Range. Only the boundary of the sketch pad kept him from reproducing the rest of the view, north past Storm King, Crows Nest, and Breakneck toward West Point. In the foreground, their once formidable redoubts reduced to grass-covered mounds, the twin Revolutionary forts Clinton and Montgomery straddled Popolopen Creek. In the middle distance behind Fort Clinton, Hessian Lake made an arc at the foot of the panorama's central and organizing feature: Bear Mountain. Broader and higher than the rest, its bare granite ledges cropping out near its summit on many of its faces, Bear Mountain (along with Storm King) held the place of honor in the imagination of most who loved the Highlands.

From his ledge perch, Dickinson could let his eye roam beyond Bear Mountain to take in the entire northern section of the Ramapo Rampart. Having sketched vistas from a hundred similar lookouts throughout the region, he could imagine the Front Range of the Highlands running south along the line of the Great Border Fault, its uniformly angled scarp face turned toward the gentle lowlands of the Newark Basin. First came the sublime summits of the Timp and Pyngyp Mountain, followed by a set of peaks with picturesque names—Horse Chock, Lime Kiln, Catamount, and Horse Stable. Across from Horse Chock Mountain is the outlier Cheesecote Mountain (commonly called Cheesecocks by locals), its name preserving the Lenape word borrowed by the first settlers. He could even see the fine stone buildings and sycamore-lined pathways of Letchworth Village, the state institution for the feebleminded, to the northeast side of Cheesecote Mountain, marking the end of the Ramapo Rampart. Interior from the peaks of the Ramapo Front, along the Mahwah River, Dickinson traced successive waves of equally high mountains: the Ramapo Torne, its high, steep cliffs overlooking the Ramapo River valley; Horse Pond Mountain rising abruptly from the river, forming the eastern wall of the "Clove" of many Revolutionary adventures. Then northeast the summits ran again in succession—Black Ash, Parker Cabin, Tom Jones, Brundige, Halfway, Diamond, Breakneck, Jackie Jones, and Irish Mountains, with the Stony, Pine Meadow and Stillwater Brooks dissecting them. These were just some of the hills he had come to know in a dozen years of hiking in the Harriman section of the Palisades Interstate Park, simply "the Park" to Dickinson and a growing number of inveterate weekend walkers.

Dickinson knew the entire assemblage of 800- to 1200-foot summits as the eroded remnants of an ancient, more majestic range of mountains worn down during the Cretaceous period to form what his physiographer friend A. K. Lobeck termed the "Schooley Peneplain." The glacially polished granite underneath him was familiar, a close cousin to the gneiss and schist that formed the foundation for the Manhattan skyline, whose angular geometry he knew even more intimately than the undulating line of the Ramapo Rampart, and which he always loved to look upon in miniature from so many Ramapo summits.[1]

Though he lived nearly his entire life in New York City, Dickinson was not born there. On the day of his birth—February 21, 1861, made doubly auspicious by the passage of President-elect Abraham Lincoln through Jersey City on the way to the White House—his mother took the ferry across the Hudson to Jersey City to have lunch with her sister. But Robert Latou Dickinson was truly a native New Yorker. His grandfather Robert Latou had at the beginning of the nineteenth century bought up all the property—then just wild, unkempt land full of goats and shacks—where the lower part of Central Park would later be developed. In 1868 his great-uncle built New York City's first skyscraper at the corner of Fulton and Broadway; from the upper of its eight stories, you could see the whole city. The building sported the city's first elevator, which anyone could ride to the top for a dollar. His parents' home was in Brooklyn, at 165 State Street, next door to the Doubledays, whose son Frank was Dickinson's age. They remained lifelong friends through Robert's forty years of medical practice and Frank's half century as one of New York's premier publishers.

After marrying a fellow New Yorker, Sarah Truslow, Dickinson continued to live in Brooklyn until the end of World War I. He had proposed to Sarah in 1888 at the "Door of the Great Spirit," a well-known traprock plateau of the Palisades that commanded exceptionally fine views of the city. (After her death, Robert scattered Sarah's ashes from there.) The columnar Palisades basalt made for an entirely different artistic subject than the gneiss of Manhattan or the Highlands. Though separated by an hour's train ride across the sandstones and shales of the Newark Basin, Bear Mountain's ledges had the same ancient quality as the outcrops along Riverside Drive from Seventy-second Street to Grant's Tomb and those in Morningside Park, Central Park, and Bronx Park. Like the Highlands rock, the edges of its layers ran north-south, paralleling the Hudson. Manhattan marked the eastern extremity of the Reading Prong of the old complex rocks of the New England Upland, while the sublime Highland summits, seen on a voyage up the Hudson, marked the midsection of the Reading Prong of that same formation.

Though far less majestic, the Highlands summits before Dickinson shared with the Adirondacks an air of the primeval. A half century earlier, as a ten-year-old boy in the Adirondacks, he had goaded his father into helping him build a canoe out of boards. When they put it in Long Lake for a test float, Robert jumped into the water and grabbed the stem of the boat to see how easy it would be to capsize. The galvanized iron stem tore open a gash in his hand which the local doctor could not attend to because of a severe bout with arthritis. Instead, the doctor called in a carpenter neighbor, who, following the doctor's direction, deftly stitched up the boy's bloody hand. The episode inspired Dickinson to become a surgeon, and 1923 marked his fortieth year as a physician. In just another month he would retire to devote himself to other work.

During that boyhood summer of 1871 Robert had filled his first sketchbook with mountains—Marcy, Butler, Slide, and many others. He had sketched French-Canadian woodcutters, white rhododendrons, deer, hedgehogs, dogs, the ever-changing sky. His draftsmanship was greatly improved by 1874, when he spent the year in Geneva at the École Privat. In the Swiss Alps he took up tramping and botany in earnest and found his greatest pleasure in making finely detailed maps of the district, known to him from countless walks, sketchbook always in hand. The sketching and mountain-climbing habits remained constant in all his peregrinations, from the Catskills, White Mountains, Green Mountains, and Berkshires to Mont Tremblant and Mount Fuji. While on a medical assignment in the Far East in 1895, his attention turned to boats on the China Sea. In Japan he had come under the influence of Arthur Dow and Japanese art, and his sketches after his Eastern sojourn were noticeably finer, softer, fuller of light. This Japanese period provided a welcome antidote to the photographic exactness of the anatomical drawings he had been making for ten years in his medical practice. A new economy enriched his drawing style; after Japan he could make two or three lines of foliage symbolize an entire forest, cast several shadows across a rock face to indicate the layered bedrock of a cliff, or with half a dozen steep bands represent shafts of sunlight striking down through the trees. In his sketches, RLD (as he had become known to his wide circle of friends, due chiefly to the three fluid initials that graced the thousands of sketches he gave away to admiring acquaintances) never hesitated to move two trees farther apart to allow a vista between them of a distant peak or to remove a telegraph pole or other eyesore that marred a view.[2]

The man-made features in the May 1923 panorama only served to heighten the beauty of the natural forms. Seven Lakes Drive appeared as a pair of parallel tracks across the open fields surrounding the Bear Mountain Inn, whose thick walls of glacial cobble topped by half-round chestnut timbers were reduced to a tiny black smudge at the very center of the sketch. The tall brick tower of the Iona Island arsenal was a minute vertical line breaking the monotony of horizontals. The causeway of the West Shore Railroad Line, running from Iona Island to the western shore of the Hudson, made only a thin gossamer thread, counterpoint to the sinuous creek running through the Iona Island marsh behind. The two massive wooden piers of Bear Mountain landing were hardly visible at this scale; the steamship *Hendrick Hudson* chugging toward them, its wake and plume of steam trailing behind in a few broken pen lines, seemed altogether insignificant, with no trace of the mechanical threat to nature that it might seem if one were standing on its deck with a thousand other passengers. The massive steel I-beams and thick bundles of cable of the new but not yet opened Bear Mountain Bridge, entering the frame almost perpendicularly, were equally diminutive, their lines equivalent to the weight of the beech, birch, maple, and oak trees that gave surface texture to the entire composition.

Before drawing the rectangular border line, RLD added the last anthropogenic detail, an imaginary one—a half dozen automobiles spaced unevenly across the span of the Bear Mountain Bridge. These and more would be there soon enough, he thought. Then he moved left to right, first across the top of the drawing, registering in his neat block script the names of the landscape features below—"Round Island, Iona Island, Doodletown Valley, Seven Lakes Drive, Playground, Bear Mt. Inn, Hessian Lake"—then repeating the process along the lower border line—"Fort Clinton, Popolopen Creek, Fort Montgomery."

He paused a moment, surveyed the drawing and its subject in one long look, then moved his pen to the lower left-hand corner where he had left ample white space below the irregular silhouette of tortured pitch pine and scrub oak. In flowing hand, fully confident of the aptness of the title, RLD penned: "Our Best Wild Up-and-Down-Country."[3]

"In the name of the State . . . "

In September 1910, directly across from Dickinson's panoramic perch on Anthony's Nose, a group made up mostly of New Yorkers gathered at the top of Bear Mountain for a ceremony that would make possible Dickinson's sweeping, uninterrupted imaginary view across the forested summits of the Ramapos. Eighteen-year-old Averell Harriman did his best to be heard by the assembled crowd: "In the name of my mother," he began, as he passed a packet of deeds to George W. Perkins, chairman of the Palisades Interstate Park Commission. Perkins took the packet, saying: "In the name of the State of New York. . . . By this act you have conveyed a fortune and a domain." The fortune was a million dollars, the domain ten thousand acres of the northern Ramapo Mountains, both acquired by Averell's father, the railroad tycoon Edward Henry Harriman. When he died in 1909, the elder Harriman left his entire $70 million estate to his wife, Mary. Besieged by hundreds of requests for funds for a vast array of projects, Mrs. Harriman rejected them all; but within a few months she made the Harriman Park endowment the first gift from her husband's legacy.[4]

Mary Harriman was honoring her husband's wishes. Shortly before his death, E. H. Harriman and George Perkins, a banking partner of J. P. Morgan and political ally of Theodore Roosevelt, had devised a grand plan to preserve the entire northern Ramapos. To New York's governor, Charles Hughes, Harriman proposed to donate nineteen square miles of his own estate plus a million dollars to acquire additional property between it and the Hudson: "I have thought possibly some of the other property owners might join me in this move, making it possible to secure practically the whole wild area between the Ramapo and the Hudson Rivers, extending from West Point down to below Stony Point, and again north of West Point, taking in the Crow's Nest." Harriman was a man who could easily imagine this sort of grand scheme. At just 5'4", the "little giant of Wall Street" was a Caesar in a city full of Gilded Age Caesars, having consolidated much of the American railroad system. The scale of his imagination was such that when in 1906 the flooding Colorado River threatened to destroy the agricultural lands of California's Imperial Valley, he organized the labor and machinery to divert the river, in the process flooding the Salton Sink instead. Setting aside a section of the Appalachian Mountains much larger than the area most of its inhabitants might even travel in a lifetime was completely consistent with his geographical and social vision.[5]

Harriman envisioned the lowlands lying below his stone mansion—situated on a saddle just below the crest of Mount Orama overlooking the Ramapo valley—as one day carpeted with people, the outer reaches of Manhattan's solid sweep of masonry and macadam. He feared that the only life in this megalopolis would be human life, "a great honeycomb of humanity creeping through an artificial world, crowded too close for the health of mind and body. It was like extending the darkest tenement zone over an area counted by the hundreds of square miles." Harriman had not been possessed of such an apocalyptic vision when he bought the land in September 1886. Then regeneration rather than degeneration was on his mind. He had gone out to Arden, New York, to attend the auction of the Greenwood Ironworks, where the last charcoal-burning furnace in the Ramapos had shut down earlier that year. Founded in 1810, the furnace had produced ordnance during the War of 1812 but did not become a major industrial site until after Robert and Peter Parrott acquired it in 1837. They eventually bought ten thousand acres of mountain land to supply both the magnetite ore—from the Bradley, Surebridge, Hogencamp, Pine Swamp, Garfield, Boston, and other mines east and west of the Ramapo valley—and the oak and chestnut timber to fuel the furnaces. The Greenwood and other Parrott furnaces were busiest during the Civil War, when they turned out tens of thousands of tons of pig iron that were shipped by rail to the West Point iron foundry at Cold Spring on the Hudson and there fashioned into thousands of Parrott guns and shells for the Union Army.[6]

A generation before 1886, Arden had been a little Pittsburgh. Two thousand men mined the ore, made the charcoal, and smelted and shipped the pigs and blooms. The hills flanking the Ramapo River were filled with their homes and hamlets, the "Greenwood" was turned black by the ubiquitous charcoal dust. When Harriman looked out over these hills, they were growing green with twenty- to thirty-year-old hardwoods, which had attracted dozens of timber speculators to the auction, keen to buy up the mountain lands to clear-cut for cordwood. Harriman spoiled their plans. As a young man he had worked as a timekeeper at the Greenwood furnace;

he was a close friend of Peter Parrott's son Richard and had hunted and fished in the area many times. His youthful experiences in the Ramapos fostered in him a deep love of the forest landscape there. Harriman bought everything on the auction block—all ninety-five hundred acres, the iron mines, furnace, and outbuildings. Fifty acres that included the Parrott home and the Arden Church were reserved for the Parrott family. Harriman's act cost him only $52,500, a price far lower than the Parrotts had expected for auctioning off their property in blocks. The Harrimans adopted a house across from the Parrotts' homestead as their summer home, but the Parrotts never again spoke to Harriman.[7]

By 1905, Harriman's purchase of about forty wooded tracts and farms had enlarged his estate to almost thirty square miles, making it the largest country estate in the vicinity of New York City. Unlike other estates in the Ramapo region—the Lorillards' Tuxedo estate, Abram Hewitt's Skylands, Theodore Havemeyer's Mountainside Farm, and Alfred B. Darling's farm in Mahwah, New Jersey—Harriman's property was not acquired with mining, farming, or timber selling as the intended activity. Though he would continue to operate the dairy farm at Arden, from the outset Harriman's principal intention had been the conservation and management of the forest lands. He took a personal interest in selecting hardwood stands for management and invited students from the newly established Yale School of Forestry to spend the summers at Arden to gain practical experience in scientific forestry.

Harriman's activity coincided with growing activism by New York preservationists to set aside the Highlands as parkland. The first quintessentially sublime and simultaneously quintessentially American landscape, the Highlands of the Hudson (more particularly the Highlands west of the river) played a seminal role in shaping the national landscape aesthetic. Before the Civil War, Frederick Edwin Church and Thomas Cole had immortalized the region in their luminous paintings. William H. Bartlett created popular engravings of Highlands scenes. Washington Irving and N. P. Willis celebrated the Highlands in prose. By the late nineteenth century, the combination of dramatic topography, patriotic resonances of Revolutionary battlegrounds, and proximity to the nation's greatest urban center assured the Highlands region a hallowed place in the American imagination. There had been a brief interlude from the late 1870s to mid-1890s when the region's reputation was tarnished by the trappings of modernity along the Hudson's shores and eclipsed by the opening up to travelers of new and sublime scenery in the West, but the early twentieth century saw the Highlands regain some of its erstwhile appeal, if perhaps for a newer class of nature worshiper than the well-educated romantics of the past. If it could not fully claim national pride of place, the western Highlands were loyally embraced by local landcape enthusiasts, particularly Manhattanites.[8]

As early as 1907, the American Scenic and Historic Preservation Society (ASHPS) had organized a committee of prominent residents of the lower Hudson River shores with the aim of preserving the scenery of the Highlands. The ASHPS, which had been instrumental in devising the plan that led to the creation of the Palisades Interstate Park in 1900, originally promoted the idea of persuading the state legislature to pass a law similar to the one that defined the limits of the Adirondack Park (that is, a life tenancy/forever wild compact). In 1908, with momentum gathering for the upcoming tercentenary celebration of Henry Hudson's 1609 voyage, support grew for a "Hudson Highlands National Park." The area proposed for the park included sixty-five square miles east of the river and fifty-seven square miles to the west. The ASHPS committee believed that many owners of large forested tracts on either side of the river—a significant number of whom, including John D. Rockefeller Jr. and J. P. Morgan, were ASHPS members—were amenable to sale of their lands to the federal government for the stumpage value of the standing timber. Others, the committee suggested, would for a small compensation be willing to give the government easements in their property, by which they would agree not to destroy their forests or take other action that would harm the region's scenic beauty. A leading proponent of the forest reserve plan was E. H. Harriman's friend Dr. Edward L. Partridge, who had discussed the idea of a Highlands park with Harriman on several occasions. Partridge promoted the idea in magazine articles that focused on the patriotic associations of the Highlands and the advantage of the fact that two federal military reservations—West Point and Iona Island—already existed in the region.[9]

In April 1908, New York Representative S. W. Bradley introduced into the U.S. House of Representatives a bill to create a "Hudson River National Park Commission" composed of the secretaries of war and agriculture, the chief forester, the superintendent of West Point, the president of the ASHPS, and the president of the National Society of the Sons of the American Revolution. When the bill failed to pass, attention shifted to a plan for the creation of a state-sponsored forest reserve. The Wainwright Forest Reserve bill, which eliminated the eastern portion of the Highlands but designated seventy-five square miles on the western side of the river as protected, passed both houses of the New York legislature on May 8, 1909. Given jurisdiction over the reserve, the New York Forest, Fish and Game Commission appointed F. F. Moon as forester of the new Hudson Highlands Forest Reservation. Moon spent the next year promoting sound forestry practices in the region; in essence this meant speaking to woodsmen in schoolhouse gatherings, where he tried to persuade them to harvest young hardwoods selectively for telephone poles rather than clear-cut them for cordwood.[10]

Preservationist rhetoric had aroused such support in the metropolitan area for more extensive Highlands protection that Moon's itinerant seminars in scientific forestry did not satisfy public expectations. This became especially clear after the public learned that the state itself intended to transform the forest on the riverside slope of Bear Mountain. On March 15, 1909, New York journalist and photographer William Thompson Howell was walking near Bear Mountain when he came to a clearing with a wooden sign nailed to a tree: "STATE PROPERTY—SING SING PRISON—TRESSPASSERS MAY BE SHOT." Within months of the creation of the new forest reservation, on the terrace where in 1776 American militiamen had bravely defended Forts Clinton and Montgomery against the invading British army, hundreds of heavily guarded convicts were clearing the land for the relocation of Sing Sing Prison. Where previous efforts to protect the western Highlands had failed, Howell's cry of alarm about the new penitentiary galvanized public opinion.

The prison plan also alarmed E. H. Harriman: the Sing Sing site adjoined his own estate's eastern boundary. Harriman's death in September 1909 put a stop to his plan to remake the Highlands landscape, but when Mary Harriman on December 15, 1909, offered her gift of land and money to New York State, one of her conditions was that construction cease immediately on Sing Sing Prison. This condition and others—that the state raise $1.5 million by private subscription within sixteen days, that it provide matching funds of $2.5 million for land acquisition, road building, and park maintenance and development, that state law be amended to extend the jurisdiction of the Palisades Interstate Park north to the Highlands and Ramapos, and that New Jersey appropriate a sum of money determined by the Palisades Interstate Park Commission to be its "fair share"—were speedily met. Ten months later the ceremony atop Bear Mountain delivered Arcadia unto Metropolis.

Building the Park

Within a year, the site once destined to become home to scores of urban criminals, a symbol of New York City's dark side, was transformed into an extension of the city's halcyon possibilities. After the mountaintop deeding ceremony in September 1910, 150 members of the official party adjourned for lunch at the abandoned warden's house of the aborted Sing Sing Prison. By the following spring, a refreshment shelter and park offices had been constructed from material salvaged from the demolished prison barracks, and the cleared land of the thirty-acre prison site was being groomed into baseball fields and picnic grounds. A steamboat dock was built on the Hudson shore, and roads were laid out to the dock and to the Iona Island railroad station. By the summer of 1911, a walking trail up Bear Mountain, docks on Hessian Lake, rest rooms, and a wading pool had turned Bear Mountain into a pleasant alternative to an outing in Central Park or at the Palisades. In 1913, when steamboat service began and camping facilities were available at the site, the demand exceeded all expectations. Between the middle of June and Labor Day weekend, more than twenty thousand passengers paid the 50¢ round trip fare (75¢ on Sundays, 25¢ for children) from the Battery to the Bear Mountain dock. More than five thousand Boy Scouts camped out this first summer, all within the area of the old prison grounds. No public roads led as yet into the park's interior.

Old logging roads did permit state employees to begin a campaign of reforestation beyond Bear Mountain. Land around many of the white cedar swamp ponds within the park was grubbed and cleared, and thousands of rhododendrons were removed from the swamps and transplanted to the slopes of Bear Mountain. Low concrete dams were built to turn a number of these swamps into ponds, with cleared areas on the shore for additional camping. The forest thinning that E. H. Harriman had begun on his estate close to his Arden home continued less intensively throughout the park, and state nurseries supplied more than ten million seedling Scotch pine, red pine, and Norway spruce for reforesting former agricultural lands. Forest roads were cleared for trampers and to serve as fire breaks, and a program was begun to clear brush 150 feet to either side of the principal roads so as to provide a "window" into the newly regenerating forest. One disappearing member of the forest community—the American chestnut—was harvested, as mature trees became diseased, to supply timber for new park buildings.

In 1914, Major William A. Welch, an engineer with wide experience in the American West as well as the Panama Canal, was hired as general manager and chief engineer of the Bear Mountain–Harriman Park. Welch immediately planned a new road through the park, to be flanked by a series of eight lakes. Seven of these were built by 1920, and the Seven Lakes Drive became one of the New York region's most celebrated pleasure drives. Welch also oversaw construction of the Bear Mountain Inn, which, when it opened in 1916, impressed visitors with its dark-stained massive chestnut-log walls and stout foundation of glacially rounded granite cobbles. In 1919, the year when Welch rechristened a number of the lakes with suitably idyllic Iroquois and Algonquian Indian names—Nawahunta, Tiorati, Kanawauke,

Stahahe—more than a million people visited the park. Welch had the dams raised to facilitate boat travel, and twenty-nine tent settlements accommodated fifty thousand people, mainly women and children from New York City, including a large number of inner-city children brought out for a week's stay by the city's many social service organizations. The park employed eighteen policemen and two motorcycle policemen to limit the speed of motorists on Seven Lakes Drive.[11]

Pathfinding

In 1921 Robert Latou Dickinson successfully combined his sketches and landscape descriptions in *Palisades Interstate Park*, the first of the American Geographical Society's "Outing" series. By that time, the southern portion of the park along the Palisades, the section that had first aroused the preservationist instincts of Manhattanites, had been a favored walking ground for a generation—so popular that its trails were suffering from overuse. By contrast, a 1920 Harriman Park annual report of activities lamented "the almost unknown resources of the interior of the Harriman Park." A new road map guided autocampers along the resurfaced Seven Lakes Drive to one of the gravel byroads where they could camp for a night, but the ten-thousand-acre Ramapo forest was virtually unknown to all but a few intrepid hikers like journalist William Thompson Howell.[12]

By the summer of 1923, the situation had changed completely. Many of the New Yorkers who arrived by automobile via the Bear Mountain Bridge, the railroad, or the twice-daily steamboats carried RLD's sketches, accompanied by his fine prose, in the form of the *New York Walk Book*. Though its subtitle—"Suggestions for excursions afoot within a radius of fifty to one hundred miles of the city and including Westchester County, the Highlands of the Hudson and the Ramapo, northern and central New Jersey and the New Jersey Pine Barrens, Long Island, the Shawangunk Range, the Catskills, and the Taconics"—signaled just how far afield it would take the walker from Gotham, the book's geographical and spiritual epicenter was probably the Ramble in Central Park, if not just south of there, at Broadway and Seventh Avenue. Home to Dickinson and his coauthors, Frank Place Jr. and Raymond H. Torrey, Manhattan anchored the metropolitan walker's outlook as surely as the Manhattan schist anchored the skyscrapers of downtown and midtown. Though born in Massachusetts, Ray Torrey had worked since the age of sixteen in 1896 as reporter, rewrite man, copy reader, night manager, and editor for New York City newspapers, including the *American*, the *Tribune*, and the *Post*. His "Long Brown Path" column in the *New York Post*, beginning in 1919, had made him the point man for outdoor recreation in the greater New York area. By the late 1920s, Torrey was active in nearly every major metropolitan conservation and recreation organization—as secretary for the Associated Outdoor Clubs of America, the New York State Council of Parks, the American Scenic and Historic Preservation Society, and the Association for the Protection of the Adirondacks, as chairman of the New York–New Jersey Trail Conference, as field commissioner of the Torrey Botanical Club (begun by his grandfather, botanist John Torrey), and as a member of the board of managers at the New York Botanical Garden. Material from Torrey's column, a rich treasury of trail lore and legend, furnished much of the trail directions in the *New York Walk Book*. Frank Place, librarian at the New York Academy of Medicine, operated a sort of clearinghouse for New York's dozens of outing clubs, whose schedules of excursions he compiled each spring and autumn. His trail notes and maps rounded out the book.

But it was RLD's pen—both in sketches and prose—that made the *New York Walk Book* an unrivaled masterpiece of the trail guide literature. Dickinson's wide view and his deep love of urban New York and its rural hinterlands gave the book a simultaneously parochial and cosmopolitan tone that drew in even the most reluctant of newcomers to the walking craze. The book's opening passage, "The Look-Off," asks the reader to look underfoot, mining Manhattan's—that is, *menahen*, the Lenape word for "island"—aboriginal past to further root the walker in place:

> Soil that ever was *Indian* seems never to lose all of that impress. On the Island of Islands, borne down at one end by the world's biggest burden of steel and stone and pressure of haste and material gain, the primitive sweep of its further free tip, with the forest trees on the stately ledges, still holds the red man's cave, the beached canoe, the air of the Great Spirit. The magic of the moccasin still makes good medicine. Fortunate we are that in civilization lurks the antidote to civilization—that strain in the blood of us, all of us, of cave man and tree man, nomad and seaman, chopper and digger, fisher and trailer, crying out to this call of the earth, to this tug of free foot, up-and-over, to this clamor for out-and-beyond. Happy are we, in our day, harking back to this call, to be part of an ozone revival that fits the growth of our desire, to see the beginning of a break-away into everybody's out-of-doors, and the happy find of a wide, fair wilderness.[13]

For RLD, the wide, fair wilderness began center city, and the reader who turned to Chapter One found that the large decorative "S" of the initial sentence—"Sidewalks for our form of outing may at first seem ill-advised"—formed the ghostly outlines of a man and a woman stylishly dressed and striding through the streets of Manhattan, the forest of sky-scrapers behind them, the man with guidebook in hand. Within the steel-and-concrete jungle that New York had become by 1923, its sidewalks nevertheless, with the help of RLD's descriptions, could trace a route back into the primeval past of the aboriginal isle: "So it comes about that below the hard concrete, beneath the remains of asphalt and macadam, down under the corduroy logs of the primitive cartway, lie the old elastic, beaten surfaces of single-file footways, worn deep into the countryside by centuries of the soft foot pads of the moccasins of the Mohegans." A section entitled "Indian Ways and Footways Hereabouts" opens with the memory of a very different sort of "100% Americanism" than the one then fashionable, one of "untrammeled summers when we were adequately clothed in moccasin and breechclout."[14]

The New York press approved wholeheartedly of the *New York Walk Book*, impressed especially by the impeccable Arcadian credentials of its authors: "It has been composed by men who are practiced out-of-doorsmen, rugged men in whom the artist tents with the scientist—'saunterers' in the etymology which THOREAU gave to the word, going afoot *à la sainte terre*, inhabitants of L. H. Bailey's 'holy earth.'" The reviewer echoed the conviction of all those who especially loved the western Highlands, quoting Henry Adams's description of lower Hudson River scenery: "A cluster of promontories, of the lost classic elegance, overhanging vast, receding reaches of river, mountain-guarded and dim, which take their place in the geography of the ideal, in the long perspective of the poetry of association, rather than in those of the State of New York." The authors themselves saw the book as a tool to help Manhattan's masses reach just such a geography of the ideal, to transcend the remarkable physical beauty of the Highlands for an even Higher Land. Dickinson, a devout Methodist, quoted Deuteronomy to Arcadian effect in the introduction, and his conclusion finishes with a phrase from Isaiah: "This is the Way; WALK ye in it."[15]

With the *Walk Book* in hand, the harried urbanite could find renewal and regeneration. Dickinson's generation may have been among the last to recognize the explicitly spiritual overtones of the word *recreation*; he hyphenated it to emphasize a meaning deeper than mere fun-filled escape: "We who go afoot to nature to get this re-creation can make good the claim to be the original open-air enthusiasts. Do not all enthusiasts take themselves seriously? Living in a world distraught, in the City of Extravagance, we are brash enough to opine that we can put up a bit of a sign on the footpath of satisfaction that is the trail to simple living, friendliness, and serenity, and that we hear the Voice behind us, 'This is the Way; walk ye in it.'" The Age of the Automobile was increasingly granting to walking the status of a sacred activity; the act itself became a sort of consecration, a rite that might be profaned only by the unthinking importation of aspects of the decaying city.[16]

For the most sacred tramping terrain in the region, the "best wild up-and-down-country," the *New York Walk Book* coauthors sent their readers north to the Highlands west of the river. According to RLD: "If some master genius of outdoor play should give himself full swing to dream of a setting that would stir the imagination, it is hard to see how he could scheme better than for the sweep of terrace in an amphitheater of mountain that New Yorkers know as Bear Mountain. Surely the whole scheme of the Bear-Mountain section of the Interstate Park is a dream come true." The prodigious *demos*, the same feature that drove New Yorkers out of the city for weekend recreation, became, in the age of mass transportation and increased leisure time, a distinct advantage at Bear Mountain, which was well equipped by nature to handle the crowds. As to why one should choose the western Highlands for recreation, RLD could trumpet:

> Scores of viewpoints, some rising to nearly 1500 feet; wide forested areas that are growing in wildness and beauty every year since timber cutting has been stopped by the establishment of the Interstate Park, the Stillman Black Rock Forest, and other agencies for their preservation; dense rhododendron swamps to hide the deer that are coming back; old military roads laid out by Washington and Putnam; Revolutionary shrines like West Point and Stony Point, whose names thrill the patriot; rock formations of the oldest periods of which we have geological record, which bear plain testimony to the mighty forces that fashioned the cliffs and ridges; safe, remote hiding places for the rarer flowers which are harried in the lowlands, and a bridge whereon northern plants carry their line to the southern Appalachian heights: these are a few of the allurements to the observant and thoughtful tramper who can appreciate the remarkable character of this region—wild and growing wilder, yet affording from its high places, on a clear day, a view of the towers of Manhattan."

Such a cornucopia of the primeval in the face of the shockingly modern laid a powerful hold on the city-weary sensibility.[17]

Though walking trails had long been available in more distant mountain regions thanks to the U.S. Forest Service and clubs such as the Appalachian Mountain Club, the Adirondack Mountain Club, and the Green

Mountain Club, these were usually too far away for anything less than week-long vacation trips. To meet the need for a trail system apart from high-ways but close by New York City, the Palisades Interstate Park became the solution. Few places in the United States saw trail construction proceed at the pace of the system in the Ramapo Mountains that stretched inland from Bear Mountain. This pathfinding was pioneered by a fairly small group of leaders, supported by a huge cadre of volunteer trail workers. Perhaps the most famous trail builder in the area was William Monroe, president of the Green Mountain Club's New York section. Monroe had previously charted the forty-two-mile Monroe Skyline Trail in the Green Mountains of Vermont and marked a trail system in the Wyanokie plateau in northern Passaic County, New Jersey. Meade C. Dobson (later president of the Adirondack Mountain Club) and Dickinson's coauthors Frank Place (leader of the Tramp and Trail Club) and Raymond Torrey were principals in trail building, as was the park's chief engineer, Major Welch, who lent all the resources at his disposal to promote outdoor recreation in the park. In 1920 Dobson organized a federation of delegates from New York City outing clubs to become the Palisades Interstate Park Trail Conference. Among the clubs represented were the New York chapter of the Appalachian Moun-tain Club, the Inkowa Club (Mary Harriman was a member), the Reptile Study Society of America (New York Zoological Society herpetologist Raymond L. Ditmars, president), the Woodcraft League of America, the Brooklyn Institute of Arts and Sciences, the New York Academy of Sci-ences, the New York–New Jersey Trail Conference, the Torrey Botanical Club, the Staten Island Institute of Arts and Sciences, the Mohawk Camp-ing Club, the Paterson Rambling Club, and the City College of New York Geology Club, as well as a number of larger national groups, including the National Audubon Society, the Boone and Crockett Club, the Boy Scouts of America, the American Game and Protective Association, and the Wild Flower Preservation Society. Leaders recruited helpers from each club and formed committees on scouting, clearing, and trail marking. Trail work in Harriman Park began in October 1920, with each worker supplying his own tools and paying his own expenses. Major Welch provided transportation within the park and shelter on some weekend working trips.

In the *New York Walk Book*, Dickinson, Torrey, and Place used the trails as a framework on which to erect a narrative of the region's human and natural history. Dickinson had a keen sense of deep time and pointed out that the Ramapo-Dunderberg Trail (the first one completed in the park, running from Tuxedo Station to Jones Point on the Hudson), in its traverse of the Bare Rocks and Hogencamp ridges, took the walker over a remnant of the old Cretaceous peneplain. He noted how the topography of the region was largely controlled by the fault lines in the edges of the fracture blocks of Precambrian times. The Highlands bedrock, so frequently exposed on ridge cliffs, stream cuts, and the ubiquitous fields of glacial *roches moutonées*, was perhaps the most essential way in which the feeling of the "primeval" was communicated to recreational hikers in the region. Layered on top of this ancient past was an array of human artifacts—tumbling-down stone walls and cellar holes of abandoned farmsteads, old mine pits, remains of iron forges and furnaces—that greatly added to this primeval feeling. The *New York Walk Book* encouraged study of the region's geology, giving tips on what to look for, a geologic time scale with sites for seeing the various formations, and a section on "The Carving of the Country," which presented a synopsis of William Morris Davis's cyclical theories of landscape evolution. To the Manhattanite who daily suffered the barrage of the *new*, trail walking at Harriman Park was imbued with a satisfying sense of permanence. "Look off from Beacon or Storm King up the valley," invited Dickinson, "and get a creepy feeling of what everlasting ages Nature takes to do her work. She is no schoolgirl with a lump of plasticine."[18]

In a section of the book devoted to the New York area's botanical character, Raymond Torrey stressed that the region was a meeting place of more northerly and southerly floras. Torrey encouraged the use of manuals to learn to identify plants, estimating that five hundred species could be easily learned in a few spring and summer seasons. He recommended that the novice plant hunter always choose some characteristic plant of the region and go looking. "It is a help, as Thoreau remarked, to receive from some friend a plant you have never seen which ought to grow in this territory. You get the appearance of it in your eyes better than can be given by any book description, and the next time conditions are favorable it leaps out of concealment where you had long sought it. That makes a good day. It is something that no one can take away from you." Torrey assured readers that within a day's excursion from New York City there were "thrills like unto the orchid hunter on the Amazon. Every remote peat bog or forest glade where one may find some rare native orchid new to him, every unfrequented ledge or cliff where an unknown fern is recognized as such and run down through Gray or Britton to its proper species becomes sure hunting ground as exciting as Central Africa or the Arctic." Torrey promised the studious walker the far reaches of space in the same way that Dickinson promised the depths of time.[19]

The Appalachian Trail and the American Primeval

Coming over the top of Anthony's Nose in early November 1924, Benton MacKaye stopped along one of its many open ledges, filled his pipe, and sat down for a mid-morning smoke. The panorama was nearly identical to the one that Dickinson had sketched for inclusion in the *New York Walk Book*, except that instead of white sprays of shadbush and dogwood flecking the Highlands slopes, patches of snow hung in north-facing hollows. Now the Bear Mountain Bridge was lined with cars and westbound freight trucks, and occasionally MacKaye could hear the piercing sound of one of their infernal electric horns. There it went, he thought, the mainstream of commercial America crossing the backbone of *aboriginal* America. He could plainly see the Bear Mountain Inn but could barely make out Major Welch's cabin. Tomorrow, he hoped, they would pick up a hundred of the "AT" trail markers Welch had designed and together mark the route that MacKaye had chosen today. The first section of the Appalachian Trail had been laid out the year before. Volunteers for the New York–New Jersey Trail Conference (founded by Major Welch, Ray Torrey, Frank Place, and others for the purpose of developing the Appalachian Trail in those states) had linked up parts of the Ramapo-Dunderberg, Timp-Torne, and Arden-Surebridge trails to form the route through Harriman Park. From the park, the trail would cross the Hudson on the Bear Mountain Bridge, ascend Anthony's Nose, and head northeast through New England toward its destination at Mount Katahdin, Thoreau's beloved mountain in Maine and the ultimate embodiment of the primeval.[20]

Although the landscape that had been MacKaye's primary inspiration for the Appalachian Trail was the Berkshires, the idea as well as the reality had been born farther south in the Appalachians. MacKaye had evacuated his cottage in Shirley Center, Massachusetts, to spend the summer of 1921 at Hudson Guild Farm, the New Jersey home of his friend and fellow regional planning advocate Charles Harris Whitaker. There, in late June, MacKaye first shared his idea; by the Fourth of July he had sketched out a preliminary draft proposing an "Appalachian Skyline"; and a week later he presented his proposal in its entirety to Whitaker and Clarence Stein, chairman of the New York State Housing and Planning Commission and author of *New Towns for America*. Whitaker, editor of the *Journal of the American Institute of Architects*, prodded MacKaye to write up his idea, and in the October 1921 issue of the journal there appeared "An Appalachian Trail: A Project in Regional Planning."[21]

MacKaye came from a long line of American visionaries. His grandfather Colonel James MacKaye, a counselor to President Abraham Lincoln, wrote the report, *The Birth and Death of Nations*, which had moved Lincoln to favor emancipation. His father, Steele MacKaye, an actor, playwright, theater designer, and inventor, had conceived of the Spectatorium, a massive amphitheater whose planned debut at the Chicago Columbian Exposition never came to pass. It lived on, however, in the pageants and epic poetry of Benton's brother Percy. Seven thousand performers presented Percy's *Pageant and Masque of St. Louis* to an audience of 250,000 in that city. Benton MacKaye's Appalachian Trail article struck its audience with the same audacious force as had the bold ideas of his progenitors. It was not so much the conceit of a two-thousand-mile-long trail; rather, the force of MacKaye's proposal lay in its conception of the Appalachian footpath as the foundation of a new social and geographic order, one that would stem the rising tide of metropolitanism washing in from the cities of the Atlantic coastal plain. Along the length of the trail, MacKaye foresaw a series of communities growing up out of the trailside shelters located about a day's walk apart. Drawing on the untapped potential of workers' increasing leisure time, this Appalachian skyline camping base would become a catalyst for the wholesale conversion of weekend campers. Transformed by their outdoor experience, these converts would choose to remain in the mountains and form the beginnings of a "counter-migration" away from the cities.

From the shelter camps would develop voluntary associations of urban refugees, which MacKaye called "community camps." Trained as a professional forester, MacKaye brought his own experience of mixing recreation with education to his proposal for activity along the Appalachian Trail: "Summer schools or seasonal field courses could be established and scientific travel courses organized and accommodated in the different communities along the trail. The community camp should become something more than a mere 'playground'; it should stimulate every possible line of outdoor non-industrial endeavor." Sustained by a mix of scientific forestry, agriculture, and other economic activity, the community camps would eventually become "food and farm camps," not unlike the Hudson Guild Farm. The only problem that worried MacKaye was the possibility that such camps might grow too large, threatening to replicate the very demographic and geographic blight they were supposed to alleviate. Like the trail itself, the communities would be harmonious models of free association: "The camp community is a refuge from the scramble of every-day worldly commercial life. It is in essence a retreat from profit. Cooperation replaces antagonism, trust replaces suspicion, emulation replaces competition." As such, the skyline refugia would have to be protected from creeping capitalism: "The enterprise should, of course, be constructed without profit. The trail must be well-guarded—against the yegg-man, and against the profiteer."[22]

This and future elaborations of MacKaye's utopian vision were given some physical substance by MacKaye's maps, which seemed to suggest that the dreams could indeed become reality. MacKaye was a compulsive cartographer; maps gave his spatial fantasies gravity, both for himself and others. His little cottage in Shirley Center was filled with hundreds of the pencil-on-tissue-paper productions of two decades of geographical observations and extrapolations. In the very first of these, from 1893, the fourteen-year-old MacKaye memorialized his many walks up Mulpus Brook and the farther explorations of the Squanacook River as a map of the surrounding forests, divided simply into coniferous and deciduous areas. His Yankee organizational bent flowed into a whole series of maps, which he eventually began to supplement with prose. Each map crystallized a particular "expedition," as Benton called his delicious part-physical, part-imaginative movements into the Berkshire hills. His brother James discovered one of these narrative geographies and delighted in quoting from its more self-consciously philosophical passages. This map commemorated the ninth of Benton's expeditions, and so James dubbed his brother's voyages "expedition nining." Lewis Mumford, MacKaye's dearest friend, described his life as "one long Expedition Nine."

MacKaye's earliest adventuring came when he was bushwhacking through the Green Mountains with fellow Harvard undergraduate Horace Hildreth along what would later become Will Monroe's Long Trail. Continuing at Harvard for a master's degree in forestry after he graduated in 1903, MacKaye honed his mapping and landscape reading skills. These were most noticeably shaped by the prodigious geographic imagination of the geology professor William Morris Davis, whose ideas about landscape form and process became second nature to MacKaye. He, in turn, passed them on to other Harvard forestry students, lecturing for a few years after receiving his degree, before spending a dozen years as a field man in Gifford Pinchot's U.S. Forest Service. From 1905 to 1913 MacKaye surveyed and mapped the forest types of New Hampshire's White Mountains; his final report was critical for establishing the White Mountain National Forest. Returning to Washington in 1913, MacKaye drafted a series of legislative proposals, including an Alaska lands bill and the National Colonization Bill, which envisioned for the Great Lakes region a redemptive project similar to the later Appalachian one. In 1919 MacKaye transferred to the Department of Labor, where he turned out a series of proposals merging his concern for environmental conservation with his ideals of conserving human labor, in the sense of making traditional productive industries— agriculture and forestry—viable community endeavors rather than exploitative capitalist ones. All of Benton MacKaye's expedition nining up until 1921 had been rehearsals for his epic production: the Appalachian Trail.[23]

Offered as "a project in regional planning," the Appalachian Trail proposal clearly was more a dramatic narrative than a bureaucrat's bold attempt at a benign form of social engineering. Camping companions knew MacKaye as a consummate storyteller. He had grown up in a family of dramatists. In addition to his playwright father and brother, his half-brother Arthur Loring MacKaye was a journalist and novelist; his brother Harold was a journalist; another brother, William Payson, was an actor and poet; and his sister Hazel, along with brother Percy, was a leader in promoting historical pageantry. Percy was Benton's constant amanuensis, and with Percy's aid, he never failed to frame his ideas dramatically. "An Appalachian Trail" concluded with a section, "Elements of Dramatic Appeal," that likened the care of the countryside to his Harvard professor William James's "moral equivalent of war": "Already basic, it can be made spectacular. Here is something to be dramatized."[24]

MacKaye's Appalachian Trail project met with tremendous approval and excitement in wide quarters but moved slowly at first from vision to reality. He carried the drama door to door for almost two years before it had its first performance. In March 1922 MacKaye went to Flushing, New York, to enlist the support of Boy Scout leader Dan Beard and to gather contacts for initiating trail construction. A couple of weeks later, over dinner at the City Club of New York with Clarence Stein, Raymond Torrey, and William Welch, the New York–New Jersey Trail Conference was founded for the purpose of building the trail in the Highlands. Major Welch, who had played such an important role in facilitating the earlier trail construction in Harriman Park, immediately found common ground with MacKaye's vision of trails as agents of both landscape and human restoration and renewal. In 1925, when the Appalachian Trail Conference was founded to ensure that the beginning made in Harriman Park would continue north and south for the length of the Appalachians, Welch was made chairman.

Welch, as the engineer of roads, dams, sewers, bridges, and other infrastructure, was the primary agent of modernization in Harriman Park; yet he saw himself as restoring the primeval Highlands landscape. Under his guidance, forestry efforts increasingly turned from the early widespread planting of exotics to an emphasis on native plantings. Native nut-bearing trees and berry bushes were planted to increase the native bird populations; native wildflowers and flowering shrubs were used along roadsides; streams and lakes were stocked with native fish. Even the nonnative Scotch broom, which still erupts golden in May on thin soils and ledge areas along the Perkins Memorial Drive near Bear Mountain, was brought into the park as a restoration of the past: Welch reminded his staff that during the Revolution, broom had arrived in baled hay for cavalry horses of the British army. Park officials always stressed how "natural" their efforts at artifice were, whether trails, inns, beaches, or parking lots. "All artificial adornment has been avoided," proudly boasted park annual reports. Perhaps the most surprising and ambitious attempt to restore the primeval landscape was the park's lake-building program. Welch reasoned that the cedar swamps and small eutrophying ponds in the region had in the Pleistocene been sparkling lakes dammed by glacial deposits, and that every concrete dam he built restored that past landscape. Now those lakes would be enjoyed by summer tent villages of campers rather than seasonal Paleo-Indian or Lenape villages. In a number of instances, Welch clearly was aware of surficial geologic indications that there had indeed been Pleistocene lakes in certain spots; in creating Lake Sebago, Welch's concrete dams across the valleys of Whitney and Stillwater Brooks restored an eroded lateral morainal deposit of sand and gravel.[25]

Welch even enlisted the aid of nonhuman engineers in his restoration of the primeval landscape. In the fall of 1920 the New York State Conservation Department gave Welch six beaver that had been trapped in the Adirondacks, where they had been reintroduced after being nearly extirpated. These were released in Beechy Bottom, a few miles west of Bear Mountain, and in Pine Swamp, north of Kanauwake Lakes. Within a decade, nearly a hundred colonies resided in the park. Although they became a nuisance to landowners along the park boundary, Welch was a tireless advocate of beaver as an essential element of the landscape. Their engineering works benefited fish, amphibians, and waterfowl, not to mention the humans who found their ponds useful for fighting forest fires. The same year the beaver were introduced, Welch brought seventy-five elk from Yellowstone National Park, hoping to reestablish these most spectacular of the aboriginal megafauna. Sadly, most of the animals died en route, and the surviving herd, kept in a pen on the western edge of the park, never reproduced in captivity. Still, the 1922 report of the Palisades Interstate Park Commission boasted that "there are few places in the world that offer more opportunity for biological study than this park."[26]

These efforts toward ecological restoration were stimulated to a great degree by the enormous sense of regeneration that Welch and others felt was engendered by the land itself. The Ramapo and Highlands forests at the turn of the century had been largely depauperate, badly abused by more than a century of repeated harvests for the charcoal iron industry. With that industry's demise, the hardwood forest was regenerating quickly, especially where it was aided by new forestry techniques. The "primeval" forests to which preservationists referred were in the opening decade of the century usually only thirty to forty years old, but to urban sensibilities they seemed spectacular, especially given the great extent of some of the forest tracts. By 1920 dramatic signs of recovery, rejuvenation, and restoration were everywhere—in the oak-hickory (formerly oak-chestnut) forests that provided ample mast and browse and the dense rhododenron swamps that provided cover for the deer that were quickly repopulating the region, in the nesting of wood duck and mergansers, and in the healthy populations of timber rattlesnakes and copperheads. Robert Latou Dickinson captured the essence of this regenerative landscape in the pen-and-ink sketches of the *New York Walk Book*. Whether of boaters on Hessian Lake, the white rumps of fleeing deer, or an abandoned log cabin melting back into the forest, RLD's sketches testified to the reality of regeneration and promised its restorative vitality to walkers. This was indeed the "best wild up-and-down country" imaginable to Manhattan trampers, who felt surrounded by the "primeval" when hiking park trails, even as they passed old iron mines, cellar holes, overgrown apple trees, lilacs, and day-lily beds, all evidence of human activity less than a century past.

Arcadia versus Metropolis

For Benton MacKaye, the "primeval" was one of three "elemental environments": the primeval ("the environment of life's resources, of the common living-ground of all mankind"); the rural ("the environment of agriculture, of local common interests and all-round human living"); and the urban ("the environment of manufacturing and trade, of the community of group interests and specialized living"). Though primarily a historical moment in the American past, eclipsed by the closing of the frontier, the primeval, MacKaye believed, was readily recoverable in the present through physical engagement with forested lands. Every inch a Yankee, MacKaye the forester and land-use planner had no experience beyond the eastern deciduous forests, and although he occasionally referred to other possible American primeval environments—the Arizona desert, the swamps of the Gulf coast, the fir forests of the Pacific Northwest—his vision of national renewal through contact with the Appalachian primeval was geographically chauvinistic. Similarly, he acknowledged other types of rural environments—"the French in Quebec and Louisiana; the Spanish in California; the Scandinavian in Minnesota"—but his model was the New England hill village of his youth, racially, economically, and culturally homogeneous. Yet, although MacKaye may have been culturally chauvinistic, his philosophy of regional planning was strikingly democratic. Feeling that the best planner is a "seeker, a revealer," he argued that one must work closely with amateurs: "the amateur revealer of Mother Earth herself . . . the would-be geographer and geologist—the 'Little Humboldt'; the student of natural history—the botanist, the ornithologist, and the others—the little 'Darwins' and 'Audubons'; . . . [and] the revealer of the story of mankind—the local historian, historical writers and dramatists." In the urban environment, MacKaye found no such indigenous revealers, only "general appreciators."[27]

MacKaye's blueprint for cultural renewal atop the Appalachian skyline began in contact with the primeval but seemed to call for a rapid transition to something like his "rural" elemental environment. He essentialized the primeval—which he alternately referred to as the "indigenous environment"—as a foundation and goal, as both natural resource and psychological resource: "The most fundamental portion of the indigenous environment consists of the primeval. . . . The primeval is 'The All' of visible creation: it is the known quantity from which we came, as God is the unknown. The primeval is bequeathed to us by God alone; all other environments are bequeathed by God with man's assistance; and with man comes in the element of fallacy." MacKaye freely mixed the transcendental language of Christianity with the language of science, often turning to biological metaphors, especially ones dealing with the structure and physiology of trees. Evolutionary ideas added further weight to his thoughts; he believed that the negative forms of human experience—toil, what he called "decreation," the opposite of true and restorative recreation—would inevitably be eliminated by evolution. He subscribed to William Patten's optimistic philosophy that "world growth" was synonymous with evolution. "*Living,*" suggested MacKaye, "*is man's part in evolution.*"[28]

In 1928 MacKaye synthesized his ideas about planning in *The New Exploration: A Philosophy of Regional Planning.* Taking his cue from T. H. Huxley's *Physiography: An Introduction to the Study of Nature* (1878), with its opening viewpoint from London Bridge, MacKaye chose for his vista Times Square in New York City. There, beneath the neon, he found the primeval's nemesis—the "metropolitan" or "wilderness of civilization." From the top of the Times Building, the reader was asked to heed not the passing river Thames but the "stream" of traffic, a "tidal" stream, with its peaks of high water at morning and afternoon rush hours, when a mass of "befuddled humanity" makes its way to and from the city, followed by a lesser surge of theater commuters later in the evening. However potent Times Square and the Manhattan theater district were as symbols of artifice, it was ironic that Benton MacKaye—having spent his first eight years growing up in this world, where his father's (and later his brother's) plays were staged—should choose them as signifiers of the evil metropolis. But he, like the rest of his family, clung to a very different model of the theater, in which drama acted as a communal rite of civic renewal. This "recreation" contrasted sharply with the "decreation," "self-abuse," or "mental opium" that issued from the commercial stage, the press, and the movies. In a January 1927 address to the New England Trail Conference, MacKaye recounted as an example of escapist self-abuse his experience of seeing Douglas Fairbanks in the film *Robin Hood*. MacKaye's ideal for walkers on the Appalachian Trail—"To walk, to *see*, and to see what you see"—was his personal philosophy, as applicable to city pleasures as primeval ones. Vicariousness, the hallmark of most modern recreation, was a sin.[29]

MacKaye's 1927 address had as its keynote his characteristic polarization of the metropolitan and the Arcadian. He drew upon ancient Rome for inspiration: just as Roman civilization had been "cleansed" by invasion from the hinterland, so must American metropoles of the day. Both "Civilizee" and "Barbarian" were Utopians, but the Civilizee was "content to be a vicarious Robin Hood," while the Barbarian was "a real (if diminutive) Magellan—a pioneer in the new exploration of a Barbarian Utopia." The Civilizee enjoyed "the throb of the jazz band," embraced "exotic metropolitan splendor," and saw "the mountain summit a pretty place on which to play at tin-can pirate and to strew the Sunday supplement." The Barbarian, on the other hand, liked "the ring and rhythm of the Anvil Chorus," preferred "indigenous colonial color," and viewed the mountain summit as "the strategic point from which to resoundingly kick said Civilizee and to open war on the further encroachment of his mechanized Utopia." When MacKaye told his fellow trail builders that the real point of the philosophy of through-trails was "*to organize a Barbarian invasion*" to counter the Metropolitan invasion, they unanimously declared themselves the new Barbarians and the Appalachian Trail the hinterland from which they would stem the tide of the modern "Romes" along the coast.[30]

Benton MacKaye and his fellow self-described Barbarians were thoroughly metropolitan, or at least *cosmopolitan*. (MacKaye was careful to distinguish cosmopolitanism—the free and selective borrowing of cultural elements—from metropolitanism—the imposition upon other peoples of the standardized manufactured items of consumer culture.) Fellow New Yorker and critic of metropolitanism Lewis Mumford once dubbed MacKaye an "aboriginal New Yorker." He had been born in Stamford, Connecticut, but until the age of nine he had lived in a crowded apartment at 46 East Tenth Street in Manhattan. His earliest memories were of rumbling elevated trains, the footlights and great satin stage curtains of the Star Theatre, and gaslit nights viewed from a hansom cab along cobblestoned Broadway. In 1888 his family had left the city for Shirley Center, where the rural and the primeval intersected outside his door. A self-conscious dweller in the primeval, MacKaye's years immediately preceding his campaign for an Appalachian renaissance were spent in Thoreauvian retreat at his Shirley cottage. He had no electricity in his own house, fetched water from the well or collected rainwater from the roof, and always took prunes for break-fast. He did not care for modern "*im-prooove-ments*," he would protest to inconvenienced visitors; modern technology was a "cancer" and "disease." Though he was the architect of the townless highway, he never learned to drive a car.[31]

Ever since he had been a boy climbing nearby Hunting Hill, MacKaye had ascended regional high points to get the lay of the land, both geographi-cally and intellectually. In *The New Exploration*, MacKaye chose to oppose the vantage of Times Square against that of the Hudson Highlands, "where, between Bear Mountain and Anthony's Nose, the mighty Hudson itself pushes through and opens the only level highway into the continent's inte-rior." There MacKaye had found "a man who recently made his first visit to New York. He had lived a long life within fifty miles from Times Square, and in spite of the Sunday supplement had no real notion of a metropolis. Yonder in the Appalachian hinterland there dwells another world. This world is the indigenous America. It is being invaded (but not yet captured) by metropolitan America." MacKaye chose a New York Metropolitan/Arcadian vantage too when he narrated a scene he had witnessed on the Erie Lackawanna Railroad while pulling out of Hoboken. MacKaye overheard a man asking whether civilization consisted of "having steam engines"; his female companion answered that no, "it is the development of our cultural possibilities." As MacKaye pondered this exchange, the train passed through the infernal infrastructure of the man's interpretation of civilization—rail-road roundhouses and train yards—to the freer domain where her vision might thrive—"the April-tinted ridges of the Ramapos against the cloud-less morning blue." Where was the couple headed? To escape Rome for a walk in Harriman Park, where they might exchange the *means* of civiliza-tion for its ultimate *ends*, namely, Arcadian contemplation.[32]

MacKaye found support for his view of the metropolitan man as in-authentic in Oswald Spengler's *The Decline of the West*. Spengler called the modern city dweller "a new sort of nomad, cohering unstably in fluid masses . . . parasitical . . . traditionless, utterly matter-of-fact, religionless, clever, unfruitful, deeply contemptuous of the countrymen." MacKaye, however, always tempered his pessimism with an inexhaustible wellspring of con-structive optimism about the possiblities for meeting modernity's challenges. Upon sending a draft of *The New Exploration* to Lewis Mumford, MacKaye took the role of reviewer to further distill his own ideas. He summarized the book as an exploration of how "the jungle of civilization has recently undergone a change called the mechanical revolution. . . . It has become a sort of barbed-wire entanglement reaching around the world. . . . Mother Earth on one side and wire entanglement on the other. Each culture and region—each 'indigenous environment' the author calls it—is being attacked by this entanglement. . . . We might in America follow up the start made in the 'Golden Day' (to use another guy's expression). This does not mean that we must all be Emersons; it means to develop potential environment just as the engineer develops potential waterpower." Drawing on his most elemental metaphorical source, he told Mumford that the book's entire intention was to put the issue of the indigenous versus the metropolitan in America "on the map."[33]

The Appalachian Trail as Epic American Drama

In March 1920 Benton MacKaye had written with characteristic optimism from his Arcadian haven in the Berkshires to his brother Percy, who was then living far from any woodland ephemeral ponds at the Player's Club in Manhattan: "I am thankful every time the spring time comes around . . . and breathe in the eternity that goes with the first peeping of the frogs. We were all born in frog time and perhaps that is what keeps us chirping through thick and thin." For MacKaye, humans—at least potentially in their primeval incarnation—were united with frogs both presently, by their perennial spring chorus, and historically, by the fact that coal-using moderns' fuel came from the Carboniferous, the era when frog voices first broke "the silence of creation." MacKaye could unite all landscapes not extensively modified by human action under the rubric "primeval" because in the forest the deep past was always present. Each tree, each frog, each mountain or pond carried within it the great saga of the evolutionary past, reminding the astute observer from whence they, and he, came. Fully conscious of historical change on the surface of the earth, feeling in his bones the ontogeny of landscapes—the cycle of youth, maturity, and old age so grandly elaborated by his Harvard mentor William Morris Davis—MacKaye was nonetheless equally convinced that Nature was benevolently static, in that it had always and would always remain apart from the Human, no matter how urbanized the landscape might become.[34]

While others worked to build his dream of an Appalachian Trail, Benton MacKaye continued to dream. In 1932, when more than half of the trail had been completed, he went on the stump again, this time to explain more concretely how the trail could bring about cultural renewal. In an article in *Scientific Monthly* originally titled "The Appalachian Trail as a Primeval Influence," MacKaye said that he had conceived of the trail as a means to "absorb the landscape and its influence, as revealed in the earth and its primeval life." MacKaye, no doubt implicitly positing an alternative to the passive windshield automobile tourism that had by then taken hold, enjoined his audience to follow in the tradition of Henry David Thoreau, who told readers that the "best way to become acquainted with any scenery is to engage in some pursuit in it which harmonizes with it." The opposite of machine influence—primeval influence—was "the antidote for over-rapid mechanization. . . . It is feeling what you touch and seeing what you look at. It is the thing whence we first came and toward which we ultimately live, the source of all knowledge—the open book of which all others are but copies."[35]

Just as walkers needed the *New York Walk Book* to know how and where to walk, hikers on the Appalachian Trail needed some written guide to know how to "read" the primeval landscape. The *Scientific Monthly* article was a brief version of that book—planned, but never published—which, in tandem with a series of fourteen nature centers along the length of the trail (the first at Bear Mountain, the rest at strategic spots along the Appalachian ridge, including Mount Katahdin, Mount Oglethorpe, and the Delaware Water Gap), would serve to teach others how to recognize the primeval the way MacKaye did. Profusely illustrated with his cross-sectional diagrams, annotated maps, and charts of earth history, the book described Appalachian geology, geomorphology, physiography, and biogeography, laid out by MacKaye as he saw it laid out along the Appalachian chain itself, that is, as a narrative. In an address to the New England Trail Conference shortly after the *Scientific Monthly* article appeared, MacKaye spoke of "The Trail as a Dramatizer of Nature." An early draft of the book, entitled "The Appalachian Revolution: A Detective Story of Nature Told by the AT," was arranged in the form of a script, with the title page identifying MacKaye only as "editor." The other dramatis personae were: the "Author—the Appalachian Trail, an antidote for the footless age; The Stage, or The Elements (air, ocean, lands, forest); The Actors, or Forces (erosion and uplift, growth and environment); the Action, or Story Before the [Permian Appalachian] Revolution; The Plot or unfolding (evolution of land and life)."[36]

The grand saga of geologic history merged with the story of the genesis of the Appalachian forest. MacKaye sketched in words and accompanying charts a seventy-thousand-year process of climate change, neatly outlining the southward and northward progression of forest types in response to the advancing and retreating continental ice sheet. Then MacKaye drew a picture of the *inside* of the Appalachian forest, its component species and their "mutual relations." His communitarian social ideas are clearly apparent in his portrait of forest ecology: the primeval forest was characterized by "cooperation and division of labor." MacKaye's text spoke of the forest as "a whole civilization; it is a close-knit society of plant and animal life. . . . Human society is an offshoot of forest society. Each has its history. To know America we must know human history, and to know humanity we must know forest history." MacKaye's forest society echoed his pragmatic view of the human social order: "The primeval forest is a balanced and independent society. It is still a warring society. It is not an Utopia, it is merely a civilization. Most of its folks live in cities—the ants and bees and hornets. Some live on farms—the lichens that first extract the food from Mother Earth. Others—like foxes—dwell part-time in subways; frogs occupy the waterfront; while songsters make their living in the skyscrapers. Each one is consumer and producer; some 'produce' by preying on others; everybody has a job; the less work the less food; resources in plenty and no markets; no middlemen, no salesmen." Visitors to MacKaye's nature centers would have found a didactic narrative that focused as much on the metropolitan political economy as on nature's primeval economy.[37]

Many years earlier, while working for the U.S. Forest Service, MacKaye had sketched out a "Drama of Conservation: A Geographic Allegory," a series of scenes, without dialogue, regarding conservation issues in the Rocky Mountain region. The characters included an eastern capitalist, land office agents, a mining expert with the Department of Interior, and a national forest supervisor. The draft drama, like all of MacKaye's projects, was a spatial affair—the script was heavily annotated with maps. It was an amateurish effort, even more heavily didactic than his playwright brother Percy's social dramas. But it represented a line of continuity with Percy's interests in the 1910s, best represented by his *Sanctuary: A Bird Masque*, written for the dedication of the Meriden (New Hampshire) Bird Club sanctuary in September 1913. Percy saw the masque as inspired equally by nature study and theater, and like Benton and his Appalachian Trail, Percy conceived of the masque as a pioneering attempt in the "redemption of leisure."[38]

The Meriden production attracted enough attention to warrant a second performance a few months later in New York, as part of a day-long "Bird Masque and Nature Conference," with Percy as the keynote speaker. Lamenting that the commercial theater took no interest in natural science, Percy envisioned a new civic theater, one that would blend theatrical art with the naturalist's vocation. Not only the popular middle-class pursuit of bird conservation, but also insects and other aspects of natural history might become the subjects of this new hybrid dramatic art: "the fascinating de-

signs, embossings, colorings, of insect forms could be symbolized in spectacles of astonishing beauty, motivated dramatically to the real and tremendous human relation which that ignored but pestiferous race bears to human
society and the state." Percy, who believed passionately in the possibilities
of the "civic theatre" to effect social change, was as convinced of his conservation drama's efficacy as Benton was of the Appalachian Trail's. Where
Benton imagined a chain of interpretive centers running the length of the
Appalachian primeval zone, Percy proposed urban centers of dramatic nature interpretation:

> If . . . every Natural History Museum had its outdoor theatre, equipped
> to set forth the multitudinous human meanings of its nature exhibits
> to the crowds that frequent its doors in their hours of leisure—if the
> directors of every Zoological Park were to provide for it a scenic arena
> and seek the civic cooperation of the dramatic poet and theatrical ex-
> pert, to vivify by their art the tremendous life stories of wild nature
> to the receptive minds of the human thousands convened to listen and
> behold—by such means, would not the disciples of nature study not
> simply adopt for their own ends a means of education and publicity a
> thousandfold more dynamic, imaginative, and popular than any of the
> static means of exhibits, lectures and published volumes on which they
> now rely: would they not also thereby splendidly assist in enlarging
> the civic scope of the theatre's art, still cramped, as for generations,
> within the walls of speculation and commercialism?

Here was an initiative to transform the metropolitan from within its own
borders, to complement the barbarian invasion being launched by his
younger brother.[39]

Percy MacKaye's theatrical vision played on the same Arcadian/met-
ropolitan tension that gave such force to his brother Benton's rhetoric of
renewal:

> For the first time perhaps in history, scientists, students of shy na-
> ture, lovers of wild remote creatures, conservators of vast, dumb-
> life forces—these on the one hand; artists of the theater, specialists
> in purely human emotions, directors of organized amusements, ex-
> perts in devising the mass-pleasure of multitudes, these on the other
> hand—meet together. . . . Here are recluse and publicist, laboratory
> scholar and footlight actor, forest builder and slum worker, repre-
> sentative of both broad prairies and Broadway: . . . says the nature
> worker: "The drama—creature of screaming bill-posters, progeny
> of reeling electric signs and congregating commuters—what is the

drama to me, except as a diversion? I never go to the theatre, unless to forget my real work."

Says the theatre worker: "Wild nature—home of unnamable birds
and beasts, hunt of lonesome unexpressive woods and mountain
faces—what is wild nature to me, unless as a backdrop? I never
go to the country, except to forget my own work."

In place of this division, Percy MacKaye prophesied a new synthesis
of the two crafts. Remembering his own childhood visits to the American
Museum of Natural History ("wistful for the wild unknown beyond the in-
sufferable city"), he asked whether the museum could fulfill its mission to
the public without bringing the exhibits to life in some dramatic form. The
same Sunday crowds who fell "under the spell of the artist taxidermist"
spent evenings from Monday to Saturday in the civic wasteland of the movies and vaudeville. His rallying cry—"art as a social science"—was familiar to many of the conference attendees, who were supporters of MacKaye
and other promoters of historical pageantry as an alternative to lowbrow
forms of recreation.[40]

Benton, borrowing perhaps from Lewis Mumford's lexical style,
termed his sort of wedding of science and art "geotechnics." Percy also
seized on the era's sense of the numinous power of the machine when he
called historical pageantry and his conservation masque "dramatic engineering." As first conceived by Percy MacKaye, Arthur Farwell, Chauncey
Langdon, and other members of the American Pageantry Association
(APA), a tremendously democratic impulse motivated the civic theater.
Metropolitan artists, happily ensconced in their Arcadian colonies—in New
Hampshire at the MacDowell Colony and with Augustus Saint-Gaudens
in Cornish, and in Vermont at Lake Fairlee—"discovered" the little community, the *Gemeinschaft*, of their host locales. But by 1920 the pageants
that had appeared in all forty-eight states were becoming routinized, weakly
participatory affairs, empty of their earlier social aspirations. Largely
through the efforts at dissemination sponsored by the APA, historical pageants tended to standardize and homogenize precisely what was supposed
to be idiosyncratic: the local place and its people. The same process could
be seen with *Sanctuary,* which was marketed from coast to coast by Ernest
Harold Baynes, president of the Meriden Bird Club, to promote "Bird Days"
and bird sanctuaries.[41]

Benton's antimodernism never quite reached the fever pitch that
erupted in Percy's early dramatic spectacles. And in the wake of World War
I's violent marshaling of community energy, the millennialist *communitas*
that marked Percy's 1914 *Pageant and Masque of St. Louis* no longer

seemed so innocent. The "primeval," in human hands, could become a thing of terror. By the time Benton was mobilizing support for the Appalachian Trail as an epic drama, Percy had retreated to the archetypal Appalachia of Kentucky for primal contact, drawing regenerative artistic strength from the "untamed" mountain people. The plays inspired by this sojourn seemed to carry the conviction that the "Megamachine" fought by Benton, Lewis Mumford, and their fellow new barbarians truly threatened to destroy the indigenous culture, the virile, archaic dialect and homespun genius of southern Appalachia.[42]

Both of the MacKaye brothers' schemas were for *secular* salvation, though their rhetoric occasionally reached past the phenomenal world they so dearly loved to something transcendental. In one of his many formulations of the necessity of recovering the primeval, Benton almost let the light of the *divinely* eternal shine on his concept: "The *primeval* influence is most embracive—something shared in common not merely by mankind but by all terrestrial life, something that links us with the stars and with the ages. The most potent field for developing this influence lies in the wild spaces, the mountain and forest spaces—the sacred remnants of our common primal world." Such sentiments echoed Romantic formulations of the previous century, but Benton MacKaye's celebration of the primeval aimed to supplant, not *supplement*, religious conviction. A single generation before, Percy MacKaye found himself uneasy with the very worldview Benton so ecstatically embraced. In the summer of 1895, after his first year at Harvard, where he received a thorough inculcation into the modern scientific ethos as he typed Professor Nathaniel Southgate Shaler's manuscript challenges to outdated Protestantism, he sent a letter to one of his former high school teachers:

> [W]hat a thing is phantasy! Let the scientist tell of our growth from dust and kinship with the chemicals, let the psychologist rave of mirrors in the brain, to me phantasy must ever be a spirit, in whose mere existence reason must see a shaming of the mean motives imputed to the universe. . . .
>
> [W]hy should not the phenomena of nature be explicable, as the realized imagination of a supreme spirit, as to be considered the blind upbuilding of senseless, unmeaning, automatic accident?
>
> . . . [This latter view] creates a void in spirit between man and his Dame Nature vaster than the breach between Christ and Caliban. Strange that man should hunt for signs of his low birth, when his own breast would reveal his kinship with the gods. Truly it is not God that drives man from his Eden, but man.[43]

The youthful Percy MacKaye's struggle to reconcile "the breach between Christ and Caliban" soon passed. His Harvard science education triumphed over the wan truths about the natural world offered by Christian evangelists, and Percy's plays and poetry, though full of Christian imagery, were largely Naturalistic in outlook, more Progressive than Congregationalist.

When a younger, less certain Percy had lamented that man, not God, drove himself from Eden, he was directing his criticism at the very heart of the new Naturalism. He scoffed at scientists' pronouncements of humans' "kinship with the chemicals" and of psychologists' talk of "mirrors in the brain." The notion of Nature as the result of blind accident was repugnant to him, the Darwinian "hunt for signs of his low birth" a terrible mistake. By 1920 an apostate Percy was allied with Benton in the search for redemption in the "natural," eschewing any need for a "supernatural." The Arcadian dramas they and their contemporaries were creating, whether on paper or on the physical landscape, were increasingly coming to fulfill any longings that modern metropolitans felt for cosmic meaning.

The primeval Appalachians and, more particularly for America's premier metropolis, the Ramapos held out in the first quarter of the twentieth century a compelling promise of Arcadian redemption. This is why Benton MacKaye's outlandish idea had first become a reality in the oak forests stretching south from Bear Mountain, over the upland terrain that Edward Harriman had dreamed into a park for the people. The metropolitan masses who sought sylvan refuge in the Ramapos on Sundays from Memorial Day to Labor Day got off at the Bear Mountain docks knowing that God dwelled in the great tidal river that carried them there from the Battery and awaited them in the green woods that clothed the Ramapo Mountains. All that was necessary to complete their redemption was a well-groomed interpretive path, some trail that could accommodate all members of the modern metropolis as it led them into the forest of natural knowledge.

CHAPTER 2

On Nature's Trail

NATURE STUDY AT HARRIMAN PARK

$\mathcal{A}$ grand physical setting with easy access to Nature was not sufficient for fully sharing the values of Naturalism with a wide public. From the outset, Harriman Park's designers aimed at the active use of the Ramapo landscape as a pedagogical tool. A decade before the birth of Benton MacKaye's dream of an Appalachian Trail, educators explored the possibilities of the park as an enormous "object lesson." Well before Liberty Hyde Bailey, Cornell University professor of botany and agricultural science, published *The Nature-Study Idea* (1903), the object lesson as a central tool for educating children about nature had been championed by educational theorists like Friedrich Froebel and Johann Heinrich Pestalozzi, who built on a tradition of object collecting for museums and cabinets of natural history. By the early twentieth century, "nature study" had come to mean the study of *living* and *local* objects, and the desire of American educators for access to outdoor settings added to the impetus for natural-area preservation already felt by conservationists. The pedagogical methods of nature study were largely pioneered in vacant lots and school gardens adjacent to urban and suburban elementary schools. At Harriman Park, educators were presented with a grander tableau upon which to work. The MacKaye brothers' emphasis upon drama was presaged by these educators, as was Benton MacKaye's focus on the walking trail as a pedagogical device. The development of nature study at Harriman Park also clearly demonstrates Peter Schmitt's contention that the Arcadian myth in America was shaped mostly by metropolitan sensibilities. In the object lessons offered at Harriman Park, the culture of automobiles and advertising were as critical as the nature of the local flora and fauna.[1]

Character Building through Nature Study

From the initial planning of Harriman Park, sponsors hoped that its benefits would be enjoyed by New Yorkers of every class, ethnicity, and race. Consequently, beginning in 1913, civic organizations were invited to join the Boy Scouts in bringing inner-city youth to park campgrounds. The campgrounds were clustered around Welch's newly restored "glacial" lakes, principally Stahahe, Tiorati, and Cohasset Lakes, and Twin Lakes at Kanawauke. In the mid-1920s, an impressive cross section of New York's five boroughs lived at two-week intervals in sylvan splendor. Camped at Stahahe were beneficiaries of the New York Association for Improving the Condition of the Poor, the Church of the Holy Trinity–St. James Parish, and the Orphan Asylum of the City of New York. Tiorati Lake hosted the Negro Fresh Air Committee, the YWCA–City of New York (Colored), the Jacob A. Riis Neighborhood Settlement, and the New York Life Insurance Company. Cohasset had the Hebrew Orphan Asylum–City of New York, the Union Settlement Association, Inc., and the New York Council of the Camp Fire Girls. Twin Lakes was the site for the Manhattan, Queens, and Bronx Councils of the Girl Scouts, the Girls' League of Yonkers, and the YWCA of Brooklyn. By 1917 the volume of campers had grown so large (about twenty-thousand from June to August) that a department was created to manage the camping program. A book about the Palisades Interstate Park claimed: "There are other great parks, great in extent and fame, and in these two points much greater than is the park which is the subject of this book; but considering its possibilities for doing good to the greatest number, it easily becomes the greatest park in the world."[2]

For all these multitudes, now provided with the opportunity of Arcadian regeneration through contact with nature at Harriman Park, there was little or no organized instruction in nature study. As with the creation of the park, the origin and growth of nature education at Harriman resulted from another antiurban, antimodern impulse born in the heart of Manhattan. During the winter of 1920, as part of the "Training Course for Leaders" at Teacher's College, Columbia University, Benjamin Talbot Babbitt Hyde, a staff member of the Department of Anthropology at the American Museum of Natural History and scoutmaster of Troop 652, New York City, addressed a group of summer camp leaders. F. Edward Brown, who was in charge of the boys' and girls' camps at Harriman, heard Hyde talk about his methods of engaging scouts in nature study and invited him to spend two weeks in the camps "telling the Nature Story." Hyde decided to spend his one-month summer vacation living with the scouts and giving one day a week to the Boy Scout camps.[3]

Hyde's affiliations with the American Museum and with Teacher's

College (where he was a trustee) stemmed from his long-time and generous patronage of both institutions. As heir with his brother to the fortune of the B. T. Babbitt Soap Company, Hyde had since the 1890s poured a substantial part of that fortune into a variety of natural history expeditions. Most notably, the Hyde Exploring Expedition had conducted archaeological excavations at Chaco Canyon, New Mexico, from 1896 to 1899 and sent tens of thousands of artifacts back east to the museum.

Hyde spent his first two weeks at Harriman Park helping to set up the "family camps," where wives of scout leaders stayed when they visited. He then began collecting materials and replicated, in a twelve-by-fourteen-foot section of the headquarters pavilion at Kanawauke Lakes, the "Children's Nature Corner" he had created at the American Museum. Since 1918, shortly after he had joined the museum staff as an unpaid associate, he had maintained a little menagerie of snakes and small mammals in the Hall of Insect Life, giving visitors an opportunity to handle and ask questions about *living* animals. Before leaving the museum for the park, Hyde had borrowed some discarded equipment, especially old insect cases, from Dr. Frank Eugene Lutz, curator of insect life. At Kanawauke Headquarters, along with several exhibits of live animals, Hyde established a small nature-study library from his own enormous collection of works in natural history. Scouts began to bring materials to Hyde for identification; the idea caught on well enough that Hyde asked permission of the museum to extend his stay for the rest of the summer, and the acting director agreed.

In the fall of 1920, when 180 scout executives met at Kanawauke, Hyde held forth for half an hour longer than scheduled on "the almost complete apathy on the part of leaders towards the bringing of Nature to the Scouts, due mostly to their own lack of training or experiences in the open to get Nature Knowledge for themselves." Despite nearly a decade during which "woodcraft" enthusiasts Ernest Thompson Seton and Daniel Beard had sought to shape the Boy Scouts into a "Brotherhood of the Backwoods," a focus on organizational efficiency and martial regimentation had stifled any real integration of the nature-study ideal into scouting.[4] Hyde outlined his ambitions for a large initiative of nature study within scouting, calling for volunteers to lead eight different science departments: birds, rocks, fishes, insects, snakes, botany, mammals, and amphibians. The next morning, thirty of the scout leaders gathered for what Hyde christened "the first Adult Nature Hike" in the Palisades Interstate Park. Hyde started off at a trot up Tom Jones Hill, stopped about half way up, and then returned to headquarters, quizzing the men on what they had observed. The hike confirmed his view of scout leaders as, at best, neophyte naturalists: "Only one knew the birds and the others almost nothing."

Hyde's anecdote suggests that scouting in the early years of its development had given virtually no attention to the place of nature study within its program of character building for the American boy.[5] Hyde had the impression that no natural history study was encouraged other than what was required in the scouting handbook to advance from one rank to the next. At that first conference at Kanawauke, the assembled scout leaders were canvassed about their preferred activities for a well-conducted scout program. After an hour of discussion with no mention of nature study, Hyde stood and announced that no camp could be complete without a nature museum. According to Hyde, "dead silence ensued." The scout leaders could not imagine how such a seemingly individualized, undirected enterprise as nature study could have any place within the daily agenda of heavily directed, drill-like group activity. Hyde's best rebuttal may have been his alarming revelation that he had discovered that most scouts were afraid of the dark and of many animals. Indeed, these city-bred members of the cult of the strenuous life did not care much for thunderstorms either. Hyde decided that the best approach to dispelling such fears would be to familiarize the boys with the most frightening member of the local fauna—snakes. After collecting snakes of the Harriman Park region, Hyde proposed to take them around to the camps and have as many children as possible handle them "and learn something of their value to mankind." When he returned for his second summer of nature instruction, Hyde arranged to have busloads of campers brought to the headquarters building to do just that—as well as to acquaint them with identification of the park's abundant rattlesnakes and copperheads and with first aid procedures.

Standing well over six feet tall, with large hands and broad shoulders, Hyde appeared supremely confident as he reached into a cage, pulled out a five-foot-long black rat snake, and held it up before an audience of gawking scouts or novice camp leaders. Frequently sharing the spotlight at lecture programs and conferences with noted naturalists and leading figures of nature study and outdoor recreation, Hyde usually stole the show with his snake demonstrations. During the winter of 1921, the American Museum sponsored a "Nature Leader's Training Course" series that featured distinguished lecturers, including Cleveland Abbe of the City College department of geology (on the mineral resources of the Harriman–Bear Mountain Park), A. Tennyson Beals, chairman of the field committee of the Torrey Botanical Club (on mosses), and Fay Welch, director of the state's conservation camps (on forestry). Members of the museum's staff also contributed: William Carr, of the education department, spoke on birds; Clyde Fisher, curator of visual instruction, gave his lantern slide show on wildflowers; Frank Lutz, always an entertaining lecturer, held forth on the life histories of local insects; and G. Kingsley Noble, curator of reptiles and amphibians, shared his wide experience in field and laboratory with exotic creatures. But none of these presentations was as enthusiastically received as Hyde's "Demonstration with Living Specimens." The brochure advertising the lecture course read: "'Uncle Bennie' Hyde believes that the study of living specimens is desirable in all nature work, but here it serves a double purpose, because the handling of live snakes releases the human mind from one of the commonest fears; and it is also a most delicate barometer to the physical and mental make-up of the person handling them."[6]

"Fear is a subtle and indeterminate source of mental distress, which may lead to an unbalanced mind and bodily discomfort," Hyde warned. From his long experience of bringing children to confront their fear of snakes, Hyde believed he had by trial and error worked out a foolproof method of banishing such disabling fears. He could cite thirty-two different common misconceptions, as well as a dozen or more fantastic "fish stories," about snakes, and he took up the conquest of the widespread fear of snakes as a personal campaign. One of Hyde's favorite exercises, carried out summer after summer at the Harriman Park camps, was to organize a snake-passing race. Two teams of campers lined up across from each other to pass along a specially selected snake. To anxious parents who believed that their children's fear safeguarded them against being bitten, Hyde offered the reassurance that only one percent of children who had received instruction from him would actually seek to pick up a wild snake, and he found that even children who had handled a demonstation snake would not pick it up again unless urged to do so by him.[7]

Beneath the scout hat, knickers, wool knee socks, and red neckerchief, Hyde looked very much the archetypal image of the slightly anxious, unmuscular, urban-softened late Victorian American male. Bald, with wire-rimmed glasses and a neatly trimmed mustache, a studious, self-consciously caring look on his face, the big man handling the big snake also was easily imagined by his audience as a fellow who very likely had himself been frightened to death of snakes at one time. Known to children and adults as "Uncle Bennie," Hyde shared with many of his era's scout leaders the mantle of benevolent paternalism worn by a generation raised mostly by stern, largely absent, and often uncaring fathers. In fact, fathers were largely absent at the park camps, where the majority of both civic leader chaperones and park camping department staff were women. Hyde, even if less impressive perhaps than the sort of male role models routinely paraded before Boy Scouts (some of whom—Teddy Roosevelt, Labrador explorer Dillon Wallace, globe-trotting naturalist and explorer William Beebe—made regular visits to the park camps for lectures), helped to ease the urban boys from the feminizing domesticity of their mothers and toward the desired ideal of strenuous manhood. Nature study in its fin-de-siècle incarnation had been a highly feminized activity; now wedded with scouting's martial vigor, nature study promised something boys need not be ashamed of. Hyde was particularly keen on reaching private school boys, knowing from first-hand experience that upper-class boys often needed to learn to think and act for themselves.[8]

Hyde embodied the tension between the traditional republican ideal of spartan virtue and the modern reality of upper-middle-class urban, commercial life. Even before he became involved in scouting, Hyde sought out authentic, primitivist experience to assuage his uneasiness about living in metropolitan luxury. Born in 1872 into the privileged world of uptown Manhattan (his parents' home was on West Fifty-third Street, not far from his boyhood Arcadian retreats of the American Museum of Natural History and Central Park), Hyde had attended St. Paul's School in Garden City, Long Island. After making a world tour in 1892–93, he and his brother Fred enrolled at Harvard, where they became devoted students of Frederick Ward Putnam, who had recently been appointed curator of anthropology at the American Museum of Natural History. Through Putnam, the Hydes met Richard Wetherill, a resident of the Southwest who had become famous as the discoverer of the Chaco Canyon cliff dwellings. The Hydes proposed to Putnam that they sponsor an archaeological excavation by the museum at Pueblo Bonito. The resulting Hyde Expedition of 1896–99, under the direction of the museum's George H. Pepper, first explored the cliff dwellings and caves of Colorado and Utah, then moved on to Chaco Canyon. Discovering that the Indian laborers on the dig would buy goods from the expedition's stores, the Hydes seized upon this potential source of revenue; their trade with the natives at the Chaco Canyon site evolved into a series of twelve trading posts on the Navajo reservation. The Hydes also encouraged blanket weaving and other handicrafts for sale to the growing tourist trade and through department stores back east. Eventually, the Hyde Exploring Expedition (the name under which the brothers incorporated the enterprise) opened a store on Forty-second Street in Manhattan where customers could watch Navajo women weaving in the store window display.[9]

Mixing commerce with science became Hyde's stock in trade. Having inherited from his father and maternal grandfather a love of chemistry, physics, and mechanics, Hyde had his own chemistry lab in his parents' home before going to work for his grandfather's company. The B. T. Babbitt Soap Company was a pioneer in the use of advertising to promote sales of its products. "Babbitt's Best Soap" was born more in the sales pitches coined by Hyde's grandfather than it was in the firm's state-of-the-art chemical laboratories. The modern sales premium owed its beginning to Babbitt's Best Soap. B. T. Babbitt conceived the idea of giving a colored illustration to anyone submitting twenty-five soap wrappers. Editions of some of these illustrations ran into the thousands. Hyde's apprenticeship as a chemist and salesman at B. T. Babbitt ran from 1897 to 1903, when the company's marketing success was at its height. Following a stint from 1903 to 1909 with the Egg Baking Powder Company, he returned to Babbitt from 1909 to 1912, serving for a time as president of the company. Hyde frequently conceived of his nature-study work as "selling" and suggested that Boy Scout leaders do the same. To make their camp a real "nature camp," Hyde recommended giving several "inspirational talks" to the entire scout group, drawing on such themes as: "the universe and earth's relationship to it; the great changes since the cooling of the earth; the ancient creatures, their life and extinction; the eons of time for life to evolve." Hyde suggested that the leader then select a few boys who showed special interest—"real naturalists in embryo"—and invite these boys to help start a museum.[10]

The foundation of Hyde's approach to nature study was his belief in G. Stanley Hall's recapitulationist theory of adolescent development. Hall viewed the transition from boyhood to manhood as analogous to the evolutionary progression from "primitive" to "civilized" man and advised pedagogical strategies that would free the adolescent boy's instinctual impulses and channel them toward social usefulness. Hyde's view of adolescence stressed two instinctual impulses that he held to be "race characteristics": the "sense of curiosity" and the "sense of possession." Both could be socially dangerous if allowed to "run wild." But Hyde believed these impulses could be developed instead into the spirit of scientific investigation (curiosity) and an ethic of conservation and preservation (possession). A nature museum, which "satisfies and directs the sense of possession," and an attendant program of nature instruction, Hyde told scout leaders and other character builders, brought both of these forces under control so that they might be harmoniously developed. The sense of stewardship cultivated by nature study could help to stave off the "cruel age" of adolescence and give the boy "a useful and pleasant knowledge of the myriad wonders of the out-of-doors and bring him in harmony with the woods and fields in a way that is vitally necessary in this age of city life and mental unrest."[11]

The late Victorian legacy of "nervousness" (a socially conventionalized malady to which Hyde himself fell victim on numerous occasions) was apparent in Hyde's prescriptions for the ideal outdoor leader. Physically, the leader should possess "steady nerves; good strong muscles; well-equipped body; good poise, not fidgety, ready to emergency." Mentally, "a right attitude toward the truth" was essential. Spiritually, the ideal leader need have "no special creed . . . to live a right life," only "a sense of appreciation to God for the greatness of life." Another anxiety characteristic of Hyde's generation and class, and one that colored his counsel to future nature study leaders, was the potential of being perceived as a huckster. Nature study, as surely as any other cultural endeavor in that commercial age, was prey to confidence men. Hyde's maxim, therefore, was: "always tell exactly what you know; do not pretend anything." In a draft of a "Fieldbook for Nature Leaders," which he prepared during his tenure at Harriman Park, Hyde broke down the reasons for undertaking nature study into two groups. In the first group, he listed conservation, research, and the "elimination of widespread superstition"; the second group contained "personal" reasons: "aesthetic appreciation of beauty and order . . . self-reliance, leadership." Nature study could of course be carried on in many situations, Hyde acknowledged, but the ideal environment for it was in camp, and for this reason scouting had a critical role to play in revolutionizing nature study. Campers had the great advantage of "study[ing] nature where nature is"; but more important, since camp life was seen to be less artificial than home life, it encouraged "naturalness." Hyde called camp-based nature study of the sort he promoted among the Boy Scouts as "more peaceful, hence encourag[ing] a receptive state of mind."[12] Nature-study instructors needed to create the same atmosphere of acceptance promoted by the Babbitt soap salesmen.

After the 1921 season, Hyde convinced park officials that, although Kanawauke had on a spectacular scale brought boys to Nature (ten thousand scouts had visited in 1921), it had not yet fully succeeded in bringing Nature to the boys and needed trained counselors to do so. The following season Hyde had a staff of seven instructors, an artist, a librarian, a "laboratory man," and a secretary. Hudson Valley conservationist Ernest Stillman donated a thousand dollars so that six female students from E. Lawrence Palmer's nature-study course at Cornell could take the nature-study program into the many girls' camps in the park. (Hyde, who was enthusiastic about getting girls involved in nature study, seeing it as an antidote to "flapperism," noted that, "because their fingers had already been trained in accuracy, care and neatness with needle and thread," the young women nature instructors created better notebooks and exhibits.) The instructors fanned out to the regional camps, spreading the gospel of nature study and initiating new museums on the plan of Hyde's at Kanawauke, which they also helped to maintain, in Hyde's words, "as a showplace, and a source of information and inspiration for the Scouts." Many of these instructors continued in the growing profession of "nature work," and some became natural scientists, among them F. Martin Brown, who worked for Hyde in 1921 and 1922 and later became a noted lepidopterist.

Hyde's activities won support from officials of the American Museum, who saw the Kanawauke Museum as spreading its influence. Director George Sherwood and President Henry Fairfield Osborn already conceived of the American Museum as "the great center for 'Indoor Field Work'"; the Harriman Park nature museums extended that tradition. In his hope that Hyde's museums would be "taken as models all over the country," Osborn fully shared with Hyde the sense that contact with the "primeval"—both in Nature itself and in Man— offered the ultimate restorative force. In 1918, writing to wish Hyde well on his recent marriage ("I am sure it will be of the greatest help to you both in your life and in your scientific work") and on his upcoming expedition to explore an Aztec ruin, Osborn assured Hyde that "it is altogether a bright and encouraging prospect, and a great relief, with our emotions stirred by the terrible condition of affairs on the continent of Europe—Nature calm, serene and beautiful, and the work of primitive man a great resource in these days of trouble."[13]

By 1924 Hyde's museum had grown well beyond its origins as a natural history cornucopia, and staff scientists at the Museum of Natural History were drawing upon Hyde's network of junior collectors. G. K. Noble had a half dozen scouts collecting salamanders in the park during the summer of 1921. F. M. Brown and George E. French organized an insect exhibit with a case of oak galls, two cases of local insects (one of moths, one of butterflies), and a specimen of carpenter bee tunnels in wood. On loan from the city, the Kanawauke Museum had an exhibit on insect life histories, including the silkworm, tent caterpillar, Cecropia moth, monarch butterfly, and honeybee. The education department also loaned an exhibit of 141 local birds, which was used by scouts to help them achieve their Bird Study merit badges. Exhibits on forestry, fungi, minerals, bird nests, and medicinal herbs also appeared in the park's museum. With the help of his growing staff, Hyde created a field extension of the American Museum of Natural History, following its method of organizing nature's variety via evolutionary theory. Charts depicted the common ancestry of contemporary reptiles and extinct dinosaurs; drawings of a copperhead among dry leaves showed the theory of protective coloration; a chart on morphological adaptations demonstrated the way in which the forelimbs of man, bat, porpoise, and anteater had been modified to suit their various modes of living. The regional park botany exhibit was accompanied by one on the evolution of the plant kingdom.

Much of summer camp life revolved around competitive sports and other activities, and nature study at Harriman accommodated itself to the competitive spirit. A nature-study emblem system modeled on the Boy Scout merit badge set goals for collecting activity, and campers were expected to keep natural history notebooks (sold to scouts for ten cents a piece at the camp store). In an effort to improve the regional camp museums, an intercamp contest was begun, with awards for the most notebooks turned in, originality in museum exhibits, and other categories. To win the coveted "nature pennant" at the end of the season, campers began to streamline their efforts by dividing the labor, such as collecting large numbers of leaves of each tree species and then distributing them in camp so that a greater number of notebooks might be turned in. Noting that the spirit of competition had been "overemphasized," camp leaders decided to end the intercamp competition in 1927.[14]

Ever sensitive to the need to market nature study, Hyde kept a full photographic record of the activity in the camps. Major Welch's staff photographer also created extensive documentation, both with still photos and motion pictures. Begun in 1921, these efforts were pursued more systematically as nature-study activity expanded beyond the scout groups. In 1925, at a three-day meeting of nature leaders at Bear Mountain, Hyde proposed a nature magazine for park campers. *The Camp Naturalist*, edited by a young Hyde protégé, William Carr, began as a standard weekly chronicle of camp news; selling for a nickel a copy, the mimeographed paper was bought by many campers eager to see their names and those of their friends in print. By 1927 *The Camp Naturalist* had become a more ambitious ten-cent affair. The focus on Harriman Park was replaced by a variety of chatty illustrated articles on natural history topics, frequently contributed by professional naturalists. Hyde promoted the publication through the Boy Scout National Headquarters, but boys lost interest.

Hyde, who had been released from his duties in the Anthropology Department of the American Museum as his nature-study activism grew, dreamed of extending nature study beyond Harriman Park. In 1923 he proposed to the National Council of the Boy Scouts of America (which had by 1920 designated him "Chief of Scoutcraft") the creation of a national program of nature instruction, to be centered at Harriman Park and including a "nature lore research laboratory" and a permanent museum building. Hyde assured scout executives that the endeavor would aid them in their effort to make New York City "the greatest center of organized scouting in the world." The estimated price tag for the first year of operation was $56,500. Undaunted by the scouting leadership's lukewarm response, Hyde in 1926 lobbied Major Welch, proposing that a $25,000 gift from Frederick Julliard, originally intended for a hospital in the park, be redirected to create the Harding School of Outdoor Recreation. Suggesting that it be constructed in the Beechy Bottom section, west of Bear Mountain, Hyde envisioned that the school would host about a hundred students and have a staff of eight to sixteen instructors. Although this initiative went unrealized, another staff member of the American Museum was already establishing within Harriman Park the foundation of America's first truly "national brand" nature study program.

"Calling Your Attention to Interesting Things"

Traveling north across the New Jersey–New York border on Franklin Turnpike, a couple of miles beyond the ivy-covered, glacial cobble-walled gatehouse of Tuxedo Park, Frank Lutz pulled the "Bee," the Model T he had rigged for collecting expeditions in the West, to the side of the road, just opposite the place where workmen were preparing to lay new macadam for the road leading west to Greenwood Lake. On this Sunday in the middle of October 1924 the turnpike was crowded with motorists, many of whom were turning east onto the Seven Lakes Drive, bound for Bear Mountain. Lutz walked through a field full of goldenrod and climbed the gravel bank to the top of the knoll. On the edge of the oak woods stood an old cabin, which he thought might serve as temporary living quarters. Lutz then walked due south down the same gravel bank, which had been cut into by Wildcat Brook on its way to join the Ramapo River just on the other side of the highway. The brook turned back on itself here, where a bed of glacial cobbles provided a convenient fording place. Crossing the brook, Lutz followed along its opposite bank for a way; the north-facing woods of beech, yellow birch, and occasional hemlocks were a welcome contrast to the drier red oak woods on the opposite bank, surprisingly warm on this Indian summer's day. As he began gradually to ascend the flank of the hill on the south side of Wildcat Brook, Lutz noted the transition first into a forest of red and white oak, punctuated here and there with the straight, limbless boles of tulip trees that filled in where old oaks had dropped out of the canopy. Toward the flat-topped, nine-hundred-foot-high summit, chestnut oaks became predominant. Lutz found one little break in the summit canopy, where an island of gneiss ringed by a few scrub oaks and pitch pines afforded him a view north across the valley to Wildcat Mountain, where that summer Uncle Bennie Hyde had carried on a forestry camp in the woods around Spruce Pond.

Lutz could make out the fire tower on Parker Cabin Mountain, just southwest of Kanawauke Lakes. Closer by, a red-tailed hawk circled the ridge to the east, and closer still, an occasional straggler Monarch headed south. Lutz noted that their population seemed especially healthy this year. He continued west along the level ridge, then descended again toward Wildcat Brook, where the ridge ended. Crossing the brook again, he ascended the opposite bank and circled back toward the place where he had begun his walk. The patchwork of field and forest in various stages of regrowth and at a variety of elevations and slope aspects, along with the riparian zone of Wildcat Brook, made for a fairly representative diversity of habitats. There were plenty of larval food plants for some interesting butterflies, wild cherry trees covered with this past summer's silken webs of tent caterpillars, even a few volunteer apple trees that would bring honeybees in May. Best of all was the steady stream of traffic on Franklin Turnpike.

On Monday morning, back at his office in the American Museum of Natural History, Lutz drafted a letter to President Henry Fairfield Osborn. His outline for a field station for the exhibition and study of insects proposed that the site would provide: exhibits of living insects like the ones he had developed on the museum's third floor (Lutz believed the field station's exhibits would be even better because they would display the insects "more attractively" in situ); a docent service for visiting scouts and other outdoor organizations, led by himself and advanced amateurs (he was thinking of his son Frank and daughter Anna, as well as other promising young naturalists); facilities for securing exhibition material for the Hall of Insect Life; and opportunities for the sort of research he had been conducting at his home insectary, but under much more favorable conditions. He expected the field station to develop along the lines of the Plummer's Island station in the Potomac River, established by the Washington, D.C., Biologists' Field Club, which hosted entomologists from other institutions there. He informed Osborn that such an enterprise would require about ten acres of "diversified" land near both Manhattan and his home, close to as many summer camps as possible, and along a much-traveled automobile highway. Finally, with Osborn's approval and help, Lutz believed he could secure such land near Tuxedo, New York, for an initial term of ten years without cost to the museum. Lutz also had high hopes that the museum would not need to increase his department's "normally very small budget for field-work," as he had the prospect of his own patrons.[15]

Osborn was delighted by the proposal, whose mix of scientific research and education accorded with many of the programs he had helped to launch at the museum. He told Lutz to discuss the plan with Director George Sherwood and Scientific Director Robert Cushman Murphy before seeking approval from the museum's trustees. Osborn also noted that he had friends in the Tuxedo district who, he was certain, would take an interest in such local educational work. Assured of Osborn's support, Lutz laid out the full plan, revealing that the exact location he had in mind was directly opposite the road where, the past July, more than eighteen thousand automobiles had entered Harriman Park, a number that would increase greatly with the completion of the Bear Mountain Bridge. Lutz pointed out that an omnibus service also traveled the route between Tuxedo and Bear Mountain, serving the Boy Scout and community camps in the park. Lutz enclosed Major Welch's 1922 map of proposed new lakes in the park, scoring in red the transportation routes and inscribing "Boy Scout Camps" prominently at Kanawauke. Having established this strategic matter of location, he went on to describe the habitat diversity that made the site so ideal.[16]

Lutz's plan followed a nearly half-century-old tradition in American biology of locating research stations close to summer resorts. Just before coming to the American Museum, Lutz had been a member of one of these unique hybrid communities, the Station for Experimental Evolution (SEE) at Cold Spring Harbor, Long Island, where he conducted research in genetics and biometrics. The Tuxedo field station—which, to win the interest and support of Harriman Park officials, he intended to call the Interstate Park Station for the Study of Insects—was similar to SEE, the Marine Biological Laboratory at Woods Hole, Massachusetts, Johns Hopkins University's Chesapeake Lab, Friday Harbor in Puget Sound, Washington, and the Mount Desert Biological Laboratory in Bar Harbor, Maine, in its proximity to a resort community.[17]

The research station envisioned by Lutz broke with tradition, however, in the degree to which it anticipated the integration of public education as part of its mission. Though partly owing to his affiliation with a scientific institution that had pioneered natural science education for "the people," Lutz's intentions were directed toward a particular public. He had been drawn into nature-study instruction for scouts through his own sons, leading their troop on local field excursions to the Ramapo Mountains and other destinations. He saw the weekend stream of automobile-borne Arcadian seekers passing his field station as an equally receptive audience for instruction in natural history. In his proposal to Osborn, Lutz quoted Osborn's friend (and museum trustee) Madison Grant, who, among his many other executive positions with metropolitan conservation organizations, was chairman of the Committee on the New York State Park Plan. Grant considered the camping facilities of "the greatest park in the world" a model operation, one that held great possibility for conservation education.[18]

Lutz saw in the camps, particularly the Boy Scout operations at Kanawauke, a resource as well as an audience. Another key component of his research station idea was to use the place as a proving ground for promising young naturalists. The coastal biological research stations counted on student workers, but drew them from undergraduate and graduate university science programs. Lutz would recruit his students from the ranks of Boy Scout troops and the type of outdoor recreation staffs then developing at Harriman Park. Faithful to field experience as a critical foundation for biological research, Lutz believed a summer spent camping close to one's subjects could be as important as a summer's instruction in a state-of-the-art laboratory. He wanted boys with pluck and ingenuity, traits he believed were encouraged in camp.

Lutz was famous for his do-it-yourself abilities. He was constantly improvising field and laboratory equipment out of the most humble materials. Without the funds to purchase a $250 Macbeth illuminometer—a device for measuring the visual acuity of insects—but needing such an instrument to carry out fieldwork in Panama, Lutz jerry-rigged a substitute made of cardboard and string. "It can be carried in an inside coat pocket, weighs only a few ounces, is unbreakable, and I thought it up all by myself," he boasted to his friend Hermon C. Bumpus, former director of the American Museum. Lutz also told Bumpus that he had spent just $53 from his museum field research budget for a ticket to Panama, where he would use his new "toy" on leaf-cutting ants. Studying insect locomotion and its relation to thermoregulation, Lutz devised a treadmill apparatus out of parts of an old typewriter, tin from tobacco cans, and other odds and ends from his home junk pile. When one of his volunteer assistants needed a quartz lens for research on ultraviolet vision in insects, Lutz supplied a pinhole cardboard lens in its place. Unable to purchase a mercury arc light for his research on diurnal rhythms in crickets and grasshoppers, Lutz contacted the General Electric plant in Hoboken, borrowed $100 worth of parts, and made his own.[19]

Though he seemed born to tinker, Lutz's ingenuity was stimulated more than he wished in the 1920s and 1930s by the museum's frugality toward its Department of Insect Life, where Lutz had been curator since 1921. (His previous positions included assistant curator of invertebrate zoology, 1906–1916, and associate curator, 1916–1921.) Lutz found it increasingly difficult to persuade museum officials to appropriate adequate funds for exhibit or research purposes. At the time of his field station proposal, he had been lobbying Director Sherwood for a small amount of money to improve the lighting for the exhibit cases in the Insect Hall; it would be three years before his request was finally granted. As the museum increasingly turned its attention to vertebrates, the stature of invertebrate zoology suffered, despite Lutz's protests about the popularity of the insect exhibits with the general public and the importance of insects as material for research in problems of general biology. By the late 1920s Lutz's research reports to Sherwood were punctuated with sarcastic self-deprecation; describing his experiments on stingless bees, Lutz told Sherwood that "the total cost of apparatus for these bits of experimental biology has been less than seventy-five cents—twenty-nine tacks, fourteen nails, about ten feet of string, nine corks, some card-board and a little watercolor paint."[20]

Lutz's confidence in the financial viability of his field station was based on the prospect of a patron, B. Preston Clark of Boston, who had offered to meet Lutz's estimate of $15,000 per year for research in economic entomology. This largesse helped clear the way for approval by the museum's trustees, but Lutz still needed the agreement of the Palisades Interstate Park Commission, because the site he had chosen was park property. On his own initiative, President Osborn prompted his friends J. DuPratt White and Averell Harriman, both park commission members, to expedite consideration and asked Edward L. Partridge, a member of the committee considering Lutz's proposal, to sound out Frederick Julliard on the possibility of redirecting his $25,000 gift for a park hospital toward the proposed research station. Partridge also suggested to Lutz that he contact Dr. Morton R. Peck of Cornwall-on-Hudson, who, Partridge said, was interested in insects: "He has means, retiring disposition, and would make an interested worker." This was the perfect formula for successful scientific patronage.[21]

In November the park commission granted a ten-year lease on the land, with the option of renewal. Averell Harriman (also a museum trustee), who owned a ten-acre parcel that was necessary to afford access to Wildcat Brook, gave the museum the same arrangement. Having no firm backers as yet to provide an endowment for buildings, Lutz intended to set up tents out of sight from the road as lab and living quarters. Whenever construction could start, however, Lutz wanted his buildings in clear view of the Franklin Turnpike, for his plan depended on the station's visibility to motorists. One of Lutz's first requests to Major Welch was for two highway signs, one to be placed with the cluster of hotel signs along the turnpike and the other at the bridge over the Ramapo, on the road coming from Harriman Park. Along with "Station for the Study of Insects, Operated by the American Museum of Natural History," Lutz suggested the wording: "For Education, Science." Lutz proved prescient about the location; in April, just as he was getting ready for his first season, the park commissioners received a proposal to lease the site for a gasoline station.[22]

Lutz expected and wanted traffic; he consulted with Major Welch about providing restrooms, benches, lunch tables, waste cans, drinking water, and even policing for his new field station. He hoped to host an overnight visit from the New York Entomological Society (he had recently been named its president) on Decoration Day, and open after that. The American Museum had circulated press releases, and he had himself given the first public announcement of the Station for the Study of Insects (SSI), at a talk in early May to the Riverdale Entomological Club. Lutz invited the club to select a talented boy to come work at SSI that summer. Albert Redmond, recommended by the museum's curator of anthropology, came to talk to Lutz; he needed to know whether he would have an opportunity to swim, because he was on his school swimming team and "did not want to go stale." Meanwhile, Lutz drew upon scout labor; taking his son Frank and three fellow scouts up to the site one weekend, Lutz paid them each a dollar and their lunch to cut trails and tenting places.[23]

The trails were the key to his plan for that summer. Having witnessed the visitor response to Uncle Bennie's live animal corner and his own success with teaching Boy Scouts some elementary natural history on camping and hiking trips, Lutz intended to devote the entire summer to an "experiment." Along the half-mile-long path that his crew had cut through the woods along the bank of and on the terrace above Wildcat Brook, Lutz attached to trees, shrubs, and herbaceous plants two-and-a-half-by-five-inch linen Dennison's labels with identifying information written in waterproof ink. A series of simple tree and shrub identifications, teaching the novice to distinguish opposite from alternate leaves, deciduous from coniferous habit, and other botanical basics, formed the main thread of the narrative. Beginning in the little clearing near the cabin, Lutz worked clockwise along the trail, pacing the labels so that they opened a subject simply, became more complex, and then closed with a short summary statement. From his experience with a numbered sequence of exhibits in the Hall of Insect Life, Lutz knew that visitors tended to disregard the numbers and jumble the intended narrative progression. Although the trail ended just a few feet from its starting point, Lutz made sure the return was obscured by vegetation so that the visitor would be certain to begin at the beginning and proceed in the right direction, amassing a concise package of natural history lore along the way. On a gnarled cherry stump at the trailhead, Lutz nailed a small sign: "The Spirit of the Training Trail: A friend somewhat versed in Natural History is taking a walk with you and calling your attention to interesting things."[24]

The "interesting things" began with a canvas tent near the start that housed common household insects like cockroaches and bedbugs; there was also a desk for one of Lutz's student docents, who would answer questions, direct visitors down the trail, and make new labels as various seasonal phenomena made their appearance. Once on their way, trail walkers passed from one chatty label to the next: "Witch hazel liniment is made from the juice of such witch hazel bushes as this one." "Notice the galls like little witches' hats on some of the witch hazel leaves." "These pointed galls formed where certain insects laid eggs." Each tag seemed to tease the visitor to read the next one. To interpret animals as well as plants, Lutz placed small screen-wire cages with accompanying explanatory labels around caterpillars and other insects on their preferred food plants. There was also a table along the brook where aquatic insect larvae from Wildcat Brook were displayed in glass jars. Lutz's assistants (the youngest thirteen, the oldest just eighteen)—his son Frank, Frank's Ramsey Grammar School friend Ken Valentine, Albert Redmond, Jim Gorham, and Anita Neu—maintained the trail and its exhibits, checking the insects, putting fresh leaves in their cages, and cleaning out the insect excrement so that the cages would not appear dirty.[25]

Lutz also punctuated the trail with occasional Arcadian literary passages, such as a quotation from John Burroughs on the pleasures of walking. Where the trail first skirted Wildcat Brook, Robert Louis Stevenson chimed in: "There's no music like a little river's. It plays the same tune . . . over and over again, and yet does not weary of it. . . . It takes the mind out of doors . . . it quiets a man down like saying his prayers." Lutz brought his wonderful sense of humor to a few labels meant to make the visitor smile. In the household insect tent, the display of centipedes asked: "Have you heard the following bit of good psychology? A centipede was happy quite until a toad in fun / Said, 'Pray, tell me. Which leg moves after which?' / This raised her doubt to such a pitch / She fell excited in the ditch / Not knowing how to run." The "friend somewhat versed in Natural History" had an altogether agreeable, inviting voice, guaranteed to gain the interest and attention of a wide variety of visitors. Lutz explained that he "wanted [visitors] to enjoy themselves, just as a radio advertiser wants his audiences to enjoy themselves."[26]

After finishing the "Training Trail," visitors could turn onto a shorter "Testing Trail," where the chatty voice turned interrogator, quizzing walkers about what they had just seen. Fifty numbered tags bore questions like "What are the pointed things on leaves of this bush?" and "What is the name of this tree?" The trail walker then took his answers to the docent to be scored. A boy from the Harriman Park camp of the Association for the Improvement of the Condition of the Poor made the summer's high score, a 99$\frac{1}{2}$. SSI ran an intercamp contest, where boys from the Lake Stahahe camps—Pequot, Ken-a-dee, Newsboys, Ne-Ha-He and Ramapo—would line up single file and alternate down the trail, having a limited time to write down their answers. The trails were popular with the campers, and even more popular with the adult counselors.

Hank Childs, one of the camp leaders, sent a memo around to all the park camp directors, calling upon them to develop nature trails at the regional museums started by B. T. B. Hyde. Lutz held a conference with them at SSI, giving them pointers on how to lay out such a trail, which by now had been dubbed the "nature trail" by some of the visiting campers. The name, and the idea, stuck. During that first season at SSI, Lutz had promised organized groups of six to sixteen one of the docent staff as a guide. But, as Lutz reported to Director Sherwood, "the docent feature was so chilled at birth that it is practically lifeless." The nature trail, however, was "really catching." In fact, as early as mid-June, he had to contact Major Welch for advice on how to handle the crowds:

> As to the crowd of motorists we are between the devil and the deep sea. Of course, no one likes to be over-run . . . however . . . we are here to help the public and to add another point of interest to this most interesting and attractive Park. . . . Now, what is the best way to get as many of these visitors as possible and still be able to stand up under the strain?

Welch advised against making the SSI attractive to motorists, saying that it would be better to restrict the parking at SSI on Saturdays and Sundays. He warned Lutz that Wildcat Brook might end up like many of the park's streams, which were becoming increasingly polluted from the "tremendous population which runs over all of our woods."[27]

By summer's end, the nature trail idea had escaped the bounds of Wildcat Brook and spread across the country. A busload of New York City teachers left vowing to replicate Lutz's idea in city parks and in vacant lots near city schools. The director and nature study counselor from Camp Calemaco, the Manhattan Girl Scout Camp in Central Valley, just north of SSI, wrote Lutz that the nature trail was of great value to the "city child": "Seeing the actual surroundings, growing conditions, and setting of the object being studied about is a wonderful help. Another thing that impressed us was the simple language used on the signs. They are not too technical, therefore easily understood by the junior and lay mind." Throughout the New York City region, nature trails sprang up at dozens of summer camps. Major Welch told Lutz that he had heard about Lutz's nature trail, and seen it imitated, all the way to the Pacific Coast. Overwhelmed by the response, Lutz sent a notice to *Science* reporting on the phenomenal success of the nature trail at SSI and encouraging its use as a tool for natural science instruction. The American Museum of Natural History also published a descriptive pamphlet by Lutz about the nature trail.[28]

Like Lutz, Sherwood was convinced that nature study in situ was a completely portable concept. To a New York City schoolteacher who wrote Sherwood to lament, "I . . . *know* that type of teaching is the only worthwhile way, but what can we do?" Sherwood replied: "One great advantage of this idea is that a 'Nature Trail' may be created anywhere, even in a city back lot." For those teachers too timid to try, the American Museum, the School Garden Association, and the Biology Teachers Association teamed up to build the first nature trail in New York City. The trailhead was at Central Park West and Seventy-seventh Street, directly across the street from the Theodore Roosevelt Memorial outside the museum's main entrance. A member of the museum's educational staff scored returns from the testing trail. In September 1925 Lutz wrote to Henry Osborn that he believed two hundred nature trails would be created around the country by the following spring. By the summer of 1926 he knew that estimate to be far too low; he told Sherwood that the number was more like two thousand.[29]

For his part, Lutz was not quite sure why his idea had caught on like it had. He thought that there was little that was novel in what he had done, knowing full well that labeled outdoor exhibits—in botanical gardens and zoological parks, for instance—had been around for a long time. He told Hermon Bumpus: "About the only merit we can claim is combining old ideas into a unified scheme and applying them. At any rate, the thing worked and there must have been something about it to arouse the flood of favorable comment that I confess myself unable to understand."[30]

Nature Study Meets the Billboard

When the Lutz children, Ken Valentine, or Albert Redmond took long drives with their parents, one of their favorite pastimes was to watch for billboards. Favorite among the American public were the serial signs erected by many gas stations and spaced strategically to keep the motorist aware of the distance to their stop. Without fail, both adults and children read these signs and found themselves anticipating the next one. Ironically, the first series of Burma-Shave roadside signs appeared in Minnesota the same summer that Frank Lutz opened his nature trail through the Ramapo woods.

At a hundred paces apart, at 35 miles-per-hour, it took three seconds to proceed from one Burma-Shave sign to the next—eighteen seconds to read the whole series of six signs. Frank Lutz knew that he was up against the same time limit with his nature trail; he had to keep visitors' attention just long enough to impart a single "interesting thing." Although Frank Lutz never singled out billboards as his conscious model for the nature trail, they no doubt influenced the style of his signage, just as surely as the volume of motorists on the turnpike had ensured that his self-serve natural history station would catch on with the same rapidity as Burma-Shave. On the highway, Lutz erected an arrow-shaped sign with the legend: "The entrance to the Nature Trails is about 210 yards west on the new Greenwood Lake Road." Without realizing it, the motorists who followed it to the parking area, dismounted, and proceeded onto Lutz's nature trail were making a seamless transition from one form of spectatorship to another.[31]

In a letter from August 1925 to his friend Hermon Bumpus, Lutz reveals the interplay between outdoor advertising and outdoor nature education that culminated in the nature trail. In pondering the best way to bring nature study to the American public in an efficient, modern fashion, Lutz told Bumpus:

> Commercial concerns pay advertising men good money. Scientists are notoriously poor advertisers but, as Jimmy O'Toole said, "It pays to advertise." Well. Commercial concerns advertise in various ways. For example:
> 1. In papers. Scientists do that to some extent (Beebe probably the most active) but they are usually advertising themselves as much as Nature.
> 2. Radio. I enjoy broadcasting nature-talks myself but I doubt if they do much good. Perhaps platform lectures are more profitable— certainly they are for the fellow giving them.
> 3. Rarely concerns join together and arrange "permanent" exhibits in large cities. Apparently these exhibits are not considered very profitable or there would be more of them. Conservative science depends largely on museums to tell the general public about its wares.

Lutz appreciated the limitations of the urban natural history museum as a device for broadcasting nature study to the masses. A museum professional for most of his life, Lutz now felt that "a 'museum' has come to mean (to me, at least) a massive building to which things are brought and in which they are stored. It is 'bringing the mountain to Mahomet' and, in spite of painted background and wax accessories, the mountain when displayed therein seems out of place." On the Nature Trail, by contrast, "one could not only see what a thing looked like but one could touch, smell, taste, or listen to it as well." A consummate field man, whose research interests tended to reflect this appreciation of the sensory dimension of the living world, Lutz was predisposed to favor a form of "advertising" that would engage the naive observer more fully than even the most artistic museum diorama might.[32]

Lutz was sensitive to the style of presentation that in situ nature study could take. Thinking back on his nature trail experiment and the voice he chose for the invisible "friend," Lutz remarked that "you would not deliver a pedantic lecture; neither would you adopt the style of a 'barker' on a sightseeing car." He was all too familiar with this latter style and feared it had crept into popular natural history interpretation. Lutz cited for Bumpus another parallel between commercial advertising and the "selling" of nature study by interpretive guides:

> 4. "Drummers" and personal demonstration by people who are ready to sell as soon as they have convinced their public that they have something worth while. Here comes in "nature guiding" and is the only kind of public speaking that I really like. It seems to me to be a very profitable way of getting our story across if we have good drummers, but a shoe-salesman, for example, should know the difference between rubber boots and bedroom slippers. Furthermore, "there is a reason" for representing drummers as having a laugh on their faces and their pockets full of cigars. Too many "nature guides" are—well, you know them.

Lutz shared with Hyde a distaste for the carnival-barking style of outdoor education. Having come of age as naturalists during the nature-faker controversy, both men were perhaps especially sensitive to the issue of inauthenticity when it came to "telling the nature story."[33]

In his survey for Bumpus, Lutz grew most excited over the possibilities for nature study as they might be developed by the most recent advertising sensation: billboards. The 1920s were truly the golden age of billboards. The economic optimism that swept across America after the signing of the Treaty of Versailles in 1919 was nowhere so dramatically evident as in the new landscape of outdoor advertising that rose across the country in perfect sync with the explosion of the personal automobile. The propaganda campaigns sparked by military mobilization during World War I had provided outdoor advertisers and their artists and illustrators with a nationwide test of the effects of synthesizing newly perceived understandings of color, word, and image into persuasive, psychologically effective messages. In 1900 the total amount spent for regulated outdoor advertising in America was $2 million; by 1925 it was $60 million. Much of that 3,000–percent increase occurred in the five years before Frank Lutz's experiment at the Station for the Study of Insects. This radical development was certainly not lost on him as he completed his analysis for Bumpus with

5. Roadside advertising. . . . Now. What would an advertising concern give for the privilege to put "They satisfy" on the lawn of a
fine hotel or other signs among the geysers near Old Faithful? They
do put them, if they dare, wherever people go and especially where
they stop. They take their story to the people instead of begging
the people to come to the story.[34]

Lutz actually envisioned the Nature Trail idea feeding back into automobile tourism to complete the loop:

What fine hotel would not be glad to have interesting things told
about the trees on its lawn? Even a road-side hot dog merchant
would gloat if his "show" were better than his rival's and his patrons would wander from one sign to another as long as their dog
lasted.

Suppose the NY State Museum took its story to the summer
people in the Adirondacks and the . . . [Catskills]. Suppose it even
cut down a little on its wonderful series of mighty good monographs
so that it could get out a million human interest "dodgers" about
NY's forest or its fight to keep out the Gypsy Moth, putting these
dodgers where the customer has the goods at his elbow.

Several years ago I flivvered to Colorado and back, sleeping every night in an automobile tourist camp. People were hanging
around wishing it were time to go to bed. Gosh! Why not have 500
outdoor museums along the Lincoln Highway?

Here was outdoor educational dreaming on a scale that would have made
Benton MacKaye blush. The coast-to-coast competition for motorists' dollars would be transformed into a grand campaign for teaching Americans
to "*see* what they see."[35]

Lutz was not alone in his understanding of or his enthusiasm for the
possibilities of intertwining nature study and roadside signage. A 1929
Cornell Rural School Leaflet report on nature trails recommended that every school could and should have a nature trail. Any doubts that educators
might have could be satisfied by reminding them how America was already
a nation that imbibed instruction in a similar fashion:

Signs that tell the tourist how to get to his desired destination are
now found on most of our highways. In the cities and large towns
these signs are supplemented by signals that tell the drivers of cars
when they may or may not cross intersections. Nature trails merely
carry this idea of directing traffic from the regular roads off through

the woods and fields and indicate on that route the things that may be most interesting.[36]

Nature trails shared with billboards an aesthetic of realism. In the 1920s, American billboards' unfailingly conservative designs were immune to European abstract or surrealist influences; realism was the style understood by the broadest mass of Americans. As veteran billboard artist Howard Scott noted, "Exhaustive surveys have been made of the merits of our point of view—realistic posters—and they have proved conclusively that as far as America is concerned we are on the right track in putting on, as I like to call them, one act plays to a five-second audience." Lutz's imperative was little different. Dishing out nature lore to the five-second audience required staying close to nature's surface, to the visual representation so matter-of-factly before the trail walker's eyes. No consideration was given to the possibility of alternate representations, of other ways of seeing. The proof of the outdoor advertiser's representational prowess was in sales volume. Lutz put his representational skills to the test on the nature trail's inner loop, the "Testing Trail," where, instead of acquiring the advertised wares, the "five-second audience" returned that which they had been given—the "one-act plays" of nature knowledge newly won.[37]

The success of the nature trail idea was proof of the era's positivist faith in the infallibility of its representations, mixed with the progressive faith in the beneficent powers of "publicity." The agreeable friend leading the way on the nature trail seemed just like the neophyte visitor, but he was different: he was a professional naturalist, possessed of privileged knowledge packaged for the average consumer.

Trailside Actions and Reactions

Frank Lutz had originally proposed a station for the *study* of insects, but he failed to carry out any systematic research at all in that first summer. He still had high hopes of getting SSI and its research mission on a permanent footing, and there were signs that this might happen. Simultaneously with his efforts to secure the research end of his original plan, Lutz moved to expand the scope of the pedagogical program. Working with Hermon Bumpus and Chauncey Hamlin, fellow members of the Committee on Outdoor Education of the American Association of Museums (AAM), Lutz offered ideas about what to call this new form of museum that would not be a museum. Lutz liked "Field Museum" best, though he admitted that "Chicago has curiously a prior claim." Other possibilities included "A-field Museum," "Trail Museum," and "Extension Museum."

Then, really letting his imagination fly: Out-lying; Out-post; Associated; Local; Topical; Special; Areal; Regional; Occasional; Johnnies-on-the-spot; Opportune; Pertinent; Relevant; and Cognate. Thanking Lutz for the glossary, Bumpus rejected all the names: "Why not call the baby a Trailside Museum? It tells the story in 9/10ths of the cases—has the proper atmosphere—needs no explanation—may be large or small." Over the next year, Bumpus, Hamlin, Lutz, and Major Welch brought the baby to term.[38]

A grant of $7,500 from the Laura Spelman Rockefeller Memorial Fund provided for the construction at Bear Mountain of a "Trailside Museum," whose purpose was "to provide for the further instruction, education, and convenience of the thousands who are desirous of extending their knowledge of the phenomena of Nature." Not intended to "merely install specimens or attempt in any way to add to the wealth of material that Nature has so lavishly provided throughout the entire Interstate Park," the Trailside Museum rather was "to provide facilities where the public may supplement their field observations and where they may follow, through the use of reference material, instruments, simple laboratory equipment, literature and personal inquiry, the ever changing appearance of the living things of the neighborhood." The AAM understood that the park was in no position to manage such a facility, having no pedagogical department of its own; AAM executives assumed (largely via Lutz's conversations with George Sherwood) that the American Museum of Natural History's seven-year relationship with the park would be continued into this new venture.[39]

*Y*oung Bill Carr, who had come up to Kanawauke Lakes during the summer of 1922 to serve as nature counselor at Camp Mattinnicock of the Queens County Council of Boy Scouts, stood on the platform at the Tuxedo station, his hand bound up in gauze. He had cut it badly on a bread slicer in the camp kitchen and was being sent home to Flushing to recover. As he waited for the train to appear, a giant in a scout uniform—Uncle Bennie Hyde—bent over and offered to carry Carr's duffel bag. On the train to New York, they talked about Hyde's plan for developing nature museums at the park, and Hyde invited Carr to visit him at his office at the American Museum.

The following winter, Carr went to work for Hyde in his "office"—the Nature Corner in the Insect Hall—and then in the spring of 1923 moved up to Kanawauke Lakes to Hyde's nascent museum. By 1926 Carr had become a paid staff member of the American Museum's Education Department, principally carrying on in New York City public schools the live animal demonstrations that Hyde had started there. Carr also gave lantern slide lectures on such topics as "Animal Stories," "Adventures of Fire,"

"Water and Force," "Foundations of Our City," "Forests and Their Uses," "Lives and Habits of Some Animals," and "The Story of Reptiles." In the fall of 1926 George Sherwood picked Carr to launch the new Bear Mountain Nature Trails and Trailside Museum. Carr and his wife, Marion, arrived there on April Fool's Day and stayed in a guest house adjacent to the Bear Mountain Inn before moving their home and office into a spare room in the Bear Mountain Bridge tollhouse. Forty-eight tons of scrap iron from the bridge construction lay about the site that was to become the heart of the new nature trails.[40]

Clyde Fisher, curator of visual instruction and Carr's immediate supervisor at the American Museum, became the young man's confidant and lifeline to the home institution. As Carr and park workers busily prepared the site in anticipation of the upcoming Conference of State and National Parks, three of Welch's gardeners worked with Carr to install 5,500 plantings of fifty-two species of native plants in the vicinity of the nature trails. For these, Carr made metal labels, cardboard signs, and wooden description tags. At the same time, Carr kept a daily checklist of birds, cataloged trees, and caught a rabbit that he intended to display along the nature trail. By the last week in May, the nature trail paths, lined in crushed rock, were complete, and Carr had fifty labels out, along with six exhibit "shrines"— small sign shelters of rustic construction for displays of live animals. Charles C. Adams of the New York State Museum had gone over the trail and made suggestions. Clyde Fisher labeled the botanical section of the trail. In its first week of operation, the Trailside Museum had more than five hundred visitors, beginning with attendees of the parks conference, a bird club, and officials from the School Nature League. On the weekend, the trails had some three hundred visitors. Carr was glad to report that none of the trail signs had been disturbed, as he was "constantly on the grounds . . . to prohibit the wholesale distribution of the many page Sunday newspaper, banana peels, pop bottles, and other material which has no place on a Nature Trail." The crowd showed the greatest interest in the shrine Carr set up with local frogs and salamanders. Carr told Director Sherwood that "living, moving things attract a crowd of this sort; a live grasshopper, properly exhibited, is of more interest to them than many labeled trees and flowers."[41]

Memorial Day weekend brought tens of thousands of holiday revelers to Bear Mountain, and thousands of these made their way onto the nature trails. Climbing the steep path from the steamboat dock, visitors came upon the beginning of the nature trail at a level spot where most paused to rest, just before they reached the enclosed overpass leading to the Bear Mountain Inn, Hessian Lake, and the playground area. A cedar arbor directed the eye toward the nature trail entrance sign. Because the trail led to the swimming pool as well as the Trailside Museum operation, it captured a large number of people who ordinarily would never have sought out this new form of nature study. Fortunately, Carr told Clyde Fisher, he had already photographed the lady's slippers: "the multitudes that swarmed over our grounds have trampled every single one; from May 29 to 31, this place had the appearance of a very active, very noisy ant hill." Carr spent the entire weekend observing the crowd, finding the average age of the visitors to be about eighteen to twenty-five, many of them couples or larger groups looking for a wooded spot to picnic. Though visitors for the most part were well behaved, a park policeman arrested eight people for breaking tree branches, trampling flowers, and acting in "unspeakable ways." Carr overheard many visitors commenting favorably on the labels, and he took notes that might help him improve upon them.[42] Carr and Major Welch thought that, in order to work, the nature trail texts would have to be tailored to the Bear Mountain throng, who were less sure of how to act and think on a nature trail than was Lutz's fully Arcadian-tutored Tuxedo audience.

When he closed up the operation in October, Carr was proud of the Trailside Museum's first run, which he estimated to have hosted twenty-three thousand visitors. The museum building, a one-story, two-winged affair with thick walls of rounded granite boulders, was not completed until the fall, so virtually all the visitation was focused on the nature trails. He had composed and placed fourteen hundred labels, experimenting with different materials, placement, and textual treatments. The trails had evolved into four separate themes—botanical, zoological, geological, and historical. He had taken two reels of motion picture film of the nature trails, another few hundred feet of beaver activity in the park, and lantern slides of skunks, all of which he added to the Education Department's enormous visual instruction collection. He also had two manuscripts ready for publication by the American Museum: a "Manual of Bird Study" and "Signs Along the Trail," his report of the first season at the Trailside Museum.[43]

The Bear Mountain nature trail differed in a number of ways from the trail begun by Frank Lutz at SSI. Carr mounted all of his labels on posts, at eye level, instead of "tagging" the natural objects as Lutz had. Thanks to Marion Carr, Lutz's thin label script was replaced with thick black block lettering, making the labels plainly visible even from a short distance. The Bear Mountain Nature Trail signs truly looked like billboards, minus the graphic art. Carr limited all label text to fewer than twenty words, and labels were placed about twenty feet apart. Some of the signs followed sequentially, approximating a narrative sequence, such as "The Story Beneath Your Feet," along the geology trail. The first sign read: "This country was very mountainous, a long time ago. The Elements . . . gradually wore down the high elevations through the ages, then from the North came a pushing Mountain of Ice: The Great Glacier." A second sign described the glacier's effects, quoted Shakespeare's "Sermons in stones and good in everything," then finished by asking: "Can you read the stories of these stones?" There were also Burma-Shave–style sequences; at an Alleghany ant mound, where the signs could not be spaced apart, Carr put three small signs on a rotating triangular platform that had to be turned to be read: "An Ant Queen started this structure about ten years ago . . . " (1); "Since then the industrious workers have toiled to build this home" (2); "The building materials are earth, sticks, and pebbles. Be careful not to disturb the Ant Colony" (3). Insects were relatively uncommon subjects of the Bear Mountain trail, which featured vertebrates—frogs, turtles, and small mammals—in its caged and aquarium-bound trailside animal exhibits.[44]

One of the lessons that Carr had learned from Hyde was the importance of story in nature study. Stories, Hyde taught, were necessary "to pass on the nature message," and he emphasized close logical sequence, a single point of view, simple language, and a clear point at the end. Carr's introductory sign kept Lutz's "friend" invitation, declaring that the "Naturalist friend" had "an interesting story to tell you." Carr titled sections of the trails "The Story of the Soil" and "The Story of the Mammals"; occasionally he brought two natural objects together to frame the drama, such as "There is a Race in Progress Here," which described the competition for sunlight between adjacent white ash and white oak seedlings. Whereas traditional nature study's "object lesson" orientation tended toward static presentation of knowledge, the activity of walking while learning added a dynamic dimension. With their beginnings, middles, and ends, walking trails were inherently narrative in structure, and the nature trail played off this narrativity.[45]

For Carr, however, the success of a nature trail depended on an element far more necessary than dramatic expression—psychology. Carr outlined his prescriptions for nature trail signage in a series of ten publications that were disseminated throughout the United States and abroad by the American Museum of Natural History. A first principle was: "It is a case not so much of what one would like to tell, but rather what the reader would like to be told." Carr likened the building of a nature trail to the building of a fire: the more carefully the kindling was laid, the more readily the fire would take. "The lack of fuel is never a worry. One cannot tag and label trees, flowers and rocks in the open as one would in a museum. It has a psychology all its own. Signs along the trail are invitations. . . . They are informal and say above all 'you may' rather than 'you must.'" For those visitors who needed a bit more kindling, Carr devised "hidden" labels, which were covered with a weighted lid that had to be lifted to find the text below. Observing the nature trail operation on a busy weekend, Carr took the sound of the doors snapping shut as "an audible sign of interest."[46]

The opening of the Trailside Museum Nature Trail in 1927 coincided with the emergence of the seventeen-year cicada, and, as he did with other periodic natural phenomena, Carr capitalized on this event as an opportunity for instruction. Though Carr, like Hyde, stressed that the nature expert must rely on "accurate accounts" written by "reputable naturalists," one could never anticipate the range of misapprehension on the part of the public. After a visitor from Idaho finished learning about the cicadas from a series of nature trail signs, she queried Carr as to whether the cicada crawled back into its shell every night. "Idaho is indeed a long way off," Carr marveled. The narrative strategy of Carr's Trailside Museum bulletins often revolved around his re-creation of conversations "overheard" on the nature trail. Naive remarks from the "spectators" were contrasted with Carr's authentic, definitive knowledge. Sometimes a visitor—always male—would serve as the voice of authority, quoting knowingly from the signage in response to his female companion's innocently ignorant remarks.[47]

Carr spoke about "advertising" the appearance of the cicada. Even more self-consciously than it had with Frank Lutz, commercial advertising provided the model for the pedagogical strategy at the Trailside Museum. In another mock conversation, Carr tells a visitor from England who has asked about the museum's interpretive signage:

> If they are colorful and attractive they will interest many people.
> In making all charts we try to remember that we must take a bit of
> a lesson from all the powerful advertising people of today, who have
> brought their art, if you would call it that, into the realm of "big
> business." These professional advertisers have learned how to approach the public, how to catch and hold their attention, and how
> to make space count for its fullest measure. If we would attract the
> public, we must also study their likes and dislikes and plan our
> charts accordingly.

The English visitor cheerfully agrees with Carr's assessment: "These advertisers are great fellows, they certainly do know how to catch the eye with their slogans and captions. They are able to describe some inconsequential little product in such a manner that fortunes are soon made for the producers."[48]

"Cheerful," "agreeable," "attractive," "appealing"—these were keywords in Carr's vocabulary. Though he stopped short of a cynical philosophy of "give the public what they want," Carr emphasized a sort of trailside market research that closely approximated the techniques of the "powerful" advertisers he so valued. Knowing that most visitors found photographs of young mammals "appealing" and "cute," Carr planned his exhibit of the life history of mammals to open with such a photograph. He advised educators planning their own trailside animal exhibits that labels should speak about the animal as a "personality." Indeed, all of the mammals and birds, and frequently the snakes and turtles as well, displayed in the Trailside Museum's outdoor zoo had personal names, and Carr frequently referred to certain animals as "stars." In a "Handbook of Nature Trails and Trailside Museums" that he was drafting for publication in the early 1930s, Carr repeated his belief that nature study should borrow ideas from "the rapid advance of the advertising world," and then he asked: "Why then, may we not 'advertise' natural history facts in a similar way and thus keep pace with the times? If a toothpaste may be made famous, why not a mouse?"[49]

Carr had the self-confidence of a Madison Avenue advertising executive: "In our efforts to discover in what channels their interests lie we have but to mingle with the crowd, listen to their remarks, and study their actions." His tendency to speak of "actions" and "reactions" of visitors firmly placed the Trailside pedagogy within the web of collaboration between academic psychology and commercial advertising that was so pervasive in the 1920s. The "city-bred people"—clerks, factory employees, and other metropolitan workers—who debarked at the Bear Mountain dock on a Sunday outing were subject to a Taylorism only slightly less conspicuous than the kind they might have experienced at their workplaces. Carr divided the visitors into three categories: 20 percent read everything; 40 percent read about half the labels; and 40 percent read only a few labels. In an effort to "attract" this last group's "eyes and minds along unaccustomed channels," Carr engineered "counter-attractions." Because young couples were hardest to attract, Carr depended on young men looking to impress their girlfriends with their knowledge: "It is all part of the world's greatest game, and therefore we have taken steps to help play that game." Carr would sometimes purposely omit labels on the cages of animals along the trail in order to observe the reactions of visitors. In one of his informational pamphlets, he tells of a young woman's delight at the "monkey" (actually a gray fox) in one of the exhibits. "What a splendid opportunity has the nature trail and out-of-door museum director to study applied psychology! The whims, the likes and dislikes of people, the inclinations to do this or that, or to notice some things and ignore others, are faithfully demonstrated. It is really a working laboratory, not only of the actions of plants and animals, but of the human animal as well!"[50]

"Nature teaching," Carr explained, was "somewhat like certain types of missionary work in far flung places. We have a great deal to offer, yet nothing to force down the throats of those with whom we come in contact. There is nothing to 'sell,' yet 'salesmanship' plays its valuable part." Carr was oblivious to any manipulative cast to the nature trails, which he saw as participating in Bear Mountain's playful atmosphere of recreational abandon. As he watched visitors "of ten nationalities" shed excess clothing on a hot day as they walked the nature trail, Carr was delighted to see them "make themselves as free as possible in the woods . . . it was a complete mental, and yes, physical relapse; a letting down of barriers demanded by rulings of social restriction." Yet freedom was in short supply in the Trailside Museum's pedagogical program. Carr's view of the human being was that of the behaviorist psychologist: individuals are bundles of habits that can be shaped by the behavioral scientist.[51]

Or the advertiser. John B. Watson's defection from behavioral science to Madison Avenue in the early 1920s was emblematic of the Faustian alliance between these twin creations of modern metropolitan America. In 1924 the *New York Times* hailed Watson's *Behaviorism* as initiating "a new epoch in the intellectual history of man." *Atlantic* called Watson's ideas "more revolutionary than Darwin, bolder than Nietzsche, and . . . more useful to the human race than the fatalistic eugenicist." Watson's employer, the J. Walter Thompson advertising agency, was equally sanguine about the prospects for the new science of human behavior. Behaviorism, like the Trailside pedagogy, was predicated on the gathering of facts prior to the attempt to predict and control human behavior. Where Hyde's and G. Stanley Hall's pedagogy rested on the right application of the knowledge of "instincts," Carr's and Watson's emphasized "habits." The Thompson agency paid Watson royally to cipher these habits so that their copywriters could effectively speak to them; Carr was a one-man ad agency, doing both the market research and the copywriting; and like Madison Avenue advertisers, he played to the public's appetite for novelty, constantly posting new bills on the nature trails.[52]

Watson held that the adjustment of the individual to the needs of society is the key to psychological health. Carr was forever sensitive to the importance of "interrelations," both in the natural world and in human society. In 1932 he opened a new exhibit, "Trailside Interdependence," which largely consisted of two pyramidal displays, one on plants, the other on animals. Each display used labeled live exhibits to demonstrate the evolutionary and ecological relations between local flora and fauna. The plant exhibit had containers with algae, mushrooms, lichens, and moss on a lower table, proceeding to ferns and grass on an intermediate table, then finally to an upper table with a pot of butter-and-eggs. The animal "interdependence" display followed the same arrangement: earthworms, millipedes, centipedes, land snails, and spiders occupied the lowest table; vertebrates—fish, amphibians, reptiles, birds, and mammals—the intermediate one; and "MAN" crowned the apex. Carr spoke of this exhibit in terms of its therapeutic value, as if viewing nature's "adjustments" would encourage visitors to better adjust to their environment: "If, through straightforward but appealing exhibits, a visitor can be encouraged to think along the lines of the interdependence of life, when in the woods, his entire viewpoint changes and he becomes mentally alert to the possibilities of more perfectly relating himself to the world about him."[53]

John Watson had very little music in him; he once wrote an article for the *Saturday Review* called "Feed Me on Facts." Like Watson, Carr's own psyche, and the one he assumed his wide public shared, lived on observation, not imagination. The Trailside Museum fed facts with a frenzy, in a prodigious outdoor object lesson that forgot that the folk who wandered onto the nature trail from the steamboat landing were *subjects*, capable of exercising their own free imaginations. Quoting in his "Trailside Interdependence" pamphlet Maxwell Bodenheim's maxim that "psychology is a rubber stamp pressed upon a slippery, dodging ghost," Carr did not take exception, but merely asserted that "some [ghosts] can be caught." Bill Carr caught the ghosts in the machine with a combination of cold facticity and warmed-over "appeal," backed by the authority of both natural and social science.[54]

The Gospel of Nature

Among Carr's unpublished manuscripts and correspondence with editors, there is also a scrapbook bulging with Carr's published articles, reviews of *The Stir of Nature* (1930), and articles about the Trailside Museum. In the large photograph of Carr pasted to the inside front cover he sits at a simple desk in the rustic interior of his office at Trailside, his hands upon his typewriter, a dictionary open beside him, a pipe in his mouth—posed as he would like to be remembered, as a writer. The photo is reminiscent of an oft-published portrait of Carr's literary hero, John Burroughs. During Carr's second summer at Trailside, he and Clyde Fisher planned a pilgrimage to "Woodchuck Lodge," Burroughs's homestead, and to "Slabsides," Burroughs's rustic cabin overlooking the Hudson, some thirty miles north of Bear Mountain.

The dramatic surge of interest in nature study and outdoor recreation in America at the turn of the century was, if not to a great degree inspired by Burroughs, at least keenly cultivated by him. Among the middle-class reading public he was universally revered as an exemplar of plain living and almost mystical insight into nature. Many found Burroughs's special writing qualities—a warm and friendly voice and a light hand when waxing philosophical—lacking in earlier American nature writers, such as Henry David Thoreau. His widely publicized friendships with two of the modern age's principal architects—Henry Ford and Thomas Alva Edison—particularly as exemplified by their auto-camping holidays (accompanied sometimes by Harvey Firestone, founder of Firestone Rubber and Tire Company), were representative of Burroughs's ready accommodation to modernity, while his long white beard, rough farmer's hands, and homespun clothing preserved his tie to America's agrarian and Arcadian past. Burroughs was made to order for an American public coming of age in the modern era, where acceptance, even if somewhat reluctant, of modern conveniences had replaced old Victorian moralizing about the dangers of luxury.

Edward and Mary Harriman were great admirers of John Burroughs. When Harriman decided in 1899 on the advice of his doctor to take a long vacation, he invited Burroughs to accompany him and his family on their cruise up the coast of Alaska to Kodiak Island, where Harriman hoped to hunt the Kodiak bear. With the assistance of C. Hart Merriam, director of the U.S. Biological Survey, Harriman turned the vacation cruise into a major scientific expedition that included twenty-five scientists from major natural history museums (the Field Columbian Museum, the U.S. National Museum, and the California Academy of Sciences Museum), three federal scientific agencies (the U.S. Biological Survey, U.S. Geological Survey, and U.S. Department of Agriculture), and six universities (Cornell, Yale, Harvard, Amherst, and the universities of California and Washington). Burroughs's friend John Muir came along, as did *Forest and Stream* editor George Bird Grinnell and photographer Edward S. Curtis. The 1899 Harriman Alaska Expedition was a gargantuan Arcadian fantasy, a last gasp of nineteenth-century frontier exploration, financed by one of the American frontier's premier conquerors intent upon bagging himself a ferocious bear. During the trip, Muir, Burroughs, Grinnell, and Curtis provided Harriman with a steady diet of nostalgia for the lost Eden of America's primeval past.[55]

For the Harrimans, as for Ford, Edison, and other Americans who were simultaneously witnessing and participating in the nation's transition to modernity, Burroughs served an even more vital purpose than to supply a comfortably vicarious experience of Nature. In his writings, Burroughs offered a Naturalistic worldview, free of nineteenth-century sentimentalism, but still emotionally satisfying. Drained of anything supernatural, Burroughs's nature was still imbued with some trace of the numinous, if only by virtue of its juxtaposition with the profane, artificial world of the human. Burroughs's accommodation to modern scientific materialism provided a level bridge across which his wide public could walk into the future.

One of Burroughs's best-known essays, "The Gospel of Nature," opens with perhaps the archetypal statement of the Arcadian sentiment:

> There can be little doubt, I think, but that intercourse with nature and a knowledge of her ways tends to simplicity of life. We come more and more to see through the vanities and follies of the world and to appreciate the real values. We load ourselves up with so many false burdens, our complex civilization breeds in us so many artificial wants, that we become separated from the real sources of our strength and health as by a gulf.
>
> For my part, as I grow older . . . I become more and more in love with simple things and simple folk—a small house, a hut in the woods, a tent on the shore. The show and splendor of great houses, elaborate furnishings, stately halls, oppress me, impose upon me. . . .
>
> How the contemplation of nature as a whole does take the conceit out of us! How we dwindle to mere specks and our little lives to the span of a moment in the presence of the cosmic bodies and the interstellar spaces!

Burroughs's gospel was founded as much upon a renunciation of traditional Christian conceptions as it was upon the embrace of unadulterated Nature. In the place of a patriarchal personal savior, Burroughs offered "the wonder and reverence and love we feel in the presence of the inscrutable universe. . . . Indeed, these seem to be renewing their life today in this growing love for all natural objects and in this increasing tenderness towards all forms of life. If we do not go to the church as much as our fathers, we go to the woods much more, and are much more inclined to make a temple of them than they were." Burroughs was quite comfortable attacking orthodox Christianity. Elsewhere he had written that God is "a fiction of our own brains. We must recognize only Nature, the All; call it God if we will, but divest it of all anthropological connections."[56]

Burroughs had imbibed along with the balsam-scented air of the Catskill summits a bit of the new psychology, and he felt sure that Nature's influences worked upon the "subconscious" as well as the conscious self. His philosophy nicely complemented the novel therapeutic ethos so dramatically evident in the new shape of nature at Harriman Park. Returning from the city, Burroughs said: "I go to Nature to be soothed and healed."

Burroughs claimed to be "saner, healthier, more contented" by virtue of his outdoor rambles, though he admitted to being less social and more likely to shirk civic duties while tucked away in his Arcadian retreat. His walks helped him in a "hygienic way," keeping him healthy and sharpening his senses. Burroughs's approach to nature study also fit Progressive ideals of combining recreation and education, and resisted laboratory science as a means of knowing Nature, "as if this kingdom could be carried by assault. . . . Biology is, no doubt, a great science in the hands of great men, but it is not for all. I myself have got along very well without it. I am sure I can learn more of what I want to know from a kitten on my knee than from the carcass of a cat in the laboratory."[57]

Burroughs's essay applauded "natural," not divine law, including the death and destruction brought by the "survival of the fittest": "I do not see design in Nature in the old teleological sense; but I see everything working to its own proper end, and that end is foretold in the means. Things are not designed; they are begotten." The "Seer of Slabsides" saw Darwinian evolution as a liberating vision, and he was one of the first popular nature writers to embrace evolutionary theory. His last book, *Accepting the Universe* (1920), was a remarkable plea both for his style of pantheism and the new scientific naturalism. "Natural selection is just as good a god as any other," Burroughs declared. "The ways of Nature about us are no less divine because they are near and familiar. The illusion of the rare and remote, science dispels." Burroughs even grappled with the puzzle of human consciousness and hinted that physical science's increasing mastery of the new "imponderable bodies"—electricity, radioactivity, magnetism—would soon dispel its lingering mysteriousness. Radio waves invited analogizing with the mind, and Burroughs wondered if both went on forever. Looking for some scientific substitute for God, the Seer of Slabsides considered whether "energy" might be Nature's ultimate principle and solace enough in the face of each individual's inevitable disincarnation.[58]

The friendly voice, the trust in natural science in situ, his stature as a regional treasure (the Nature he celebrated was that of the lower Hudson River valley) as well as a national hero—all this made John Burroughs the writer most often quoted on the nature trail and museum exhibit labels at Trailside. In November 1940 the spirit of Burroughs was joined on the Bear Mountain Nature Trail by the spirit of an old friend, Walt Whitman. The two men had become acquainted during their Civil War sojourn in Washington, D.C. Burroughs wrote the first book-length appreciative critique of Whitman's *Leaves of* Grass, and he served as Whitman's source for natural history knowledge whenever he needed it.[59]

Whitman's gospel of natural, democratic man was a bit too libertine for the New York City park commissioners, who had refused sculptor Jo Davidson's designs for a statue of Whitman to be placed in Central Park or Battery Park. On a visit to Davidson's Paris studio in May 1938, Averell Harriman proposed that if New York City would not have Walt in their parks, perhaps he could come to Bear Mountain, in memory of Mary Harriman's gift of the land for the park. In New York that autumn, Davidson spent Thanksgiving at Arden House with the Harrimans, and Averell Harriman took him over to the Appalachian Trail section that coincided with the first leg of the Bear Mountain Nature Trail. Finding just a few feet from the trail's edge an enormous granite boulder that he thought perfect for use as a pedestal, Davidson tried out some enlarged photostats of a sketch he had made of the statue and took a mold of the top of the boulder. He sent the mold back to his Paris studio and began work on the eight-and-a-half-foot-tall statue.

At the end of February 1939, Percy MacKaye and his wife were staying with Davidson for a week or so, on a visit from Dornach, Switzerland, where they had been staying since October 1938. Davidson told MacKaye of having passed along to Averell Harriman a copy of the play that MacKaye had written while teaching at the Craigie School in Manhattan, in which Harriman had played a part. Davidson was delighted to report that the statue in which MacKaye had always shown such a keen interest was to find a home, thanks to Harriman, at Bear Mountain. Percy told his brother Benton of his visit and of how in Davidson's studio, along with busts of Gandhi, Mussolini, Rockefeller, Roosevelt, La Follett, and nature-mystic Rabindrath Tagore, he had had the great pleasure of seeing Walt Whitman Appalachian Trail–bound: "Watching old Walt Whitman emerging in bronze (nine feet of him!) all smeared over with black, baked mud of the mould he was cast in . . . to rise up, stalk over the Atlantic, and stand for centuries, at the trail entrance on Bear Mountain." Before Percy returned to Dornach, Davidson sketched him and made MacKaye a present of the drawing, inscribing it to "Our Walt."[60]

After a stop at the New York World's Fair, where he seemed to be striding from the New York City pavilion to the General Electric pavilion, Davidson's Whitman arrived at Bear Mountain in November 1940 for the ceremony commemorating the thirtieth anniversary of the day when young Averell Harriman had stood on the top of Bear Mountain and presented the deed and check to the Palisades Interstate Park commissioners. A commissioner himself now, Harriman recalled in his dedication address how "fifty years ago the rocky hills and lakes seemed of little or no value, but they appealed to my mother and father and it was here they made their home." After citing his father's promotion of better roads in the county, Harriman rather ironically noted that the statue would stand off the road, on a base provided by glacial ice: "Whoever should see it must come here on foot." Lieutenant Governor Charles Poletti took note of the radical changes since 1910—the two world wars and the many modern inventions. He then focused on the most transformative development of the twentieth century—the automobile—which in 1910 was still a curiosity, a "devil buggy." He told the old joke about the Yankee farmer who bought up all the livery stables for a song, waiting for the day when the automobile fad would die down. "Who could have believed that from 1910 to 1940 motor vehicles in the state would have increased from one car to every 145 persons, to one car for every 5 persons, and that more cars than there were in the whole state would now visit Bear Mountain Park in a single day?"[61]

In 1910 many observers had been skeptical about the accessibility of Harriman Park and wondered whether the state should burden itself with such a large piece of forest, so remote from the populace that might find recreation there. By 1940 the Appalachian Trail, along which the huge bronze Whitman seemed to stride, was itself a highway, heavy with "through-hikers" who raced from end to end, oblivious to the original intent of Benton MacKaye's long leisurely route into the primeval. (Benton MacKaye used to lament about the through-hikers: "They'd say: 'I did the trail in three days.' Dreadful! I want to take the *longest*. I want them to *see* what they *see*.") The automobile's ever-increasing velocity moved inexorably into the rhythms of its drivers, who now took billboard text at twice the speed they had when Frank Lutz put up the arrow-shaped sign on Franklin Turnpike. When the drivers got out to walk the nature trail at Bear Mountain, they were full of speedy radio jingles that made the static trailside labels seem more labor than amusement.[62]

The through-hikers as well as the day visitors to the nature trails typically stopped to read at least a few lines of Whitman's "Song of the Open Road," carved into the granite boulder upon which he stood.

> Afoot and light hearted I take to the open road,
> Healthy, free, the world before me,
> The long brown path before me leading wherever I choose.
>
> Henceforth I ask not good fortune, I myself am good fortune,
> Henceforth I whimper no more, postpone no more, need nothing,
> Done with indoor complaints, libraries, querulous criticisms,
> Strong and content I travel the open road.
>
> The earth, that is sufficient,
> I do not want the constellations any nearer,

I know they are very well where they are,
I know they suffice for those who belong to them. . . .

you road I enter upon and look around, I believe you are not all
that
is here,
I believe that much unseen is also here.

Whitman's "Song of the Open Road" carried within its meter the pulse of the walking man of the nineteenth century, and in its text the spirit of an age that still believed the unseen to hold a redemptive promise. When Walt and his poem were set astride the trail in 1940, walkers had within them a faster meter and a different measure of the open road before them. The Bear Mountain nature trails and trailside museums, though promising Arcadian redemption, were utterly modern creations, destined to augment rather than diminish the frequency of the pulses issuing from the top of the Radio City tower. The spirit of that Radio Age had no heart for, and no belief in, any unseen other than the fourth-dimensional ether that carried jingles and jazz. The faith was fully visible on the signs along the nature trail, which itself was an artifact of an age of *fact*. The labels all proclaimed the importance of the seen, treating the trail's myriad object lessons as if they constituted their own gospel. The nature trail became a successful tutor of novice naturalists because most all of the trail walkers were already Naturalists, subscribers to a philosophical system devoted to the preeminence of perceived phenomena. Devoid of transcendental, divine, or metaphysical dimensions, the Naturalist/naturalist world could be neatly laid out as data points on nature's trail.

CHAPTER 3

Science and the Sensible

Seeing, Hearing, Believing

Nature-study promoters frequently offered their brand of knowing nature as an alternative to the heartless and artless reductionism of laboratory-oriented natural science. Yet nature study's factual repertoire was almost entirely the product of scientific observers, not poets like Walt Whitman. The popular enthusiasm for the easy instruction of trailside-style nature study developed simultaneously with a forensics of nature possessed of increasingly more powerful investigative tools. Just as nature study wedded the narrative style of the old natural history to the new psychology, biology in America was rapidly diversifying, in the process distancing itself from the qualitative and descriptive science of the nineteenth century.[1] Physiology, the organismal science that had seen such progress in the closing decades of the 1800s, penetrated deeper and deeper into the mysteries of the plant, animal, and human. The new science of genetics offered a promise of understanding the mechanisms of evolutionary change. Another new biological science, ecology, proposed to detail organismal interactions with their physical and biological environments in such a way as to give a more complete picture of nature. The prodigious expansion of biological science in America in the opening decades of the twentieth century took place from coast to coast, in the laboratory and in the field, in metropolitan as well as Arcadian settings. Though marked by a complex process of intellectual and cultural change, this transformation paralleled developments in natural-area protection and in nature study in its contribution to a widespread acceptance of Nature as normative.

John Burroughs acknowledged that human striving after the "Infinite and the Eternal" still lent a certain "dignity and sobriety" to modern humanity, but Burroughs was a realist, certain that "the other world fades as this world brightens. Science has made this world so interesting and won-

derful, and our minds find such scope in it for the exercise of all their powers, that thoughts of another world are becoming foreign to us. We shall
never exhaust the beauties and the wonders and the possibilities of this."[2]
Natural science's new powers of discovery and explanation reinforced the
Naturalist ethos, driving Americans deeper into the sensible world, so that
the possibility of a world beyond the senses seemed illusory. As it brought
a greater sweep of the natural world under its gaze, natural science bol-
stered both of the naturalisms—recreational field study of nature and philosophical foundation—to which John Burroughs and his peers aspired. Given
the intensity of cultural activity along the Arcadian/metropolitan frontier
of Harriman Park, it is not surprising that these developments found local
expression there.

Adapting Radiation

When Frank Lutz founded the Station for the Study of Insects (SSI)
at Harriman Park in 1925, he did so partly as an experiment in boys' work
in nature study, for he saw the degree to which modern life separated children from vernacular contact with the natural world. Similarly, his *Field
Book of Insects* (1918) was intended primarily to reach young people, to
answer their questions and guide their observations regarding insects. (The
book was phenomenally successful; sales of this and successive editions
in 1921 and 1935 put all four of Lutz's children through college.) Though
the human world had changed since Lutz's boyhood, the qualities that recommended insects, traditionally the most familiar objects of nature study,
as the ideal organism upon which to come to an understanding of general
biology—from anatomy and physiology to ethology and ecology—had not.
Insects were ubiquitous, easy to catch, inexpensive to maintain alive, and
just the right scale for children. If earlier generations of American farm
children had come to know insects mainly as pests, they had at least done
so only after first gaining a more sympathetic acquaintance with the six-
legged class of invertebrates. Lutz was convinced that in the growing field
of nature-study instruction, insects would play a large role as subjects of
study, and he argued that instructors would be required to know entomology to be fully qualified.[3]

For its second summer of operation, Lutz closed the SSI site to the
automobiling public so that he and his students could undertake a full program of entomological research. Lutz intended to stress what he called the
"three P's": physiology, psychology, and pathology. From the park camp
department staff he recruited F. Martin Brown, who taught at St. George's
School in Newport, Rhode Island. Known as "Mitzi" around SSI, he was

exactly the sort of protégé Lutz was looking for—bright, quick to take up new initiatives, and nearly as playful as Lutz. William S. Creighton, a doctoral student in zoology at Princeton University, and Brandt Steele, an undergraduate in zoology at Indiana University, were Lutz's other principal coworkers, and they were joined by a number of "junior guests"—teenage boys who were kept busy about the station and learned some entomology along the way.[4]

Always wary of "common sense," Lutz was bothered by the suspicion that "insect galls" might more directly be the result of infection by fungi, bacteria, or viruses that were carried by injurious insects. Having befriended the head of the bacteriological laboratory at the Tuxedo Hospital, who put the lab at the disposal of SSI, Lutz invited Brown to undertake research to test the theory. Starting as ever with problems close at hand, Lutz set up Brown with a collection of gall-infested twigs from a witch hazel that grew at the corner of their cabin. From the tissues of the gall, Brown isolated strains of a bacterium caused by *Hamamelistes spinosus*, an aphid, and found the same bacterium to be present in galls that he collected in Newport. Though attempts to cause the formation of galls by inoculating witch hazel with a saline solution of the bacteria proved unsuccessful, Brown and Lutz concluded that it was possible that the bacterium and not, as common sense assumed, any enzyme or other chemical injected by the gall-forming insect was responsible.[5]

William Creighton received his assignment in a similarly commonplace fashion. One afternoon, as Lutz and his son Frank were returning to the cabin, they noticed a hundred or so large red ants congregated at a spot in the driveway. When Frank asked his father what the ants were doing, Lutz, uncharacteristically absentminded, said that the ants were "swarming." "Guessing is not always safe," Lutz said upon thinking back to the incident, "and absentminded guessing is decidedly risky when a boy is asking questions." Young Frank stopped to look more closely, and his father did also. As they watched, the red ants simultaneously disappeared into an opening, and suddenly reappeared, carrying black ant pupa in their jaws. The "swarming" ants were really "slaving." While Lutz returned to the cabin, his son followed the line of marauding ants into the woods, across Greenwood Lake Road, and up a steep bank to an opening where they entered their own nest. Lutz put Creighton onto identifying the slave-making ants. It turned out that these ants, *Polycergus lucidus,* were commonly believed to steal other species' food, not their young.[6]

Lutz was as cautious about the language he used in describing insect behavior as he was about the manner of observing it: "Whether 'slaves' is a good name for them I shall not say, and neither shall I yield to the often-yielded-to temptation to draw comparisons between such slavery and human conduct, past and present." In a discussion of another ant species, Lutz noted that it had become so specialized that it could not even attend to the rearing of its own offspring. He drew attention to the ease with which zoologists moved from descriptions of animal to human behavior: "I almost wrote that sentence 'so far degenerated that it does not attend to the rearing of its own children,' but that might be construed as drawing comparisons between human conduct and the affairs of ants." Having been immersed in the rhetoric of "degeneration" while working under Charles Benedict Davenport at the Cold Spring Harbor Station for the Study of Experimental Evolution between 1903 and 1909, Lutz was leery of using the word in a biological context. The entire language of the "social"—spoken particularly by invertebrate zoologists acquainted with the Hymenoptera—made him uneasy: "It is too bad that there is a confusion in the usage of the word 'social.' As applied to human affairs it means cooperation between offspring of different parents and is usually primarily for selfish ends of the cooperators but resulting in good for the species as a whole. Ants are not social in that way. Their society, like the human one, is built on selfish motives, but, unlike human society, cooperation, when it is not enforced 'slavery,' is usually confined to close relatives, usually a mother and her children."[7]

Lutz was himself a keen student of the Hymenoptera, the order of so-called 'social' insects, especially for the opportunities they afforded for biological research on "invisibles"—the portions of the electromagnetic spectrum beyond human detection. In 1923, in the yard at his house in Ramsey, New Jersey, he had begun tests to see which insects were sensitive to ultraviolet light. By putting glass of different colors at either end of a box, Lutz could determine which color was brightest to the insect trying to exit the box. Honeybees, bumblebees, wasps, and two different species of solitary bees all sought out the ultraviolet windows over the (humanly) visible colors of the spectrum. Lutz also enlisted the aid of physicist F. K. Richtmyer of Cornell University to determine the ultraviolet reflectivity of certain insect-pollinated plants, as a beginning toward discovering whether the UV sensitivity of insects was a factor in pollination ecology. The publication describing the results of their work was awarded the A. Cressy Morrison Prize of the New York Academy of Sciences in 1923.[8]

At SSI in 1927, Lutz continued his work on the ultraviolet sensitivities of insects, choosing to work with honeybees. Lutz constructed a wire maze whose routes were marked by different colors, only one of which led to a dish of sugar water. Once certain bees were regularly making their way along the correct route, Lutz changed the colored lines to see if this would confuse the bees. Though it did, they soon learned to follow the new route. This exercise in operant conditioning was paired with one that used a dish of sugar water and several dishes of plain water. All the dishes were placed on plaques painted white, but only the plaque under the sugar water reflected ultraviolet light; when the UV plaque was moved under the dishes of plain water, the bees visited them instead.[9]

In the summer of 1926 Lutz and Mitzi Brown had spent a number of days assisting Tuxedo Park resident Alfred Lee Loomis with some of the experimental work he was beginning in his home physics laboratory. Loomis had made a fortune as a Wall Street attorney and financier with the firm of Bonbright and Company. Just as Lutz was turning his attention at SSI toward physics, Loomis was shifting his scientific interests from physics toward biology. The "Glass House," Loomis's laboratory at his huge stone castle, had more scientific apparatus than many well-equipped college labs. Although Major Welch would build a sixty-by-twenty-five-foot laboratory for SSI the following summer (calling it a "patrol station" so as not to draw criticism of the park for its use of state funds to build a scientific facility for the American Museum), Lutz made extensive use of the Loomis lab. Lutz and Loomis were fast friends. An accomplished stage magician who loved to entertain children with card and coin tricks, Loomis, like Lutz, thrived on intellectual challenges and was a "gadgeteer," playing at building gliders, model airplanes, and radio-controlled automobiles. And with a mind even more wide-ranging than Lutz's, he mastered new fields remarkably quickly. The very new field of biophysics seemed ideal for both men.[10]

One problem of insect physiology that Lutz had always wished to investigate was the relationship between temperature and locomotion. Over the years Lutz had made periodic attempts to devise some form of treadmill that could allow insects to walk straight ahead indefinitely in an environment whose temperature could be controlled. The many prototypes had all proved ineffective. He needed a device that would be frictionless enough to move under the weight of a fruit fly but retain enough friction to require the insect to expend effort to move it; and and the device would have to record automaticaly both the speed and direction of turning. Lutz had arrived at a gadget—"something like an automobile tire with the insect inside of it"—made of very thin transparent celluloid, with a tiny sliding celluloid door for allowing the insect in and out. The wheel's spokes were fine silk threads, and the axle either a needle or the shaft of a hat pin. At the suggestion of physicist R. W. Wood (who in a sense had been the original inspiration for Loomis's lab and was the other principal occupant during the summer of 1927), Lutz added an electromagnet controlled by a rheostat, so that the friction on the ball bearings could be adjusted for the particular insect and its activities.

Experimenting with carabid beetles, yellow jackets, and fruit flies, Lutz found *Spirobolus marginatus*, a large brown millipede of the late-summer woods, to be the ideal insect athlete for the treadmill. After determining that, as expected, its speed increased with increasing ambient temperature, Lutz availed himself of one of Loomis's vacuum pumps to see what effect low atmospheric pressures, mimicking conditions at high altitudes, might have on the millipede. From the standard sea-level barometric pressure of 760 mm, Lutz took the millipede through a graded series of descending pressures; the millipede continued to saunter all the way down to 22 mm, equivalent to a balloon ride up to fifteen miles above sea level. Its pace actually increased up to the point where two-thirds of the air had been removed from its bell jar container. Exhilarated by the physiological endurance of the millipede, Lutz subjected a number of other insects to similar treatment. First he took ten *Drosophila* "aloft," this time decreasing the atmospheric pressure from 760 mm to 22 mm in ninety seconds. Finding that after four minutes they all walked about uninjured, he repeated the "aerial adventure," stopping only after twenty trials, when only six of the ten were still walking. Placed on some ripe banana, the flies started breeding the following day.

Continuing his atmospheric assaults, Lutz made the ten-minute automobile drive in the "Bee" from SSI to the Loomis lab with two genera of solitary bees, two species of mound-building ants, a beetle, a grasshopper, a bumblebee, and two species of butterfly. Loomis's vacuum pump was capable of evacuating the air to a pressure of one ten-thousandth of a millimeter. Lutz engineered an apparatus that would permit the insects to be subjected to this super-vacuum while still supplying them with some atmospheric moisture so that they would not simply dry up and expire from desiccation. Casualties of an ant and both butterflies did not keep Lutz from marveling over these "wonder creatures." Slightly self-conscious about the "use" of such experiments, he unself-consciously declared that they were "amusing."[11]

In 1927 Loomis and Wood published the foundational paper in what would become the field of ultrasonics, having spent the summer using a six-foot-high ultrasonic generator to kill mice and fish and nearly all manner of insect in pursuit of the question of the biological effects of physical extremes. Before Lutz closed SSI for the winter, he went back to the Loomis lab with his trusted research associate, the cricket *Gryllus*, for some supersonic experiments of his own. Placing a cricket into a beaker and then placing this into a container of water through which a 50,000–volt generator sent waves oscillating at frequencies of 200 to 500,000 alternations per second, Lutz found that the cricket merely moved about when the generator was started, then stopped when it was shut off. Then Lutz placed the cricket directly into the water; instead of the "death whisper" given by vertebrates, *Gryllus* chirped happily after it had dried off. Lutz then sent four-meter-long radio waves through this same cricket, as well as X rays. Up on the high ridge overlooking Tuxedo Lake and the Ramapos, Lutz grew giddy on science's new electromagnetic toys, adapting radiation to curiously diabolical ends.[12]

Championing Evolution

The experiments at the Loomis lab were not merely the result of technological euphoria; behind most of this research lay questions about evolution and the action, if any, of natural selection upon insect physiological characters. Lutz framed his early work on ultraviolet light as a challenge to the theory of natural selection. Strong selectionists held that nearly all of nature's hues were "useful," from the protective coloration of animals to the attractive coloration of the Angiosperms, and hence were designed by the blind watchmaker of natural selection. Lutz, inspired by physicists' increasing penetration of the realm beyond the sensible, used new tools to interrogate whether the wealth of professional and popular assumptions about the "attractiveness" of the variegated pigments and patterns of flowering plants were actually confirmed by experiment. Having demonstrated the deceptive limits of using the human visual spectrum as a yardstick for insects, Lutz went on to investigate whether the invisible (to humans) colors of UV reflective flowers actually conferred some advertising advantage upon them. Wishing to determine for flowers of varying UV reflectivities the number of insect visits per unit time, Lutz fell back on the simple method of random five-minute observation periods of individual flowers. After many hours of observation, Lutz reported that, contrary to his expectation, highly UV-reflective flowers were no more popular with insects than their non-UV-reflective neighbors.[13]

Once Lutz had shown that a variety of insects can detect ultraviolet radiation, their entire perceptual world demanded reconsideration. All other assumptions about coloration, whether protective or attractive, seemed suspect. A yellow garden spider, to human eyes exquisitely matched to the corolla color of the host plant upon which it patiently awaited its unsuspecting prey, might in the UV-sensitive eyes of a potential prey insect stand out in high relief against its background. The same relation would hold for many insects thought to be camouflaged for protection from predators. That many of the color patterns of insects were not quite what they seemed once one took UV radiation into account threw open to question another cliché of Darwinian thinking—mimicry. Viceroy butterflies photographed in the UV range of the spectrum were not as impressively matched to their monarch models as in the humanly visible range.[14]

All of Lutz's research convinced him that floral colors were not products of natural selection but developed as byproducts of plant metabolism; at most they were only of incidental and minor service to their insect visitors. His research on X rays, though showing conclusively that photopositive insects reacted to them, emphasized that the rarity of X rays as natural occurrences made them unimportant biologically and hence a poor candidate for the agency of natural selection. In 1927 Mitzi Brown's father, F. W. Brown, a commercial chemist, joined the summer staff at SSI and began to throw suspicion on the assumed role of floral scents as insect attractants. The radical environmental conditions survived, even enjoyed, experimentally by the insects at the Loomis lab suggested that if natural selection was the master designer, it was prone to considerable "overdesign" in the realm of physiology. All in all, Lutz's SSI research contradicted the ancient dictum that "every existing thing is for some good." Yes, there were no blue roses in nature, but there was no justification, Lutz was certain, to using the idea of natural selection to explain this fact.[15]

Despite all his contrariness when it came to the limits of natural selection, Lutz was no antievolutionist: "Evolution there certainly has been, and without doubt natural selection has placed limits beyond which variation may not go. . . . It is also quite conceivable and altogether probable that certain variations are of so great a benefit to a creature that natural selection favors that variation." In the mid-1920s natural selection was receiving more critical scrutiny from biologists than it had in several decades, but evolution by some yet-to-be-confirmed mechanism was hardly in doubt.[16] Even Henry Fairfield Osborn, president of the American Museum of Natural History, though he could not accept a purely naturalistic mechanism of chance variation, was prone to the strong adaptationist stance. Lutz's biological logic frequently bumped up against Osborn's notions. One day in 1925 the president met Lutz in the corridor and asked him about possibly editing some of the text in the new exhibits in the Insect Hall to address evolutionary themes. Lutz's response was characteristically contrary:

Is the long hind leg of the cricket physical or mechanical? The venation of an insect wing? The presence or absence of hairs? The presence or absence of simple (as contrasted with compound) eyes (the ocelli)? How about the presence or absence and shape, if present, of teeth on mandibles and spines on legs? Would you say that the fact that one caterpillar eats nothing but oak while another confines itself to willow is chemical (it may be psychological) or would you say that it is not a character, although it is characteristic?

As apparent from my NY Academy Morrison prize paper and from my recent bulletin "Insect Sounds," I am somewhat heterodox concerning Adaptation. I think much of it is human imagination and a large part of the remainder is adoption of structure by a creature for its needs—a structure that was really forced upon the creature by its internal forces; we can call it orthogenesis if we must—rather than adaptation of a structure to a creature's needs.[17]

Osborn emerged as America's most famous champion of evolution in the summer of 1925, when, as a scientific advisor from the American Association for the Advancement of Science, he assisted the American Civil Liberties Union in its representation of John Thomas Scopes against the state of Tennessee. On Sunday, July 12, just after the trial began, the *New York Times* devoted most of one section to the Scopes trial, juxtaposing on the front page photographs of Osborn and William Jennings Bryan. On the same page a "family tree of man" and drawings of prehistoric men clearly showed the *Times*'s support for scientific over revealed knowledge. Throughout the trial, the *Times* stories were disdainful of the fundamentalist argument against evolution. The July 12 issue carried an editorial giving the *Times* imprimatur to the Osborn cause: "Educated men think unconsciously in terms of evolution. The idea of it and the applications of it are woven into the intellectual life of the whole world today." During the twelve days of the trial, the *Times* moved more than a hundred thousand words over the news wires, all of them championing Clarence Darrow and the "facts" over Bryan's dubious unseen.

Darrow's defense of Scopes was classically empiricist. Rather than presenting evidence to prove the truth of evolutionary theory, he offered facts that cumulatively served to reject the null hypothesis—special creation as described by Genesis and subscribed to by Bryan. Bryan attempted to present evidence in favor of his hypothesis, but that evidence was fatally flawed, based in revelation rather than observation. In terms of communicating a narrative of the trial, it was difficult for the media to represent Bryan as anything other than a pathetic arcane caricature and Darrow as the scientific vanquisher. Though ridiculing Bryan's fundmentalism, the journalists of the *New York Times* and other newspapers engaged in their own brand of fundamentalism—an irrational faith in the news-gathering process. Newspapers and modern science were a perfect match: equally dedicated to the hypothetico-deductive method of acquiring knowledge, the modern press, like modern science, was fact-based, not idea-based, and thus constantly validated their shared epistemological underpinnings.[18]

Throughout the summer months Osborn received letters of support from scientists and educators congratulating him on his testimony and encouraging the museum's role in spreading the gospel of evolution. Ernest Hopkins, the president of Dartmouth College, stressed the museum's importance at this moment, "when so much ill-feeling and controversy has arisen over the life of past ages; the American people are largely dependent for fact on those evidences painstakingly gathered or exhibited by the Museum." Just at this time Lutz's new additions to the Hall of Insects had recently opened to the public. Where Osborn's Hall of the Age of Man (newly refurbished the previous year) at every turn advanced Osborn's racialist and classist notions of human evolution, Lutz's dioramas—habitat groups of the tiger swallowtail, Baltimore, European cabbage, and monarch butterflies, and the Japanese and ladybug beetles—presented simple life history information, with no grand evolutionary narrative or even incidental remarks about evolution.[19]

Both Lutz's hesitations about the ubiquity of natural selection and Osborn's confidence about the certainty of a teleologically driven process of biological evolution were equally symptomatic of the state of evolutionary theory in the mid-1920s, just as the Scopes trial was dramatic evidence that belief in evolution among the American public was not as yet universal. George Hunter's *Civic Biology*, the text from which Scopes taught and which put him outside the bounds of Tennessee law, was fairly short on evolutionary theory, though it assumed some version of evolution as a scientific fact. If anything, the Scopes trial served to make high school textbooks treat evolution more explicitly than they had previously done. Even by the time Osborn celebrated his seventieth birthday in 1927, the consolidation of modern sentiment in favor of Darwinian theory seemed imminent, and within a generation the previously unsettling issue of how to reconcile Darwinism with Christianity would become mostly moot.[20]

However much they may have differed on the fine points of evolutionary theory, Osborn approved of Lutz's style of zoology. Despite his enthusiasm for experiment, Lutz remained faithful to the principles and spirit of in situ nature study. Osborn in the mid-1920s was fond of pointing to Lutz's work at SSI as a model of biological education. Lutz certainly attracted the right kind of young men, for they were uniformly upper-class. Among junior staff members for the summers of 1927 and 1928 were: David Rockefeller and a schoolmate, De Veaux Smith; Coolidge Alden, a student at Kent and the son of the dean of the law school at the University of Buffalo; Francis Evans of Philadelphia (about whom Lutz reported that he was "a descendant of the stock that gave us Cope and other, not so widely known naturalists"). Osborn fully believed that these boys were getting the opportunity to master both nature and their developing selves by camping out at SSI, where they would learn that evolution was progressively ascending, despite the retrogressive lapses of modern society.[21]

Whereas Lutz's experimental approach to insect biology pushed up against the borders of the unseen, Osborn's philosophy regarded the unseen as a bulwark against the moral and spiritual transgressions of modernity: "nature never relaxes but always reinforces moral and spiritual laws . . . in other words, there can be no contradiction between nature and religion, because primitive religion issues out of the heart of nature in reverence for the powers of the unseen." For Osborn, the unseen was truly beyond human investigative powers; for Lutz and Loomis, it was just a matter of the right technological invention wedded to the right inventive spirit. By the 1930s, Loomis's Tuxedo lab would become the site of extensive research on a newly discovered invisible—brain waves. As he turned his machines upon himself, it seemed only a matter of time before man caught the ghost in the machine.[22]

Surveillance and Spectatorship

Early in 1926, Lutz was offered the directorship of the New York State Museum in Albany, challenging Osborn's commitment to his insect curator's blend of natural scientific research and pedagogy. Keen to keep Lutz in New York, Osborn approached Mary Harriman with a proposal for an endowment of $100,000, which would enable the museum to hire two assistants for Lutz. Osborn stressed the important work that Lutz was carrying out "on your 'Land of Eden,'" that is, Harriman Park. The endowment failed to materialize, but Osborn promised Lutz an augmented budget with new scientific staff, and Lutz declined the Albany position. Lutz was not as concerned about funding for SSI. Frank Johnson, owner of the National Pneumatic Company, was paying the expenses of the student workers and scientific guests at SSI, Alfred Loomis was meeting all of Lutz's needs for apparatus, and the park's virtual gift of the patrol station/lab made any building fund unnecessary. Lutz was an improviser and felt no great interest in trying to establish an impressive physical plant. His commitment was to create a fertile environment for collaborative work on insect biology between physical and life scientists. "Biology needs the invigorating effect of outbreeding," he maintained. "[P]hysicists, chemists, and mathematicians . . . know their subject and it is a bit embarrassing to a biologist to see how easily they punch holes in the physics and chemistry of apparently first-class work in which biologists have ventured by themselves to apply those sciences." He was willing to see such collaboration established under any one of a number of scenarios, not just as an SSI endeavor.[23]

Still, there were real limitations on Lutz's ability to attract scientists to the Tuxedo field station. He understood that the most accomplished professionals were already attached to institutions with more resources than SSI could offer and that those with the freedom to pursue summer research might well prefer to join the seashore labs or simply stay at home with their families. New opportunities in conservation and nature education work meant that students frequently could get summer jobs that paid them a small salary as well as room and board. He had been successful with those students he had attracted, fledging both a small cohort of promising natural scientists and, in David Rockefeller, cultivating a future patron of entomological research at the American Museum.[24]

In October 1928 Lutz closed down the SSI cabins, moved most of the lab's apparatus to his home in Ramsey, and returned the SSI lease to Averell Harriman. He told museum director George Sherwood that this would be best, considering the presence of two squatters on the property and the chance that some incident might generate adverse publicity for the museum. Lutz planned to invite some of the "strictly scientific" amateur natural science organizations from New York—the New York Entomological Society, Linnaean Society, and Torrey Botanical Club—to take over the SSI site as a naturalist's field club, but he confided to Major Welch that he had little hope for this arrangement, as "so many of these fellows have trouble seeing farther than from one field trip to the next." It would be three years before the park found a tenant to preserve the Arcadian heritage of the SSI site—the Federation of the German Youth Movement in North America.[25]

*O*ne of the last research projects carried out at SSI was a survey of the insect fauna in the immediate environs, undertaken by Charles Curran, Lutz's colleague at the American Museum. In nine weeks Curran collected 540 species, 97 of them new to New York State and 30 wholly new to science. He reported that almost all the collecting was done within a half mile of the station, and most of it in the little clearing just outside the cabin door. Considering that the insects of the New York City region were perhaps the most intensively collected in the country, Curran and Lutz were delighted with the survey. The history of scientific collecting in the Ramapo region was a long and fairly august one, given the proximity to so many leading institutions of natural science; but the golden era of collecting had really begun almost simultaneously with the first Arcadian migrations to the region, around 1880. The sense of the Ramapos as a refuge for Manhattanites was based on more than just the purely aesthetic draw of the mountain topography. The amateur and professional naturalists who regularly scoured the cliff faces, bogs and swamps, mountain brooks, and variegated forests of the Ramapos and the rest of the Highlands added detailed knowledge of just which species were present, giving specificity to the urban refugees' sense of sylvan regeneration.[26]

In 1898 Lieutenant Edgar Mearns of the U.S. Army, who had been born just two miles south of West Point and had spent twenty-seven years in the Highlands, published the first survey of Highlands vertebrate fauna. In the late nineteenth century, vertebrates—particularly mammals—were the main index for popular conceptions of the relative vitality of regional environments. This notion was especially widespread among the metropolitan men who came to the Highlands to hunt. A big-game hunter's prospects in 1898 were not particularly good. Deer had been locally extinct for some time, as were lynx (though local counties were still paying bounties of $25 for lynx hides in the 1870s), beaver (gone even when Mearns was a boy), and bear (Mearns's grandmother remembered seeing bear occasionally early in the century). Mearns noted other faunal declines typical of the northeastern forest: rarely seen were a number of birds—particularly raptors—and rattlesnakes. But Mearns's survey also testified to a certain basic health of the Highlands ecosystem, as he reported on the populations of fish (collected in 1877–1878 with C. Hart Merriam along the Hudson shore and up Popolopen Creek), amphibians, reptiles, birds, and mammals. Bear Mountain was a favorite collecting location, yielding specimens of the marbled salamander (*Ambystoma opacum*) and the red-backed salamander (*Plethodon cinereus*). Delightfully exotic, but nonetheless native, creatures like the "blue-tailed lizard" (*Eumeces fasciatus*) and even "tree lizards" (the northern fence lizard, *Sceloperus undulatus*) were seen every year by Mearns.[27]

Mearns's report was punctuated with anecdotes about particular animals that he had collected. Speaking of a pair of five-lined skinks that he shot near his Highland Falls home and deposited in the American Museum's collection, Mearns noted: "They were together, sunning themselves on a rock. This beautiful and entertaining animal lives among rocks, under buildings, walls, etc. It is exceedingly swift, but often surprisingly gentle, coming out of its hole and close to an intruder as often as driven in, but usually so nimble as to avoid capture." He described box turtles eating wild strawberries and mushrooms, and the antics of red squirrels and chipmunks. Mearns found a population of albino red squirrels on Constitution Island in the Hudson and noted that William Church Osborn had brought him a perfect albino specimen of the Brewer's mole, shot near Osborn's estate in Garrison. Frequently Mearns wrote in almost clinical detail about the reactions of animals to being shot.[28]

Mearns's activities coincided with regional collecting by mostly local naturalists like Osborn and Theodore Roosevelt (whose naturalist stripes were earned as a boy in the Highlands). This generation was followed by many naturalists from Manhattan and its suburbs; they had not grown up in the region but found it a desirable place to carry out fieldwork. The creation of Harriman Park in 1910 created an artificially bounded region within the Highlands; as the focal point for outdoor recreational activity, it attracted natural scientists wishing to paint a truly comprehensive picture of the region's flora and fauna. In 1919 Charles C. Adams of Syracuse University outlined a plan for an ecological survey of the Palisades Interstate Park, stressing the uniqueness of such a heavily forested region—the "wild woods"—in such close proximity to a major metropolis. Adams believed that, while making a scientific contribution, an inventory of the park would aid outdoor education: "The beautiful ponds, lakes, brooks, ravines, and forest trails and paths, mountain outlooks, and similar attractions furnish innumerable invitations for natural history field excursions and tramping trips, if the city dweller can learn to take advantage of these." An inventory would also assist management of the park and could lead to applied research, such as the problem of accelerated eutrophication in park lakes due to the huge volume of summer campers or the eradication of leeches, which were an annoyance to this same group.

Adams wished to build on previous survey work done in the park, particularly P. M. Silloway's 1918 study of the birds of the Bear Mountain and Little Long Pond areas of the park and his own work with T. L. Hankinson and A. E. Fivaz on park fish populations. While sampling fish populations in Kanawauke Lakes, the biologists had been tailed by 150 Boy Scouts, whom Adams put to work collecting: "We wanted them in their bathing suits and in the mud and water. Their joy knew no bounds when they caught the squirming bullheads and 'sunnies,' and when they watched them swim about in our tubs and glass jars." From these and future field studies, Adams foresaw a series of publications, both technical reports for park administrators and popular field guides for visitors. However, drawn increasingly into fieldwork at Alleghany State Park, which was closer to Syracuse, Adams never carried out his plans for a grand inventory of Harriman Park.[29]

After its establishment in 1927, the Bear Mountain Trailside Museum became the clearinghouse for field studies of park flora and fauna. Within a few years Bill Carr had come to feel that the pedagogical program at Trailside become estranged to a certain degree from "honest-to-goodness nature work itself," and he was anxious that intensive field surveys begin immediately, building on the episodic beginnings made at the time of Adams's interest. Trying to convince Major Welch to propose to President Osborn that his time would be well used in coordinating such surveys, Carr asked Welch to designate him official "Chief Naturalist." Always the aspiring author, Carr proposed a series of "non-technical yet thoroughly accurate" guides on the animal life of the park as an adjunct to the survey.[30]

Carr's proposals, coming at a time when both the museum's and the park's budgets were under Depression-era tightening, went unheeded until 1934, when Harriman received two "wildlife technicians" under the Civilian Conservation Corp's Emergency Conservation Work (ECW) program. Administered by the Branch of Education and Research within the National Park Service, the ECW program vastly augmented the labor force in the national parks (employment went from 2,200 in 1933 to almost 7,500 in 1940) and also revolutionized the landscape of many of the country's state parks. Within this program of landscape transformation wildlife technicians were meant to prevent CCC construction activity from adversely affecting park natural resources, particularly wildlife.[31]

The two young ECW technicians assigned to Harriman—Dan Beard's grandson D. Bartlett Beard and Albert Hochbaum—were under the supervision of park naturalist Carr, but their work methods were largely dictated by the CCC supervisor. Carr found the technicians' work wanting and felt the entire ECW program was a pointless exercise in paperwork. Rather than being a truly field-oriented enterprise, he told Major Welch, it was "a mass of generalities" lacking "scientific acumen" and completely ignorant of the tremendous volume of amateur and professional fieldwork that had been carried on in the park since 1920. Carr insisted that the program be run according to his initial plans: daily recorded observations of wildlife, region by region; daily study of wildlife feeding habits; a survey of predominant plant associations; and a well-organized filing system to store the field observations made. Carr voiced his objections to the head of the ECW program, NPS Assistant Director Conrad Wirth, and confided to Welch that he saw the whole program as typical of the "ever-broadening rule over local units by an ill-equipped central power."[32]

By spending one day a week in the field with Beard and Hochbaum, and dispatching members of the Trailside Museum staff to assist them, Carr managed to bring the bureaucratic apparatus under his direction to a certain extent, so that the survey became more than a make-work exercise. Assembled into a three-volume report, the survey divided the park's forty-two thousand acres into twenty-one districts, each of which was sampled by Beard, Hochbaum, and the Trailside staff. In his introduction, Carr related that it had long been his ambition to tie together the threads of natural history information contained in the various surveys done within the park, to create "a rounded story." This desire for narrative completeness was accompanied by a strong impulse toward geographic integration. The ECW survey repeatedly stressed how unified the fabric of the landscape would become once the last farms within park boundaries were abandoned, securing the park's sanctuary function. In Region Twelve, the Beaver Pond area, Carr and the technicians noted that some logging was still going on and that hunters and trappers frequently poached on park property. Although the CCC was building dams to construct lakes to replace the patchwork of wooded swamps and was carrying out extensive clearing for the recreational camps they would build, these activities were regarded as benign because they were nonconsumptive. The landscape integration that gripped the nature workers and scientists was one that—other than the study skins collected for the Trailside Museum's scientific records—conceived of wildlife as something to be watched rather than consumed.[33]

Spectatorship and science increasingly went hand-in-hand as the park's Arcadian landscape was consolidated. The scientific surveys gave interpreters like Carr a sense of authoritative knowledge of the park landscape, down to the level of individual copperhead and rattlesnake dens, wood duck nests, and winter deer yards. With the ECW maps and record cards, Trailside's "signs along the trail" were backed by definitive empirical observations from within the park rather than secondhand reports of a vaguely generic Nature. The progress of scientific knowledge within the park received ample public attention through the journalistic efforts of Ray Torrey, the park's publicity coordinator. Torrey's own expertise in botany and his wide acquaintance with naturalists of the metropolitan region, uniquely qualified him to report on developments in the scientific understanding of the park's natural resources. Throughout the 1930s, his weekly press releases regularly described topics well beyond the ken of the reporting staffs of daily newspapers. In an October 1936 article on fall foliage, Torrey communicated a wealth of natural history information about the tulip tree, *Liriodendron tulipifera*. Along with guiding motorists to the best spot to see the lovely display of the tulip tree's gold "blending with the dogwoods' scarlet [and] the red and gold of soft maple," Torrey reported on the history of the tulip tree within the Highlands forest, its importance to the mountain people as a source for woodenware, and Major Welch's conjecture that it had largely replaced the ecological niche formerly occupied by the American chestnut. Another piece drew upon his discussions with Welch and park forester Raymond Adolph about the composition of the Highlands' original forest. Torrey's historical knowledge was also apparent in his articles on the archaeological investigations (in which he was often a participant) undertaken by the Trailside Museum at Forts Clinton and Montgomery and at prehistoric rock shelters within the park.[34]

Torrey's articles celebrated the continuing sense of restoration that had marked the park since its birth in 1910. In 1936 he reported that pileated woodpeckers and little blue herons were beginning to reappear. Roger Tory Peterson had recently spotted a Blackburnian warbler near Cohasset Lake, and even loons were sojourning on park lakes in their spring and autumn migrations. When Major Welch gave a speech at Bear Mountain Inn to more than five hundred members of organizations affiliated with the National Federation of Garden Clubs of America, Torrey emphasized that Welch told the women that "he knew the forest would come back, even after the injuries it had suffered, if properly protected. . . . [Even] the rarer, more delicate plants began to come back too. Some of them had survived clearings and burnings, in remote swamps and bogs, and when the forest was protected and began to revive, they ventured out from their refuges and began to reappear in their ancient stations." When an enormous bronze elk head— a gift of Palisades Interstate Park Commissioner Victor Berman—was installed on the cliff face high above the Bear Mountain steamboat docks, Torrey captured the sense of regeneration experienced by the dedications' participants. Clyde Fisher's address painted a picture of the original wildlife of the Highlands, of the elk once native to the region, and of the hope that through Welch's restoration program it would again roam the Highlands forest.[35]

Photographic documentation of the landscape restoration program at the park was remarkably complete; a staff photographer recorded the construction of every one of Welch's roads, lakes, and buildings. The nature-study program was also fully captured on film, in photographs and, increasingly after 1925, in motion pictures. The motion picture camera, which held such promise for Fisher, Carr, and other nature workers, was enlisted at the park as a tool for scientific investigation as well. Carr thought of his many hours spent wielding the camera, especially in his observations of beaver, both captive and wild, as "research." He was especially proud of his color films of beaver working at night, which he claimed were the first ones ever made. In 1944 Carr wrote two scripts for a motion picture series planned by the New York Zoological Society. As a method of scientific instruction, motion pictures seemed limited only by the camera person's ability to find subjects. As with the ecological survey, the researcher merely needed to record and file the data to circumscribe the organism completely.[36]

All the forms of scientific surveillance did little to bring the scientist or the visitor into a closer relationship with the regenerating park landscape. As the forest came back in full force, and with it the suite of flora and fauna characteristic of the pristine past, the scientists and nature workers were left standing outside looking in. In his effort to train young people to observe accurately, Carr exhorted his charges to "see what you are looking at." He advised nature counselors to teach by the Coué method, making children repeat the phrase six times before conducting an object lesson. Carr believed that "the art of seeing things as they are is possessed by but a few of us, and by none of us perfectly." But one clear rule of thumb for achieving clarity of vision was to temper the "desire for the sublime" with "the unbiased light of rationality." Scientific vision should never be supplanted by mere storytelling.[37]

Modern Nature-Fakers

Science had a tremendous role to play in an age and culture so rich in flim-flam as America in the 1920s and 1930s. The anxiety about "nature-faking" that had animated naturalists like John Burroughs and Theodore Roosevelt a generation earlier was even more acute for Carr and his peers. Perhaps Carr, as a popular interpreter with meager scientific credentials, was especially sensitive to the pitfalls of embellishing on the facts, for he was nearly manic about "untruths" circulated within the lay world of natural science. Most exasperating to Carr were tales that prejudiced naive people against wildlife—the child-snatching eagle, the blood-sucking bat, the many myths circulated about snakes. Much of the animus in the original nature-faking controversy had been directed against sentimentality in the portrayal of animal behavior, and Carr also objected to "cute" newpaper and magazine tales that bent the truth to win reader empathy for animals. Because of their conspicuous impact on the landscape, beaver, Carr's favorite creatures, were especially prone to misrepresentation, and Carr was forever trying to replace fiction about them with facts.[38]

For Carr the key to accurate reportage of animal behavior was faithful field observation, beginning with correct identification. The aspiring naturalist had to develop the habit of mentally dividing the animal into a set of discrete anatomical parts, each with its own descriptors. Novice birdwatchers were instructed by Carr to note the bird's size, form, location, movements, flight pattern, song, and other characteristics. The key to understanding nature was the eye: "There is no better way to reach the boy's mind than through his eyes, for after all, the eye is not only the brain's eye, but the eye also of the mind." Through the eye, the mind could be "impregnat[ed] . . . with facts." Carr seemed to believe that understanding nature was a straightforward affair of collecting enough "facts" to subdue any gullible tendency toward untruth.[39]

When he occasionally spoke of nature's "mysteries" or "secrets," Carr was hardly echoing the traditional sense of medieval natural philosophy, which held that behind the physical surface of nature were occult patterns that demanded alchemical alterations of individual consciousness to be detected. Carr merely referred to the wholly exoteric "life-stories" that emerged additively from repeated passive observation of nature in situ. Replete with "signs," nature just had to be attentively read, not unlike the method employed on the nature trail. Studying nature as a hobby would be endlessly rewarding, Carr promised, because one could never learn all of its signs. Rather than referring to nature's semiotic complexity, this promise sprang from Carr's awe for the sheer number of facts lodged into their respective niches in forest, field, and stream. In the introduction to his handbook for young naturalists, Carr took a pair of waterfalls from an Adirondack stream remembered from his boyhood and turned them into a metaphor for two approaches to nature. The "big falls" represented "inspiration"; the "little falls," "information." Inspiration—nature's grandeur and power—was communicated principally by physical forces: tectonic and erosional events, the hydrologic cycle, weather. The little falls of the biological world spilled over with the data of ethology, ecology, life history, anatomy and physiology, taxonomy, and the other approaches to nature's factual cornucopia. Nowhere within his metaphor did Carr allow for significance. He substituted fact for meaning, as if meaning could come from the facts themselves rather than from human cognitive effort.[40]

Carr's rare allusions to the "unseen" in nature always meant that a certain behavior or episode had gone unrecorded by an individual observer or that science had not yet devised the necessary technology to make visible some still invisible aspect of nature. A bit of Ramapo Mountain lore related in *The Stir of Nature* illustrates the intersection of Carr's faith in fact, his disdain for myth, and his opaqueness to the possibility of a supersensible realm standing behind nature. Noting the ancient belief that salamanders can withstand fire, Carr told how a group of German ironworkers near the Ramapo Torne had in their native country put out their forge fires once every seven years to forestall the evil influence of the salamander who was believed to dwell in the fire. Hugo, the owner of the Ramapo furnace, refused to allow the workers to extinguish the flames, and soon they saw the salamander looming from the forge. Hugo was knocked unconscious from his encounter with the salamander; his wife, sprinkling holy water to appease the demon, was killed; and seven years later their young son disappeared. The entire tale was related by Carr as an example of the uselessness of prescientific knowledge of nature.[41]

The story retold by Carr originated with a group of the Brothers of the Rosy Cross who had settled in the Ramapo valley in the mid-1700s. The "salamander" in the story refers to one of the four classes of elemental nature spirits that in Rosicrucian tradition were understood to stand behind the physical world. Gnomes inhabited the earth, sylphs the air, undines the water, and salamanders fire. No relationship existed between the supersensible salamander and the sensible ones collected by Carr for display at his Trailside Museum. His own assertion that there was an ancient belief that salamanders could live in fire was itself a commonly held but wholly erroneous interpretation that mistook a supersensible being for a real animal. Carr's use of this anecdote encapsulated the entire historical inversion of the relationship between fact and imagination, the seen and unseen. The Rosicrucians, wedded to a view of nature that held both its origins and its significance to lie in the spiritual realm, were seen by Carr as fanciful dreamers uninfluenced by sensible facts. The Rosicrucian outlook held the same belief about modern science—that its knowledge was deeply flawed, blinded by its own seemingly fantastically successful empiricism.

The once-esoteric knowledge of nature cultivated by the Brothers of the Rosy Cross had by the 1920s become wholly exoteric, as the "occult revival" of late-nineteenth-century Europe had reached America's shores. Through the efforts of the Theosophical Society of America and other organizations, ancient alchemical, gnostical, and other esoteric systems of knowledge were being elaborated in modern language for a lay public and disseminated in books, magazines, and lectures throughout the United States. New York City was a prominent center of American popular occultism; the Theosophical Society had been founded there in 1875, and noted occult writers were regulars on the New York lecture scene. Like the rest of the American publishing industry, the occult press had its principal home in New York. The vast majority of this occult literature, although it routinely criticized materialist science in a general way and singled out Darwinian evolutionary theory in particular, had little to say about nature, preferring to dwell on the marvels of supernature. Thus it found its principal audience among artists and intellectuals seeking an alternative to reductionist science's denigration of imagination and emotion.[42] Though some American natural scientists found Henri Bergson's "creative evolution" attractive or countenanced John Burroughs's parallel improvisations—such as "Creative Energy" and "Universal Intelligence"—to retain some semblance of telos in a blind Darwinian universe of chance, few were attracted to occult science, for there seemed to be no *science* in it.[43]

Occult writers who did engage directly in natural scientific research usually had very little to offer in the way of empirical evidence to contradict materialist observers of nature. Journalist and occultist P. D. Ouspensky, seeking examples to discredit the utilitarianism of Darwinian explanations of biological form, took up the subject of mimicry in *A New Model of the Universe* (1931). He cited the same sorts of objections that antiadaptationist biologists like Frank Lutz voiced: the lack of usefulness of intermediate forms in a scenario of gradualistic evolutionary change and the "overdesign" of some devices for deception, such as the mock fungus spots and grazing scars on cryptically patterned leaf insects. Ouspensky had no observations of his own to add to scientific knowledge of the puzzle of biological mimicry and preferred to think that the artfulness of adaptive coloration and form derived from some purposeful intelligence dwelling in the "Fourth Dimension." To anyone who had vernacular knowledge of insects in their natural environments, Ouspensky's theory held absolutely no explanatory power.[44]

Episodic outbursts of popular interest in "nature mysticism" in the 1920s suggest that not all Americans accepted a completely Naturalistic nature. In 1920 the *Atlantic Monthly* serialized the "Journal of an Understanding Heart," by Opal Whiteley. Written when she was seven years old, the diary spoke a child's animate language of nature but was punctuated with startling attention to natural history detail. Digging potatoes in Oregon with her grandfather, Opal observed:

> Potatoes are very interesting folks. I think they must see a lot of what is going on in the earth they have so many eyes. . . . To some [potato] piles I did stop to give geology lectures. . . . Too, I did have thinks of all their growing days there in the ground, and all the things they did hear. Earth-voices are glad voices, and earth songs come up from the ground through the plants; and in their flowering, and in the days before these days are come, they do tell their earth-songs to the wind. . . . I have thinks these potatoes here did have knowing of star-songs. I have kept watch in the field at night, and I have seen the stars look kindness down upon them

Opal, who had made a tremendous impression on Ellery Sedgwick, the *Atlantic Monthly* editor who brought the diary into print, fascinated a wide American and European audience with her naive nature mysticism.

Henri Poincaré and Lord Rayleigh wrote her admiring letters of congratulation, and the English naturalist Sir Edward Grey wrote the preface to the British edition of her diary after it was brought out in book form. A great flurry of press attention followed the diary's appearance, much of it focusing on her mysterious identity and the possibility that she had really written the diary as an adult. Opal insisted that she had been born to French naturalist Henri D'Orleans, and that after his death in 1904 she had been adopted by the Whiteleys in Oregon.[45]

In 1914, when Opal was seventeen, her mother took her to visit the University of Oregon. For a number of years she had maintained her own nature museum in her home and had given classes in nature study to local children. She dreamed of becoming a nature writer and had written a book and enlisted subscribers (including the vanquisher of nature-fakers, Theodore Roosevelt). The head of the geology department at Oregon declared after meeting Opal that she knew more about geology than many of his graduate students, and the chairman of the botany department was reputed to have lamented: "Is all our great system wasted? Is it hindering normal development?" The Oregon girl's knowledge of the natural world was disturbing both in its precocity and in its suggestion that plants and animals could communicate with humans. Even more unsettling was Opal's conviction that all natural events had a close correspondence with spiritual events.[46]

By 1940, Opal Whiteley—blind, seemingly schizophrenic, and in poor health—was living in a ward in Napsbury Hospital near London. Skeptics felt satisfied that her state confirmed their suspicions that her nature mysticism was merely the result of mental illness.[47] The entire affair echoed events that had transpired almost simultaneously in London in 1920, when Sir Arthur Conan Doyle and the Theosophical Society had trumpeted two young Cottingley girls' photographs of fairies.[48] A great rush of hopeful believers had in both instances interpreted the animate nature perceived by the girls as an intimation of a sacred, animate Nature beyond the bounds of natural science's secularizing onslaught. Empirical science, supported by the popular press, had quickly regrouped and debunked the authenticity of both Opal's diary and the Cottingley fairy photographs. Bill Carr's nature study, founded as it was upon modern natural science's empiricism and modern social science's view of the human as a puppet of instinctual urges, could never approach the invisibles that Opal Whiteley seemed to sense. The scientific study of nature within Harriman Park was also a two-pronged attack, coming from the level of the individual organism and its sensory embeddedness within its life world and from the level of the landscape unit that acted as a bounded "container" for an enumeration of those organisms. From either direction, it was clearly a science of quantities, even if its descriptive language and its reliance on the observer's eye rather than some technological intermediary gave it the appearance of a relatively qualitative body of knowledge.

Modern science's extension of the human senses, through improvements in the technology to penetrate both the microscopically and the macroscopically insensible, promised the naturalist the possibility of conquering any vestige of a transcendental unseen behind nature's appearances. Frank Lutz's experiments in insect physiology were also experiments in determining the limits of sensible Nature, and they suggested that the limits were fast disappearing. The rapacious inventory of Harriman Park's flora and fauna was another step on the road to natural science's global panopticon of remote sensing. When suspicious manifestations of an unseen appeared, like Opal Whiteley's talking potatoes or the Cottingley fairies, the guardians of Naturalism could quickly marshal their technological and philosophical apparatus to dispel these dangerous illusions. As it cunningly decoded the nonhuman world, science seemed to elevate the humble status of fruit flies, beetles, and bees. At the same time, the new Naturalism diminished the status of the human being, or at least certain human beings. In the Ramapo Mountains, where naturalists found so much of the nonhuman primeval worthy of salvation, they also discovered a human primeval that demanded eradication.

CHAPTER 4

Caught between Nature and History

*L*ong before the "back-to-nature" movement sent Manhattanites and other metropolitans over the Ramapo fault line in search of Arcadian refuge, the Ramapo Mountains had served as a haven for another population. If the restorers of the Ramapo's primeval quality went to great lengths to reestablish all the flora and fauna they believed to be native to the region, their enthusiasm for the human natives was decidedly different. The movement across the fault in the late nineteenth century brought people of modern urban sensibilities into direct contact with rural people, contributing to the invention of "feeblemindedness" as a social and intellectual category. From the Jukes family study of the 1880s, to Henry H. Goddard's Kallikaks and Pineys, and finally to the many early family studies conducted by the Eugenics Record Office at Cold Spring Harbor, Manhattan Island was the epicenter of eugenic interest in rural feeblemindedness. Other of the region's geographical features—the Pine Barrens of New Jersey and Long Island, the swamplands of the lower Hudson, the Catskill Mountains—were sites of eugenics field activity, but the intensity in the Ramapos had no equal. As surely as metropolitan naturalists found the Ramapos a rewarding field for natural scientific study and teaching about the nonhuman components of the landscape, they also extended their Naturalism to the human occupants, in a local expression of the widespread early-twentieth-century cultural confrontation known as eugenics.

Lucy DeGroat's Hoevenkopf Kin

Lucy DeGroat was just five years old in 1911 when she arrived at the Training School for the Feeble-Minded in Vineland, New Jersey.

Authorities from the New Jersey Children's Home Society had responded to a sensational newspaper report about a destitute woman living in a woodchopper's shack in the Ramapo Mountains near Oradell, New Jersey. Among the "litter of neglected, sick animals" they found Lucy ("a pitiful little idiot girl"), her seven-year-old brother (placed with a farm family), and her two younger sisters (adopted by childless couples). Having heard stories of a mixed-race, degenerate clan of people known as the "Jackson-Whites" living in the mountains, Dr. Henry H. Goddard, superintendent at the Vineland Training School, sent social worker Jane Griffiths to the Ramapos to research the DeGroat family history. Following Goddard's instruction, Griffiths began a card file. Pasted to her first card, a photograph of Lucy shows a sandy-haired girl with bright eyes and a warm smile wearing a calico dress under a dark jacket. She had a bow in her hair. The record card description reads: "eats naturally and well; helps dress and undress herself; hard to manage at times; bites; bad habits; tries to do something; cheerful, affectionate, excitable, quick-tempered."

Griffiths's preliminary research led her to focus on Hillburn, New York, as a promising area to find members of the DeGroat family. There, in November 1911, Griffiths located Lucy's paternal grandparents—Isaiah and Lucinda DeGroat—who turned out to be well behaved and generally respected by their neighbors. The farmer for whom they had worked for ten years told Griffiths that he had been unable to find anyone who would care for his land or his cattle as well as Isaiah had. Lucinda had been a fine housekeeper for the farmer's wife, and she kept her own place on the farm neat and clean. But the farmer had to let the DeGroats go after some of their shiftless children moved in with their parents. On the file cards, Griffiths recorded that Lucinda was only "slightly defective," as was her husband. They certainly could not be described as normal, but Griffiths felt it unjustified to call them feebleminded. Though poor, at least they were gentle and harmless, living decently and providing for themselves.[1]

Griffiths found no actual "colored people" in Lucy's paternal family, but there *were* traces of African-American ancestry in the fair, kinky-haired, brown-eyed children, some of whom were quite attractive. Griffiths had begun to trust in the guide provided for her by Nora Snow, daughter of the owner of the American Brakeshoe foundry, just down the Ramapo River at West Mahwah, where so many of the families from Hillburn worked. But the families who lived up on the Houvenkopf—the steep mountain that rose on the southwest side of the Ramapo River, marking the entry of the Ramapos into New Jersey—were entirely different from their relations down in Hillburn, West Mahwah, and the other valley towns. The only way to gain admission to the homes of these remarkably shy people was to go with someone they knew.[2]

As winter closed in on the Houvenkopf, Griffiths put away the DeGroat case until the following summer of 1912. By that time, she had already begun to sketch much of the DeGroat family tree, based on the interviews she had conducted with Miss Snow, Miss Wright, a teacher at the school on the Houvenkopf, and Mr. and Mrs. Francis Wheaton, who began a school for the mountain children in their cabin in 1902, the same year that Miss Snow built a new school and settlement house on the mountain. Returning to the Houvenkopf in June 1912, Griffiths brought a new tool for recording data—a camera—which proved to be a great help in making friends with the mountain people. They were delighted to get prints of her photographs, which often included three generations and typically were taken in front of the family home. She had photos of Isaiah DeGroat's sister Lizzie, his grand-niece Mary Elizabeth (known as "Old Fanny"), and her common-law husband of twenty years, Old Jake DeGroat. Jake and Fanny owned the best house on the Houvenkopf, a three-room log cabin. Griffiths had a wonderful photo of Jake's brother Richard—"Punkin' Dick"—dressed in a felt hat, white shirt, and dark tweed coat. He had taken one of his pole-like crutches and rested it across his shoulder, while holding the other out in his right hand, so that it looked like a gentleman's walking cane. He looked for all the world like a country squire, which his father, Richard, had nearly been. When he died in 1894 at the age of ninety-two, he owned almost three hundred acres of the mountaintop south of the Houvenkopf. A photograph of another of Richard Sr.'s sons, Owen, was taken near one of the mountaintop fields the father had worked for seventy years. Griffiths was especially fond of her photo of Owen's wife, Old Nance, who looked up proudly from a wooden chair with a carved back that they had set outside the cabin. Her daughter Henrietta stood behind, along with a handsome grandson; Henrietta's youngest daughter, a ribbon in her hair, stood alongside her.[3]

A photograph of Anna DeFreese DeGroat with two of her grandchildren showed just how mixed-up the family's blood was. The little girl, in her best white dress, was as black as coal, with tight, kinky brown hair. The little boy, on the other hand, was strikingly Indian in all his features, from his straight, jet-black hair and copper complexion to his aquiline nose and eyes, which were almost black. Anna told Griffiths that her husband was "pure Indian" and that as a boy he had straight red hair. Her grandmother was a "white French woman, a real lady," who had married a colored man. Four of her ten children were albinos, Anna affirmed, but she seemed sensitive about their condition, so Griffiths did not inquire further about photographing them.[4]

Some of these albino children appeared in the pedigree chart published by Charles Benedict Davenport with his 1910 *American Naturalist* article on the heredity of skin pigmentation. In March 1909 Davenport, director of the Station for the Study of Experimental Evolution (SEE), sent his colleague Sumner Meringham to Hillburn to gather family history information for Davenport's research on the heredity of albinism. Davenport had achieved little success with the questionnaires that he had been sending to "defectives" as part of the survey he was conducting as a member of the American Breeders' Association's Subcommittee on Feeble-Minded Children. He was excited to learn that Goddard planned to put fieldworkers on the road to make inquiries about each of Vineland's nearly four hundred inmates. In particular, he encouraged Goddard to alert Jane Griffiths to instances of albinism, and he was delighted at Goddard's offer to pass along any information Griffiths gathered. "We have an unlimited appetite for data," Davenport assured Goddard.[5]

"A RED-LETTER Day for Humanity"

As of February 16, 1910, Davenport had the means as well as the appetite for collecting eugenic data. On that "RED-LETTER Day for Humanity," as he noted in his diary, Davenport lunched with Mary Harriman, who agreed to contribute $10,000 toward Davenport's idea for a survey of feeble-mindedness in America. In August, Davenport sailed out of Cold Spring Harbor with Mrs. Harriman on her yacht *Sultana*, and they had a long discussion about the name for their fledgling enterprise. Mrs. Harriman definitely objected to anything with the word "laboratory," for she liked everything "as simple and direct as possible." This settled the matter for Davenport, who proposed "Eugenics Office of Records" and "Office of Eugenics Records." Mrs. Harriman chose "Eugenics Records Office."[6]

Davenport had first met Mrs. Harriman in June 1907, when she and her husband sailed the *Sultana* into Cold Spring Harbor to visit their daughter Mary at SEE, where she was attending Davenport's summer lectures on heredity and eugenics. Davenport used this meeting to ask Edward H. Harriman if he might loan the *Sultana* later that summer to ferry visiting zoologists at the International Zoological Congress in New York out to Cold Spring Harbor for a tour of the SEE labs. Davenport flattered Harriman by alluding to Harriman's worldwide fame among zoologists for having sponsored the Harriman Alaska Expedition. Though the *Sultana* was otherwise committed, Harriman made available the steamer *Isabelle* in its stead. A year later, Davenport solicited a contribution from Harriman for a one-hundredth anniversary celebration of Charles Darwin's birth sponsored by the American Association for the Advancement of Science, and his letter suggested that the Harrimans shared their daughter's eugenic interests (her nickname at Barnard College was "Eugenia"). Davenport noted the importance of Darwin's contribution to agriculture (Harriman was an avid breeder of premier animal stock, particularly harness horses), and also the revolutionary impact of the theory of natural selection on philosophy and religion: "We understand now that the evil in man is often an inheritance from animal ancestors, and that moral delinquents and mental and physical defectives are reversions to remote ancestral conditions. Even the idea of evolution in the practice of the business worlds has been animated by the introduction of the idea into philosophy."[7]

Darwinian or not, Harriman's conquest of American rail traffic begat its second legacy: on October 1, 1910, just two weeks after the ceremony that bequeathed Harriman Park, the Eugenics Records Office (ERO) opened for business, housed in a building up the road from SEE. Mrs. Harriman preferred to emphasize eugenics fieldwork. She had promised Davenport that she would fund both a summer training course for fieldworkers and, afterward, the expenses of five or six of the best, whom Davenport was to choose and assign to the most promising locales. "This is a national matter, not only a private or purely scientific one," she wrote Davenport from Arden House, itself a testament to her belief in a purely American cultural impulse. Davenport was equally patriotic, pledging to do his best to further Mrs. Harriman's ideal "to develop to the utmost the work of the physical and social regeneration of our beloved country through the application of ascertained biological principles." They were not alone in feeling the necessity of a concerted research effort in eugenics. Thomas Henry Morgan had recently presented a plan to the president of Columbia University to undertake eugenic research, and Mrs. Harriman was watching that proposal with interest. David Starr Jordan, president of Stanford University, had visited Mrs. Harriman at Arden House just after the Fourth of July and counseled her that Columbia would not be the best place to develop such a program. Davenport now had her undivided support for his plan of "uplifting . . . our country by improving the blood of the nation."[8]

Davenport's lectures to the first class of ERO fieldworkers were full of earnestness for the eugenics cause. Reminding the students that loyalty to the ERO and its directors was "the highest virtue," he cautioned them against the peculiar dangers of the eugenics fieldworker. They were pioneers in this important work and would be carefully watched by those with a nose for scandal. Because their research touched on human reproduction, there would be plenty of prurient journalistic interest. Newspapermen, always looking for "hot stuff," should be avoided. "Be always businesslike in your dealings with men and women and the matter of sex will be forgotten," he told the group, only one of whom was male. He assured the women that, as proven by the experience of women census takers, even single women could visit homes in rural villages and small towns without incident; still, they should be "prudent while courageous and businesslike." Rather than "blab," it was imperative for them to listen. When in the field, "go primarily for the specific facts sought but be a good listener and report to the central office other facts in which it is interested." "The discovery of truth," Davenport told them, "is a noble occupation; but truth is not lightly got at."[9]

By using the correct approach with potential informants, preferably by demonstrating at the outset some recent contact with relatives, the fieldworker could soon become regarded as "a friend of the family," even a "confidant." Informants had rights, of course, including the most valuable right to personal privacy, but it was possible to gain information without being offensive. Two principles operated in favor of the fieldworker: first, people like to talk about what they know, and family traits were universally the most familiar topic of conversation; second, people would often give "facts" about "defects" in the family because they believed that the facts would be used to aid the afflicted person. Once collected, these facts were to be "sacredly guarded," and the fieldworker should assure informants of their confidentiality. "Remember you are after the truth; spare no pains to attain it," Davenport challenged them. So far as determining what constituted the truth, Davenport made only one recommendation: seek out a second witness to corroborate statements. Davenport placed remarkable confidence in the self-evidence of "facts."[10]

Davenport and Harry Laughlin, superintendent of ERO, also led the aspiring eugenics fieldworkers on a variety of field trips. On one outing the group inspected Sing Sing Penitentiary, toured the Matteawan (New York) State Hospital for the Criminally Insane, and then visited an albino family studied by Davenport in Millerton, New York. On another trip, to Connecticut's only school for the feebleminded in Lakeville, they used the institution's records to plot a map of inmates' birthplaces. Davenport was struck by the disproportionate percentage of inmates who came from rural communities.[11]

The Geography of Feeblemindedness

Davenport's perception that the rural feebleminded posed a threat to the nation determined the assignments of the first class of ERO fieldworkers. Brown University graduate Florence Danielson ("Fieldworker #1" in ERO records) would go to Connecticut to work up the pedigrees of some of the Lakeville "imbeciles." Fieldworker 2, Sadie Devitt, would return to her native Minnesota and pursue similar work there. Fieldworker 3, Mary O. Dranga of Indiana, had the important task of following up on Oscar McCullough's 1888 pioneering study of the "Tribe of Ishmael." Similarly, Arthur Estabrook, Fieldworker 4, would head for the Catskill Mountains to see if he could locate the descendants of the "Jukes," made famous by R. L. Dugdale in 1902. Helen Reeves would return to Vineland to carry out fieldwork directed jointly by Davenport and Goddard.

In his 1911 book dedicated to Mary Harriman, *Heredity in Relation to Eugenics*, Davenport devoted a chapter to bringing together geography and human heredity to help explain the geography of feeblemindedness. Seeming to grasp for the sort of biogeographic rule that his fellow zoologists were proposing based on their field observations of widely distributed fauna, Davenport stated that negative human traits multiplied most dramatically in long-established, relatively isolated communities with much inbreeding, while positive traits multiplied most rapidly by emigration. By this reasoning, Davenport believed that a country with "a restless people" (like the United States) would show a small percentage of negative traits and a high percentage of positive ones. Within America, however, pockets of defectiveness could be explained by geographic isolation, typically enforced by water or elevation. Davenport illustrated this principle with a section from a topographic map depicting a steep mountain surrounded by a lowland, which he identified as the Catskill home of the infamous "Jukes."

Interest in the biological effects of geographic isolation was widespread among early students of evolution, but Davenport was particularly sensitive to this dimension of biogeography, having been influenced directly by the landscape evolutionary ideas of his University of Chicago colleagues Rollin D. Salisbury and Thomas C. Chamberlain and indirectly by his sometime field partner Henry C. Cowles.[12] Davenport was most keenly interested in the effect of geography on "consanguinity," particularly the conspicuous defects that consanguinity had produced in islands and other isolated regions. The assignments of the first class of ERO fieldworkers reflected this interest. Though he could not spare a fieldworker in 1910, Davenport hoped eventually to send one or more of his graduates to one of the eastern seaboard's trouble spots: Martha's Vineyard (where, he was told by ERO board member Alexander Graham Bell, deaf mutes constituted 11 percent of the population); Point Judith, Rhode Island (where 13 percent of the population was supposed to be composed of idiots); Block Island (where there was a pronounced loss of fecundity); a peninsula on Chesapeake Bay (where he had been told about "dwarfness of stature");

the Outer Banks of North Carolina ("suspiciousness; inability to pass beyond the third or fourth grade"); or islands off the coast of Maine (where consanguinity produced "intellectual dullness"). The observation about Maine had been made by Davenport during his vacation in the region the previous summer, a trip motivated by a desire to see for himself if there might be promising sites for fieldworkers.

That these reputed pockets of genetic chaos were also the locations of maritime resorts was hardly a coincidence. The ERO enterprise was set in a very particular historical moment, when educated professionals of urbanizing regions in America turned their attention to nearby areas that were resistant, for a variety of environmental, historical, and cultural reasons, to modernization and urbanization. The favorite sites of eugenic attention were typically uncomfortably close to the apotheoses of the turn-of-the-century Arcadian aesthetic—Cape Cod and its outlying resort islands (Martha's Vineyard and Nantucket), Bar Harbor, Long Island's North Shore, the Catskills, Saratoga, Tuxedo Park. Nearly all the key figures of the American eugenics movement were enthusiastic participants in the Arcadian movement "back to nature" and so had firsthand experience with the jarring juxtaposition of their genteel Arcadian ways with the rougher rustic habits of indigenous neighbors. John D. Rockefeller, Madison Grant, and H. H. Goddard all had summer places in the Bar Harbor region, where after 1900 it was still possible to find the odd island that had not been turned into a private retreat by some newly made millionaire. The backwardness of the inhabitants of such places appalled the summer colonists. But rural regions far from urban, suburban, and resort communities simply did not attract the scrutiny of ERO and state-level eugenic institutions. For eugenicists, the working premise truly was "out of sight, out of mind" when it came to rural degeneracy.[13]

The transportation revolution precipitated by the automobile accentuated this clash of Arcadia and Metropolis. Between 1900 and 1920, before the explosion of automobile ownership, the motor-tourist who ventured off the macadamed main highway onto dirt roads frequently encountered country people unfamiliar with metropolitan lifeways. As more and more upper-middle-class metropolitans bumped up against rural folk, both near suburban garden housing developments and summer resort areas, the rhetoric of "the menace of the feeble-minded" began to find a wide audience. Like the Arcadian myth, eugenics in America grew up with the automobile, and the focus on degeneration among rural families was possible only because these regions could be reached by automobile. None of the female ERO fieldworkers owned a vehicle; unless Davenport provided a budget for an automobile, they depended on the generosity of local middle-class informants, such as ministers, physicians, school principals, and others who might serve as chauffeur and scout. When Jane Griffiths first arrived in Hillburn, her first stop (following Goddard's advice from Davenport) was Nora Snow's home; Snow told Griffiths that it would be impossible to conduct her work without an automobile to reach the scattered mountaintop dwellings on the Houvenkopf. Fortunately, Snow provided one, along with a guide. The ERO summer field school relied completely on the automobile to access its study areas; one of Davenport's favorite locales was the Shinnecock Indian Reservation, inaccessible from the Long Island Railroad but an easy day trip in an auto.[14]

Eugenicists were often among the early and enthusiastic automobilists. Davenport selected the Maine islands for fieldworker Mary Sturges after his ten-day summer automobile trip through the region. In 1915 Harry Laughlin wrote to Davenport from southern California, where Laughlin and his wife were visiting his brother. Reporting that they had traveled some seven hundred miles in the last ten days by automobile, Laughlin told Davenport that if he would come to California, they would "show him the country—eugenically, biologically, and scenically." Ichthyologist David Starr Jordan, another leading American eugenicist, claimed to have made the first automobile tour in America, in 1892. Davenport and Jordan both refined their motoring skills on biological field trips, where the geographic compass provided by the automobile was a tremendous boon to the naturalist interested in gaining a cosmopolitan view of biological distribution. If the automobile revolutionized the surveillance of America's flora and fauna, it also brought the human within the scope of systematic science.[15]

Davenport translated his natural history training into techniques for his eugenics fieldworkers. Frequently his pedagogical instruction at the ERO summer school echoed rules of thumb he might deliver to young biologists at SEE. The greatest asset of the eugenics fieldworker, as of the field naturalist, was keen observational prowess. Where the naturalist was to be ever aware of new phenomena for investigation, the eugenics fieldworker must stay alert to new leads for hereditary inquiry. Davenport told the ERO students: "In conversation with persons seek to collect facts concerning other family traits than that which you are at the time studying. Be on the lookout, all the time, for interesting families." Data recording was of paramount importance, and Davenport suggested that the eugenics fieldworkers follow the habit he had developed as a naturalist: "At odd times, while waiting for trains, at ends of days, during rain, and if necessary during the evening, before your records grow cold, make out pedigree charts in triplicate . . . on quadrille-ruled paper." For identification assistance, eugenics fieldworkers carried Davenport's *Trait Book*, a massive inventory of the variegated signifiers of degeneracy, from polydactyly and albinism to alcoholism and epilepsy.[16]

The fact that the pioneers of rural eugenic research in America—particularly Davenport and Goddard—used the term *fieldwork* suggests the degree to which natural history served as the model for eugenics family studies. Although fully infused with the ethos and aspirations of experimental science, eugenics also partook of the culture of criminology and urban sociology, where the term *agent* was nearly universally employed to describe investigative workers. From the outset of their professional relationship, Goddard and Davenport spoke of "fieldworkers" engaged in "fieldwork." Goddard, Davenport, and other American eugenicists assumed both that eugenics fieldworkers were subject to the same standards of rigorous empiricism expected of field naturalists and that, occasionally, they would be subject to the same hazards—inclement weather, strenuous physical activity, remoteness from the conveniences of the metropolis. For eugenics fieldworkers, as for field biologists, raw encounters with the natural world, especially given the "primitiveness" of many of their subjects, were only to be expected. During his second summer of fieldwork, Arthur Estabrook battled with Davenport over the publication of his Catskill investigations. Davenport intended to put himself as first author of Estabrook's report, even though he had done nothing more than assign the research and serve as advisor. Estabrook's strident letter of protest to Davenport began by reminding him of the strenuous conditions suffered by the eugenics fieldworker: "While the work in the field is most interesting, a field-worker endures many snubs and unpleasant experiences."[17]

During its first decade of operation, ERO in many ways followed the model of nineteenth-century natural history museums and herbaria when they were in their descriptive phases. Davenport was the all-knowing "systematist" standing at the center of a network of field collectors. Just as Asa Gray, Louis Agassiz, Spencer Baird, and other systematists had to keep in close communication with their field representatives, Davenport was obliged to monitor his surveyers constantly. Every morning in the field, each ERO worker was expected to send a postcard reporting location and plans for the day. Davenport kept up a steady correspondence with his fieldworkers, answering questions, suggesting avenues of inquiry, and providing moral support. Though the fieldworkers occasionally had the opportunity to publish their own results, Davenport, like his systematist counterparts in biology, was the only one to make wide use of *all* of the field reports in constructing his synthetic works. Even more so than the museum-bound zoologist or botanist, Davenport risked errors in judgement because he lacked firsthand experience with the "specimens" in the field.

Though he often lectured and wrote about the "Jackson-Whites" and other rural degenerates, he relied on his extension workers for his data, never having met a Jackson-White himself.[18]

Hunting the Hovel Dwellers

The two principal sponsors of eugenics fieldwork in America—Mary Harriman and John D. Rockefeller Jr.—had entirely different philanthropic philosophies. Rockefeller's strategy of efficient giving was to hire professional managers who, together with corporate boards, would decide where best to spend some of the immense Rockefeller fortune. Mary Harriman disapproved of this new style of giving, preferring to involve herself personally in any charitable endeavor she supported. From the beginning of her relationship with Davenport, she took an interest in every aspect of ERO's operations, and Davenport came to rely on her for encouragement as well as for financial support. He sent her a copy of his paper on the Hillburn albinos, providing her with the surnames that were symbolized only with single initials on the pedigree chart, and explained how "the tribe" was given to consanguineous marriages, increasing the chance of "two similarly defective germ cells uniting." Mrs. Harriman was especially keen to learn of the progress of individual fieldworkers, and Davenport provided her with quarterly reports on their activities, as well as the occasional sketch map showing the routes they had traveled. Davenport also kept his patron abreast of legislative and research developments in other states regarding eugenics. After the first year of ERO's operation, Mrs. Harriman was entirely satisfied with the beginning Davenport had made. On Thanksgiving Day 1911, she wrote to him after having read the proofs of his *Heredity in Relation to Eugenics*: "Your book is certainly a nice starter not only in eugenics but for a proper understanding of the great national care of and responsibility towards the American people. The decay of the human race before death is so much more terrible than after death, and the debasing of moral life by the degeneration of the physical system so appalling, so I am glad to have my name added to those hoping to stem the tide . . . we were meant to be wholly pure beings and an understanding of the laws of nature must help to keep us pure."[19]

In 1912 Mrs. Harriman carried her zeal for eugenics research to Letchworth Village, the New York State Department of Mental Hygiene's new state-of-the-art facility for the feebleminded in Thiells, adjacent to the Harriman Park property. Mrs. Harriman was enthusiastic about establishing a program of scientific research at Letchworth, both in a medical laboratory and in fieldwork. Offering to underwrite the salary, she asked

Davenport to select his best ERO fieldworker for assignment to Letchworth Village, someone who could begin research on the rural defectives—the "Jackson-Whites" and other degenerate peoples of the Ramapo Mountains—Mrs. Harriman knew so well. Before he died, Edward Harriman had attempted to improve the mountaineers by encouraging them to relocate to the more settled lands in the Ramapo Valley. Davenport had applauded the effort: since "the Ramapo Mountains had been recognized as a source of defectives," he told Mrs. Harriman, her husband had done "a very practical piece of work in eugenics when he had the hovel dwellers go to the villages." Mrs. Harriman had also sought to better the mountain people, having introduced home economics and industrial arts into a number of the one-room schoolhouses on or near the Harriman estate.[20]

By early 1913, Davenport had dispatched Fieldworker 32, Florence Smith, to Letchworth Village. Upon Mrs. Harriman's recommendation, Smith began her investigations in the little community of Sterling Mines, only three miles south of Arden House (and just a mile north from the future location of Frank Lutz's Station for the Study of Insects). One of the few mines still operating in the Ramapo region, Sterling Mines employed 168 men—42 "native" Americans, 48 Slavs, Hungarians, and Russians, and 78 Italians, all of whom were paid between $1.80 and $2.50 per day. Smith followed the procedures she had learned at the ERO field school, beginning with interviews of local authorities: the overseers of the poor in the nearby towns of Southfields, Monroe, and Highland Falls; the physician in Monroe; and officials at the Bedford Reformatory, the Middletown Children's home, and the State Charities Aid Association. On rainy days she read the reports of the overseer of the poor in the Tuxedo Town Hall or brushed up on local history in the Tuxedo Library. Throughout the summer of 1913, Smith alternated between walking door-to-door in Sterling Mines, interviewing the inhabitants and photographing them and their homes, and driving to the scattered locations of family members, both in isolated mountain cabins and in neighboring towns. As Davenport taught at Cold Spring Harbor, she took special note of the "tidiness" and "thrift" of the homes and their inhabitants:

> Dewitt Decker never works steadily, is fond of fishing and trapping . . . wears his hair long and has a most unkempt appearance. Is boy-like in his lack of responsibility, good-natured, and unreliable. When in town is the butt of jokes at the corner grocery. . . .
>
> Sadie Hovencamp's early environment was poor in every respect. Her family lived in one of a group of five log huts in a small clearing about a mile up on Pochuck Mountain. . . . Those from the

mountain who worked out did so very irregularly and usually only when they were in need of some immediate necessity. They never worked during the hunting season or when food was plenty, depending upon fishing, small game, what they could gather from their small clearing, and what they could get from the orchards and fields of their more thrifty neighbors. The farmers never made complaint when they helped themselves to food and in fact never interfered with them if they could help it, being thankful if their barns escaped burning. The people were practically always mated after they reached maturity and changed consorts whenever it suited their taste or convenience. They lived in every way in a most primitive fashion. On the whole they were fairly capable when they chose to work, were skillful at hand work, were rather shrewd and cunning, prided themselves upon having enough knowledge of the law to escape punishment, were independent and child like in their inability to keep things to themselves.[21]

Smith's report stressed how "unattractive" Sterling Mines was, due to the "low standards in social conditions," the "isolation of the place," and the fact that it was a company town, so that none of the miners could own their own homes. As a result, Smith reported, Sterling Mines attracted a rather "shiftless, unambitious class of people." Her primary piece of data was a pedigree chart and a map of the village with all the houses numbered. This was accompanied by an inventory for each dwelling: the number of rooms; number of beds; condition of the house as to repair and housekeeping; size of the family; number of domestic animals; type of water supply; presence or absence of a garden; and total weekly income of the family. Few of the dwellings met Smith's standards of domestic economy; invariably, where she did encounter a neat and thrifty homestead, its inhabitants' moral economy also proved to her liking. Typically these homes belonged to the company storekeeper, clerks, or mine foremen. Mrs. Harriman was dismayed to discover from Florence Smith's report that the American workers were the least thrifty and the most inclined to become dependent. In the fall Mrs. Harriman arranged for Smith to administer Binet intelligence tests to all the children at the Sterling Mines school, as well as at seventeen other rural schools in the area. At Sterling Mines, Smith determined that of the forty children, one was "normal" and another "above normal"; the other thirty-eight were "backward" or "defective" to varying degrees.[22]

Among the "native" Americans of Sterling Mines were many who avoided the mines, working instead at woodchopping, making spoons, bowls, and baskets, gathering bark for local tanneries, and charcoal making. These had been the traditional cash-earning activities of at least two previous generations of Ramapo mountaineers. The stories told about such "bockies"—a Dutch word (*bockje*) for a small basket that came to signify anyone who lived an independent subsistence lifestyle in the Ramapos— were invariably the richest in idiosyncratic local lore. Stories about deceased relations distilled individuals down to wonderful caricatures, often told "warts and all" but with great love. Bill Van Tassell, for instance, who was nicknamed "Black Hawk," had been born in 1818 and spent his life around Greenwood, Arden, and Sterling Mines. Tall and lithe, with straight black hair, sharp dark eyes, high cheekbones, and light brown skin, Bill was, "according to all descriptions" Smith heard, active, energetic, and "naturally intelligent." Though he could read and write, Bill insisted on keeping his children from learning to do so because he was convinced that such knowledge "would make devils out of them." People remembered his droll humor and described him as an expert ax man and a good hunter. Bill died in 1883 of tuberculosis and was buried in Harriman, in the James Wilkes Burying Ground. People at Sterling Mines remembered Bill's grandchildren when young as having lived very much like Indians, going about in summer with no clothes on: "they were so shy and suspicious that they would disappear as if by magic when a stranger appeared, and keep perfectly quiet until they were gone." Someone described them as like "a nest of small partridges," and another said they were "as shy as rabbits."[23]

The Ramapos in the vicinity of Arden House were home to a sizable population of mountain folk whose hamlets were much more remote than the village at Sterling Mines. When Edward Harriman acquired the Parrott estate, nearly every hollow and ridge harbored a bockie squatter or two. Most of them were single men who had drifted away from settlements like the one at Beaver Pond, a swampy area of ridgetop whose springs made up the headwaters of the North Branch of Minisceongo Creek, which passed right through the center of the lushly landscaped grounds of Letchworth Village. Shortly after Florence Smith began her fieldwork on the western flank of the Ramapos, Davenport sent Fieldworker 48, Ethel Thayer, to Beaver Pond to take up another "special assignment" from Mrs. Harriman. After a year of fieldwork, she produced a ten-foot-long pedigree chart, showing all the "bad blood" in a particular family from the area. All eugenic family narratives begin with a "progenitor," some individual cast as the primordial source of the tainted protoplasm that ran down through the generations. The progenitor identified by Thayer for this Beaver Pond family was one Jacob Rose Jr., who was "reported to have been a shiftless, worthless individual, as indeed he must have been to choose for a home a place having nothing whatever to attract a man of any ambition." Thayer proceeded to paint a picture of Beaver Pond as a place where all the residents were cut from the same cloth as the "shiftless" progenitor:

> All the families being related, practically no outside influence is brought to bear, and except in rare instances, the "mountaineers" are left to follow their "natural bent" which is a crooked one. Several detrimental facts concerning them are known in a general way, and long residents of the county are not inclined to make any exceptions in their accusations of the community. For instance, they are known to steal timber in great quantities from the adjoining mountain sides, and at one time certain individuals were brought to trial for it. There are known certainly to have been several stills in the vicinity.[24]

Like the Sterling Mines study, the Beaver Pond report offered a curious mix of present depravity and past glory, confirmation of the progressive degeneration from the hardy, sober stock of the eighteenth century to the shiftless, alcoholic, and frequently feebleminded folk of the twentieth. Jacob Rose's father had fought with the Second New York Regiment in the American Revolution, and in 1785 he and his brother, a fellow patriot, had been awarded twelve hundred acres in the Ramapo region. In 1809 Jacob had left the entire homestead to his wife and seven sons, giving his sloop *Sallie* to his eldest son Jacob. Jacob Jr. lacked his father's ambition and "left much to be desired in the matter of morals," according to Thayer's informants. But for the most part, all of Jacob Jr.'s descendants, though successively degenerating from the original stock, lived in towns, where they were "watched" by authorities, who kept their tendencies somewhat in check. Jacob's brother John, on the other hand, lived up in the mountains, and clearly his kin—who made up a large part of the Beaver Pond community—were free from any civil restraints.[25]

Wild Nature, Wild Histories

"Wild Men Within Commuting Distance" proclaimed a front-page headline of the *New York Tribune* in June 1921: "Thirty-five miles from New York City, with its man-made skyline, seats of learning and citizens of culture, towers a range of mountains which shelters an assortment of humans . . . wilder than any people [in] the Tennessee Mountains." The article noted sarcastically that the mountaineers had "entered into the 'back to Nature' idea with the fullest enthusiasm." There was something simultaneously fascinating and repulsive about the wildness of the Ramapo's "native" people that could not be ignored by journalists or the eugenics fieldworkers. Arriving in their Model Ts in full metropolitan dress and outlook, they were unaccustomed to the rural ways of the mountain folk. By the time Jane Griffiths reached Houvenkopf, metropolitan distortions of mountain lifeways were decades-old clichés. In 1877 a New York City journalist published a sketch of what he referred to as "a community of outcasts." The article began with a romantic description of the Ramapo River valley, a "paradise" just ninety minutes by rail from the city, so "peaceful and ennobling" that the author wondered whether there could be any region that could inspire "more purity and virtue." But suddenly his tone changed: in this region, he declared, "there dwells a race of people of such brutal manners, such savage natures, and such foul corruption, that the inhabitants of the valley look upon them as outlaws, and apply to the region they inhabit an epithet which is equivalent to 'hell.'"[26]

The picture the journalist drew was representative of how, just a decade after the Civil War, outsiders were coming to perceive the people of the Ramapo Mountains. "The actual spectacle of these creatures is terrifying. Their dress is made of any thing which has breadth and flexibility—cloth, bark strips, fur, or leather. Their manner is rough, their eyes furtive, their faces stolid. Their bearing is that of children who have continually been overridden and subdued. They have no elasticity of step, voice, or expression." He ridiculed their manner of speech, their physique, and especially their work habits:

> Here it is that one may find a perfect example of that shiftlessness called living from hand to mouth. Give any of these wretches the certainty of a meal, and he will fall into a state of sloth equaled only by a Digger Indian. . . . They lay up nothing. . . . Their clothing costs them nothing but a present of a few trout to some of the world's people in the valley; a few chaldrons of charcoal, or a bundle of brooms, purchases the tools they require, and their woodcraft brings them food. Their desire is simply to live. That they must live for something never occurs to them. The machine named perhaps Conklin or De Groot, has been set going by Nature, and following the life-preserving instinct, also fully possessed by the pig, they supply it with fuel, and further are irresponsible.[27]

Soon newspaper accounts were referring to the people of the Ramapo Mountains as "Jackson-Whites," a derogatory name that spread as quickly as the fanciful and frequently hateful tales that went along with it. Applied first and most often to the mixed-race folks of the Ramapos south of the Ramapo Clove, but also often used for the mostly white mountaineers north of the Clove, the term had two folk explanations. According to one version, it was a contraction of "jacks"—a common name used by white northerners to refer to freed slaves—and "whites"—the white mountaineers who lived in the region and intermarried with the freed slaves. Another increasingly more popular version was that during the American Revolution a man named Jackson had contracted with the British to supply West Indian prostitutes to their fleet and army occupying New York City in 1776. After the British evacuation of the city in 1783, the women scattered into the hills. One variant explained the Dutch surnames of the people—DeGroat, Van Dunk, DeFreese—by claiming that the women married Hessian mercenaries who had deserted the British army to settle in the mountains.

Elizabeth Kite, who in 1917 finished editing the original manuscript drafted by Jane Griffiths (who left Vineland for the Waverly School for the Feeble-Minded in Massachusetts), favored the first explanation. Following the narrative style of Griffiths's earlier work for Henry Goddard on the "Kallikaks" of the New Jersey Pine Barrens, Kite portrayed the people of Hillburn and the Houvenkopf as more animal than human:

> Protected by the inaccessibility of their mountain fastnesses, these people are free to live as they please. Without the common impulse of morality or decency and with little to fear from outside interference, they are existing to propagate their kind. Unless they get into some serious mischief the law seldom bothers with them and so they live, apparently asking nothing from the outside world except that it leave them alone. Their huts are of gruesome squalor and filth though often situated high up among the clouds amid the unsurpassed beauty of the Ramapo Mountains. . . .
>
> In spite of the degradation of the people the picturesque beauty of the Houvenkopf remains.

Along with this contrast of human squalor amidst such natural splendor, Kite stressed a more ambiguous aspect of the animal nature of the Jackson-Whites. Throughout Griffiths's biographical accounts and Kite's editorial commentary, the people of the Houvenkopf are characterized as having a "care-free nature" and a "desire for physical freedom," and also as being "born lovers of nature." Though constantly caricatured as "childish," and thus seemingly *dependent*, the mountain people, the eugenics fieldworkers had to admit, maintained a fierce *independence*. Kite exclaimed about "Old Fanny": "Wild she was born and wild she will remain until her dying day and no man can change her."[28]

Kite and Griffiths assumed that the natural sovereignty displayed by the Jackson-Whites signaled their Indian ancestry. Depending on the need for a particular narrative turn, those Indian traits could appear threatening. One of Lucy DeGroat's uncles, Ransom DeGroat, was described by Griffiths as an "able-bodied man of Indian type, with receding forehead and chin, high cheek bones and the general appearance of a lawless, desperate character." The fieldworkers, like their mentor Davenport, practiced the most fluid of physiognomical interpretation, shaped more by fear and misunderstanding than by empirical knowledge. And yet their language gave them all the authority of science. Elizabeth Kite construed the entire Houvenkopf community as a "natural experiment": "We have here a complete experiment, a group of abnormal individuals who would commonly be described as intensely immoral and degenerate. A most up-to-date means of regenerating them has been tried . . . [the] result: failure. Shall we try the same experiment in other places, if the essential conditions are the same? What hope that the results be better? . . . Before we attempt to accomplish any great results, it is desirable to understand the material with which we are working. And this is just as true when the material is human beings as when it is animal, vegetable, or mineral."[29]

The Burden of Biography

Both Charles Davenport and Mary Harriman were deeply interested in biography, Mrs. Harriman as a reader, Davenport as a writer. Both believed it to be an uncanny indicator of hereditary fitness, and both accepted fieldworkers' reports—whether in the form of pedigree charts, index cards, or the brief biographical sketches of individuals in the Sterling Mines or Beaver Pond studies—as capturing the essential measure of a man or woman's life. Only rarely did the lives weigh out as worthy, for the fieldworkers' task was to uncover all that marked the rural dweller as delinquent, defective, and degenerate—the "three D's," as Davenport liked to say.[30]

In the effort to understand the burden of biography, ERO carried out a program of what was commonly called "negative eugenics." In the wake of the very first meeting of the operation's board of directors in 1910, board member Alexander Graham Bell had protested that the ERO research program was really one of "cacogenics," not eugenics. "[I]t is the fostering of desirable characteristics that will *advance* the race," Bell told Davenport, "whereas the cutting off of undesirable characteristics simply prevents deterioration." Bell sought a eugenics in the spirit of Greek idealism, not Spenglerian pessimism. This same desire motivated Percy MacKaye to write his play *To-Morrow* in the fall of 1910. MacKaye had been keeping a scrapbook devoted to developments in genetics and eugenics for at least four years, and he was especially fascinated by the work of "plant wizard" Luther Burbank in California, who argued that the wonders that he had produced in plants through careful selection could be replicated in humans. Here was a "positive eugenics" worthy of dramatization, unlike the negative eugenics that was the dramatic focus of French playwright Eugène Brieux. Although negative eugenics might hold more dramatic interest, given its inherent tragic conflicts, MacKaye held high hopes for his positive drama. "Of all the demonstrable visions," MacKaye wrote in his preface to the play, "the truths of biology give perhaps the securest pledge of beauty and happiness for the race—a pledge more fair and true than the earlier prophecies of a poetry divorced from science; for the social, political and religious aspects of our life are radically conditioned by the biological."[31]

Mendelism, MacKaye believed, had begun to demystify the workings of fate, the prime mover of all human drama. The mathematical nature of the "law of Mendel," so well known to Burbank in his horticultural work, "appears to radically modify the human meanings of fate, and permanently to condition predestination by the growth of reason." MacKaye predicted that Mendel's discovery would one day be ranked with those of Copernicus and Newton, and though Mendelism had as yet hardly begun to influence art, it would inevitably do so. MacKaye's play was meant as a tentative first step toward that future art. The study of eugenics, he declared, was "certain to illumine the age-worn adage: 'The proper study of mankind—is man.'"[32]

MacKaye had paid a personal visit to the man he clearly believed to be Mendel's brightest disciple: Luther Burbank. In 1910 America was still awestruck by Burbank's apparently magical ability to transform the colors, forms, tastes, and textures of so many vegetables, fruits, and ornamental plants. Burbank seemed to embody the Arcadian version of American Prometheanism, his horticultural discoveries in the fruitful land of California promising the restoration of a lost Eden. *Burbank* had already entered the American vernacular as a verb meaning to modify and improve not only horticulturally but in any domain, including human breeding. Along with Davenport, David Jordan, and Alexander Bell, Burbank was a member of the American Breeders' Association's Committee on Eugenics, but his membership was almost entirely honorific. His pronounced Lamarckian view of evolution combined with his sunny naiveté to give his eugenics a decidedly benign cast compared to the harsh hereditarianism of Davenport. In a May 1906 *Century* article, "The Training of the Human Plant," Burbank declared that "environment is the architect of heredity" and that as with plants, so with people: all manner of weak, unpromising, and even abnormal children could be improved by careful tending. Burbank's greatest enthusiasm was for extending the human seedling's period of exposure to the restorative powers of light, open air, and nourishing food. He recommended that children not be sent to school until after age ten. "Every child should have mud pies, grasshoppers, water-bugs, tadpoles, frogs, mud-turtles, elderberries, wild strawberries, acorns, chestnuts, trees to climb, brooks to wade in, water-lilies, woodchucks, bats, bees, butterflies . . . hay fields, pine cones . . . sand, snakes, huckleberries and hornets." This philosophy appealed deeply to MacKaye, who felt that his early years of poking about in Poog's pasture along Wilder Brook at his parents' summer retreat in southern Vermont had imbued him with some of the qualities for transcendental communication with nature. He felt that Burbank was possessed of such knowledge, as he wrote to his wife: "I have had a not-to-be-hoped-for, delightful long visit with Burbank—an hour and twenty minutes. He is my hero—scientist or no scientist—and I am not so sure that he does not know a heap about the deeper qualities of Nature that he has done so much to reveal."[33]

MacKaye began his play just a month after his trip to Santa Rosa. The main character, Peter Dale, was inspired by Burbank, to whom MacKaye dedicated the drama. *To-Morrow* (changed from *The Thoroughbred* before publication) opens in Dale's California garden, where Rosalie, a little blind girl, is singing "Starfish, Starfish, / Answer me the wish I wish!" Peter Dale, his daughter Mana (for *mañana*), and his foster child and assistant Mark—described as a rugged California Adonis—are also there. Peter recounts a myth about "Mother Morey" (Mother Nature) and her husband Phœbus, who produce the first living organism—"a wee mite of a rolypoly jelly-belly water-baby," Amœba—who then splits in two. The party in the garden is joined by Professor Raeburn, Mana and Mark's former biology teacher, who had high praise for Mana as a naturalist: "She was one in a lifetime. Do you know, before she came to my class, I had taught biology for years, and never knew it was poetry. She taught me that!" In admiring Mana's mix of reason and poetic spirit, Raeburn seems to give voice to the desire for a rational biological science touched by the sort of pure, unadulterated nature mysticism that MacKaye and so many others found in Burbank.[34]

When Raeburn learns that Rosalie is the adopted daughter of Senator Julian Henshawe, he declares his intention to speak to Henshawe about passing a new eugenics bill that would prevent the congenitally blind "from ever being created." Following on the heels of a pair of lumbermen who have been lobbying Henshawe to support a forestry bill that would provide for breeding experiments, Raeburn tells the senator that what goes for plants also goes for people: "So with men and women, Americans, our people—breed is the sinew and soul of us: Sound Americans, Senator, better Americans—we must learn to breed them, scientifically." *To-Morrow*'s characters are all comfortable speaking about the "laws of nature" that, seemingly, are fully known to Mendelians like Dale. MacKaye's faith in biological science led him to portray "Father Peter" as having raised Mana and Mark on bedtime readings of Darwin's *Descent of Man* and having provided them with early training on the microscope and thorough instruction in the keeping of aquaria and paleontological collections. Mark reminisces about how "the master" used to tell them when they were young that one day they would go to the Arizona desert, where they would breed thornless cacti (at the time, one of Burbank's most famous—and suspect—horticultural "inventions") and where each would find the perfect mate with whom to start a utopian colony. "[T]here we'd teach our children to live simply, and to go on selecting wisely other mates." His heart sinks when Mana tells him that Senator Henshawe has asked her to marry him.[35]

Peter Dale refuses Henshawe's request for his daughter's hand, saying that he knows from the village minister that Henshawe had two blind sisters, one of whom was also epileptic. He also knows that Rosalie is Henshawe's child by an illicit affair with a girl who died in childbirth. In the play's second act, Henshawe confesses his dysgenic past to Mana; by marrying Mana, he hopes to purify "the taint." Mana is appalled at the prospect of union with such a man, and in the play's most melodramatic scene, Mark appears out of the Monterey cypresses and throws Henshawe off a cliff. "I pulled a weed," he declares to Mana. In the third act, just as Mark is about to confess that he attacked Henshawe out of jealousy, Dale intervenes to reveal that this has been his eugenic plan all along, that the virile sapling he adopted and raised should be joined with his own pure offspring, Mana. When the minister advises Mana to marry the dying Henshawe to redeem her womanly honor, she lashes out at him. The minister has profaned matrimony by allowing dysgenic unions: "there was a priest named Mendel. Flowers were his flock. Reason was his holiness. The law of heredity was his prophet's staff."[36]

Many reviewers panned the play after it was published, savaging MacKaye's mix of melodrama and social prescription. The *New York Times* said that the play sported "the most despicable group of hypocrites that ever trod the stage," while the *Los Angeles Times* judged that *To-Morrow* "attains the well-earned pre-eminence of being the most vapid and absurd play which America has yet produced." Despite the poor reviews, it found a wide audience, and dramatic readings of the play were given in many notable theater clubs in New York, Boston, and Philadelphia. Winthrop

Ames, manager of The Little Theater in New York, loved the play but was reluctant to produce it because he feared that it was too much ahead of its time for public acceptance. In Minneapolis, *To-Morrow* was recommended by the city's educational extension department as suitable reading for high schools, but the board of education banned it. The play received its first and only production in 1913 at The Little Theater of Philadelphia, where it received similarly mixed reviews.

MacKaye sent copies of the play to a wide range of public figures whom he knew were supportive of the eugenics cause, among them William Dean Sumner (dean of the Cathedral of Saints Peter and Paul in Chicago, who had recently refused to perform marriage ceremonies unless couples had a certificate of health), eugenicist Irving Fisher (then chairman of the Hygiene Reference Board of the Life Extension Institute), Theodore Roosevelt ("Of course I heartily agree with its purpose," he assured MacKaye), John D. Rockefeller Jr., Luther Burbank ("[the play] meets with my approval in all respects"), and Charles Davenport.[37]

Davenport assured MacKaye that he had "given the public an insight into Eugenical principles in an artistic fashion," and he agreed to meet MacKaye in New York to discuss their ideas about the prospects for eugenics. The MacKayes were just the sort of American family in which Davenport had taken so much interest over the years—a prolific family of prodigious talent, whose achievements showed up clearly in each generation. This same dimension of the apparent physical inheritance of talent— in the MacKayes' case, the gift of the Muse—was clearly behind Percy's other eugenic literary creation, *Annals of an Era, Percy MacKaye and the MacKaye Family 1826–1932: A Record of Biography and History* (1932). Having devoted some thirty years to collecting material for a biography of his father, Steele, Percy became almost obsessed with its execution after signing a contract for its publication in 1923. By the time that work was finished, in 1926, MacKaye had accumulated a mountain of manuscript material that chronicled much of his entire family. He spent another four years organizing this material into the *Annals*, which in some sense is an elaborate pedigree chart of the MacKayes.[38]

For each member of the MacKaye family directly descended from Percy MacKaye's paternal grandfather, lengthy hagiographic entries describe the individual's "literary, dramatic, artistic, scientific and cultural contributions." MacKaye had collected virtually every laudatory comment ever written about his family, from personal correspondence as well as from published reviews. Advertisements suggest that the compilation was a model of "positive" eugenics. Biographer Gamaliel Bradford was quoted as saying that a "special interest attaches to cases of genius, in which a father transmits creative gifts to children and even grandchildren. Such a striking case was the Bach family in Germany, and another was the tribe of Kembles on the English stage. Assuredly the story of the MacKayes in America has something of the same family significance." Walter Lippman raved: "The best argument I ever saw for an aristocracy of birth is a family which preaches democracy. The MacKayes, all, have achieved distinction in art or science. They publish books as a matter of course. . . . That is the MacKaye inheritance—plays, novels, poems, acting, scientific research: 'fun, fishing, and philosophy' for all the world. It is in their blood."[39]

Facing the title page of the book, photographs of members of four generations "in direct descent"—Colonel James MacKaye (1805–1888), Steele MacKaye (1842–1894), Percy MacKaye (b. 1875), and Percy's son Robert Keith ("Robin") MacKaye (b. 1899)—form a diptych. Percy and his grandfather face right, their thick gray hair and mustaches showing clearly a family resemblance. Steele and his grandson Robin look slightly left, their poses nearly identical—at a desk, with books close at hand, the universal literary posture. Here the physical resemblance—thick hair (tousled and dark this time), dark mustache, strong jaw, and penetrating eyes—is uncanny, a testament to the power of biology in the destiny of a family. As he was working on *Annals*, Percy's old eugenics imaginings were rekindled, and he wrote to Davenport to suggest they meet to discuss "certain experimental ideas which I am inclined to think would interest you in your own studies and experiments." After publication of the Annals in 1932, Davenport and MacKaye met again, and Davenport responded to MacKaye's request for a meeting also with Henry Fairfield Osborn, on the heels of the Third International Congress of Eugenics at the American Museum of Natural History.[40]

The Natural History of Man

MacKaye visited the American Museum to see the exhibits installed for the congress and found them to be fantastic portrayals of the sort of positive eugenics that he had always envisioned. Visitors entering the Main Hall were greeted by a portrait gallery of Charles Darwin's family, including a painting of Darwin that had never been published, loaned for the exhibit by Darwin's son Leonard, who had come from England to give an address to the congress. Nearby, a pedigree chart showed the distribution of the salient traits of the Galton-Darwin-Wedgewood clan, and there was a bust of Francis Galton, Darwin's cousin, who had coined the term *eugenics*. Another wall featured a pedigree chart for Thomas Edison's family, along with a graph of "Race Descent: American Statesmen." In the Main

Hall, MacKaye found more of these graphic tributes to the power of heredity, the west wall being devoted to similar treatments for Abraham Lincoln, George Washington, and Theodore Roosevelt. At each marble column within the hall, Harry Laughlin of ERO had set up mechanical demonstrations of genetic principles: a shot machine showed Mendelian segregations and ratios in successive generations; a sort of mechanical loom of rattan and pegs illustrated the interaction of heredity and environment; another machine used colored cylinders and glass tubes to portray the segregation of chromosomes. Laughlin also had set up a table with piles of dried peas to demonstrate random sampling in Mendelian ratios; on another table a pair of dice illustrated pedigree selection.

At the entrance to the Education Hall, next to impressive busts of Davenport and Osborn, a Kodascope stereomotorgraph displayed an endless peep-show illustrating a variety of eugenic subjects. In the second booth in the hall MacKaye found a large exhibit of Davenport's research on body build (mainly a collection of photographs of naked men from Letchworth Village posed next to anthropometric yardsticks). Nearby, the FBI had a large exhibit on fingerprinting, and a number of German scientists displayed their work on twins and various anthropometric topics. A motion picture in the third booth illustrated the research at Letchworth Village, including a section on the various types of feebleminded inmates there. MacKaye found considerable space devoted to negative eugenics. One of the most prominent displays was the ERO exhibit on the historical development of both the medical techniques of and the legal initiatives for sterilization, illustrated by large maps and the drawings of Dr. Robert Latou Dickinson, who was attending the congress in his capacity as secretary of the National Committee on Maternal Health.

In the south corridor of the third floor of the museum, William King Gregory's new Hall of the Natural History of Man had opened to coincide with the Eugenics Congress. Although the exhibit began with a portrait of man as machine—the text spoke of man as "a living engine which derives its working capital from the sun" and described the heart as "the main pump," the lungs as "living bellows"—its overall message was of man as *animal*. The first wall chart paid homage to Darwin for having transformed the study of human anatomy into part of the story of vertebrate evolution. In exhibits such as "Organ Systems of Dogfish Shark and Man," "Elements of the Locomotor Apparatus," "Hands and Feet of Primates," "Maintenance of the Upright Posture," "Comparative Embryology from Fish to Man," "Man Among the Primates," and "Rise of the Human Brain," skeletal remains, reconstructions, and graphics were used to demonstrate conclusively that man is a risen quadruped. A large wall painting of "Man Among the Primates" showed Gregory's view of human evolution: men occupy the upper branch of a tree whose lower limbs bear lemuroids, tarsioids, Old and New World monkeys, the anthropoid apes, and, just below contemporary men, Piltdown Man, Peking Man, and Java Man. Way out on a lone limb above them stood a bent-over Neanderthal clutching a stone club, and just above him a wildly painted Australian aborigine was poised to throw a boomerang. Almost level with him, a Cro-Magnon sketched a mastodon on a cave wall. At the apex of the tree were four figures, the "African," "Red," "Yellow," and "White" races. The figure of the white race, in the classic pose of a Greek statue, was carefully placed at the farthest remove from his anthropoid ancestors.[41]

Gregory's interpretation of human evolution differed radically from Osborn's. As portrayed in the Hall of the Age of Man, Osborn held to an older notion of a separate lineage for *Homo*, and his hall, which had undergone major renovations just before its reopening for the Second International Eugenics Congress in 1921, spoke the language of hard-line eugenics. Its exhibits, most powerfully in Charles Knight's murals of Paleolithic men, conveyed Osborn's conviction that the natural men of old had been racially pure, unlike the unnatural practices of contemporary metropolitan man, whose mixing was on the verge of causing "race suicide." In his address at the opening of the 1932 congress, Osborn made a wild rhetorical gambit, quoting at length from Aldous Huxley's shocking new novel, *Brave New World*, to paint a grim futuristic picture of "chemo-mechanically" controlled conception. Invoking his personal memory of the young Huxley's illustrious grandfather Thomas H. Huxley, Osborn declared that Darwin's bulldog would join him in shuddering at the prospect of an artificial future. Their common Naturalistic philosophy proclaimed that "whatever is natural in the wondrous and beautiful order of nature can not be fraught with danger." Birth control, maintained Osborn, was unnatural, while "birth selection"—the ultimate aim of all eugenic efforts—was "natural" and hence to be fostered by all means possible.[42]

Davenport presented this same maxim to the congress delegates, that while the mixture of northern European peoples produced especially virile individuals like Theodore Roosevelt, unrestricted racial mixing was proving disastrous, that the only hope for racial progress was to base social policy on the "laws of biology." As he had been a quarter century before, when he began to combine natural history with eugenics at Cold Spring Harbor, Davenport was firmly convinced that human beings fall under the domain of natural law as known to contemporary science. He told Osborn:

If the congress was successful it was due to the grand setting and prestige that the Museum gave. One can hardly estimate the advantage of the surroundings for the eugenics congress since they put it at once on the plane of natural history, rather than of sociology or economics. . . . It serves still further to strengthen the correlation of eugenics as a branch of the natural history of man. . . . When I look back over the 11 years since the last congress I realize that great steps have been taken in placing eugenics in its rightful place in relation to the natural history of man

Davenport, Osborn, MacKaye, Dickinson—all these metropolitans demonstrated their faith in the redemptive powers of the natural as fully in the corridors of Mammon's most artificial edifices as they did out on the trails through the Ramapo forest.[43]

Landscapes of Living Flesh

The fantastic visual artistry on display at the 1932 eugenics congress—representing the "facts" of race suicide and rural degeneracy, the power of science in detecting Mendel's laws, and the titanic struggle between cacogenesis and aristogenesis—though impressive, was a wholly theoretical demonstration. Both Davenport and Mary Harriman had *living* canvases upon which to paint their eugenic aesthetic. Mrs. Harriman, in her patronage of eugenics fieldwork in the Ramapos, had carried on the ambitious landscape alteration project her husband had begun when he first swept up the Parrott lands in 1885. With the help of eugenics and Arcadian idealists, she could now motor from Arden House to Bear Mountain and see hardly a single tarpaper shack marring the green scene. Though he lacked her resources for landscape alteration, Davenport had his own landscape "laboratory" where he could put into practice the abstractions of eugenics.

In March 1913, just as Florence Smith was beginning her Ramapo work, Davenport attended a meeting of a dozen or so of his Nassau County neighbors to organize the Nassau County Association. Its committees—Care of Dependent Children and Outdoor Relief, Health and Eugenics, Good Roads and Public Utilities, and County Research—suggest the scope of its reform efforts. Handling the pressing problems of both mosquito eradication and the rural feebleminded, Davenport's Health and Eugenics (later Sanitation and Eugenics) Committee was the most ambitious. Besides Davenport himself, the association's most active member was its president, Mary Harriman Rumsey. Before "Eugenia" and her family moved to Nassau

County, she had been one of the many recent wealthy immigrants to Westchester County, and through her activism Davenport had sought funding from John D. Rockefeller Jr. for a eugenics survey there in 1911–1912. In her new home, Mary Rumsey refocused her enthusiasm toward a Nassau County survey. Her donation of $1,000 to the committee became the seed money necessary to attract other Nassau County donors. With the addition of Rockefeller support, funneled through the National Committee on Mental Hygiene, the "Nassau County Survey of Mental Defectives" began in 1913 with Davenport as chairman.

In his proposal to the Rockefeller Foundation, Davenport listed a number of geographic reasons that made Nassau County an ideal "natural laboratory" for a county-wide eugenics survey. It was of a convenient size and population (10,000) and contained a considerable farming region but also suburban towns with populations over 5,000 and both native- and foreign-born residents. The county's proximity to New York City made it "possible to utilize in the survey interests centered in the City," and the nearness of one of the larger institutions for the insane (Kings Park Hospital) was also convenient. Not long after the survey's fieldworker began to send in her reports, Davenport moved to take action on them. He wrote to the board of overseers for New York's new sterilization law, recommending five individuals from Nassau County for sterilization. He also wrote to the superintendent at the newly opened Letchworth Village to ask that a local teen, Ray Brower, be committed there. Frustrated that there was not enough room for Brower, Davenport took steps to organize the New York State Committee to Investigate Provision for the Mentally Deficient (whose initial meetings were held at Arden House). In 1914 the committee began to lobby the legislature for a series of eugenic measures, including increased appropriations for institutions for the feebleminded. The fact that Letchworth Village had to turn down Ray Brower was the first step in transforming the facility from a state-of-the-art, one hundred-bed institution into a three thousand-bed community in 1933. By 1937, with 3,655 children and adults in residence, Letchworth was again exceeding its capacity and was well on its way to becoming a social service nightmare.[44]

When Letchworth Village opened in 1911, sixty-three boys and girls arrived to take up residence—neatly segregated into two "colonies" by Minisceongo Creek—on what looked like a model farm. Its lovely stone buildings and gracious agrarian landscape had been laid out by Frederick Law Olmstead Jr., and the board of managers was especially proud of how "natural" the site appeared. The decentralized design mimicked a rural village rather than the tenements of lower Manhattan. Inmates worked in the fields, mingled with farm animals, and received the hygienic benefit of the sylvan setting, adjacent to the regenerating forest of Harriman Park. Margaret Bourke White's publicity photographs of Letchworth Village made it appear to be a serene, Edenic place, and the inmates, dressed in neat white outfits, seemed hygienically angelic. When Mary Harriman joined the board of managers in 1913, Charles Davenport and Henry Goddard had already been appointed as medical advisors to Letchworth. The board was well aware of the need for a research extension to the facility: "when we realize that four to six children of the same family are here, and those families extend back into the past beyond the reach of obtainable histories, the importance of scientific study becomes clear."[45]

The original purpose of Letchworth Village had been "to limit the propagation of genetically inferior stock by segregation," the tried-and-true method of eliminating the feebleminded blight upon the landscape. At the time Letchworth opened, however, there was great optimism that segregation would soon be joined by a more forward-looking method: sterilization. America's two most ardent proponents of sterilization—Harry Laughlin and Charles Davenport—relied on the medical advice of the man most knowledgeable about the surgical procedure of sterilization, Dr. Robert Latou Dickinson. Dickinson had been studying the details of human sexual anatomy for three decades. Early in his obstetric and gynecological practice, he had installed next to the examining table a square white pillar that looked like a pedestal for a flower pot but was actually a hiding place for a camera for photographing patients. With the aid of these photographs, Dickinson could detail each fascia of flesh in his drawings of the many techniques of female sexual sterilization by salpingectomy: ligation and section ("Pomeroy"); the Pfannenstiel abdominal incision; crushing and section ("Madlener"); stump burial; cornual resection; and the inguinal and vaginal routes. Dickinson's drawings rendered the female anatomical landscape as artfully as his Ramapo panoramas and served a similar purpose of highlighting only those essential features that demanded attention. RLD entered these landcapes of the flesh as if he were walking them; indeed, he called his massive two-volume compilation of human sexual anatomy *A Topographical Hand Atlas*.[46]

Dickinson's imagination was remarkably three-dimensional, and he employed it to wonderful ends in medicine. He made his own models of anatomical parts for instructing young surgeons and fabricated rubber dolls to teach delivery procedures. At the 1940 World's Fair in New York, Dickinson exhibited twenty-four life-size models illustrating conception, fetal growth, and birth in what may have been the most successful single effort at sex education in American history. Dickinson carried these sculptures to the fairgrounds at Flushing Meadow on the subway; he would sit in the corner and slowly unwrap them, a pixie gleam in his eye. A few passengers would start asking questions, and eventually he would lecture to the whole car on human reproduction. To produce the World's Fair models, which afterwards were donated to the American Museum of Natural History, Dickinson used measurements gleaned from Davenport's longitudinal studies of developing children at Letchworth Village.[47]

In 1950, after nearly half a century of activism for eugenic sterilization, Dickinson teamed up with fellow physician and sterilization advocate Clarence Gamble to provide a primer for the lay public on techniques for permanently controlling conception. The doctors had to admit, "To rescue humanity from harmful fertility [is] no simple problem." (The capital T was one of RLD's trademark letter-pictures; the curved arm of the T's upright cradles a naked infant leaning on his clenched fist, studying an open book). Whereas eugenicists had been working for only thirty years to foster "breeding for quality," "Dame Nature" had a million years' head start, "selecting for survival the most prolific, the toughest and smartest—and she had a planet for laboratory and all races for experiment." The doctors gave a list of those conditions that indicated the advisability of sexual sterilization: "undesirable heredity," including mental deficiency, mental diseases, epilepsy, and inheritable diseases; "indications pertaining to upbringing of potential children," primarily feeblemindedness in the mother herself; "conditions affecting the community," suggesting vaguely that if parents had produced "all the children they [could] rear with health, happiness, and usefulness," it was for the community's benefit as well as their own that they be prevented from becoming parents again.

Along with these particular indications, the doctors found sterilization fairly advisable "in general," citing in particular a German source that concluded that one of every two hundred persons should be sterilized. The study had been published in 1936, three years after Hitler's Hereditary Health Law had gone into effect, and in postwar New York the doctors were not unaware of the extremes to which the National Socialist regime had gone in its landscape alteration efforts. In an appendix enumerating the number of sterilizations carried out state-by-state in the United States, Dickinson and Gamble also surveyed the German experiment. Their description stressed the safeguards of the German law: "elaborate case histories" were required before a recommendation for sterilization could be submitted to one of the 203 hereditary courts; these courts were composed of a district judge, a public health official, and a physician specialist; expert witnesses were called; there were twenty-six courts of appeal. According to the doctors, of the 250,000 cases recommended, only 87,000 operations were performed in the first fifteen months, nearly half of them for feeblemindedness. They cited the finding of their friend Walter Kopp, who had found in Germany the "fullest appreciation of the thorough-going American initiative." Regarding "the very secret executions by gassing late in the war for some of the worst mental defects such as marked idiocy," the doctors protested that these could "hardly be called sterilization."[48]

"A Simple Gospel"

When he was out hiking the Ramapos, Robert Latou Dickinson would often surprise his walking companions with full-throated exclamations of joy: "Glory to God—what a sunset!" "Glory to God—see that tree—what a beauty!" A consummate sensualist, Dickinson knew well the physical ache that could be inspired by a beautifully lit and framed landscape, its harmonic dimensions entering into his very bones. His invocation of "God" was not disingenuous; he was as devout to his God as to his Earth. In his pocket he carried a little prayer card with a verse from Corinthians: "Wherever I go, thank God, he makes my life a constant pageant of triumph in Christ, diffusing the perfume of his knowledge everywhere by me."[49]

When Dickinson first began teaching medicine in the 1880s, his students asked him if he believed in the Virgin Birth. In response, he challenged them to join him in putting together a version of the synoptic Gospels (finding it hard to come to terms with John's text), *omitting every miracle*. By the end of the school year, they had assembled a bulging scrapbook, and Dickinson took it around to a few New York publishers, including his old friend Frank Doubleday, offering it as a text that "skeptical scientists might welcome in time." Doubleday and two other publishers agreed it should be published but declined to do so themselves, certain that sales of their other religious titles would suffer severely. In the early 1940s, in his eighties, having finished revisions for the *Walk Book* and made progress on his "Balk Book"—*The Doctor as Marriage Counselor*—Dickinson turned his attention once more to this old and important project. He wrote to Edith Hamilton, whose "scientific" take on the prophets of Israel he had recently read, telling her that he believed such a gospel would be readily accepted now for publication and that she was just the right person to author it.[50]

Dickinson sent along his draft manuscript from 1924—"A Simple Gospel: The Life of Jesus of Nazarene in the words of the Synoptic Gospels, the Miracles Being Omitted"—and publication proposal to Hamilton. "A Simple Gospel" looked back to Thomas Jefferson's writings about Jesus as an antecedent of the progressive view of a de-supernaturalized Christ. Jefferson's beginning needed revision:

To increasing numbers of people the reading of the life of Christ is hampered by the need of extracting the incomparable example and inspiration from that very large proportion of the story which elaborates and emphasizes physical marvels. Those to whom these constitute a stumbling block are, moreover, handicapped in giving the book to their children because the explanation of many of its most dramatic episodes brings into question the authenticity of the whole. They are commonly willing to waive questions of historicity and credibility. What they seek is a certain selection, with the emphasis not on the eliminations, but on the parts set forth.

Dickinson proposed to arrange the text so that the climax of Christ's story would come not at the tomb but at the Sermon on the Mount, emphasizing the secular inspiration over the supernatural mystery of Golgotha. The book should be of a size "such as to fit the pocket, the type large enough to read in moving train or trolley, the style to carry distinction." RLD wanted the book illustrated with modern paintings because "the Old Masters had too long mislead with their depictions of the miracles." He wanted modern typography too, to give the book a conversational character. "A Simple Gospel" would be in the spirit of the *New York Walk Book*, eminently utilitarian but elegant. As an example of how the book would bring the New Testament up to date, he worked over a bit of the Gospel of Mark. Though to Mark "wonderful cures of mental and physical ailments proved everything," to Dickinson and his imagined readers "they were never the ground-work for our belief in the Master, for our loyalty to him, for our deepest heart's desire to learn his secret and follow his method—to cleanse the inside of the cup—to find our life, losing it—to learn of Him, the mild and lowly of heart, that we may find rest in our souls."[51]

Dickinson's Christ was not the Savior peddled by Bruce Barton in *The Man Nobody Knows* (1924), which characterized Jesus Christ as history's greatest ad man. Though it was full of well-meaning piety, RLD's simple gospel was part and parcel of the Naturalist project to strip the world of spirit. "Feed Me on Facts!" cried John B. Watson—and America with him. Still, there was an undeniable desire for magic in the midst of the rationalizing of the Ramapo landscape. Bill Carr and Ruby Jolliffe lamented the absence of an indigenous folklore in the Ramapos. Jolliffe, camps director at Harriman Park, felt there was "something lacking" in the camps; she wished for picturesque stories that her camp counselors could tell around the evening campfire.

The character builders wanted something suitably primeval, something aboriginal and endemic to impart to the campers, to match the primeval landscape. But by then the Conklins, Odells, Babcocks, Roses, and other white mountaineers had all been pushed to the margins of the park, the squatters removed by park police, and the landowning natives bought out or broken by the state's power of eminent domain, the power that Mary Harriman had insisted be available to enlarge the park's boundaries so that it might encompass that entire upland block of terrain that her husband had seen whole, an unbroken forest primeval. Most of the mountain hamlets that had harbored indigenous folklore were long gone, drowned beneath Welch's sylvan lakes.

In the 1920s, one of America's most ambivalent modernists, William Carlos Williams, was also in search of something archetypally indigenous to give meaning to America, both geographically and chronologically. The Paterson, New Jersey, physician turned to his own backyard—the Ramapos—through the person of his Jackson-White housekeeper. "To Elsie" caught the people of the Ramapo Mountains in his gaze, but through a eugenically warped lens that left him profoundly disappointed:

> The pure products of America
> go crazy—
> mountain folk from Kentucky
>
> or the ribbed north end of
> Jersey
> with its isolate lakes and
>
> valleys, its deaf-mutes, thieves
> old names
> and promiscuity. . . . [52]

What Williams and the character builders were seeking was soul, something that endless miles of aimless walking on mountain foot trails just could not generate. The Arcadian pioneers' hope of hopes was that by marking trails upon the land, they would themselves be marked by the land. This had been Benton MacKaye's quest: through a combination of walking and watching, both to preserve that which was primeval from the metropolitan and to make over the metropolitan in the image of the primeval. As he walked, the metropolitan would escape modernity, tread back to a time when an authentic soul seemed more possible for America. But by 1934 MacKaye's Appalachian epic drama, rather than captivating metropolitans, had been captured by them. Under the direction of Myron Avery, president of the Appalachian Trail Conference, the trail became a metropolitan plaything, an episodic site of adventuring to soothe the tired nerves of the city dweller, another apparatus of modernity's therapeutic culture.

Like Bill Carr's nature trail at Bear Mountain, the Appalachian Trail became more an agent of modernity than a creative response to it. When in *The New Exploration* MacKaye recalls meeting a man who, though living but fifty miles from Manhattan, had just made his first visit there, he remembers also one of the people he met in the Ramapos while scouting the route for the Appalachian Trail. The man was a mountaineer, a bockie, someone the modern world had left behind or, perhaps more accurately, someone who chose to take only so much of what modernity offered, so as not to jeopardize his independence and his relationship to his natal place.[53]

The people of Halifax and the Houvenkopf, of Sterling Mines and Beaver Pond and all the other Ramapo Mountain hamlets, both within Harriman Park and without, were in the first half of the twentieth century caught between nature and history. "In" nature in a more authentic fashion than the back-to-nature enthusiasts, they were seen to be in nature *in the wrong way*. Their log cabins, weedy front yards, work habits, kinship relations, marriage customs, educational traditions, and, especially, their physical appearance all marked them as alien. To the metropolitan mind, the indigenous people of the Ramapos just did not belong there. Certainly there was no place for them in the park, a neatly rationalized landscape where regeneration, not degeneration, was the leitmotif. The Ramapo natives were in nature the wrong way because they were in history the wrong way. They "belonged" to the past, the same way that abandoned iron mines, charcoal pits, redoubt ruins, and old logging roads did. These landscape features, inanimate and mute, added vital texture to the region's primeval atmosphere. The holdouts against modernity, animate and vocal, disrupted that texture and that atmosphere.

The mountaineers' metropolitan peers were just as tightly pinned between nature and history, but none of them seemed to realize that. Having succeeded spectacularly at shaping a landscape of biological and personal regeneration, erecting an empire of empirical knowledge of nature that was beginning to penetrate old sensory boundaries, fashioning a pedagogical system to instruct even the disinterested, and implementing a system of social engineering consistent with their vision of natural law, the Arcadian architects could feel great optimism for the future. Only at odd moments might their confidence falter, as they caught some unsettling suspicion that perhaps the triumph of naturalism as both epistemological and personal style was a chimera. Something demonically deterministic arose alongside the new Arcadia, subjecting nature and history—and with them, the possibility for meaningful human redemption—to its cold and calculating will. Despite liberation from an instrumental relationship with nature and from merely suffering history, the modern metropolitan seemed superfluous, a reader of billboards and user of soap, wholly cosmopolitan but by no means a Cosmos. Having set out for the Ramapos to restore their humanness, the Arcadians had instead substituted a picture of the human as a mere animal. The American Museum of Natural History proclaimed it in state-of-the-art exhibitry; the museum extension at Bear Mountain echoed it in behaviorist treatment of its nature-seeking public; the eugenicists implemented this diabolical fallacy's apotheosis in their campaign against the indigenous human communities of the Ramapos.

PART II

CHAPTER 5

Not an Earthly Service

*A*mong the dozens, perhaps hundreds, of Arcadian experiments carried out in the New York metropolitan region in the opening decades of the twentieth century, the convergence of personalities and events in that part of the Ramapo Mountain landscape transformed into Harriman Park was unique. No other place witnessed quite the concerted effort at restoration and integration or so distinctly expressed the new ethos of Naturalism held by its shapers. In the 1930s, at almost the exact moment when the metropolitan naturalists felt most assured of the success of their venture, just across the Great Border Fault a much smaller band of Manhattanites was directing its efforts at rescuing humanity from the very triumph of Naturalism celebrated by its Arcadian neighbors. Though sharing their Naturalist peers' commitment to the scientific reshaping of the individual and society, these men and women blazed a radically different trail into modernity. They called themselves "anthroposophists," a name that denoted their allegiance to a spiritual science that placed the human being at the center of knowledge, radiating out into the natural world, contrary to the Naturalist stance of defining the human being out of knowledge derived from nature.

Threefold

By Sunday afternoon, the field beside the oddly shaped green three-bay garage at Threefold Farm was filled with automobiles, most of them with New York plates. Many of the newly arriving nonmotoring guests had come via the Erie train from Jersey City or by bus from the Astor Hotel Bus Terminal at Forty-fifth Street, between Broadway and Eighth Avenue. Ralph Courtney and other residents of Threefold Farm periodically made the two-mile trip in his roadster to the Spring Valley station to bring them out to the farm. After signing in at the main house, where they purchased their lecture tickets (at 25¢ per lecture), overnight guests headed across the orchard, past the greenhouse and gardens, into the oak woods, where twenty canvas tents (at thirteen dollars per week, including meals) accommodated participants in the two-week Anthroposophical Summer School Conference of 1933, the first to be held in America.

The conference had opened the night before with a lecture by Dr. Christoph Linder on anthroposophical medical science. On Sunday morning Dr. Linder led a discussion of his lecture, following the established tradition of summer conferences at the Goetheanum, the administrative, cultural, and spiritual center of anthroposophy in Dornach, Switzerland. Even for those who had not been to the Goetheanum, it was understood that this practice was based on the anthroposophic principle that "sleeping on it" allowed newly heard concepts to imprint themselves on the invisible nexus of cosmic forces to which Dr. Linder's lecture had frequently alluded. The ninety-minute discussion was followed by a lecture by Dr. Maria Roschl, a teacher from the Waldorf School in Stuttgart, on "Ways of Inner Development." A vegetarian lunch was then served in the dining hall of the main house. All afternoons were free for reading, meditation, and tea under the trees, a tradition introduced by Threefold founder Ralph Courtney, who had picked up the habit during his student days at Oxford. Activities resumed at 4:30 P.M. with a painting or eurythmy lesson, and after dinner came the evening lecture. There was also plenty of time for a swim in the pond, which had been created by damming the Oost Val, the little brook that bisected the farm's thirty-two acres. A photograph of the pond, sporting a diving board and sandy beach, was featured on the front cover of the conference brochure, which advertised the farm as a "delightful vacation spot . . . lying in the foothills of the Ramapo Mountains." From the top of a nearby hill, one could look due north to the front range of the Ramapos.

The conference brochure's photos of apple trees in blossom, its notice that the farm eschewed the use of poisonous sprays and mineral fertilizers, and its invitation to all those interested in "a Spiritual Science which can flow as a revitalizing force into every domain of human life" marked Threefold Farm as an Arcadian enterprise. Incorporated as a village within the township of Ramapo, New York, in 1910, Spring Valley had been drawing refugees from New York City for three decades. The source of its principal attraction, its many restorative springs, lay in the Ramapo Mountain forest just across the Great Border Fault. By the turn of the century, metropolitan visitors to the springs who had once stayed in the area's resort hotels were buying up lots for summer homes set in the midst of a bucolic patchwork of pastures, orchards, and woodland. In 1926 Charlotte Parker, one of the original members of the Threefold Group of the Anthroposophical Society in America, had come to Spring Valley searching for a place where she and her fellow anthroposophists could escape the stifling city heat and begin to put into practice in a more convivial setting some of their ideas for regenerating modern metropolitan American culture. One of Ralph Courtney's priorities was that the site should be suitable for the eventual development of summer conferences to disseminate anthroposophical knowledge. Parker thought the modest farmhouse on the brow of a hill overlooking the unpaved Hungry Hollow Road had real possibilities for becoming the American equivalent of the Goetheanum.[1]

Charlotte Parker had first come to know Ralph Courtney in another Arcadian setting, an Adirondack summer camp, during the terribly hot summer of 1922. There Courtney had put up a sign outside his cabin: "Lectures by Rudolf Steiner read here every evening." She recalled that only one person usually attended the evening readings. In light of his own first reaction to Steiner's ideas, Courtney fully understood the lukewarm response. Though he had moved to England as a child, he had been born in Texas and retained a Texan sensibility about the world as an impressively physical place, with no need for lunatic occult ideas to help explain it. After graduating from Brasenose College, Oxford, his first job in London with a literary agent brought him into contact with publisher Max Gysi, who was looking to acquire the copyright to Steiner's *Way of Initiation* so that he could publish it in America. Upon reading Steiner's work, Courtney wondered how anyone could take it seriously; but after reading some early lectures by Steiner, he got hooked and began reading everything available in English. While in Paris to cover the Versailles Conference as chief European correspondent for the *New York Herald-Tribune*, Courtney mentioned Steiner to the head of the local Associated Press office, who thereupon pulled open his drawer to reveal a collection of Steiner's works. Knowing that Steiner was passing through Paris that day on his way to Dornach from London, the journalist invited Courtney to accompany him to hear Steiner lecture.[2]

Courtney was especially intrigued by Steiner's ideas about the threefold social order, upon which he lectured widely between 1919 and 1923. Pointing to the devastation caused by World War I, Steiner argued that social life should conform to an essential principle of human nature—its threefold organization of thinking, feeling, and willing. Steiner called for a future where universalism replaced nationalism; but rather than founding this universalism on collective principles, the threefold social order intended to recover the original meaning of *liberté, égalité, fraternité*. Liberty was to prevail in the domain of cultural and spiritual life, such that individual freedom of thought was ensured. Guaranteeing equality of rights would become

the sole task of the state, while fraternity would become the guiding principle of economic life, so that material needs of all humanity would be met
through the free exchange of goods. These three domains of social life were
to be kept totally independent, but always in balance. Anxious about the
political compromises at Versailles, Courtney was drawn to Steiner's threefold idea and conducted two interviews with Steiner in 1921. At their second meeting, as they said good-bye, Steiner helped Courtney put on his
overcoat. Courtney was overwhelmed by a feeling that he found impossible to describe but that seemed to recognize Steiner as the representative
of the very universalism for which his threefold idea called. Courtney
formed an inner resolve to devote himself to nurturing in America the idea
of the threefold social order.[3]

When Courtney moved to New York City in 1921, the General Anthroposophical Society could claim no more than about a hundred members in
the entire United States. The greatest concentration, however, could be
found on Manhattan Island in the blocks just south of Central Park, where
the first anthroposophical group in America was formed. At first glance,
the Saint Mark Group (the name had been chosen because Mark's concise,
analytical writing style was thought to be well suited to the American mind)
appeared to be an urban art colony. Meeting since 1910 in the Carnegie
Hall studio of Herbert Wilber Greene—president of the National Singing
Teachers' Association and associate editor of *Étude*—most of the members
were aspiring musicians, singers, and artists, many of them former or current students of Greene's. Courtney first attended the group's Tuesday
evening meetings at Carnegie Hall but soon was giving his own readings
of Steiner's works, emphasizing his vision of social renewal. In November
1923 Courtney founded the Threefold Group.

Courtney's first step in creating a new social order was to lease an
apartment building at the corner of Sixth Avenue and Fifty-sixth Street, a
block below Carnegie Hall, and rent its rooms to members and friends. Before long, floors in a second building were occupied, and Courtney talked
art student Charlotte Parker (who had never cooked before in her life) and
piano students Louise Bybee and Gladys Barnett into preparing an evening
communal meal for the tenants. Courtney also instituted afternoon teatime.
By January 1924, the dinner group outgrew its room and began renting
the building's basement space to open the Threefold Vegetarian Restaurant.
Given its proximity to Carnegie Hall, the Art Students' League, and Broadway theaters, the restaurant mainly attracted artists, musicians, and actors;
as business boomed, lunch was added. Patrons could choose from items
like the daily vegetable plate (40¢), vegetable casserole (20¢), and, for des-
sert, cranberry sundae (15¢). Because the predominantly female clientele

could not persuade their boyfriends and husbands to frequent a place with solely vegetarian fare, a daily meat dish was eventually offered. The Three-fold Restaurant—which a *New Yorker* food critic characterized as a "tearoomy cellar, which looks so ridiculously like a student lunching and dining place that it is difficult to believe it really is one"—regularly had two hundred customers at lunch and a hundred at dinner. Patrons uninitiated into the esoteric world of anthroposophy received a gentle introduction: the small grocery store in front of the restaurant sold products from Weleda, an anthroposophically oriented pharmaceutical company; distinctively ethereal anthroposophical artwork graced the restaurant's walls; and the wooden chairs and tables built by Threefold members Carl Schmidt and Fritz Westhoff were anthroposophically sculpted, their curved design intending to reflect the cosmic formative forces rather than contemporary furniture fashion.

Threefold members, especially given their self-consciousness about the source and quality of their food, were keen to extend their urban efforts at social renewal into a rural setting. The purchase of the Spring Valley farm in 1926 provided a landscape close enough to Manhattan to allow them to engage fully in an effort to renew both nature and culture. But the Arcadians assembled at Threefold Farm were far from going "back to Nature." Rather than seeking to be redeemed by Nature, they sought to become redeemers of Nature, aiming to reclaim for human beings their central role as the intermediaries between the sensible and supersensible worlds. While their contemporaries just a few miles away in Harriman Park were reshaping the physical landscape in hopes of drawing modern metropolitans into closer contact with the sensible, the Threefold anthroposophists directed their efforts at a wholly supersensible landscape. In 1924, when Rudolf Steiner had carried out the rededication of the General Anthroposophical Society, he had declared: "This anthroposophical movement is not an earthly service; this anthroposophical movement, in every detail of its totality, is a divine service, a service of the gods." Of the eight hundred anthroposophists present at that gathering, only a handful were at Three-fold Farm in 1933, but the others understood Steiner's declaration to have signified humanity's first attempt to ally itself consciously on the side of the Powers of Light in the titanic battle waged behind earthly events across the divide of the visible.

Making the Unseen Seen

The audience for the evening lecture that Sunday in 1933 was very large, as it was to be the first American lecture given by Ehrenfried Pfeiffer, who had pioneered the Biologic Dynamic agriculture practiced at Three-fold Farm. In 1927 Threefold members Gladys Barnett and Elise Stolting had visited Count Carl Keyserling's estate at Koberwitz, Silesia, where Rudolf Steiner had given his famous agricultural course in 1924. Upon their return, they started a Biologic Dynamic vegetable garden on the side lawn of the main house at Threefold. A year later the farm had one cow from Switzerland, and soon goats were added. Later during the conference, Pfeiffer was to give a pair of lectures on the practical applications of bio-dynamic methods to agriculture, but tonight his topic was a more funda-mental one—"Making Visible the Formative-Forces in Nature."

In the large circus tent that had been erected in the oak grove beyond the farm buildings, Pfeiffer began with an indictment of contemporary natu-ral science, which he characterized as an entirely analytical enterprise that turned nature into a corpse. Pfeiffer also spoke of modern science's inves-tigation and society's utilization of the subearthly forces of nature—elec-tricity, magnetism, and gravity—forces he knew well from his boyhood fascination with them and his year working as a toolmaker for the Bosch Manufacturing Company in Stuttgart. Enlisting at age eighteen in the Ger-man Army Corps of Engineers, Pfeiffer was sent to the war front to super-vise the construction of bridges and forts, as well as the destruction of these structures and a host of others. In 1919, back at Bosch, he attended a lec-ture on the threefold social order given by Rudolf Steiner to the Bosch em-ployees at their union hall. According to Steiner, the subearthly forces around which the modern world revolved, and which Pfeiffer had learned to harness and direct, were responsible for the social chaos enveloping Eu-rope. Steiner emphasized the need to discover new forces that were life-enhancing; until humanity reckoned with them, modern social structure would continue to mimic the disintegrating forces upon which modern civi-lization was based.

While Steiner spoke, the workers sat at tables drinking beer, some of them arguing. It was a hot summer day, and Pfeiffer noted that the long lecture had already left the speaker hoarse and perspiring. He asked a wait-ress to set a bottle of soda water on the speaker's platform, and Steiner immediately drank it. From that moment on, Pfeiffer devoted himself to serving Steiner's work. In 1933, eight years after Steiner's death, he was at the beginning of a relationship with the American anthroposophical com-munity that would echo Steiner's twenty-five-year relationship with Euro-pean seekers of a spiritual science. In that quarter century, Steiner had written forty books, given more than six thousand public lectures, and founded a diverse array of practical social and cultural initiatives. For the next twenty-seven summers, Pfeiffer would open the Threefold summer conference and, along with the biweekly Sunday lectures he gave after coming to live at the farm in 1942, pour forth a remarkable body of knowledge about nature and history in his own right.

Few if any students of Steiner were as qualified to speak about an anthroposophical understanding of nature as was Pfeiffer. As a twenty-one-year-old student at the University of Basel, Pfeiffer had followed Steiner's advice to major in chemistry, although he had earlier completed two semesters in physics and electrical engineering at the Technical College in Stuttgart. Each term, Steiner suggested which courses to select, adding mineralogy, botany, plant geography, ecology, economics, sociology, and psychology to Pfeiffer's already heavy load in chemistry. Having designed a curriculum that recapitulated to a great extent his own wide training, Steiner impressed upon his young protégé that he must master the modern sciences if he was to "disprove materialism with its own weapons." Special emphasis was placed on laboratory instruction and practical as opposed to theoretical training. Steiner further advised Pfeiffer that he must keep a double-entry notebook, one side listing the interpretations of orthodox science, the other those of spiritual science. At the end of each semester, Pfeiffer was to give Steiner a full report of what he had learned in each course. Finally, Steiner instructed Pfeiffer to cultivate a regular and intensive practice of meditation, by which he would begin to bridge the gap between the visible and invisible worlds of nature.[4]

During this intense period of personal discipleship, which lasted from 1919 until Steiner's death in 1925, Pfeiffer actively participated in the life of the Goetheanum. The focal point of the enormous, hand-carved wooden building was the stage, which was conceived of primarily as the site for the performance of Rudolf Steiner's mystery dramas. After he moved to Dornach in 1920, Pfeiffer directed the installation of the stage's lighting and ventilation systems. Pfeiffer's other principal activity was to begin natural scientific research at the Goetheanum. From his study of Steiner's work, Pfeiffer knew that central to understanding the interplay of the sensible and supersensible worlds was the concept of *Bildekräfte*, the "etheric formative-forces." These forces were posited by Steiner to be the mediator by which the spiritual-supersensible gives form to the physical-sensible. In keeping with the spirit of anthroposophy's emphasis upon knowledge of and through the human being, Steiner's principal indications about the earth's etheric forces focused on the *Bildekräfteleib*, the "body of formative forces," most often referred to by Steiner and his students as the "etheric" or "ether" body. Steiner explicitly distinguished the etheric body from both the hypothetical

ether of nineteenth-century physics and from the lineage of nineteenth—
and twentieth-century conceptions of a vital force.[5]

In his *Occult Science: An Outline* (1914), Steiner described how the
etheric body appeared to supersensible perception: "All the organs of the
physical body are maintained in their form and configuration by the currents and movements of the etheric body. Underlying the physical heart
there is an 'etheric heart,' underlying the physical brain an 'etheric brain,'
and so on. . . . And where in the physical body there are distinct and separated parts, in the etheric everything is in living flow and interpenetrating
movement." Plants and animals also possess an etheric body, but it is the
uppermost member of the plant's organization, merely giving form to the
physical, whereas in animals the etheric body is shaped by an additional
supersensible member—the astral body. The human etheric body alone is
shaped by the uniquely human supersensible member—the "I" or "ego."
In *Occult Science*, Steiner described the "involution" of each of these organizational principles from out of the cosmos, right up to the time of their
materialization in actual physical beings upon the earth. In direct contradiction to the fundamental precepts of modern science, Steiner's cosmology
held that matter had itself evolved and that the principle of uniformitari-
anism applied neither to time nor to space.[6]

The qualities of the human etheric body—which Steiner variously
characterized as "flowing," "humming," "singing," "radiating," and other
terms intended to communicate the *living* nature of the etheric—were the
manifestation of the thoughts of a particular class of spiritual beings, the
Exousai (Hebrew: *Elohim*), frequently referred to by anthroposophists as
"Spirits of Form." In turn, the etheric body was seen as the vehicle for human thought, by virtue of its interaction with the astral and ego bodies.
Western science's conception of the physical brain as the seat of consciousness was its grossest materialist error; instead, anthroposophy held that
thought takes place via the etheric body. In the anthroposophical conception of history, humans in the year 1413 C.E. entered the age of the "Consciousness Soul," which, over its 2,160–year duration, would witness the
gradual "loosening" of the human etheric body and, as a consequence, an
increase in supersensible experience by human beings. The era of materialist natural science, which began at about the same time, was believed to
be a result of the configuration of the etheric body during the preceding
epoch of the "Intellectual Soul" (747 B.C.E.–1413 C.E.), when the etheric
body became most closely bound to the physical body. Anthroposophists
of the 1930s believed that the cultural milieu in which they found themselves—where Watsonian behaviorism, Darwinian determinism, and hereditarian social policy were the order of the day—was the absolute height of

materialist thought. The Great Depression had only slightly subdued the unabashed cultural materialism of the Roaring Twenties; thinking remained stubbornly materialist, particularly as shown by the increasingly mechanistic and naturalistic trends in scientific thought.[7]

In 1933 only a handful of human beings over the entire earth possessed sufficiently fluid etheric bodies to achieve supersensible perception. Anthroposophists saw their world-historical mission as guiding humanity toward a fully conscious response to this incipient enlivening of thinking that would transpire as the etheric body freed itself from its two-thousand-year imprisonment in the physical. Although most of the anthroposophists gathered at Threefold Farm had a clear understanding of the role of the etheric body and the etheric formative forces, few as yet enjoyed the ability to perceive the etheric, so Ehrenfried Pfeiffer's lecture subject attracted a great deal of notice. Conscientious anthroposophists who had not achieved supersensible perception consoled themselves with the knowledge that even the active attempt to understand the reality of the spiritual world was a step on the path to gaining direct knowledge of it. But the possibility of somehow developing a technique to make the formative forces visible was tantalizing; to make the unseen seen gave hope to their own aspirations toward internalizing supersensible capacity. Pfeiffer told the gathering at Threefold Farm how in October 1920 he had asked Rudolf Steiner if there might be some way of using the constructive, synthetic forces as the foundation of a new altruistic technics that would have within itself the impulse of life rather than death. Steiner replied that the etheric forces needed first to be demonstrated and that Pfeiffer should work to develop a "reagent."

How to create a suitable reagent? The only suggestion Steiner gave Pfeiffer was that he and his Goetheanum colleague Guenther Wachsmuth should observe the process of crystallization that would take place when plant substances and blood were added to certain salts. Asking for more details, Pfeiffer was told that he would have to discover them for himself. Pfeiffer's first experiments at demonstrating the etheric formative forces were conducted in a box under his bed. From his knowledge of anthroposophical theories of the etheric body, he assumed that in "capturing" etheric processes, they would be connected in some way with the imagination, so he could neglect the third dimension and confine the crystallization procedure to a plane surface. Pfeiffer visualized a setup in which the crystallization took place in a glass petri dish. The crucial matter of the correct salt was similarly intuited by Pfeiffer's coworker Erika Sabarth, who immediately chose copper chloride and also gave the proper solution concentration. Working first with extracts from water lily and chamomile, they produced clear crystallizations—grayish blue patterns like frost on a windowpane—on their very first attempt. Pfeiffer told the audience that the odds against such serendipitous success were incalculable, that they had succeeded because they followed Steiner's advice to make the laboratory a place where the elemental beings of nature would feel comfortable.[8]

This meant establishing a suitable spiritual atmosphere through prayer and meditation, and a meditative state was also required to interpret the crystallization images, which to the untrained eye of the flesh appeared as little more than crystalline Rorschach blots. There was some visually detectable difference in the crystallization images: healthy plant extracts or blood from healthy subjects produced radially symmetrical crystallizations, while chaotic patterns were characteristic of ill plants or people. Pfeiffer used the simple crystal patterns to diagnose the nature and location of inflammations, infections, even cancer. The key to this unorthodox diagnostics was proper mental preparation; Pfeiffer found that the best results came from "a pure phenomenology combined with intensive meditation."[9]

Pfeiffer's inquiry into the etheric formative forces had begun with an eye toward a new and benevolent technics, and he told his audience how he had initially performed experiments in the application of this force. When he reported the results, Steiner interpreted them as indicating that the time was not yet right for humanity to make use of the etheric force. When Pfeiffer asked when that time would come, Steiner replied that it could only be when social conditions were such that no misuse could be made of etheric technology for selfish purposes, a situation that would come about only when the Threefold Commonwealth was instituted in at least a few regions on earth. Until that time, Steiner advised Pfeiffer, no experiments toward an etheric technology should be conducted. Pfeiffer confided to the conference audience that, despite the earnest efforts of anthroposophists— including the members of the Threefold group, whose diverse initiatives were founded to advance the principles of the Threefold Commonwealth— he doubted that he would see the advent of the necessary conditions in his own lifetime. He felt sure that he would go to his grave keeping secret the little knowledge he had gained of the application of the etheric forces.[10]

The crowd under the circus tent was unfazed by such an unorthodox approach to the science of life. Whether engaged in painting a landscape, practicing eurythmy, or planting a garden, the anthroposophists gathered at Threefold Farm were constantly mindful of the invisible dimensions of their actions. The gathering itself they conceived of as an event with spiritual consequences, bringing into being definite spiritual entities. Perhaps only a hundred people attended the conference over the two weeks, but the participants believed themselves joined by a host of others—the dead who looked upon their actions from the spiritual world and who could be called upon for assistance. Among the small group who had founded Threefold Farm and had spent six summers in Hungry Hollow, there was a firm sense that the spirits of the Hessian soldiers said to have died there one hard winter during the Revolutionary War were overseeing the small band of idealists, giving life to their anthroposophical aspirations. Indeed, the millions of soldiers and civilians killed during World War I were also thought to help prepare the way for the new etheric perception.

Another way of making the unseen seen was through the practice of eurythmy, an art form first developed by Rudolf Steiner in 1911. Smoothly and gently moving their arms in accompaniment to spoken texts, eurythmists strove to represent the spiritual world via a suite of very precisely executed gestures. Performed in loose-fitting colored veils almost exclusively by women, eurythmy appeared to the untutored onlooker to be a variation on the modern dance techniques popularized by Isadora Duncan —a number of the Threefold eurythmists had been Duncan enthusiasts. (Summer outdoor eurythmy practice gave Threefold's Spring Valley neighbors another caricature to add to their images of the community; motorists on the Hungry Hollow Road did a double take when they came upon the ghostly gatherings in Threefold's meadows.) Calling eurythmy "visible speech," Rudolf Steiner had identified the new art form as one that developed, as did all the arts, out of spiritual sources. Consistent with his conception of the evolution of consciousness through a sevenfold process, Steiner envisioned a distinct hierarchy of the arts that mirrored the members of the human being. Architecture manifested the laws of the first member, the physical body; sculpture, the etheric body; painting, the astral body; music, the ego. Poetry and drama sprang from the "spirit-self," the member yet coming into being amidst humanity; and eurythmy, whose full expression lay in the future, manifested the "life-spirit." As with each of the other anthroposophical initiatives—agriculture, the threefold social order, Waldorf education, medicine, natural science—eurythmy had been carried from Dornach to America by a single individual, Lucy Neuscheller. She began to teach eurythmy to Saint Mark members in Manhattan in 1923 before beginning a summer camp for eurythmy instruction at Connla's Ard in the Ramapo region at Monroe, New York.[11]

The gestures of eurythmy were employed also when members of Threefold Farm enacted Rudolf Steiner's mystery dramas. These exceedingly long (performances required an entire day) and difficult plays portrayed a group of individuals over successive lifetimes, with the action alternating between physical and spiritual beings and events. Collectively narrating the tale of how supersensible perception is to be regained by contemporary individuals who once possessed spiritual faculties in earlier incarnations, the mystery dramas were performed in the hope that they would help audiences to understand their own interpersonal struggles as they too moved toward recovering the ability to perceive the supersensible. Like eurythmy, the mystery dramas impressed outsiders as peculiar avant-garde forms, analogous to the attempts of Symbolist playwrights to create alternatives to realistic drama. For Steiner and the anthroposophists who enacted them, the invisible spiritual events and beings were as "real" as the physical ones, and of far greater significance. Lucifer and Ahriman, the two great spiritual beings who figure so importantly in anthroposophical thought, appeared in all of the dramas, along with lesser beings like sylphs and gnomes. As a technique of representing these supersensible beings, Steiner employed the gestures of eurythmy. Ahriman, the embodiment of intellect, moved in rigid linear fashion, while Lucifer, the embodiment of will, moved in flowing curves. Gnomes combined the two forms, and sylphs spiraled around in airy freedom. These movements were meant to be strictly representational.[12]

As fully convinced as anthroposophists were of the reality of the unseen realm, there was always at the Threefold summer conferences some uncertainty about just who was clairvoyant and who was not, and to what degree. As a member of Rudolf Steiner's inner circle, Pfeiffer was widely understood to possess clairvoyant abilities. Many in the audience had heard stories of Pfeiffer's magic jackknife: when consulting with farmers, Pfeiffer was reputed on occasion to draw from his pocket a knife, dig it into the soil, and then hold up the soil and pronounce in great detail the land use history of the site—which crops had been grown there and when—in a manner well beyond the ability of more conventional agronomists. There were also rumors—among both believers and unbelievers—about Pfeiffer's ability to see "nature spirits," the elemental beings of field and forest. In his Sunday talks Pfeiffer frequently made assertions that, seemingly, could have been derived only from clairvoyant experience.[13]

During Pfeiffer's debut lecture at the 1933 conference, a wave of silent confusion passed through the audience under the tent. Extremely dogmatic even as a young man (he was thirty-three at the time of the conference), he was overly confident of his command of English and spoke with a heavy German accent. At one point, he spoke about the "gawds ov de pascheur"; the audience heard this as "goats in the pasture," which made no sense in the context of his subject. Then suddenly a look of enlightenment came over many of the faces: Pfeiffer was speaking of "the Gods of the past." Even the sensible world could be profoundly mysterious.[14]

A Science of the Insides of Things

To a great degree, the atmosphere at the Threefold Farm summer gathering was of a time out of time, for the ideas circulating there were so far removed from those prevailing in contemporary society. Only occasionally did a lecturer point to peers whose work supported his or her own views. There were minor intersections of anthroposophical perspectives with more widely held ideas: biodynamic agriculture shared with a number of contemporary agricultural reform movements a trenchant critique of industrial agriculture; the Waldorf school movement often found itself in conversation with other progressive educational initiatives, like the Lincoln School of Columbia's Teacher's College; and Ralph Courtney circulated his ideas on the threefold social order to a wide network of American intellectuals and social activists. But these intersections tended to stay at the surface of the anthroposophical worldview. Behind all of the more easily acceptable ideas and institutions fostered by the American anthroposophists stood a formidable esoteric intellectual edifice that usually met with slack-jawed stupefaction from outsiders. That kind of incredulity informs a *New York Herald-Tribune* report from the 1933 conference. The glib correspondent, who attended the second Sunday of the conference, saw Threefold Farm as "the nearest thing to Brook Farm that America has seen since Bronson Alcott gave up at Concord." His piece began with a biographical sketch of Rudolf Steiner: "the self-educated son of a railway worker, [Steiner] was always an independent theosophist, but so great was his mastery of the mysterious forces of the universe that the German branch of the cult made him its head. He was deposed when Mrs. Besant brought Krishnamurti out of an Indian hat as the new savior. Then Dr. Steiner borrowed a part of the theory of the transmigration of souls, elaborated other theories of his own, and produced anthroposophy."

In a sense, it was remarkable that a metropolitan newspaper gave the summer conference coverage at all. (The local weekly *Rockland County Leader* took no notice; its front page during the initial week of the conference was devoted to one of Ray Torrey's press releases about happenings at Harriman Park.) It seems likely that Ralph Courtney, given his former association with the *Herald-Tribune*, arranged the reporter's visit. Courtney briefed the reporter on the concept of the Threefold Commonwealth, which he described as a spiritual reality perceived by Steiner's "more than human senses." Courtney outlined the history of the Threefold initiatives in Manhattan and also spoke of his recent effort to replace currency with scrip within the group's economy. (Courtney had recently persuaded a number of business owners in Spring Valley and neighboring towns to accept the scrip.) From summer conference lecturer Ernst Lehrs the reporter garnered a headline-worthy phrase: anthroposophy was the "science of the insides of things," while natural science was the science of the outsides. Lehrs contextualized anthroposophy by explaining that just as natural science had arisen at the end of the Middle Ages, so the spiritual science of anthroposophy had been discovered suddenly in this century. The *Tribune* journalist noted anthroposophy's elucidation of the etheric forces and, in spite of his own skepticism about this new science of insides, reported that there were currently more than twenty thousand anthroposophists worldwide.

A sensible, rather than supersensible, aspect of Threefold Farm made the most distinct impression upon the *Tribune* reporter—the eccentric architecture. The "anthroposophically-architectural garage" sported "outcrops of wood jut[ting] in every direction [and] in which every window has its curve," while the greenhouse was constructed on "wavy anthroposophical lines." Oddest of all were the little cottages tucked into corners here and there: "Curved lines in windows, roofs and doors, even in walls, prevail, and the furniture is knobbed and twisted unexpectedly to express dynamic forces. The general effect is that of the Gingerbread House to which poor Hansel and Gretel found their way." All of these structures had a single inspiration: the Goetheanum, designed by Rudolf Steiner as the principal building at the anthroposophical community in Dornach, Switzerland. Seen by some historians as a spectacular example of the early-twentieth-century culmination of the widespread late-nineteenth-century impulse toward the *Gesamtkunstwerk*, or as a highly idiosyncratic modification of an emerging Expressionist impulse within European architecture, the Goetheanum was much deeper in both its influences and aspirations. In later years, some of the Hungry Hollow community's larger buildings—the auditorium (completed in 1954), Pfeiffer's laboratory, a Waldorf school, and dormitories for Sunbridge College (a Waldorf teacher-training college)—would continue to be designed along the lines Steiner pioneered with the Goetheanum. The buildings at Hungry Hollow were meant to foster the same effect as eurythmy, anthroposophical meditation, and even the lectures, that is, to stimulate the awakening of the perception of the etheric world. Just as the physical body of the human being was the creation of cosmic formative forces, so too should architecture mirror these forces. Rudolf Steiner believed that the built environment had specific spiritual effects; modern utilitarian architectural forms, he said, were designed principally "in the best possible way for the eating of roast beef." Anthroposophical architecture was intended to counter such grossly materialistic effects.[15]

The completeness of anthroposophy as a system of knowledge, its assertion of a specialized and privileged outlook upon absolutely everything from agriculture and architecture to zoology, frequently opened it to ridicule in America, where the pragmatic bricolage of vernacular commonsense was valued most highly. Anthroposophy's pronounced mixing of esoteric Christianity with idiosyncratic speech and dramatic technique, pedagogical principles, house building, gardening, medicine, and a host of other domains violated American propriety, which demanded the separation of the sacred and the secular. Usually highly educated and often upper-class, American anthroposophists also seemed suspiciously elitist to many outsiders. The writer of an article surveying "fringe religions" in America was obviously irked by the economic status of anthroposophists: "from an American headquarters in a very swanky section of New York's Madison Avenue, [the Anthroposophical Society] propagandizes the upper classes with a steady stream of pamphlets from the pen of the late Rudolf Steiner, a German philosopher and occultist." Anthroposophists were forever explaining that anthroposophy was not a religion but a *Geisteswissenschaft*, a spiritual *science*. The fact that very few individuals appeared able to verify personally the spectacular contents of knowledge brought forth by Rudolf Steiner bothered not only critics of anthroposophy but anthroposophists themselves, most of whom never mastered the methods of producing supersensible perception. Still, they were heartened by Steiner's assertion that even the critical weighing of the supersensible facts brought forth by anthroposophy was a step on the path toward winning this knowledge for oneself.[16]

Despite anthroposophy's claim to be a science, many of the summer conference attendees had distinctly antiscientific sympathies. They saw modern science as "Ahrimanic," influenced and inspired by the spiritual being who sought always to turn humanity away from the spirit and toward the material world. Many anthroposophists, particularly those whose relationship to anthroposophy was primarily through art, even regarded the scientific research carried out by the Natural Science Section of the Goetheanum (begun by Ehrenfried Pfeiffer and Guenther Wachsmuth) as an Ahrimanic pursuit. And yet the summer conferences were dominated by scientists. The other principal lecturer of the 1933 conference, Dr. Ernst Lehrs, was science master at the Stuttgart Waldorf School and had extensive training in science and engineering. In 1921, while pursuing doctoral research on the uses of high-frequency electric currents, Lehrs attended a lecture in Stuttgart by Dr. Elizabeth Vreede, leader of the Mathematical-Astronomical Section of the Goetheanum. The lecture—"The Overcoming of Einstein's Theory of Relativity"—was part of a conference at which Rudolf Steiner gave a series of eight lectures on "Mathematics, Scientific Experiment and Observation, and Epistemological Results from the Standpoint of Anthroposophy." Lehrs, already to a great extent disenchanted with science's inability to bring harmony into modern social life, was impressed with Steiner's critique of contemporary science, especially in light of his obvious command of scientific knowledge. Steiner's conviction that the contemporary mathematical interpretation of nature was a thoroughly necessary transitional stage in the history of human consciousness captivated Lehrs.[17]

In his lectures at Threefold Farm—"Knowledge of the Body, Soul and Man," "The Relation between Natural Science and Sociology," "The Threefold Organization of the Earth and Humanity," and "Metamorphosis of the Social Organization During the Development of Humanity"—Lehrs frequently used Steiner's term *onlooker* to describe the condition of consciousness that had come to prevail since the advent of the "Consciousness Soul" (1413 C.E.). Widely read in both pre—and post-Enlightenment natural philosophy, Lehrs saw René Descartes among those taking the first steps toward the modern malady of onlooker consciousness. His bold assertion of the objective reality of human thought ("Cogito ergo sum") was followed by the revelations contained in Robert Hooke's *Micrographia*, whose copper engravings of the sensory surprises of the microscopic world undermined confidence in the trustworthiness of the human senses in representing reality. From there, according to Lehrs, it was a small step to David Hume's universal skepticism, which modern scientific thought had fully inherited.[18] Like Steiner, Lehrs regarded this three-century passage through the abyss of onlooker consciousness as a necessary step on the way toward a new relationship with nature.

The Reappearance of Christ in the Etheric

Anthroposophy, though sharing many superficial resemblances to a variety of contemporaneous Arcadian impulses toward cultural and personal renewal, was unmarked by any antimodernist outlook. Founded upon a theory of history that acknowledged the spiritual gifts of earlier stages of human consciousness evolution but clearly saw these as outmoded, anthroposophy was distinctly forward-looking. Human beings' separation from Nature and their loss of an enchanted, largely sacred and reciprocal relationship with their surroundings was concomitant with the separation from the Divine. What to the romantic mind seemed lamentable losses were seen by anthroposophists to be critical gains by human beings on the road to spiritual freedom. Sharing with Theosophy the conviction that the *Kali Yuga*, the "dark age" of human consciousness evolution, had ended in 1899 and that humanity was now in the process of developing a new and higher clairvoyance than the one shared by premodern civilizations, anthroposophists believed that the year 1933 would witness the culmination of the spiritual seed planted two millennia ago, at the moment that each individual at the conference believed to be the turning point in human history.[19]

As surely as Rudolf Steiner's teachings began with an affirmation of the etheric formative forces in the physical world, his work culminated in the conviction that in the twentieth century the resurrected Christ would be united with the earth's etheric realm, bringing to all human beings the possibility of experiencing for themselves the mystery of Golgotha, just as Steiner himself had in 1899.[20] "In our age it is essential that Christ shall be proclaimed in his etheric form, and this is the task of anthroposophy," asserted Steiner, who began in 1909 to speak about Christ's Second Coming as a supersensible event.[21] In these initial lectures, Steiner pointed to the 1930s and 1940s as the years when Christ would appear in the etheric; also in these years there would be a noticeable increase in clairvoyant experiences. During a lecture tour through Scandinavia, Germany, and Italy in 1910, Steiner predicted two particular manifestations of this etheric clairvoyance: some people would have visions of "the second man within the physical man" (that is, perception of the etheric body), and others would see "dream pictures" showing the effects of certain actions in the future.[22] Contradicting the notion that "Nature makes no leaps," Steiner asserted that in fact it makes many, especially in the appearance of new human spiritual and cognitive capacities. Although the new clairvoyance would in the twentieth century appear in only a few hundred individuals, over the next twenty-five hundred years it would become the common heritage of all people.

For those in whom nature had made no leap, the task was to study, and the mood of the summer conference was one of serious scholarship as well as of Arcadian repose. Many of the conference participants carried their well-worn copies of *Knowledge of the Higher Worlds and Its Attainment* (1904), which was Steiner's first full elaboration of the anthroposophical path of inner development, in which an attitude of intense devotion was wedded to disciplined study. The book carried simple instructions for exercises to prepare for anthroposophical meditation, and throughout the conference participants stole moments to practice. The first of the exercises, which consisted of choosing a mental image of an object and concentrating on it, was meant to develop inner certainty and, after a period of time, to help slightly loosen the etheric body from its imprisonment in the physical body. The second exercise, pursuing some unnecessary task at the same time each day, helped to develop initiative but also had an "etheric" goal—to strengthen the interaction between one's etheric body and the larger etheric world. Exercise three required the practice of equanimity by cultivating a calm, listening attitude; this was intended to awaken an awareness of the astral world. The fourth exercise cultivated positive thoughts, the fifth, openmindedness; and the final exercise asked the student to bring the other five together in an orderly way, to achieve inner equilibrium.[23]

Having mastered these exercises, the anthroposophical student could progress to the first meditation, the *Rückschau*, a review of the day's events. This meditation was to be done in great detail, so that all perceptions and actions were included. The successful practitioner eventually came to develop a spectacular memory. Some of the conference participants who had heard Steiner lecture had witnessed his ability, upon returning to a lecture venue he had not visited for years, to begin exactly where he had left off.

The intention of the *Rückschau* was not to achieve extraordinary mnemonic ability but to lead the student out of the physical world's forward stream of time and into the etheric time stream, which flowed in reverse, from future to past. This was the stream of time that Steiner regularly entered in order to bring forth knowledge of the past and the future. And among all the remarkable revelations he made during his lifetime, none carried more significance than his indications about the Second Coming, which, as he announced in 1910, would occur in the year 1933. In contrast to the many prognosticators of Christ's *physical* resurrection in the twentieth century, Steiner spoke of Christ's *etheric* return. In the same manner that witnesses at Christ's tomb experienced the Resurrection, Steiner taught that humanity in the twentieth century could develop the supersensible organs necessary to perceive Christ's etheric reappearance. This was the very heart of Steiner's mission and the ultimate goal of the practice of anthroposophical meditation—to develop etheric clairvoyance in order to unite oneself with the Christ impulse in human history.

The summer conference participants, though deeply committed to the regeneration of Nature through such wholly exoteric activities as organic gardening, nature study, and wildlife conservation, also devoted themselves to the esoteric task of aiding the inevitable degeneration of the planet Earth. In the anthroposophical conception of cosmic history, the physical Earth was but one of seven planetary evolutionary stages, destined to pass away in C.E. 7894. After a long *pralaya*, or resting phase, human consciousness evolution was expected to resume again in a future "Jupiter" stage.[24] While Earth's evolution up until the present had been directed toward the physicalization of the planet from out of etheric formative forces, now Earth was moving toward "disincarnation," a slow dissipation of its former physical vitality, a return from matter into the etheric from whence it came. Christ's entry into human history would prepare all humanity for this eventual disincarnation, and consequent respiritualization, of Earth.

Like so much of anthroposophical thought, the macrocosmic process of Earth etherization had its microcosmic reflection within the domain of human life, in the process that Rudolf Steiner christened the "etherization of the blood." In 1911 Steiner outlined the esoteric physiology that stood behind the incipient etheric clairvoyance to be developed by humanity. Steiner maintained that human blood, the "noblest instrument possessed by man," was the bearer of the human ego, mirroring in its circulation the flowing of the etheric forces beyond the physical world. Interaction between the heart and the pineal gland, the second of the seven etheric organs of the human body, led to the etherization of the blood.[25] As a clairvoyant, Steiner could perceive the etheric currents passing between the heart and the head's pineal gland region, as the blood was transformed into etheric substance. This transubstantiation of matter into spirit within the human body echoed that of Earth.

When Christ's blood flowed from his wounds into the soil on Golgotha, it began to undergo the exact same process of etherization; now, in the twentieth century, that process had completed itself, making it possible for each human being to unite his etheric bloodstream with Christ's.[26] Such a union would effect the acceleration of a person's spiritual development, leading to more pronounced clairvoyance than could be accomplished through meditative activity alone.

Occult Significance of the Blood

"Blood" was a throbbing refrain at Threefold Farm during July 1933. In his lectures, Ehrenfried Pfeiffer frequently reminded his audiences of occult physiology and the responsibility of anthroposophists to pursue this union of etheric blood as the necessary path toward effecting the proper respiritualization of the Earth. Among the Steiner lecture pamphlets for sale at the 1933 conference were "The Mystery of Golgotha" and "The Occult Significance of the Blood." Each morning of the conference, however, the *New York Times* brought an altogether different image of blood in brief but chilling reports of Nazi activity in Europe. Nazi storm troopers tortured trade unionists in Austria. Swastikas were paraded menacingly everywhere in Germany, painted on streets, walls, even mountain crags, and flotillas of burning swastikas were sent down rivers. The day before Pfeiffer's Sunday lecture, the *Times* reported that a New York businessman and his wife (the uncle and aunt of a friend of some of the conference participants) committed suicide in Berlin following a savage beating by storm troopers.

For the anthroposophists at Threefold Farm, the events in Europe were a terrible but unmistakable confirmation of Rudolf Steiner's corollary prognostication about the year 1933: adversary spiritual powers would set in motion events to turn humanity's attention from Christ's etheric return. Anthroposophists understood the timing of the etheric reappearance of Christ to be a function of the archetypal rhythm established by his life of 33¹/₃ years. The fifty-seventh cycle of this rhythm had begun on January 8, 1933, the date of the "etheric remembrance"—that is, the inscription in the backward-flowing etheric time stream—of Christ's Resurrection. Just twenty-two days later, Adolf Hitler was named chancellor of Germany, and the twentieth-century echo of Herod's massacre of the innocents began.[27] In the 1940s and 1950s Ehrenfried Pfeiffer often remarked how World War II successfully interfered with the recognition of Christ's reappearance in the etheric realm.[28]

On the last day of the summer conference at Threefold Farm, the magazine section of the *Times* carried an article by Waldemar Kaempffert, "Can the Stock Be Improved by Weeding Out Non-Aryans?" Kaempffert noted that twenty-seven states had passed sterilization laws and that by 1930 more than ten thousand sterilizations had been performed. Though Kaempffert conceded that marriage restrictions should be enforced "where hereditary feeble-mindedness has been clearly established," he cautioned that "weeding out the unfit" was not an easy task and that Hitler's yet-to-be-approved eugenic plan was unlikely to succeed. Two days later the left-hand column of an inner page of the *Times* carried a correspondent's report of a recent tour of the Dachau concentration camp. The tone of the article was unthreatening, indeed, reassuring. The prisoners ate the same food as the guards, and no prisoner spoke of mistreatment. On the right-hand side of the same page a small headline read: "Reich to Sterilize Undesirable Groups." The accompanying article noted that Hitler's Hereditary Health Law would be enacted the very next day. By the end of 1933, fifty thousand "defectives" had been sterilized in Germany, the first step toward the death camps and genocide.[29]

Given their view of the human being, anthroposophists were particularly resistant to the application of Darwinism in the form of eugenics. Steiner had lampooned eugenic ideas at an early date. In a 1917 lecture that took up the familiar theme of the waning of former etheric clairvoyance, he characterized much of modern thinking as dead, because it lacked any spiritual content. As an example, he cited Woodrow Wilson's political idealism, then went on to an extended discussion of eugenics:

> In 1912 a science called eugenetics was established in London. People tend to use high-falutin' names for anything which is particularly stupid. The ideas you find in eugenetics really came from

people's brains and not from their souls. What are the aims of this science? To ensure that only healthy individuals are born in the future and not inferior ones; economics and anthropology are to join forces to discover the laws according to which men and women are to be brought together in such a way that a strong race is produced.

People are really beginning to think in this way. The ideal of the London congress, which was chaired by Darwin's son, was to examine people of different classes to see how large the skulls of the rich were compared to those of the poor, who have less opportunity for learning; how far sensibility went in rich and poor; how far the rich could resist getting tired and how far the poor would do so, and so on. They want to gain information on the human body in this way which may at some future date enable them to establish exactly the following: this is how the man should look, if they are to produce the human being of the future; he should have such and such a capacity for getting tired and she such a capacity; this size skull for him, and a matching size for her, and so on.[30]

Steiner strenuously warned against the introduction of human thoughts into the actual evolution of humanity, saying it was necessary to renounce the practice of eugenics.

Steiner saw a contemporary "mechanization" of the human being— Taylorism—in a similar light, characterizing Frederick Winslow Taylor's calculations of ironworkers' productivity as an abomination. "The others who could not constitute their force in the given period were now simply thrown out . . . those who were sifted out on the principle of selection were . . . very well satisfied. But the unfit—let them starve." In both eugenics and Taylorism Steiner saw more than the mere application of flawed scientific ideas. He believed these ideas to be especially dangerous because of the incipient development of new forms of etheric clairvoyance. "It would be possible to acquire a vast power over men, even if only by selection of the fittest. But we should not stop at selection of the fittest, but by seeking occult means to make the fit ever more fit, we might reach a tremendous exercise of power which would be diametrically opposed to the good impulses of this epoch."[31]

For all of their attention to the necessity of cultivating etheric clairvoyance, the anthroposophists at Threefold Farm were well aware of how in a previous period of human evolution the mastery of the etheric had brought about catastrophe. Steiner often described how during the last period of the Atlantean Epoch (ending around 8000 B.C.E.) the selfish use of the etheric formative forces in "mechanical," "eugenic," and "hygienic" occultism had brought about the final cataclysm that destroyed most of Atlantean humanity. Eugenics—both in its American manifestations and in its diabolical form in Nazi Germany—and Taylorism were seen by anthroposophists as twentieth-century equivalents of the black magical practices of Atlantean times.[32]

Anthroposophy's critique of eugenics was accompanied by a remarkable social and scientific program of its own for the feebleminded. In his early twenties, while studying in Vienna, Steiner supported himself by tutoring students in subjects ranging from math and chemistry to Greek and Latin. In 1883 he became tutor to a family with four boys, one of whom was severely hydrocephalic and considered ineducable. Carefully cultivating a loving relationship with the boy, Steiner at first gave him very brief lessons, then slowly engaged him with more and more challenging concepts, until his pupil was able to join a class in a secondary school. He went on to university and became a physician.[33]

Throughout his adult life as a teacher, Steiner occasionally spoke about medicine and the need for new healing impulses developed out of spiritual science. In 1924, in Arlesheim, Switzerland, a group of anthroposophists had begun a home—the "Sonnenhof"—for children in need of special mental and physical care. The doctors and teachers there invited Steiner to lecture them on how to meet the needs of these children. Once again, the key concept in Steiner's approach was the etheric body. He stressed that every child's "right relation to the cosmic ether" be understood; children with backward or distorted thoughts had etheric bodies that had not been formed correctly. Steiner discussed schizophrenia, hysteria, autism, epilepsy, and albinism, and he made diagnoses and prescribed remedies for a number of the children at Sonnenhof.[34]

In the audience at Threefold in 1933 were Roger and Marian Hale, who three years before, based on the recommendation of their German housekeeper, had taken their brain-damaged child to the Sonnenhof. Their son thrived in the loving atmosphere there, and the Hales became important patrons and promoters of anthroposophy in America.[35] Another conference attendee, Bill Hahn, soon became involved in curative work with children; later that year he married one of the founders of the Threefold Group, Gladys Barnett, who traveled to the Sonnenhof in 1934 to attend the course in curative eurythmy. In 1935, at Lossing Farm in Copake, New York, the Hahns started the first anthroposophical curative home in America. The Lossing School was small—the Hahns never took in more than ten children at one time—and each child received the same loving attention that Rudolf Steiner had devoted to his pupil in Vienna. The brochure advertising the school read: "We have started a new school. It is for children whose parents feel as we do: that however 'abnormal' a child may seem to be, this is not necessarily his final personality; behind the physical or mental handicap there is just as warm and sensitive a soul as in the so-called normal child. One has to take more trouble to reach it, perhaps; more 'special care' in helping it to become free and to evolve at its own tempo."

The Workings of Karma

Like Lucy De Groat and all the children and adults studied by American eugenicists, the children who came to the Lossing School arrived with histories, but here their histories were viewed as extending over several lifetimes. Their soul heredities, not their physical heredities, were of paramount concern to Gladys Hahn and the other teachers at Lossing. Steiner stressed this attitude in his curative education course. The improperly formed relationship between a child's physical body and his or her subtle bodies— etheric, astral, and ego—was the result of karma. The anthroposophical conception of karma was largely consistent with ancient Eastern ideas; but as with all of his other expositions of esoteric knowledge, Steiner integrated karma into a modern, Western epistemological framework. The doctrine of karma and its inseparable twin doctrine of reincarnation, though so wholly alien to Western sensibilities, were as central to anthroposophy as the expectation of Christ's etheric return.

The "connection of a being with the consequences of its actions is the universal law of Karma. Karma is activity which has become destiny," declared Steiner, who likened the cause-and-effect relation between a human being's present and past incarnations to that between yesterday's actions and today's: "My actions of yesterday have laid down the preconditions for my actions of today. . . . I myself have created the causes of which I am now to add the effects. . . . My past remains associated with me, lives on in my present, and will follow me into my future." Applying this reasoning to the case of a feebleminded child, anthroposophists could only be outraged by the claims of eugenics. Steiner maintained that it was not uncommon for a person believed to be insane or feebleminded to have been a genius in a previous incarnation: "We need to look upon insanity with love, and to inquire after the karmic connections of such people."[36]

Gladys Hahn was acutely aware of the workings of karma in her own life. At the age of fourteen, while traveling with her father on a train, she had witnessed him rise from his seat moments before a splinter of steel came shooting through the window. In 1926, when she had gone to audition as accompanist for Vittorio Giannini's concert tour to Japan, she was incapacitated by severe cramps. She went to Dornach instead, and the events of that year were critical in defining the rest of her life. She had lost most of her hearing by 1926, and though devastated by the effect on her musicianship, she looked upon her deafness as a meaningful condition of karma. She also attributed to karma the help that came to her "out of the blue." In 1934, when she decided to attend the Sonnenhof curative course to prepare for the establishment of the curative home at Lossing, she was totally deaf and had no idea how she would be able to participate fully. The day before she was to leave New York for Switzerland, she met two women who had recently come to New York from California. They told her about Bakelite, the ceramic substance that would soon revolutionize the manufacture of hearing aids. The next morning, before the ship departed, Hahn went to the Bakelite manufacturer and bought a piece for a quarter. Holding the Bakelite sheet between her teeth (which conducted the vibration from the Bakelite sounding board to her jawbone and inner ear) for the entire course, she was able to hear everything said by the lecturers. She never saw the two California women again, or even knew their names.[37]

Karma intervened for another participant in the 1933 conference, unexpectedly bringing his life into service to anthroposophy. Henry Barnes had just graduated from Harvard University and landed a position for the following fall as assistant to the headmaster at the Choate School. The previous January, Henry's roommate, who had also been his best friend when they attended the Lincoln School of Teacher's College in New York City, had disappeared from Cambridge and was later found to have committed suicide on the shores of Lake Huron. Determined to maintain contact with her dead son as he entered the spiritual world, the friend's mother had studied Steiner's *Knowledge of Higher Worlds* and eventually encountered the Threefold Group in New York. A few weeks before the summer conference began, she invited Barnes to come to Threefold Farm. Deeply impressed by the anthroposophical vision of education and of the human being expressed by Ernst Lehrs and Maria Roschl in their lectures, Barnes decided to go to Stuttgart after the year at Choate. When he informed the headmaster of his desire to study Waldorf education the following year, the headmaster encouraged Barnes to pursue it immediately. Following his training under Lehrs and Roschl, Barnes became a teacher in the Stuttgart Waldorf school. After the Nazis closed the school in 1938, he moved to the New School, the first Waldorf school in England. Returning to the United States in 1940, Barnes joined the faculty of the Rudolf Steiner School in New York City.[38]

In Stuttgart, Henry Barnes met Percy MacKaye's daughter Christy. Along with her sister Arvia, Christy had begun to study anthroposophy a decade before, after Arvia, in Europe as Radcliffe College's representative to an international conference on the youth movement, had made a visit to Dornach. By 1933, Arvia was living and working at the Goetheanum, while Christy was teaching at the Rudolf Steiner School in New York. Their father found much to be admired in anthroposophy, particularly its nurturing of art, poetry, and theater (via the mystery dramas). In 1933 the MacKayes' destiny became more closely connected with anthroposophy, when, upon Arvia's recommendation, Percy and his wife Marion placed their son Robin in the Wiesnick Sanatorium in Freiburg, Germany. Under the direction of Dr. Friedrich Husemann, the sanatorium approached the psychiatric problems of adults from the same standpoint of anthroposophical curative work for children—with attentiveness to the karmic dimension of each patient.

Even more so than his father, Robin MacKaye had had an intimate relationship with the natural world. He grew up out of doors, tramping the New Hampshire countryside day after day with his dog. At age eight he built a small cabin, which he filled with natural history books and a collection of rocks, arrowheads, animal skeletons, and other found objects. He became friends with a lumberjack named Ben Jorden, who took him on hunting trips, introduced him to his backwoods friends, and told tales of his boyhood. Robin and his sister Arvia were also befriended by Robert Barret, a neighbor whom they called "Brown Beard." An explorer who had been to China, Japan, Africa, and Tibet, Barret gave them lessons in tracking and campcraft. When Robin finally began to attend school at age thirteen, he did poorly.[39]

Robin MacKaye often wrote and spoke of the "Green God," whose works he had come to know intimately as a child and continued to marvel at as an adult. He combined his uncle Benton's empiricist eye with his father's transcendentalism: "Words are beyond me to describe the beauties of Nature after a rain. Take the twig of butternut with the catkins broken from it by the drops. What can picture to you the irregular symmetry of its wavy, olive-brown stem, that undulates, indented alternately with the hollows of last year's fallen leaves? What is the spirit of those hollows; the noble expression of this record in wood?" Like his father, he mused perennially upon the evolutionary riddle of where Nature ended and the human began. "Brackish Water," was among a small collection of his poems that won the Albert Stanburrough Cook Prize, offered annually at Yale to the best unpublished verse:

Brackish water, brackish water,
Like a glass among the sedges,

Fumed with brown, and amber-tinted,
Black in shadow 'long the ledges
Where old leaves, for ever stepping
Back the mirror of the forest!

In thy depths a constant creeping,
Teeming life in silence keeping
Countless generations crawling,
Darting, streaking, meeting, blending,
Becoming past without an ending;
Following an unknown music,
Like a maze of motes that eddy
To an air-swirl in a sunbeam.

Pollywog and caddis-wormling,
Beetle-boat and tiny squirmling,
All sunning in a sultry vintage—
Slumbrous brew of endless ages
That confounds the wisest sages.[40]

Like his father, Robin also looked to the future of human evolution
as well as its past, as in his poem "Wings for Hands: Grist for a Crow Play
in the Theatre of Evolution":

He began as black, swift dust
thickened into the night of the oils and the oozes,
somehow shook free into a cool eddy,
and from the shattering pulsations of his journey
built him—a gut of clay, where he progressed
by gathering to him that which ever fell
behind—
in the first circle of the jellyfishes,
till in the sea, mimic of the earth, traveling
under bright stars,
he found a shorter course amid the oceans
than among the stars—
and felt at home.

 . . .

Black
in steep quest up the black curved cataract,
Caa, the Crow,
perhaps the oldest of earth's portion,
playing his forgotten Drama

on his crumbling stage of falling clay,
forever doomed to play roles evolving:
mind of the old world
still bantering each curtained sunrise across the footlight of the
Alps,
which he has deserted:
to the sea, from which he withdrew
to costume peopling waters with clownish glory,
returns he.

But now
beside him all things are new
and beetles honor the mightiness of his lone, circular
six-fingered hand
which once quivered the triad of the earth
in those dim, distant, mundungoidous days.

In his play, ring-master, author, interlocutor,
he knows not heaven—save two wings
wherewith forever he falls, but is borne up by the wind:
a new wind, full of fruited fragrance,
needing him
still.[41]

Robin MacKaye found Nature more perfect than the human, but he saw that humanity's role was "to know for all lesser creation."[42]

At age twenty-eight, the promising young poet whose photo had formed one corner of his father's eugenic family portrait on the cover of *Annals of an Era* suffered a nervous breakdown. The move to Wiesnick came after years of fruitless psychiatric treatment in the United States. Percy at first refused to admit that there was anything wrong with his son, preferring to view Robin's state as typical of a young artist. Other members of the family saw Robin's breakdown as the consequence of the irreconcilability of his intuitive relationship to nature with the reductionist scientific training he received during college. To Arvia and Christy, who knew firsthand that the primary goal of Waldorf education was to nurture the feeling dimension of soul life as the intellect was built up, their brother's mental breakdown represented the catastrophic possibility faced by twentieth-century humanity.[43]

In 1936, after more than three years of separation from Robin, the MacKayes planned a European tour, which would begin in Dornach so that they might be reunited with their son and their daughters. Three days after their arrival in Europe, they attended the opening night of Albert Steffen's drama *Peace Tragedy* in Basel. From Arvia, MacKaye already knew of the poetry and essays of Steffen, president of the General Anthroposophical Society. MacKaye sat riveted as a series of tableaux unfolded on the stage, opening with President Woodrow Wilson and his wife in the White House in December 1918, passing through the Peace Conference in January 1919 and the fateful treaty negotiations at Versailles, and ending in January 1924 with the anguished ex-president confronting the wreckage wrought by the League of Nations. Throughout the play ran the theme of Wilson's *Doppelgänger*, or "etheric double," which was considered by Steffen to be the spectral presence that played a primary role in leading Europe into World War I, due to Wilson's abstract idealism.[44]

The very next day, All Souls' Day, the MacKayes attended a program in memory of the dead at the Goetheanum; then, a few days later, Percy MacKaye met Albert Steffen for the first time. "First Meeting," the poem he wrote to commemorate the occasion, suggests that the anthroposophic concept of karma and reincarnation was already beginning to find a receptive listener in the former advocate of eugenic destiny:

> I have seen you, long ago:
> Seen you smiling—even so—
> With an enigmatic glow,
>
> As a lonely poet smiles
> At his own allusive wiles
> Luring him to occult isles.
>
> I have felt your sentient hand
> Touch my own (as now we stand)
> Long since, in another land—
>
> On some threshold of the air—
> In a glimmering doorway, where
> The soul is of itself aware.
>
> Was it in a Doric wood
> Of some Delphian solitude
> So we met—and understood?
>
> Or in some old Gothic pile,
> When deep organ played the while,
> I caught that candle-flickering smile?

Or beside an Orient well
Where the Bethlehem shepherds dwell
First we felt this starry spell? . . .

Still you smile, through all the lore
Of long ago, while at the door
They say, we've never met before.[45]

In 1938, Percy and Marion MacKaye returned to Dornach. Particularly through his literary friendship with Albert Steffen, MacKaye's views of nature and history were radically reshaped. A new spirit appeared in his writing, which on occasion sounded "anthroposophical," as in the poem "Metamorphosis," which became part of a volume written jointly with Albert Steffen:

Four-mold are all living things:
The egg, the worm, the chrysalis,—the wings;
Four-fold in unfurling power:
The seed, the stem, the sealèd bud,—the flower;
Four-pleated in one whole:
The self, the sense, the sharded brain,—the soul;
Four-compassed, all in one,
With womb, warm earth, enschrouding mist,—and sun.

So even with us two:
Like worm and stem and groping sense, we grew—
Grew till we died of pain
In chrysalis, shut bud, and sharded brain—
Died, till the All-Knowing One
Freed us to find ourselves in the encircling Sun—
Ourselves in each other—freed
To know our oneness with the immortal Seed.[46]

Letters to his practical Yankee brother Benton show little evidence of the new outlooks on nature and the human being that Percy was gleaning from his residence in Dornach, though he sent Benton a copy of Ehrenfried Pfeiffer's new work, *Using the Bio-Dynamic Compost Preparations and Sprays in Garden, Orchard, and Farm*, and encouraged Benton to contact Pfeiffer when he made his next lecture tour to the States.[47] Then, in June 1939, Marion died, and Percy was devastated. If he had not already embraced anthroposophical concepts of the soul's immortality, he moved closer toward acceptance in the wake of her death. Writing to Benton a few months later, the old refrains of antimodernism mingled with the desire for the infinite:

We lead such blind lives, my dear boy. Death is all that gives dignity to life—yet we give him the cold shoulder, and go our petty, overbusy, rattly, raucous little ways, till we bump into his great silence, without ever having learned to love and emulate it.

What are we anyhow? Just June bugs? Or are these gossamer thoughts, that we pack away down into our bellies so hard—angel wings?

* * * * * * * * * *

There are no radios here Ben. There are no movies. There are no roaring motors.

There are only mountains—-and the eyes of the midnight—stars . . . stars . . . stars.[48]

Little asterisk stars fell down the page until they coalesced in the letter "P" for "Poog." Once Percy had seemed convinced that from dust he had come and unto dust he would return. His encounter with anthroposophy would likely have been more like his brother's relationship with it—at arm's length, largely disinterested—had his son not needed special care. And it transformed his image of human fate. In Dornach, Percy came to see humans as having come from the stars, not from the soil of earthly heredity, and he knew that it was unto the stars they would return.

The World's Hidden History

Percy MacKaye left no explicit record of his reflections upon what effects his encounter with anthroposophy had upon his former eugenic ideals. Given his experience with his son's illness and his embrace of the possibility of reincarnation, he may well have looked back upon his eugenic enthusiasm with some degree of dismay. His daughters understood his enthusiasm for eugenics as having been shaped by his unique karmic context, one seemingly shared by many generations of MacKayes. The MacKayes were fervently "Greek" in their idealism, in their artistic goals, even in their countenances, and Percy's Burbank-style eugenics seemed a twentieth-century recapitulation of the Greek striving for physical perfection.

At the Threefold summer conferences, it was not unusual for anthroposophists to speculate about others' previous incarnations. Such conversations ran the gamut from somber ruminations to good-natured kidding, but the largely unspoken rule of thumb held it in bad taste to pronounce upon one's own imagined karmic past. Rumors abounded as to who Rudolf Steiner and his inner circle of anthroposophical leaders—including Ehrenfried Pfeiffer—had been in previous lives. Pfeiffer actively discouraged this sort of karmic gossip. In a lecture at one of the summer conferences, he told the audience: "Either we understand Rudolf Steiner and the position he takes in Christianity, and we will keep quiet and restrain from speculating, or we don't know and had better not speak."[49]

Pfeiffer himself was deeply involved in karmic research, traveling widely in Europe and the Middle East to visit the most important mystery centers of past ages and the locations of important events in the earth's spiritual history, such as the site of Christ's baptism in the Jordan. Egypt held a particular fascination for Pfeiffer, and he supplemented his trips there by delving deeply into scholarship on ancient Egypt. Occasionally his lectures on topics seemingly unrelated to Egypt would pour forth in tremendous detail knowledge about Egyptian esoteric practices. At these times, friends and colleagues noticed how there would appear to be a change of consciousness that came over Pfeiffer, as if fragments of another life were coming through.[50]

Over the years at the summer conferences, one illustration appeared perhaps hundreds of times on blackboards and drawing pads: the concave arc describing the pendulum swing of post-Atlantean Earth history. Its left-hand apex marked humanity's beginnings in the first epoch, the Ancient Indian; its right-hand terminus reached out to the seventh epoch at the end of the eighth millennium. At the bottom of the arc, a little hachure marked the "Abyss," the middle of the fourth post-Atlantean epoch, when humanity reached its deepest descent into the physical realm before beginning the journey back into spirit. Frequently, lecturers drew a descending wedge down to the hachure, to signify the earthly incarnation of Christ at exactly the midpoint of the Greco-Roman era, saving humanity from the Abyss.

One of the laws embraced by anthroposophy was that at all levels of history, from cosmic creation to the unfolding of the post-Atlantean periods, an inviolable "mirroring" process occurred, by which events on either side of certain moments of time reflected one another. The third post-Atlantean "Egyptian" epoch (2417–747 B.C.E.) was understood to be reflected in the present epoch, the fifth post-Atlantean. In the Egyptian epoch humanity began a more intensive engagement with the physical world, most dramatically expressed by the Egyptian practice of mummification; thus, by the spiritual law of reflection, the task of humanity in the present, fifth post-Atlantean epoch was to retrace, but *transform*, the impulses of the third epoch. The Threefold anthroposophists saw their "new alchemy," particularly the scientific research of Pfeiffer, as a seminal agent of such transformation, and, like Pfeiffer himself, they believed that this individuality who was such a powerful force at Threefold was in the process of transforming deeds he had likely performed as an Egyptian priest thousands of years before.

In his lectures at Threefold Farm, Pfeiffer often told members of the audience that their destinies were linked particularly to the eighth and ninth centuries, when they had incarnated to participate in the Christian heretical movements. At that time, the Archangel Michael made preparations for anthroposophy through his inspiration of Scotus Erigena (833–877), who introduced reason into Christian thought and belief. In a manner very different from exoteric intellectual historical practice, Pfeiffer interpreted Scotus Erigena's Scholasticism as bearing fruit in Rudolf Steiner's foundational work, *The Philosophy of Spiritual Activity*, and he traced the origin of the biodynamic agricultural method to the gardens and fields of the Cluny Monastery, founded by the Scholastics in the early tenth century.[51]

Pfeiffer's biweekly outpouring of historical revelations at Threefold Farm came in the wake of his near fatal bout with tuberculosis in 1946. While recuperating in a sanitarium in Pomona, New York, Pfeiffer had pored through a prodigious sampling of historical literature, making a world historical review of human activity since the time of Atlantis. Upon this knowledge he brought to bear the wide-ranging historical research of his mentor, Rudolf Steiner, including the remarkable karmic investigations that Steiner had revealed in a series of lectures the year before his death in 1925. Pfeiffer synthesized his own esoteric and exoteric research into an enormous chart, which began in 500 B.C.E. and ended in the late nineteenth century. In Pfeiffer's minute script, in columns labeled "Political History," "Migrations-Invasions," "Religion-Art-Philosophy-Mystic," and "Philosophy, Alchemy, Science, Trade, Architecture," all the chart's text pointed toward the right-hand column, "Spiritual Science," where the meaning of historical events was interpreted according to anthroposophical concepts. Disparate dates and events were linked by Pfeiffer's simple system of red, blue, and yellow pencil markings. The chart was a familiar feature of Pfeiffer's Threefold lectures after 1946.

The right-hand column was truly a wonder to behold, with its stunning compression of the vast corpus of Rudolf Steiner's historical revelations, particularly his karmic research. Noted were the incarnation of the nineteenth-century French occultist Eliphas Levy in the fifth century B.C.E. and his participation in the "decadent" Mesoamerican mysteries of that time. Georg Wilhelm Friedrich Hegel's former incarnation during the period of the Eleusinian mysteries and the later incarnations of a number of Plato's pupils as the German Romantics Goethe, Robert Hamerling, and Friedrich Hölderlin were revealed. The chart identified a former incarnation of Victor Hugo in Ireland during the third century B.C.E. and Swiss educator Heinrich Pestalozzi's incarnation as a Greek slave overseer in the first century B.C.E. Following the mystery of Golgotha, there were such revelations as Rabindranath Tagore's fourth-century incarnation, the identification of a fifth-century initiate of Asia Minor as a former incarnation of Henrik Ibsen, and the discovery of an individual in the eighth century named "Moawija," who was said by Steiner to have been a previous incarnation of Woodrow Wilson.

Even a glance at a single recent century left one breathless. The eighteenth-century section began by identifying Voltaire as the reincarnation of a Mohammedan Kabbalist (as was Emanuel Swedenborg) and Frederick the Great (who wrote the tract "Anti-Machiavelli") as a reincarnation of Machiavelli. Immanuel Kant was a reincarnated Chinese individual who had previously experienced very few incarnations. Many notations referred to contemporaneous doings in the spiritual world of the Archangel Michael's cult, such as the inspiration of Goethe's *Märchen* and the witnessing of the returning etheric Christ by the soul individuality who had once been Tycho Brahe. There were also references to the adversarial spiritual powers and their machinations, such as the Luciferic inspiration of Hegel and Jean-Jacques Rousseau, the latter noted as the same impulse as the one that had led to the French Revolution instead of the Threefold Order. One year bore the notation that the Comte de Saint-Germain, identified as the incarnation of Christian Rosenkreutz, had warned Marie Antoinette that she would perish unless a new social order was introduced. Victor Hugo earlier lived as an initiate into the Hybernian mysteries, and an unidentified crusader against slavery in America was the incarnation of the Master Jesus.

Charles Darwin's former incarnations were faithfully noted on Pfeiffer's chart, as were those of Germany's leading advocate of materialist monism, Ernst Haeckel. One brief line near the conclusion of the chart summed up the modern human predicament: "Man between illusion about Nature and hallucination of the Spirit." World history culminated in the twentieth century, when the illusion about Nature—materialism—reached its terrible apotheosis in natural scientific thought.[52]

Pfeiffer's lectures frequently attacked the illusion that physical Nature offered humans any guidance to social action. This was the work of Ahriman and his host of "abnormal" spiritual beings, whose influence was especially apparent in the application of Darwinian logic to humanity. Eugenics was not merely some aberrant application of unsound science but the inevitable successor to the Ahriman-inspired notion of natural selection.

The Mission of America

America's place in the spiritual history of the world was conspicuously absent from the lectures at the 1933 conference. This oversight largely reflected the relative ignorance of America among the founding generation of anthroposophists. Rudolf Steiner's esoteric history, though wideranging and "ecumenical," was still the product of a European sensibility. Steiner's pronouncements about America, aside from his karmic research into the previous lives of Woodrow Wilson, provocative lectures on Aztec mystery practices, and even more provocative statements about the tenth-century discovery of America by Irish monks, were limited. With the establishment of anthroposophical initiatives in the New York area, an effort was made to "Americanize" anthroposophy, and the summer conferences at Threefold Farm were essential to this process. In 1934, owing in part to the success of the first summer conference, an American lecture tour was scheduled for three leading German anthroposophists, Hermann von Baravalle, Guenther Wachsmuth, and Ehrenfried Pfeiffer. Arriving in New York on Columbus Day, the trio spent two months spreading anthroposophical seeds throughout the country, wherever the soil had been prepared in advance by the handful of anthroposophists living outside the New York City region.

Just as Pfeiffer, under Steiner's tutelage, had developed the crystallization methods for perceiving the action of the etheric forces at an organismal level, Wachsmuth had pioneered etheric perception and interpretation at the level of the physical and biotic landscape. Wachsmuth's etheric geography led him to a "threefold" interpretation of America: eastern cities he found to be more like Europe, living more in the nerve-sense pole; in the "tropical vegetation of the West," and most of all in California, "where the pioneer type is the strongest," he observed the vital pole; between them lay the equalizing pole of the Middle West. Wachsmuth found Steiner's indications confirmed repeatedly as he made his way across the Plains, then the Rockies and the Sierra Nevada to California. From the life ether in the Midwest, as evidenced by the fruitfulness of the cornfields on the plains of the Missisippi and Missouri Rivers, to the life ether at the Rocky Mountain front in its mineralizing aspect, to the warmth ether in the Sierra, evidenced by renewed vegetative growth, Wachsmuth saw America as "a living piece of 'ether-geography.' "[53]

Their American travels confirmed for the two students of the etheric realm that Rudolf Steiner's indications about America were true: there the forces of the *Doppelgänger*, the etheric double, were pronounced. The double, according to Steiner, is always at work in every human being. It does not have a heart and so lives only in the head and the will, not in the mediating realm of the rhythmic system. With its very strong connection to the forces that ascend from the earth—magnetism, electricity, and the "third force" (unknown in Steiner's lifetime, but manifested a decade later as atomic energy)—the double has the goal of binding human beings to the earth forces, so that their thinking and willing receive direction only from the earth.

"Back to Nature," the slogan that embraced such positive associations for the Arcadian proponents who were near neighbors of Threefold Farm, was a phrase that carried for anthroposophists a chilling picture of a possible future. If the work of the etheric double was not countered, human beings would go "back to Nature," become prisoners of the earth forces, and lose all consciousness of higher worlds. This was precisely the goal of Ahriman, and the etheric double was a microcosmic replica of Ahriman, devoid of the heart forces that kept man from becoming a mere material being. In the anthroposophic view of history, supported by an esoteric reading of the Book of the Apocalypse, earth evolution would come to a close at the end of the seventh post-Atlantean epoch, known to esoteric history as the "American" cultural epoch. In the sixth millennium, America would either fulfill or fail its mission in world history, just as Germany had in this century. At that future time, as described in the seventh ("Leodicea") letter of the Apocalypse, mankind would split into two streams, one descending to a state between man and animal, the other ascending to become the Tenth Hierarchy and join the angels, archangels, and other spiritual beings in their task of guiding the earth on its proper evolutionary course back toward its etheric origins.

Although this apocalyptic moment lay long millennia away, Rudolf Steiner, and Pfeiffer after him, taught that all of the signs of the times indicated that the twentieth century was witnessing a foreshadowing of that Apocalypse, that the salient developments of their own lifetime indicated a turning point in time. Nowhere was this clearer than in America, where the Ahrimanic double increasingly seized hold of every domain of human life, borne on the obliging back of natural science. The pedagogical practice of nature study, the investigative apparatus of natural scientific research, and, most diabolically, the application of Darwinian theory to the human social realm—these three seemingly sunny trails through America in the early twentieth century were actually paths to the dark death of the living forces of the spiritual world. No one was immune from the tentacles of the Ahrimanic double. Good men and women—Robert Latou Dickinson, Frank Lutz, Bill Carr, Mary Harriman, Benton and Percy MacKaye—easily fell prey to its relentless inspiration of materialist thoughts.

Guenther Wachsmuth returned to the Goetheanum in 1934 with a collection of lantern slides he had made of America's physical geography in order to illustrate the country's etheric geography. From east to west, he had photographed America's mountain ranges, wave after wave of them running in a north-south direction. Rudolf Steiner had repeatedly connected this geographic feature to America's spiritual destiny, stressing that electromagnetic forces—the forces of death and the power behind the etheric double—were particularly strong wherever mountain ranges were oriented north to south. Anthroposophy sought to provide the enlivening heart forces to keep the American people from going "back to Nature."

Whenever the Threefold anthroposophists looked northeast toward the Ramapo Mountain front, they were reminded of their region's, and their nation's, unique etheric geography and of their apocalyptic task to save America from its tendency to unite with the earth forces. Imagining their way across the great border fault that separated the supersensible world from the sensible one, the Threefold community saw a very different high ground than the builders of the Appalachian Trail, the founders of the Trailside Museum, and the patrons and fieldworkers of the Eugenics Record Office. They saw Heaven, not Arcadia, as their true home, and with heart-strengthened thought they tried to blaze a trail there for all to follow. Dwelling in the same Arcadian hinterland as Harriman Park's Naturalists, the Threefold anthroposophists saw that the heavenward trail started right underfoot and demanded the study of the nonhuman nature that surrounded them.

CHAPTER 6

Spiritual Science and the Redemption of the Senses

*D*uring the opening decades of the twentieth century, American zoologists, who only a generation earlier had eagerly emulated their European counterparts, established and elaborated their science so that it soon surpassed its exemplar in scope and ambition.[1] By the opening years of the anthroposophical summer conferences at Threefold Farm, zoology in America was a fully fledged discipline, not only confident of the detailed picture it might offer Americans of animal life but also increasingly certain that contained within animal behavior and evolution was the history of the human being. The zoology offered to participants of the Threefold summer conferences, like the anthropology taught there, centered around the concept of a subtle body, imperceptible to the senses as currently developed. This zoology required new senses, to be developed not in proxy through the invention and refinement of instrumentation but through the human mind's engagement with its own sensory apparatus.

A New Zoology

Out in the garden behind the main house at Threefold, a small, round man with alert eyes moved up and down the rows, surveying the many stages of growth. Peapods hung from their chicken-wire trellis; beans were elongating earthward beneath the dark and furrowed leaves; the sulphurous yellow flowers of the broccoli were in various states of bloom, attracting scores of cabbage whites; zucchini and summer squash grew enormous even as their vines produced new flowers; the corn still held within its skyward-reaching shoots all of the flowers and fruit. The soil below, lovingly nurtured with Dr. Pfeiffer's biodynamic preparations, teemed with earthworms.

183

On this morning's walk Hermann Poppelbaum moved like a honeybee among the June flowers, collecting fresh mental pictures to bring to the hive of listeners who would hear his first address at the 1939 summer conference later that day. His own pictures were wholly European. Though here in the garden he met many familiar plants and animals—the honeybee being perhaps the most evocative of his homeland—there were also new colors, new forms, new behaviors and habits unknown to him.

Never having met the ruby-throated hummingbird, Poppelbaum still felt it familiar, and he compared its iridescent emerald plumage and roseate throat patch to the patterns of European hummingbirds. After a moment, he realized that one "hummingbird" was actually a hawkmoth out on an early morning nectar run. Many of the butterflies that made their way in and out of the garden were nearly identical to species he knew from Germany—swallowtails, whites, sulphurs, coppers, hairstreaks, blues, and brushfoots. He recognized the monarch and the viceroy, knowing them as spectacular exemplars of mimicry. From the nearby woods he heard a cuckoo call and wondered which bird served as the obliging host to its interloper chick. Bees and butterflies, hovering hawkmoths and hummingbirds, cuckolding cuckoo—all were more "awake" than the comparatively sleepy green world below them, and all brought before Poppelbaum's mind's eye the unmistakable image of the "awakener," the astral body. While his colleagues Ehrenfried Pfeiffer and Guenther Wachsmuth had made great strides in elucidating the etheric formative forces, Poppelbaum's contemplation of animal form and function sought the higher principle of the astral, which, through the etheric formative forces, brought the animal into exquisite fittedness to its surround. Whereas plants were merely embedded in their environment, animals experienced, and hence more fully expressed, the qualities of the environing world.

The close, seemingly obligatory reliance of the butterfly upon its particular food plant, the tailored fit of hummingbird beak and butterfly proboscis to their tubular flower feeders, the painterly mimesis of monarch by viceroy, the cuckoo's parasitism of some songbird's nest—each was a superb illustration of the pervasiveness and artfulness of the astral world. At each stage of the butterfly's life, the astral took hold of the animal's etheric body and wed it to the plant's: the egg, resting upon the leaf or stem of the future host plant, already placed its destiny in the care of the plant; the growing caterpillar, consuming the flesh of its vegetative host, wove its astral being even more closely into the invisible fibers of the plant's etheric body; the chrysalis, though seemingly asleep, came close to becoming a plant organ, the bud; then, at the apotheosis of lepidopteran transformation, the imago burst forth like a blossom and took flight, a flower set free to seek again its host as it fed upon blossom-borne nectar or exuded sap. The animal-to-plant matching of feeding tube to floral tube, most extravagantly developed in the orchids and their pollinators, showed the astral penetrating even more deeply into the plant etheric world. The mimetic dance of viceroy and monarch, and the parasitic dance of cuckoo and host, were apt pictures to suggest that the astral's power of "belongingness" reached its baroque extreme when expressed within the animal realm alone, apart from plants.

As he left the garden for the forest, Poppelbaum noticed a procession of ants carrying chrysalids away from one nest entrance toward another and immediately recognized them as one of the "slave-making" species. Here was another perfect picture of animal astrality. Ants, bees, termites—all the so-called "social insects"—showed the limitations of traditional zoological thought, for the individual organisms were incomplete in themselves. Possessed of all their necessary physical parts, still they lacked completion without the entire suite of component players—worker, guard, king, queen, and so on. In the case of the slave-making ants, the incompleteness was carried even farther, across the species divide. Poppelbaum would direct his listeners once more to seek for the solution to such riddles in the astral realm, the molder as well as the awakener of all forces peculiar to the animal kingdom and absent from the plants.

Poppelbaum had practiced this new style of zoological observation to such an extent that he could *see* these astral relations. And this was his objective for his course of lectures at Threefold: to cultivate such pictures so as to lead his audience to freshen their perceptual styles, to abandon the automatic corruption of their perceptions fostered by decades of Darwinian training. The "struggle for existence" was a heinous illusion, as was the notion of "gradually acquired mutual adaptation." Darwinism's incessant quest for shared lines of descent dulled one's perceptual acuity. To know insects, one did better to study closely the plant and its metamorphoses, seeking there in Goethean fashion the key to seemingly unrelated biological events. What was the butterfly if not a "summed up" plant, its egg a seed in both appearance and function, the caterpillar wholly belonging to the foliage, the chrysalis to the bud, and the imago to the blossom? While the plant continued to hold the picture of its unfolding in time in its vertical arrangement of the various organs, butterflies and other insects "consumed" their histories as they lived.

This imaginative picture could be carried to the moths, whose ascension into the realm of the formative forces was stepped down to a lower level; except for a few crepuscular hawkmoths, they eschewed the light. Moth larvae likewise sought out unlit spaces—within the soil or, as in the case of the cutworm moth, within the cabbage head. Beetles lived their life cycles largely within the realms of the fruit and root; grasshoppers lived almost exclusively within the leaf realm, and the absence of a pupal stage within the Orthoptera appeared to Poppelbaum a confirmation of their "incompleteness." Worms put the hierarchical arrangement of life stages down another step, so that both the pupa and imago forms were suppressed entirely. As a realm of ennobled shapes, thought Poppelbaum, the insects arise from the dark netherworld of the worm as "blossoms" of the worm world. In remaining behind to husband the physical and etheric forces of the soil, the earthworm had its own nobility, sacrificing beauty for productive work.

Surely these pictures would stretch his audience's capacities enough, but Poppelbaum hoped to add just one more image. Where, he would ask, did the sacrificed formative powers go? Was there perhaps an invisible corresponding imago of the earthbound worm? And where might one find it? Poppelbaum trusted his audience to know to seek within the human all the answers to nature's mysteries, and he felt he could direct their attention to the region of the human form that had so fascinated Goethe: the union of the head with the neck and trunk. He knew that the Threefold anthroposophists would be familiar with Rudolf Steiner's idea that the metameric nature of the trunk was a function of the etheric formative forces, which were responsible for the production of all forms in the nature of repetition. The abrupt transition to a wholly different architecture at the head suggested the intervention of astral forces, which in nature operated always to bring rhythmic sequences to their necessary end and subsequent supercession.

Poppelbaum intended to present a challenging picture of the organ within the vaulted dome of the skull. In embryonic development, the human brain began as a wormlike set of three vesicles, then became five, after which a contraction of the axis and a swelling of the third and fifth vesicles occurred. Finally, the terminal vesicle divided itself into two, the left and right halves flaring up and back like a pair of puffy wings. Here in these wings, the two lobes of the expanding cerebrum, Poppelbaum saw the missing imago of the worm. The brain acted as if it were a larva prevented from hatching. Instead of unfolding into the light of the sun as did the butterfly imago, the human brain/grub remained imprisoned in the dark and watery depths of the skull. This backward-stepping metamorphosis ensured that the formative forces were prevented from expression in man's bodily nature and were saved for the faculty of imagination. "What the worm gives to the soil, the imprisoned larva of the brain gives to the human entity." This was the picture he intended to leave with the Threefold audience, to work upon their imaginations.[2]

Man and Animal: Their Essential Difference

The orgy of nationalism that Rudolf Steiner had foreseen in the absence of the implementation of the Threefold Commonwealth led to an event that had important consequences for the dissemination of anthroposophic teachings. In 1938 the National Socialist leadership in Germany outlawed all anthroposophic activities; Waldorf schools were closed, study groups and lectures were banned, and the members of the executive council of the German Anthroposophical Society went into exile. Hermann Poppelbaum, chairman of the executive council, migrated with his family to England, where he gained a reputation as a lecturer, study group guide, and trainer of future leaders of the Anthroposophical Society in Great Britain. Invited to the United States in 1939 for the summer conference and a continental lecture tour, he was caught by the outbreak of World War II and remained in America for nine years. In July 1939 Poppelbaum joined Ehrenfried Pfeiffer under the canvas tent in the oak grove at Threefold Farm to bring to American anthroposophists an entirely new way of looking at the animal world around them.

Before Poppelbaum's arrival in the United States, American anthroposophists were familiar with his ideas from a 1931 translation of his 1926 work, *Man and Animal: Their Essential Difference.* Having completed his dissertation on gynandromorphic butterflies under Richard Goldschmidt at the University of Frankfurt in 1916, Poppelbaum came to maturity as a natural scientist at the very moment when natural science was most confident of man's animal origins. Called into the German army as a cavalry officer in 1918, Poppelbaum served on the eastern and western fronts, and he was captured by the French a few months before the armistice. Poppelbaum learned of anthroposophy from a fellow prisoner, Otto Palmer, and during their months of captivity, Palmer tutored Poppelbaum in Steiner's philosophy. Returning to Frankfurt after the war, Poppelbaum envisioned a new zoology based on Steiner's work: "Man, no longer the accidental *finis* to the animal species, but the centre of gravity in the kingdoms of nature. . . . Man, not the final product of evolution, but from primordial time its hidden source. . . . The human soul, no longer a further and more highly developed animal soul, but the harmonious and uncorrupted archetype in which the animal soul is contained as a part. . . . The human spirit no longer the reflex of the nervous system, but the microcosmic reflection of the Divine. . . . The whole man the key to the physical and spiritual universe."[3]

The centrality of the human being was the alpha and omega of Rudolf Steiner's anthroposophy. In dozens of books and thousands of lectures Steiner had given innumerable indications about the distinction between man and animal, yet he had never systematically worked through the animal kingdom in the manner of a contemporary zoologist. Poppelbaum's entire scientific oeuvre drew upon a familiarity with contemporary factual discovery and theoretical issues while hewing closely to an anthroposophical outlook. His lyrical descriptions of the natural world, startling and seemingly abstract to the vast majority of his professional colleagues, were remarkably free of abstraction, and Poppelbaum frequently framed his own observations in opposition to what he believed to be error-ridden biological abstractions: natural selection and genetics.

"Adaptation"—like Frank Lutz, Poppelbaum always placed the word in quotation marks—as perhaps the most sacred Darwinian dogma, received considerable rethinking by Poppelbaum. Working from an understanding of the astral body as the molder of characteristic animal shapes, Poppelbaum developed an approach to animal morphology that was free of the deterministic overtones of natural selection. Poppelbaum was just as astounded as any of his Darwinian peers by the fantastic fittedness of organisms to their environment, but he contemplated this amazing fact completely independently of any hypothetical struggle for survival. Form, that essential aspect of organisms that continues to elude mainstream biology, and that in the 1920s and 1930s was leading some biologists to reach for the concept of a morphogenetic field, was seen as a product of an additional supersensible member of the animal constitution—the astral body. Plants, possessed only of an etheric body, had no true physiognomy, only differing architectural plans. Animals, on the other hand, because their astral bodies welded their shape into an inseparable unity with their behavior, were seen by Poppelbaum as having distinct physiognomical characters. Each of the major animal phyla, classes, and families bore a characteristic "stamp."

As surely as Pfeiffer looked to Rudolf Steiner for indications as to the nature of the etheric formative forces, Poppelbaum relied on Steiner's teachings about the astral body to support his interpretations of animal morphology and behavior. Poppelbaum conceived of the astral body as an "individualizer," its principal function being to bring the environment into a deeper relation with each individual animal. A spider's web "belonged" to the spider's astral body, a hummingbird's beak to its preferred flowers, a cuckoo to its parasitized host. The entire realm of insect-plant mutualisms—from the exquisite fit between orchid corolla shapes and the heads of their pollinators to the striking instances of camouflage, mimicry, and other varieties of adaptive coloration—was seen as a consequence of the astral body. Within the bodies of individual organisms, the interrelation of organs was likewise understood to derive from the pervasive influence of the astral body.

Outrageous as the concept of the astral body may have appeared to his scientific peers—a sort of supersensible neo-Lamarckism—Poppelbaum's new zoology directly contradicted the crowning achievement of Darwinism: the insertion of the human being into the animal lineage. The hiatus between man and animal, as distinct as that between animal and plant, was marked by the addition of a final supersensible member—the "Ego." With the appearance of the Ego, the tyranny over animals by astral influences of the past and future was understood to have been overcome. In the space that the Ego created for itself, the free individual human being unfolded. As the most dramatic expression of the freedom of the human being from the deterministic confines of the animal, Poppelbaum pointed to the human form, whose very "non-adaptedness" he saw as the key to human freedom. Darwinians were wrong to assume some stage of incongruence between animals and their habitats, however fleeting; all animals are completely equipped, both morphologically and behaviorally, for the tasks that face them. For humans, however, there is always a gap between abilities and demands, and this inadequacy and incompetence, which in the animal would prove fatal, become the wellspring of each individual's humanness. On the human level, "life ceases to become a sequence of biological facts . . . [and] becomes a story, a biography." For animals, biography is impossible, because each individual animal is merely a specimen of a type. In humans, however, all that is generic becomes real only in and through the individuality.[4]

Poppelbaum, though turning mainstream zoological thought upon its head, credited Darwinism for its detailed portrayal of human history via the elucidation of biological lineages. But rather than seeing humans as a highly contingent uppermost branch on the tree of life, Poppelbaum—always acknowledging Rudolf Steiner's spiritual science as his guide—saw evolutionary history as the story of the absolutely inevitable becoming of human beings, "the changes of animal forms within successive geological epochs mark[ing] the drawing away of one veil after another from man's emerging image." To effect such a reorientation of outlook upon the evolutionary panorama, Poppelbaum asked his students to draw upon their newly awakened eye of the spirit, brought to life via the contemplation of human biography as a record of individual spiritual deeds. Just as one met the spiritual essence of a person in the record of his or her deeds, one met in nature the record of the deeds of higher spiritual beings.[5]

In Steiner's *Occult Science: An Outline* (1909), Poppelbaum and his audience found support for this radical approach to the history of life, both in its descriptive contents and in its methodological suggestions. As with all of Steiner's works, the book carried within itself the key to acquiring the very same knowledge outlined in the book. Available in English translation since 1914, *Occult Science* was considered one of the "basic texts" of anthroposophy and always enjoyed brisk sales at the summer conferences. Poppelbaum, more fully versed than Steiner in the details of the fossil record, elaborated upon the founder's narrative framework but remained faithful to its central idea that the most advanced forms of each geological epoch form a line describing the inevitable path to the human being. Conceiving of all of earth evolution as a materialization of the thoughts of spiritual beings, both Steiner's and Poppelbaum's occult evolutionary science emphasized the evolution of consciousness. At the beginning of the Paleozoic era, the Cambrian period was noted by Poppelbaum not for the explosion of biological forms but for the picture that both hard- and soft-shelled organisms gave of "trance-consciousness." The largely aqueous constitution, radial symmetry, and complete immersion in its surroundings that characterized the jellyfish, Poppelbaum asserted, was indicative of the weak degree to which the jellyfish was distinct from its surround. Perfectly integrated into its environment, the jellyfish was also perfectly unaware of its perfection. Poppelbaum interpreted the absence of a medial plane as a telltale sign of its lack of a focal consciousness. The hard shells of clams, trilobites, and other creatures marked a measure of opposition to the environment, but the outward rather than inward skeleton limited their independence and thus relegated them to the trance-consciousness stage.[6]

In the occult scientific view of evolution, humans were present from the very outset of the earth's evolution, but not as physical beings. Poppelbaum followed Steiner's chronological language in terming the Cambrian the "Polaric" age, and, like Steiner, he spoke of the material forms dwelling on Earth as a reflection of man's contemporaneous status, cradled as yet in the spiritual world.[7] While man held back from assuming a material form, the myriad invertebrates that made their appearance in the early Paleozoic did not. The advent in the Ordovician period of the first vertebrates—fish, with their axial skeletal organization and lateral line indicating a slightly more focused, "sleep-like" consciousness—Poppelbaum took as the beginning of the "Hyperborean" age. In the third stage of earth evolution, the "Lemurian" (Mesozoic), ethereal man slowly achieved selfhood and upright posture while his animal contemporaries dramatically pictorialized the struggle toward his advent. Poppelbaum interpreted the nightmarish contradictions of the saurian forms—atavistic elements, such as their relation to water, scaly bodies, and reptilian organization, combining with incipient developments, such as upright posture, supportive limbs, and even aerial forms (*Pterodactylus* and *Pteranodon*)—to represent premature expressions of the emergent human form.[8]

Toward the close of the Lemurian age, the modern classes of vertebrates were still "mixed" to a certain degree, as shown by intermediate creatures like the *Trachodon*, whose open pelvis, reduced dentition, and duck bill allied it with birds, its crude hands with the mammals. Only when the true birds and recent reptiles appeared in the Tertiary did the Lemurian end and the mammals emerge from the space between them. Poppelbaum marked as important the fact that man did not physically appear on Earth until there had been a full radiation of mammalian form. Then, in the "Atlantean" age (equivalent to paleontology's Cenozoic), after this "unfolding" of the mammals, nature's oldest creation, which had held back from physical incarnation, stepped forth as the human being. This notion of holding back was the key to Poppelbaum's human-centered zoology, for it explained all manner of animal forms. The creatures considered by conventional zoology as most manlike and thus fairly heroic—monkeys and apes—were regarded by Poppelbaum as pitiful shortfalls before the triumph of man. Their lack of individuality, semi-uprightness, limping, bent-kneed gait, and half-hands, half-feet were cruel reminders that they had not held back sufficiently. The tragedy found its most poignant expression in the transformation of the nearly human features of the fetal ape into the beastly visage of the adult.[9]

In his lectures on the new zoology at the summer conferences, Poppelbaum repeatedly described the fossil record as successive waves beating against the rocks of time, until man finally stepped ashore. His capacity for imagination was such that he discovered in each phylum forerunners of the individual elements of the human being's threefold nature. In shellfish, cuttlefish, and snail he found a metamorphic series developing the "formative gesture" of secrecy and repose that would find its final perfection in the human head. The segmentation of the worms, arthropods and vertebrates elaborated the architectural principles of the human trunk, the middle element of man's threefold organization. Only the highest vertebrates—birds and mammals—illustrated the third architectural element, man's supporting limbs.

Different Natures

Hermann Poppelbaum's new zoology differed as much from that practiced by mainstream scientists as anthroposophical ideas about curative education differed from eugenics. Poppelbaum argued that the need of scientific research was not for more facts—the Holy Grail of the Trailside Museum's pedagogical program—but for a radical reorientation of natural science. The foremost question facing natural scientists, Poppelbaum believed, was the relation between man and animal, and the solution to this question would conclusively overturn a whole host of the present era's predominant zoological theories and interpretations. Unlike his contemporaries at the American Museum of Natural History and elsewhere, Poppelbaum studied the human in order to understand animals, not the reverse.

As with the scientific research carried out by Frank Lutz at SSI, much of Poppelbaum's inquiry was directed toward understanding the nature of biological adaptation (the anthroposophic scientists actually eschewed the word *adaptation*, preferring *manifestation* instead). Adaptive coloration, for example, was explained as resulting from the animal body not being interpenetrated directly with an Ego, as the human astral body is; the animal was thought instead to be "in the grip" of its experiences, in a sort of dream state. The close interpenetration of the physical body by the astral in all animals accounts for the fact that an animal's experiences imprint themselves physiognomically into its shape, bringing the animal's morphology and physiology into supreme harmony with its environment. Although superficially appearing to be neo-Lamarckism, the fourfold conception—of a physical, etheric, astral, and "ego" body—distinguished the work of the anthroposophical scientists from their neo-Lamarckian contemporaries.

Poppelbaum shared Frank Lutz's fascination with animal sounds, but approached them through the concepts of anthroposophy. According to Poppelbaum, the toneless animals—those that can produce sound only with the outer parts of their bodies (cold-blooded animals, including crickets, cicada, grasshopper, frogs, salamanders, and snakes)—still retain in the present day the pictorial consciousness possessed by all animals at a former period of the earth's history. Only warm-blooded animals (birds, mammals, and man), free to varying degrees of this atavistic style of consciousness, could achieve genuine intonation.[10]

This picture consciousness was one in which an unequivocal correspondence existed between object and image, and as a theoretical underpinning it led to explanations undreamed of by behavioristically oriented ethologists. All of the striking "errors" of instinctual animal behavior, believed by behaviorists to be completely mechanical "reflex arcs"—a spider spinning silk around a vibrating tuning fork touching its web or dragonflies laying their eggs on freshly tarred roofs instead of calm pools of water—were not reduced to mechanical explanation. Rather, Poppelbaum and his students defended the life world of animals from mechanization; though certainly less "conscious" than the waking ego consciousness of humans, it is hardly machinelike. He also confronted the puzzle of the simultaneous rigidity and flexibility of animal behavior. Conventional animal psychology lacked a theory that could account for both kinds of behavior, the exquisitely adapted and the equally exquisitely unadapted.

Poppelbaum proposed an analogy with plants in the relationship between morphological types and their environment. Transplantation experiments showed that plant form is plastic; varying environments rapidly produce pronounced phenotypic variation. According to Poppelbaum, "the variation itself is no less peculiar to the genus than are the differentiae which determine it; another kind of environment evokes yet other modifications; until gradually, by multiplying the different external conditions, the invisible realm of innate tendency can be step by step explored and marked out. . . . The circumstance does not create the type; it only makes it visible; it assists it to manifestation." The reference to "type," "innate tendency," and the quest for the time sequence of form all marked Poppelbaum's thought as thoroughly "Goethean."[11]

Whether contemplating plant, insect, animal, or man, Poppelbaum never strayed far from the Goethean fascination with metamorphosis. His most familiar pedagogic gesture at the summer conferences was to sketch out on the blackboard some seemingly arbitrary biological sequence—at any one of a number of levels of organization, from individual organs to organisms, genera, or even phyla—and then proceed to knit them together into a whole. He approached each subject as if he were an artist, attentive to the myriad qualities of animal form.

Looking at mammals through the lens of metamorphosis, Poppelbaum might arrange such disparate species as a horse (hooved), a lion (predatory), a mouse (rodent), and a bat (flying mammal), seeing in the series a progressive mammalian leap from earthbound gravity to merger with air. Poppelbaum found the horse best viewed in profile, because its body is closely associated with the median plane; the observer best approached and understood the other animals of the series from the front, because each carried in its face, hands, and ears more of the characteristic stamp sought in this artistic search for the true nature of the animal. Surveying the shapes of aquatic mammals, Poppelbaum perceived a series leading down from the seal—bearing the unmistakably taut body of the carnivore—to the manatee—its body puffed up into formlessness—and ending in the whale, in whom the absence of hind limbs signified the severance of all relationship to the terrestrial environment. The brief embryonic vestige of teeth and their replacement by baleen in some whales Poppelbaum took to mean that "the earth-bound lime substance has lost its power over the skeleton." This reduced ossification was a result of the interplay of etheric formative forces, while the exaggerated size of the whale expressed the degree to which the astral body penetrated the physical-etheric organization.[12]

Poppelbaum took the same tack in his morphological analysis of individual animal organs and structures. Eschewing the Darwinian view of horns and antlers as primarily shaped by their use as weapons, he saw the horns as "dams" of the formative forces, stopping the growth of the front of the skull as did the teeth from below. Following Rudolf Steiner, Poppelbaum saw this barrier as indicative of the "reflecting" role of the horns, whose possessors—buffalo, bison, cattle—all had consciousnesses turned back upon themselves and thus took little interest in their environment. Antlers, on the other hand, reached out to the environment like antennae, expressing in physical form the greater "vivacity, awakeness and even nervousness" of the deer family: "The antlers open the organization of the bearer, the horns close it to the surrounding world." In such poetic formulations, Poppelbaum offered a different avenue for exploring the nature and action of the etheric formative forces.[13]

Each class of vertebrates was presented by Poppelbaum as having met, exceeded, or fallen short of, the human "level." The "rudimentary and smooth forebrain . . . primitive character of the excretory system . . . and the 'crippled' structure of the feet" told of birds having prematurely "rushed into a higher phase of existence" without having sufficiently shed their reptilian status. Reptiles, on the other hand, had fallen from the middle level of the human as far as birds had striven to rise above it. Turtle and tortoise shrunk the human form "to a lump of rock," while lizard and crocodile stretched it out into a tail. The snake abandoned all relationship to the earth, and hence lost its limbs entirely. The bird was a trunk which functionally had become a head. The tortoise carapace was molded in skull fashion. Lizards, with their candy-colored metallic dewlaps, went beyond birds "into the realm of the butterflies . . . [seemingly] painted by the luminous atmosphere itself." Finding "precursors" in the *Stegosaurus's* comb, *Corythosaurus's* crest, and *Pteranodon's* backward-pointing bony plate, Poppelbaum dismissed as superficial any argument that extant and extinct reptiles shared such structures with birds. All these vertebrates (and with these he also included the headgear of the Tibetan lama and other human adornments) drew upon the same "treasury of motifs." Members of Poppelbaum's audience frequently smiled nervously at such eccentric formulations and yet, with reflection, came to find them to possess their own wisdom.[14]

To illustrate his lectures, Poppelbaum never exhibited any live animals or even any skulls, skeletons, or stuffed specimens, native or exotic. Rather, Poppelbaum's menagerie was conjured in colored chalk. Silhouettes and skeletal structures appeared and then disappeared, as if fleeting phantoms of the etheric formative forces that produced them rather than the quick, certain motions of the lecturer's hand. On each day of the eight summers that Hermann Poppelbaum brought forth these forms for the small audience of anthroposophists at Threefold Farm, half an hour away, at the Trailside Museum, Bill Carr and his assistants would hold regularly scheduled demonstrations with native animals. While thousands of spectators were treated to an array of facts about the living animals at Trailside, at Threefold the listeners learned to bring Dr. Poppelbaum's living pictures into play when they met animals on their own in the field or in the silent setting of their minds.[15]

Snakes, the stars of the show at Trailside, were not left out of Poppelbaum's procession of animal form. The way downward into limblessness Poppelbaum painted through another metamorphic series, passing from the characteristic lizard of the Ramapos—the blue-tailed or five-lined skink, which, although preserving a lizard look, hinted at the snake in its elongated shape—to the short-tailed, Old World forms bearing stumps for legs, and finally to those that have only hind limbs or none at all. Poppelbaum stressed that in every one of these lizard lines the number of vertebrae increased as the extremities decreased in size. Limblessness, like all expressions of the animal form, was not mere adaptation. It was a degeneration: "The way towards the snake form must be viewed as the countermove to the contrasting ascent of the other reptile families and genera toward the realm of the birds."[16]

The innocent observer might have as easily accused Poppelbaum as Uncle Bennie Hyde or Bill Carr of projecting his inner attitude upon snakes, rather than reasoning his way to their true nature. Poppelbaum spoke of snakes' "devious stubbornness," of how "their whole being appears as the very embodiment of greed." He seemed to attribute a weird agency to snakes: "They treat all elements as if they were not yet divided. They behave as if the structure of nature's kingdoms still lingered on in an ancient chaotic phase. Indeed, the snakes have never actually set foot on the earth." While Uncle Bennie and Bill Carr attempted to exorcise humans' irrational fear of snakes, Poppelbaum found such fear wholly justified. Its lack of all head adornments—collars, combs, and crests of the sort found in lizards—indicated to Poppelbaum that the snake's astral body penetrated less fully into the formative forces of the body's periphery and was instead manifest in its urges and instincts, its motion and behavior. "In snakes . . . ferocity continues as a relentless drive which is prevented from running into form. . . . The snake . . . is malicious and treacherous, even in the morphology of its body. It refrains from fully manifesting its nature in the body, but keeps a large part of it lurking in the background." Upon hearing this, any zoologist from the American Museum of Natural History would have surely believed that it was Poppelbaum, not the snake, who lacked earthly grounding. To orthodox scientific contemporaries, this "new zoology" smacked of equal parts *Naturphilosophie* and sheer pseudoscience, seemingly having taken flight of its senses in its sincere striving for the supersensible.[17]

Goethean Science: A "Gentle Empiricism"

Poppelbaum, remembered by many as the most effective lecturer at the summer conferences, owing to his precise, clear, and economic use of his second language, easily mixed poetic images with scientific exactitude. He spoke of the animal as a "consummate response" and "a cue for which the life-sphere is waiting." Frequently his metaphors were full of pathos: "The animal form is like the goal for which the plant reaches out, but in vain." Although Poppelbaum took the human as the template for animal development, his language never turned into easy anthropomorphism; indeed, he chided those who claimed to portray individual experience among animals, saying that the so-called biography of the individual animal is actually "an exemplary life story of the species." Poppelbaum found in the Romantic musical metaphors of German ethologist Jakob von Uexküll a completely congenial and accurate vocabulary for overcoming the mechanistic conceptions of adaptationism. Von Uexküll spoke of "form-melodies" or "scent-and-color melodies" to portray the interconnected details of anatomy and function in the snapdragon; in adding to these the attunement of the bumblebee, von Uexküll heard a "duet, the musical score of which was pre-existent and has laid down the pattern for all future duets of the two." Poppelbaum felt that von Uexküll was intuitively groping for the concept of the astral body, which Rudolf Steiner had even spoken of as woven from "cosmic music."[18]

Each summer, Ehrenfried Pfeiffer brought to the plant world the same Goethean approach that Poppelbaum brought to the animal realm. Holding aloft one after another common garden or roadside plant—peonies, buttercups, shepherd's purse, and other mustards and cresses were favorites—Pfeiffer would ask his audience to follow the metamorphoses of the plant from cotyledon to seed: reduction in form, complication in form; expansion and contraction. Pfeiffer likened the polarities found in these serial vegetative transformations to the polarity of light and dark found by Goethe in his investigations into color. Polarity was a "creative principle," showing up at all levels of biological activity. The green plant experienced a "refinement" of form, color, and scent as it reached its final expansion into blossom before its final contraction into seed.[19]

Such language, along with a host of other expressions—"threefold" morphological schemata, "formative forces," and, particularly, the emphasis on polarity and metamorphoses—marked Pfeiffer's and Poppelbaum's science as a twentieth-century survival of eighteenth-century German *Naturphilosophie*. Or so it would appear from the outside looking in to the strange "science of the insides" cultivated originally at the Goetheanum in Dornach and now transplanted to American soil in Spring Valley. Indeed, the frequent hearkening to Goethe's spirit of scientific inquiry by Poppel-baum, Pfeiffer, and a host of other Threefold lecturers explicitly linked them to that paragon of Romantic natural science. Certainly Rudolf Steiner spared no effort to identify his spiritual science with "Goetheanism."

As might be expected, anthroposophists had (and continue to have) a view of *Naturphilosophie* very different from that of their peers. Rather than seeing this blossoming of German Romanticism as an embarrassing episode in intellectual history, they understood Goethe and at least some of his fellow *Naturphilosophen* to be both products of a long-running spiritual current in human history and antecedents of Rudolf Steiner's spiritual science.[20] If mainstream historians of science regarded Goethe and his rival Lorenz Oken (who claimed priority in the discovery of the vertebrate origin of the skull) as merely fellow travelers on the idealist path, anthroposophists forging a "Goethean" artistic or Steinerian "karmic" reading of Oken and Goethe would place these Jena neighbors on widely divergent roads.

During his years in America, Poppelbaum lectured on this subject on numerous occasions. Poppelbaum interpreted the battle between Oken and Goethe as something more than a clash of personal differences. Rather, he saw it as a battle over the very nature of natural science. He characterized Goethe's approach as a slow and careful consideration of phenomena, saying that, like the Greeks' form of haptic perception, his method of seeing was actually a "feeling into" nature. In Oken, ideas sprang forth fully formed, a vestige of the old intuitive knowledge and more like the subsequent barren scientific consciousness. Goethe's inflexibility, according to Poppelbaum, whether directed at Oken or Newton, expressed his firm belief in his own science as the one true path, a path that first Rudolf Steiner and, after him, Poppelbaum himself, along with Pfeiffer, Wachsmuth, and others, had taken up.

Poppelbaum showed a nuanced understanding of what is usually assumed to be the universal assumption of progress among the *Naturphilosophen*. He understood that there are always varying degrees of development, so that an individual might simultaneously be markedly advanced and retarded in different arenas of activity. Poppelbaum saw Oken as having failed to absorb the impulses of the Greek (fourth post-Atlantean) epoch; he was instead still in the karmic grip of the third post-Atlantean epoch, the Egypto-Chaldean-Babylonian. When Oken, the transformed Egyptian, encountered Goethe, the representative of the newly transformed Greek consciousness, sparks inevitably flew. As evidence of Oken's sensibilities, Poppelbaum noted that Oken published a magazine called *Isis* that carried pictures of Egyptian divinities on the masthead.[21]

This sort of historical explanation, like Poppelbaum's zoological observations, was within the realm of plausibility as an object of thought. To replicate such perceptions, or to add to them, the Threefold audiences understood that they had to cultivate a different state of consciousness. At the summer conferences, along with his zoological lectures, Poppelbaum also conducted a class on anthroposophical meditation. Meditation was the methodological hallmark distinguishing anthroposophy's occult science from orthodox natural science; it produced a state of being in which the knower could reach beyond the sensible to the supersensible. But even the manner of Poppelbaum's lectures, and particularly his endless formulations of metamorphic series in the animal kingdom, were cast in such a way as to facilitate the new consciousness. The fluidity of thought activity necessary to follow the sorts of sequences Poppelbaum outlined on the blackboard was an important bridge toward full etheric thought.

Rudolf Steiner had termed this new capacity of consciousness *Imagination*. But Steiner, Poppelbaum, Pfeiffer, Ernst Lehrs, and other spiritual scientists never hesitated to point out that Goethe had clearly identified his own form of cognition as *exakte sinnliche Phantasie*, "exact sensorial imagination." By this *zarte Empirie*, "gentle empiricism," Goethe had been led to a profoundly new understanding of nature, the one that permitted him to discover the vertebral origin of the skull, the intermaxillary bone, the archetypal plant, and the true nature of color. All of these were "boundary phenomena," instances where the seeming divide between subject and object yielded to the realization that the observer's intentionality is always present. Scientists working within a Goethean framework followed Goethe in their manner of foregrounding their own epistemological style when discussing their observations of natural phenomena. A critical philosophical premise of Poppelbaum and his peers was that contemporary human consciousness splits the world into concept and percept, giving rise to the illusion that man imports from "within" something that is foreign to the world "without." This epistemological premise meant that in studying the consciousness of animals, scientists had to be sensitive to the fact that their subjects are all blind to the concept. Poppelbaum used as an example Wolfgang Köhler's work with chimpanzees, which Köhler believed to show that chimps cannot "pick out" objects and thus cannot suitably substitute the proper tools when faced with certain mechanical problems. Poppelbaum framed his explanation of Köhler's experiments with this objection: what appear to be "new ideas" to animals—substituting a stick for a branch and so on—are not really concepts. Animals cannot unite percepts with concepts, thus penetrating reality, as humans do.[22]

Though few of the practitioners of Goethean phenomenology at Three-fold Farm thought of the observation exercises they followed under Poppelbaum's tutelage as "experiments," Goethe himself used this term to refer to the first stage in studying phenomena. Relying on the most vernacular, but most precise, apparatus—the senses—Goethe began his experiments by opening his senses as fully as possible to the phenomenon in question, while working to ensure the exclusion of theoretical constructs. Where Frank Lutz and Alfred Loomis put massive machinery between themselves and their subjects as they searched for the "invisibles" of nature, the scientists at Threefold were faithful to Goethe's maxim that "insofar as he makes use of his healthy senses, the human being is the greatest and most precise scientific instrument that can exist." There was no visible laboratory at Threefold Farm until 1952, but "experiments" in the Goethean sense went on invisibly.[23]

Anthroposophists understood Goethean science as a redemption of both the sensible and the supersensible. They also understood Goethe's as the archetype of the new etheric cognition for which they all strove. Indeed, Rudolf Steiner had explained Goethe's revolution in scientific thinking as a consequence of, as well as a path to, an etheric body freed from its physical fetters. Steiner, whose karmic research revealed to him that Goethe's desire to penetrate nature had been carried over from a previous incarnation, maintained that a severe illness that Goethe had suffered while in Leipzig as a young man had acted to loosen his etheric body. This illness was unmistakably karmic as well, since it prevented Goethe from becoming too deeply bound to the physical world he so wished to fathom. On the heels of this etheric loosening, Steiner said, at about the time of his encounter with Johann Gottfried von Herder, Goethe had been able to formulate a "systematic spiritual world conception," the first such formulation in modern times. Goethe's loosened etheric body created a condition whereby impressions from the physical world did not immediately make an impression on the physical body but rather produced a "softer," fluid thought pattern.[24]

Goethe was the precursor of the "water-man," bearer of the etheric consciousness that anthroposophists sought in themselves, not only to see Nature truly but also to go through Nature to God. Saint Paul's "Not I, but Christ in me," was a common goal at Threefold, but not in the sense of common Christian piety. To see Nature truly would lead to an experience of the Christ within, the watery man of the future, and from Poppelbaum and Pfeiffer the dedicated anthroposophist received essential training in becoming that water-man. As with the daily practice of the *Rückschau*, daily engagement with Nature's metamorphic activity—the contemplation of both the emerging and withering blossoms on plants, the artful picturing of series of animal morphologies, the observation of cloud forms—would precipitate the new consciousness of Nature and History the world so desperately needed in the twentieth century.

Spectatorship and the Battle for Human Consciousness

No one at Threefold Farm expected the new view of Nature to be easily won, any more than they expected an unimpeded path to a new view of History. If the adversarial powers were waging war to prevent the widespread recognition of Christ's etheric return, then they were sure to have prepared some means of derailing humanity from its proper task of gaining exact sensorial imagination of Nature. Once again, a mere glance across the Great Border Fault to Harriman Park brought the manifestations of this derailment into high relief. Instead of gentle empiricism, the natural scientists at SSI applied the thumbscrews of X rays and ultrasound to crickets and other creatures. In his entomological investigations, Frank Lutz employed the motion picture camera to freeze time, rather than cultivating the etheric capacity of creating one's own inner moving pictures, as Imagination led to the ability to enter into time. Bill Carr and the Trailside Museum staff each summer took natural history films to all of the park camps, letting the campers in on Nature's "secrets."[25]

Since coming to America, Hermann Poppelbaum had been greatly troubled by the triumph of passive spectatorship over active sensory cultivation. At the summer conference in 1940, he delivered a lecture entitled "The Dimming of Consciousness by Technology—in Particular by Motion Pictures." He began with a review of Rudolf Steiner's sensory and cognitive theory, and noted the error of nineteenth-century psychology in confusing the simple impression with the perception, and consequently failing to grant an active power to the soul. As an example, he pointed to the commonly accepted scientific belief that complementary colors arising in the eye are merely a quirk of the organism rather than, as Goethe believed, an indication of the active nature of the organ of perception. Poppelbaum saw this error as symptomatic of the fact that the active participation of our being in cognition had already begun to deteriorate. The onlooker consciousness theorized by nineteenth-century psychology had become the "gruesome" reality of the twentieth century: "In the nineteenth century people thought of themselves as spectators of their lives; in the twentieth century, through the catastrophes of the world wars and their sequel, they have become spectators in fact."[26]

All about him, Poppelbaum saw indications that the former vitality within human observation was being eclipsed. "Impartial observation, once the pride of the natural scientific age, is dwindling. . . . In the exact sciences it has become the ground rule to exclude as much as possible the supposedly subjective perception. It has become almost an obsession to replace the observing human being by recording instruments. Even in the field of biology man's distrust of the senses is increasing—a distrust which Goethe already felt to be an injustice perpetrated against our humanity." The journalistic obsession with facts combined with humanity's superficial reading to erode the human memory capacity critical for the new etheric consciousness. Photographs only added to this erosion: "They become a surrogate for inner living pictures, won from an active experience of reality. Unrelated to us, still they sink down into us, impairing our vitality." Urban life's visual gewgaws—shop windows, signs, and, in particular, advertisements—"sink down in us unexperienced, and slip away, separated from the 'I,' a reservoir of disease-breeding waste products in the living body."[27]

The most destructive of influences, however, the technology that virtually embodied the antithesis of all that Goethean and spiritual science strove for, was the motion picture. Billboards, newspapers, and magazines merely gave single vicarious pictures to the modern person's dulled consciousness. But film's "flood of impressions intrudes between the viewer and his world at such speed that any response by the soul is made impossible." Poppelbaum's critique was based on film's effect on the etheric body: "Instead of being bound to man's living time-nature [the etheric body] each single picture sinks down into that isolated region below memory, the gathering place of all our undigested impressions and reactions." Poppelbaum believed that modern humanity's sense of time was also being corrupted. He condemned slow-motion and time-lapse photography: "Though people say 'Wonderful! Now I can see how a flower grows!' precisely the opposite occurs, they see how a flower does not grow. It belongs to the nature of the plant for its shape and growth to be motionless for a beholder." As when Goethe grasped the nature of the archetypal plant, etheric cognition properly supplies the movement from within, rather than consuming it from without.[28]

Indeed, many of the activities at Threefold Farm—eurythmy, form drawing, Poppelbaum's observational exercises—were explicitly directed toward counteracting the deleterious effects of the modern world's harmful schooling in perception. Every human mind was a battleground where the new etheric consciousness would be either won or lost, and natural science as presently constituted was a formidable enemy. In the anthroposophical view of history, this battle had been going on forever. In order to understand the history of natural science, Poppelbaum, like Pfeiffer, challenged his audience to abandon conventional history and attempt a morphological reading of the past, in a manner not unlike the method he taught of reading the contemporary natural landscape. The historical portraits Poppelbaum drew were as artful and outlandish as those he offered for zoological contemplation. To explain Charles Darwin's theory of natural selection, Poppelbaum began with a blackboard illustration of an elaborate ornamental Islamic arch of the eighth century C.E. Next to it he drew a simple Romanesque arch of the same period. Although the Islamic ornamentation at first glance looked more "alive," with the arabesques mimicking plant tendrils, further study showed them to have a "sham vitality" because the whole form was composed of mere mechanical repetition rather than organic growth.[29]

For his next picture of medieval Arabic thinking he brought forth a mechanical horse from *A Thousand and One Nights*. Arabian culture, he noted, along with being the first to introduce mechanical toys, invented the "abstract doctrine of a single God." Mohammedism taught that everything, including human fate, was blindly subject to this singularly remote Allah. This fatalism drove Arab fanaticism in battle, and Muslims quickly conquered northern Africa and penetrated into Europe, prematurely bringing to that region of the world the first formulation of modern natural science. Although this Arab onslaught against Middle Europe was eventually repulsed in the physical world, it continued on the spiritual plane. A thousand years later, when the Consciousness Soul—the proper fashioner of modern natural scientific thought—was destined to be born, individuals were incarnated who bore within them the Arabian spiritual impulse from a former earth life.[30]

Evolutionary theory, the "child of the eighteenth century," was meant to be brought to term by Goethe's science, which had been nurtured previously during the Greek cultural epoch. Goethe's living thinking, his sense of inner plastic forms, was the rebirth in human thought of the living Greek dome. The arid, abstract intellectual system that supplanted Goetheanism—Darwinism—was more like a "vault made of stalactites." Whereas Goetheanism brought the observer within the flow of actual biological processes, Darwinism developed completely out of thinking and established not what *is* but what is merely thinkable: "Darwin is not interested in structural laws, but in deviations of individuals. His law is not developed, but deciphered from a mosaic-like arrangement of a multitude of data." Poppelbaum characterized Darwin's *Beagle* journey, his relentless collect-

ing activity, and his embrace of Malthus as full of intellectual power, particularly in its deductive capacity. But he lamented that "it presents only
the plausible. It does not examine and contemplate, it only calculates from
detachment." Darwin's huge accumulation of facts, and his attempt to digest these economically in the *Origin of Species*, Poppelbaum likened to
the endless variations on the same theme so apparent in Arabic art, "the
filling out of large surfaces with the repetition of a single motif."[31]

As he did in nearly every one of his Threefold Farm lectures,
Poppelbaum asked his audience to allow the picture he had given of Darwinism to "work on" them. Doing so, they would find that the implication
of natural selection is that life is dictated by "an infinitely remote, invisible, and incomprehensible will. . . . An Allah, translated into total abstraction, who reigns with a fickle will among the vast and implacable laws of
nature" is the spirit of the theory of natural selection. As such, Darwin's
theory of natural selection was the reincarnation of the medieval Arabic
doctrine of predestination. Like that doctrine, Darwinism "reduces the
whole process of evolution to an absurd and insulting futility, which might
amuse some far-detached being, but which, for its incomprehensibility, men
can only fear." Darwinism, the fundamental underpinning of the modern
world-conception, obliterated freedom, obliterated meaning, and darkened
the human spirit at a moment when, through Goethean science, it was meant
to enter an age of light.[32]

Poppelbaum noted one final tragic similarity between modern scientific thought and the influence of "Arabism": the lack of representation of
the human being in Islamic art. Centuries later, at the hands of Darwin and
other reincarnated spirits of the medieval Arabian cultural epoch, humanity was once again banished from its rightful place in the cosmos. Directing human attention to Darwin's "tangled bank," scientific Naturalism in
the early twentieth century aimed to exact a full picture of the world's biotic complexity from the physical senses and their technological extensions.
Especially in America, the beauty and integrity of that tangled bank was
felt to be most sublime when human beings were banished from the scene.
Even as the Ramapos became the playground for millions of metropolitans, the *idea* of wilderness, and the occasional opportunity for serendipitous encounters with the nonhuman Other, made Harriman Park a perfect
setting for the new Naturalism. The natural science cultivated at Threefold
Farm also aspired to a correct and complete view of the tangled bank, but
sought to keep the human being always part of the picture, not as a *product* of nature but as the *producer* of nature. Engaged in a battle to van-
quish Arabism, to defeat Darwinism, to restore and re-enliven nature and

history through the redemption of the senses, the anthroposophists at Three-fold Farm, like the scientists of the American Museum of Natural History, were keen to develop pedagogical strategies to pass along the tools and methods that would enable a correct understanding of nature and of the proper place of humans within nature. Goethean science began its course of nature-study instruction for children with fairies instead of facts.

CHAPTER 7

Reenchanting Nature

ANTHROPOSOPHICAL NATURE STUDY

Created Out of Light

At the edge of the lawn spilling down from the front of the main house at Threefold Farm, Virginia Birdsall gathered a dozen children around a daisy. She asked them to turn and lift their faces, like the daisy, toward the sun: "See how the daisy longs to give itself up to the sun. Like us, plants are children of the Sun, and though their roots bury themselves deep in the dark ground, the blossom lifts itself into the light." Just then a Poplar Admirable danced past the group and landed briefly in the nearby grass before lifting off again, and the teacher recited from memory a few lines of Rudolf Steiner's poem, "A Secret of Nature": "Behold the plant! / It is the butterfly bound fast to earth / Behold the butterfly! / It is the plant set free by the universe." As this poetic image sank in, Miss Birdsall reached down and with her fingernail sliced open the seedpod of a nearby cress, spilling the tiny ripening seeds into her palm. She likened the seeds to butterfly eggs and then suggested that the caterpillar who emerged from the egg eventually came to look like the tender new shoot of a green plant, that the chrysalis could be likened to a swelling flower bud.

Miss Birdsall guided the children's attention toward a half dozen turtlehead plants along another margin of the lawn, noting the way the upper flowers remained closed, chrysalis-like, while the lower blossoms opened out into face-like forms, complete with lips, tongues, mouths, and throats. As they inspected the plants, one child cried out in delight, having found a golden chrysalis clinging to the stem below the blossoms. Miss Birdsall told the children how the earthbound caterpillar was drawn to the sunlight by the same urge that drew moths and other insects to throw themselves into the candle's flame; but because the chrysalis could not reach the sun, it spun its own body into light in the form of its silk cocoon. "When you find a chrysalis you are finding pure sunlight spun into gold. When the butterfly emerges from this chrysalis, it is created out of light. All animals are created out of light, and so are we human beings."

Miss Birdsall said nothing of the etheric body of the caterpillar or of the astral forces that worked into the chrysalis, weaving the colors that would shine forth in the imago. She did speak of the ego, the "I." While they had their "I" inside them, she told the children, the butterfly had its "I" outside, in the light that brought forth the brilliant hues of the butterfly. "Every time you say 'I' to yourself a little invisible flame lights up in your brain, and it is this same light that colors the butterfly's wings. If the light inside us were not held fast, but could spill out in to the whole world of Nature, it would create butterflies. We could all make real butterflies with our 'I.'"[1]

Skirting an area of rich damp soil flanking Oost Val Brook, the group encountered a thicket of stinging nettles. This was a plant "full of fire," Miss Birdsall warned the children; it wasted none of its fire in flower production, for its flowers were tiny and almost colorless. A few of the children accepted their teacher's challenge to experience the plant's fire by striking their flesh against the nettle's stinging leaf-hairs. Miss Birdsall pointed out that almost no flying insects visited the nettle's flowers but that two beautiful butterflies—the Peacock and the Small Tortoise-Shell—laid their eggs in the nettle. The caterpillars took into themselves the fiery force of the plant, becoming after metamorphosis the nettle's flowers flying about in the air. "The nettle reminds one of those people who, unnoticed by anyone, are always doing good. They are, like the nettle, possibly even disregarded and misunderstood, because they seek no renown and no position. But if you consider what they bestow upon other human beings, then you recognize how worthy of reverence they are."[2]

Education as an Art

In the early 1920s, Threefold Group member Virginia Field Birdsall had been on the staff at Miss Baird's School, an exclusive elementary school in Montclair, New Jersey. In 1923, while attending an educational conference in Ilkley, England, she heard Rudolf Steiner deliver an inspired course of lectures that was later published as *A Modern Art of Education*. Along with a dozen or so other New York City–area anthroposophists who taught at "progressive" private institutions, Birdsall longed for a school where she might fully practice Steiner's pedagogical ideas. In 1929, with Irene Brown, Arvia MacKaye, and others, she helped found the Rudolf Steiner School in Manhattan. Although she left the New York area in 1941 to help start the third American Waldorf school, Kimberton Farms in Pennsylvania, Birdsall was an important pioneer in the planting and nurturing of anthroposophical nature study in its formative American environment, namely, Manhattan and its Ramapo hinterland of Threefold Farm. Whether in the Ramble in Central Park or in the oak woods of Spring Valley, Virginia Birdsall could often be found leading nature walks of a very different sort from the ones conducted at the Trailside Museum.

As with American anthroposophists' understanding of etheric geography, esoteric history, and the new zoology, nature study for children came to America directly from Dornach and Stuttgart. When the Rudolf Steiner School was founded, most of Steiner's pedagogical lectures, and all of the works by European authors inspired by his ideas, had yet to be translated into English. In developing her nature study program for the Steiner School, Birdsall turned particularly to the work of Gerbert Grohmann, whose *Kleine Pflanzenkunde* (*Little Plant Studies for Children*) closely followed the indications given by Steiner. Grohmann, who had studied natural sciences at the University of Tübingen and received a doctorate in botany from Leipzig University, published his first book, *Die Pflanze*, in 1921, after he was already well acquainted with anthroposophy. He wrote seven more books and many essays, all on botany and pedagogy. Virginia Birdsall's Goethean approach—her close attention to qualities and her phenomenological language, which was almost intuitive for the children—was mediated largely through her acquaintance with Grohmann's writings, which she energetically translated.

Until Hermann Poppelbaum arrived in the United States, Virginia Birdsall almost single-handedly carried on anthroposophical nature study in America. Her attendance at Steiner's 1923 lectures had placed before her a pedagogical philosophy and methodology very different from the ones she knew from American developmental psychology of the day. Instead of G. Stanley Hall's crude evolutionism, Steiner's "Modern Art of Education" lectures were imbued with a spiritual scientific viewpoint. Still, they were everywhere "evolutionary"; indeed, the entire thirteen-lecture sequence unfolded in an evolutionary fashion. The introductory lectures looked back to Greek times, when pedagogy was still a unity of knowledge, art, religion, and morality; but they also looked to the present necessity of reactivating the creative fundament of Greek thought in its modern, sense-free form of Imagination. The middle lectures covered the ways in which the physical changes in the growing child both reflected and initiated transformations in the child's relationship to the spiritual world. The theory of the etheric body was central to these lectures, which covered such key topics as the shedding of the first set of teeth and the transfer of physically con-structive forces into the power of thought. During the child's second seven-year period, marked by the onset of puberty, astral forces were set free of the body, and Steiner counseled the assembled teachers on how to aid the independence of this second supersensible member of the growing child.

Steiner's pedagogical lectures alternated between topics in the same sort of living rhythmicity that anthroposophy claimed to be the goal of the new etheric thought, and they were filled with suggestions about how best to cultivate the timely and proper emergence of each child's potential. Com-pared with many contemporaneous educational philosophies, Steiner's ideas seemed simple, if not simplistic. Steiner maintained that the three funda-mental faculties each child needed to develop during the first three years of life were walking, speaking, and thinking. Speaking was seen as a prod-uct of walking, and thinking, a consequence of speech. Careful attention to the teaching of walking, and to the manner of speech in a child's pres-ence, were essential steps on the path to healthy cognition. Above all, Steiner warned of the dangers of promoting intellectual training prematurely; such training before the age of five would lead to the development of material-ism in the child. Each child must be left in his or her "gentle, dream-like existence as long as possible," declared Steiner.[3]

Throughout the Ilkley lectures, and throughout the Waldorf schools, the teacher's attention always returned to the manner in which art was to be employed in education. Steiner spoke of the ideal teacher as a sculptor, forever aspiring to release the forms inherent in each child. Releasing the forms through artistic activity extended to the teaching of reading, writ-ing, and nature study, which Steiner considered together in a single lec-ture. In Waldorf pedagogy, reading came only after the study of writing, which was approached pictorially, encouraging the child first to picture mentally a variety of physical qualities: "water" and "wave" led to the draw-ing of the "w"; "mouth" to the "m"; "fish" to the "f." Vowels were intro-duced by their respective gestures—"a" ("ah") communicating wonder, for example—that expressed the human's inner being. Only after these ex-tremely concrete steps had been mastered was the abstraction of reading introduced.

The measured introduction of abstraction was especially apparent in Steiner's approach to nature study. Placing the advent of the self/not-self distinction by the child at age nine, Steiner stressed that, up until that age, all outer elements of Nature should be met as living beings, not abstrac-tions. This stricture was especially critical for the child's encounter with plants, which formed the basis of anthroposophical nature study in grades one and two. Steiner was adamant about avoiding all modern geological concepts in the early years, because they led to the erroneous conception of the earth as a mineral entity rather than a living being. Steiner's lectures were filled with critiques of the "scientific" method of nature-study pedagogy: "Living ideas cannot be roused if we only give the child what is nowadays called 'science'—the dead knowledge which we so often find teaches us nothing! Rather must we give the child an idea of what is living in nature. . . . We shall foster a living, growing soul in a living, growing physical organism—and this alone serves a true development."[4]

Animals joined the nature-study curriculum only after this first year of immersion in the green, watery, etherically formed world of plants. Just as Grohmann's fundamental principles were contained in Steiner's brief indications in this single lecture, the entire research program that Hermann Poppelbaum would conduct in later years was distilled into seminal formulations in this same lecture. Starting from the human being's threefold organization, Steiner sketched out the beginnings of anthroposophical biogeography, paleontology, and ecology. Clear foreshadowings of Poppelbaum's ideas were everywhere apparent: the perception of the "headlike" forms of primitive invertebrates; the threefold partitioning of taxonomic groupings of vertebrates; and, most important, the human being as the synthesis of the three systems—head, chest, and limbs/metabolism—reflected in the animal world.

Waldorf teachers aimed to guide students to learn to read two "books": the Book of Nature (Geographia) and the Book of Civilization (Historia). In the Geographia curriculum, grade one introduced the plant world, grade two, animals; grade three revolved around the seasons; grade four began a study of geography. The Historia curriculum recapitulated the evolution of human storytelling, from fairy tales (grade one) to fables and legends (grade two) to the Hebrew Bible (grade three) and Greek and Norse mythology (grade four). The two curricula were paced to nurture the imagination and culminated, in grade four, with the beginning of the "Man and Animal" curriculum developed by Poppelbaum, Eugen Kolisko, and other associates of Steiner. Waldorf teachers were trained to make every effort to give children the opportunity to observe phenomena for themselves before drawing conclusions. This Goethean phenomenological approach extended to the common practice in upper grades of refraining from discussing an experiment until the following day, when the necessary etheric impression had matured.

Systematic, taxonomic study of plants was introduced in grade five, and study of the physical sciences—geology, mineralogy, chemistry, physics—commenced in grade six. These sciences were also approached in an evolutionary, recapitulationist fashion, beginning with acoustics, since

Pythagoras' laws of acoustics were the first natural laws established. Chemistry study avoided all mention of atomic and molecular theories because these violated Goethean phenomenology. In high school, the succession of subjects was reversed, beginning with nonorganic nature and concluding with animals, plants, and earth history. This reversal reflected the increasing ontological distance from the surrounding world won by the mature teenager.

Facts versus Fairies

Rudolf Steiner was relentless in his critique of modern science's "disenchantment" of Nature, ironically suggesting that in its quest for "fact" science actually had created a completely erroneous picture of the natural world. Modern biological theory's ignorance of the role of the etheric formative forces in the creation and maintenance of life, Steiner likened to medieval notions of preformation:

> The professor . . . still believes in the egg as containing everything. . . . Contemporary science no longer has any knowledge of what works in air, light and water. It knows nothing at all about it. You see, this is something which already sorely rankles our social life; this fact that on the one side we have a science that really disregards the entire cosmos and only has eyes for what can be seen through the microscope and, on the other side, a State that takes no interest in the pensioner nor has any further use for him beyond paying his pension. The same thing applies in the case of the scientist who extracts means of nourishment from Nature, but no longer understands its working and only concerns himself with the microscope, in other words, just with parts. Science today really regards the whole cosmos as an idler who has been pensioned off. . . . Nature is referred to as someone now "on the shelf." Thus the whole of our spiritual life is being swamped, and the time has now come when we must emerge. We do not progress for the simple reason that the general public finds it easier to accept what it hears. The truth today is told only by Anthroposophy![5]

For early childhood study of nature, Steiner stressed the need to present the natural world in the form of stories:

> This is how we must teach children, instead of the horrible way in which elementary zoology is drubbed into them! We must tell of special things done by the lion, the fox, the ant, the ladybird, and

so forth. Whether these things have actually taken place, is not the chief point; what matters is that they should be full of sense. What we drive into children's heads today, is an extract of natural science; this must come later, when the children have fed themselves on tales which deal with the individual aspect in animal-life.

Mainstream nature study in the early twentieth century, such as the program developed at Trailside Museum, intuited this need for narrative and the usefullness of relating to the "individual" in animals. But Steiner's program called for stories far outside the parameters of his contemporaries: "It will be very important to consider the life of the plants also in this way . . . to tell [children] long, long stories of how the little spirits leap over the flowers when we go across a field, and similar things. Botany should be taught to children in this way."[6]

In addition to her efforts to bring European scientific ideas into the American sphere, Birdsall, along with fellow Steiner School teacher Margaret Peckham, worked to build a complementary body of nature stories. For the early grades, Steiner had stressed the importance of "fairy stories," not the sort fashioned by writers like J. M. Barrie, but fairy tales that communicated the original sense of both a diversity of fairy forms and the important creative role played by fairies within Nature. In "The Four Elements," a boy who committed a selfish act was deserted by his fairy helpers, but he was later saved from a giant's kettle by a gnome. Children learned how each of the four elements—earth, air, water, and fire—had its respective fairy form in gnome, sylph, undine, and salamander. In "How the Little Flowers Grow," the springtime awakening of plants was presented not as the result of inanimate forces of energy but as the particularized task of animate beings. Gnomes awakened the seeds and rootlets out of their winter sleep and taught them how to grow and transform themselves into the variegated shapes of growing plants. Undines created just the correct sap for each plant and collaborated with the gnomes to ensure that the right amount of minerals were taken up. Then the undines handed over the labor to the sylphs, who had the task of "painting" the leaves and flowers and deciding upon the proper perfume. Finally, Fire Spirits (salamanders) formed the fruit and seed: "They gathered warmth and loaded it on the filaments of the blossoms as though on tiny ships. Then the warmth of the sylphs drew down into the calyx of the flowers and created the fruit out of the fruit knot. They turned the blossoms into all the good cherries, pears, apples and thousands of other fruits and little seed cases and penetrated them with warmth inside and outside so that they might ripen."[7]

In fact, this fairy tale distills the fundamental tenets of anthroposophical views of the "elemental beings," the variety of etheric entities that together sustain Earth as a living planet. Rudolf Steiner taught that just as there is an etheric body behind the human physical body, there is an etheric body behind the whole of physical nature. In humans the etheric body is a unity; Nature's etheric body, on the other hand, is "infinitely multiform," a plurality consisting of many differentiated etheric beings. As in his formulation of so many other modern spiritual scientific concepts, Steiner employed the traditional language of Middle Europe for his vocabulary of the elemental world. Indeed, the term *elemental world* is itself drawn from medieval European writers like Paracelsus. When he spoke about the fairy world, Steiner claimed to be working out of the same absolute empiricism that informed his descriptions of the angelic hierarchies or the Akashic Record; he swore to present only "the dry facts."[8]

Steiner's preliminary statements about "nature spirits"—which he qualified as an inadequate name, given that elemental beings consist only of body and soul, not spirit—conformed to traditional accounts associating gnomes with earth, sylphs with air, undines with water, and salamanders with fire. But they also systematized the elementals' activity in relation to the organic substrate upon which all animal life depended—green plants. Just as in Birdsall's fairy tale "How the Little Flowers Grow," Steiner told how the gnomes could be found working within the earth, undines in the growing and transforming plant, sylphs at the blossoms, fruit, and maturing seed, and salamanders at the germination of the new plant. Steiner's descriptions seemed to hover between the phantasmagoria of folk accounts of fairies and the dry factuality he always strove for in his presentations of the supersensible world. Though ordinary science conceived of plant growth as directed upward from forces below, Steiner saw the undines—who were especially active outside the plant world at springs, waterfalls, and other sites of falling water—as "drawing forth" the plants. Sylphs "have no form of their own at all . . . flashing up like lightning . . . [they] flit over the earth, flashing and vanishing like meteors or little will-o'-the-wisps." Salamanders were actually created by the formation of intimate relationships between humans and animals—a rider and his steed, the shepherd and his flock, a child and her pet. Salamander elementals found "nourishment" from these relationships and in return, gave to humans helpful "recipes or prescriptions." Gnomes, which could be seen at many spots in the depths of the earth, "appear to 'burst asunder' when the earth is broken into, from an original clustering together in vast numbers. They actually become larger rather than 'fly apart.'"[9]

Like all other creatures in the Great Chain of Being, nature spirits had a discrete hierarchy of bodily members. Gnomes, the lowest of the elementals, did not possess an ego, astral, or etheric body; the physical body was their highest member. Undines ranked next, with two bodily members at the level of the physical. Sylphs ranked above them, and salamanders approached the human being, since all four members of their body were at or above the level of the physical world. Lacking egos of their own, all of the elemental beings were under the direction of subangelic astral beings called "devas" (drawn from Hindu terminology, the Sanskrit word meant "shining ones"). To become useful to the devas, nature spirits had to permit themselves to be "enchanted" by the devas into the physical world. (Steiner also decribed elementary beings as "charmed," "bewitched," "chained," and "imprisoned.") By this enchantment—really a form of sacrifice on the part of the elementals—the physical world took on its forms.

The devoted sacrifice of elemental beings into states of enchantment is symmetrical with the activity of all spiritual beings, including humans, in that they ultimately seek to become unified with the Hierarchies. Nature spirits were seen by Steiner to bring knowledge of the earth to the devas, thus placing the lowly elementals and the mighty shining ones in a symbiotic relationship. Steiner spoke of how salamanders, sylphs, undines, and gnomes all delighted in their own demise: "Undines and sylphs have a need for death. They feel they only have a life when they die. Dying is really the beginning of life for them as they stream out of earthly matter to offer themselves to higher beings as nourishment." Steiner described how in summer, as the Baltic Sea "blossomed" with the odor of putrefying fish, undines ascended toward the Hierarchies, borne aloft on the dissolution of matter. Elementals participated in the spiritual ascension of bird song, which rose to the highest level of the Hierarchies, the Seraphim, and then was sent back "as a blessing for man." Dying birds poured astral substance into the air, and sylphs bore this astrality aloft, "flash[ing] like blue lightning through the air . . . and dart[ing] up like lightning flashes to be inhaled by the beings of the hierarchies."[10]

Steiner's extravagant descriptions of elementals were not unprecedented. In their basic outlines—the association of each class of nature spirits with one of the elements, the ability of gnomes to change their size instantly, their helpfulness to human beings and the gods—these descriptions were consistent with ancient hermetic tradition, as well as with the growing body of modern theosophical teachings concerning nature spirits. But while authors like Helena Blavatsky, Charles W. Leadbeater, Edward L. Gardner, and Geoffrey Hodson offered detailed accounts of the nature spirits in settings from all over the world, their descriptions lacked Steiner's systematic incorporation of these etheric beings into a compelling drama of world evolution. As demonstrated by his elucidations of human and cosmic evolution, Steiner had a stunning vision of the evolutionary history of one class of elementals, especially in their relationship to human progress. Each human being, ever struggling to resist the temptations of Ahriman (to go too deeply into the physical world) and of Lucifer (to flee the physical for the spiritual world), had sixteen possibilities to merge his individuality with the leading spirit of humanity—Christ. Those who faltered, taking the "sixteen paths of perdition," fell out of the evolutionary process, to appear in some later epoch with the characteristics of an earlier age.

Subsequent to the earth stage of human evolution, once humanity had completed the development of the fifth bodily member—*manas*, or "life-spirit"—the leading race of humanity would no longer possess a physical body. In this future "Jupiter" stage, only those humans who had taken the "sixteen false paths" would remain at the level of the physical body. They would appear as "the hideous forms of the retarded beings with egoistic demands for love and they will be the devastating powers in the Jupiter existence." Steiner explained that some of the nature spirits of our present time had arrived at their rank within Nature via this same process of "falling behind" the proper tempo of evolution toward the higher hierarchies of the spiritual world. "Thus we see how the world is woven, harmful elements as well as beneficent; we have a moral element woven into the world process."[11]

Reenchantment and Redemption

While Virginia Birdsall and Margaret Peckham were cultivating a nature-study curriculum founded upon respect for and understanding of the fey folk of the etheric world, American educators were consciously striving to banish fairies from the mental world of the child. Contemporaneous with Bill Carr's efforts to "feed 'em on facts" on the nature trails at Harriman Park, articles in professional journals and popular magazines polemicized against folklore and fairy tales for fostering illusions about the physical world. None of the advocates for fairy stories ever suggested that such beings as nature spirits actually existed and that fledging children on fairy tales prepared them to understand the natural world properly; their argument invariably centered on the desirability of imaginative tales as aids for encouraging creativity in children.[12]

In the early twentieth century the Brothers Grimm remained the richest source of fairy lore, and Waldorf-educated children in both Europe and America were most likely to learn about the "little people" from retellings of their tales. But beginning with the phenomenal popularity of theatrical performances of J. M. Barrie's *Peter Pan* in the 1910s and 1920s, and culminating in Walt Disney's domestication of the fairy world in the animated films *Snow White and the Seven Dwarfs* (1937), *Fantasia* (1940), and his own rendering of *Peter Pan* (1953), fairies experienced a rapid process of "disenchantment" in the modern world. Although theosophical writers and romantics like William Butler Yeats and Walter Yeeling Evans Wentz celebrated nature spirits as real, and folklorists continued to collect descriptions of fairies from traditional cultures around the globe, the Western imagination denied the existence of such beings while at the same time creating a sentimentalized caricature as a substitute.

At Threefold Farm, fairies were not merely for children; the adult curriculum of nature study also incorporated fairies and other elemental beings. Ehrenfried Pfeiffer routinely referred to elemental activity in his lectures, and when out walking with certain people, he would stop and describe his past experiences of elementals at particular sites.[13] Pfeiffer described gnomes as protean beings whose heads shape-shifted in relation to the task being carried out; thinking of a triangle, sphere, or pyramid, the gnome changed its head to assume that shape. Because of their variability of form, one could frequently become confused, believing that one had observed different gnomes when really there had been only one. One sure field identification mark was that the gnomes' appearance reflected the local bedrock type. While limestone regions were inhabited by "pure and transparent" gnomes, gneiss areas like the Ramapos supported less beautiful gnomes.[14]

Pfeiffer emphasized the degree to which all gnomes—those of Hierarchical origin, those born of the fallen angels Lucifer and Ahriman, and particularly those created by human beings' thoughts and feelings—experienced to a certain degree the inner activity of the human race: "In its outer work this gnome would depend entirely upon the particular forces of nature. In its inner development, however, this gnome would be influenced by the thought life of man. He would feel or think, or rather, experience pain or joy in connection with his surroundings or his particular task. The gnomes are especially sensitive to theoretical, abstract thoughts which are not connected with reality. They are especially amused by man's so-called scientific theories." In Pfeiffer's experience, "Everything connected with materialism and intellectualism, the hunt for money, questions of physical power on this earth (political questions), all thoughts and emotions of men regarding this sphere increase the disturbance in the elementary world. . . . If there are one or more human beings devoting their thoughts to questions of eternity, the elemental beings feel a relief and lose more or less of their worries."[15]

When human beings were wracked by materialistic, selfish, fearful thoughts, the elementary beings who were charged with maintaining the proper relations of the earth's etheric body went wild, and the results ranged from cancer to insect and fungal infestations to the disruption of regional and global climatic patterns. A close observer of local weather conditions and their influence on his biodynamic garden at Threefold Farm, Pfeiffer regularly reported that abnormal weather resulted from human action. The freak weather patterns in the spring and early summer of 1941, he explained, were caused by a group of elemental beings who were charged with providing Europe and America with adequate moisture and warmth; their aberrant activity he attributed to human behavior "a few years back," no doubt referring to the eruption of fascism and its companion pathologies in the mid-1930s.[16]

On his very first trip to America in 1933, Pfeiffer had executed a comparative study of the elementals of Europe, the Atlantic Ocean, and America, making a series of drawings that he occasionally used to illustrate his lectures. His observations confirmed Steiner's research, which posited that the elementary world of Europe—save certain remote regions like northern Scotland, Norway, and the Swiss Alps—was more "refined" than that of North America, which tended to be "rather uneducated and naughty." Though this sounded like unabashed German chauvinism, Pfeiffer explained that the difference was based upon fundamental variations in geological forces and upon the spiritual background of the two continents. American elementals were "younger" in both respects than their European counterparts. The relatively younger age of the North American landscape, particularly in its more extensive region of Pleistocene glaciation, was compounded by the relatively youthful age of human settlement upon the continent. In Europe, many millennia of human cultural achievements—from Greek art and architecture to the music of nineteenth century composers—had "educated" the elementals, refining and spiritualizing them:

> [Elementals] find . . . [recreation and balance] in the contemplation
> of human art. . . . All this explains why certain European elemen-
> tal beings are old, i.e., wiser or more educated, as compared with
> certain beings especially living in water or air in the North Ameri-
> can continent. The latter have not had the chance to see the beauty
> of art and have not been present at one of those mystery
> centers . . . [such as Ephesus or Delphi]. To give an example in the
> form of a picture, they make hungry and pitiful impressions, often
> behaving in a rather crude and impatient way.[17]

From Asia to western Europe, and particularly in any of the shrines connected with the mystery of Golgotha, those elemental beings associated with mystery centers were "filled with energy, harmony, peace, balance and health." The "wildness" of North American elementary beings, on the other hand, was actually exacerbated by the cultic activity of the continent's original occupants: "The elemental beings had only the thoughts and pantheistic relations of the Indian as their education, not much of a Christian impulse." In particular, the Ahrimanically materialistic mystery centers of Mesoamerica—the Toltec and Aztec centers at Teotihuacán and Tenochtitlán and the Olmec and Mayan centers in the Yucatán Peninsula—had powerfully retarded any evolutionary development of the New World elementals: "[T]he old Central American mystery centers with their rites, magic and cruelty, cast . . . a dark shadow which penetrates every elemental being, every moral effort, every human being in the North American continent, even in our day." In more modern times, new forms of materialism continued to hold back the elementals, or drive them away entirely. Pfeiffer pointed particularly to the technical developments of the last two centuries—that is, since the Industrial Revolution—as a bane for nature spirits. Throughout America, he had witnessed places where elementals had abandoned their former localities, becoming "homeless." New York City, for example, had been deserted by legions of its original elemental denizens.[18]

A New Gospel of Nature

To attempt imaginative perception of elementary beings was particularly difficult in urban areas, but Pfeiffer stressed that the effort was uniquely rewarding, amounting to a redemptive act. Indeed, the redemption of Nature by human beings, through the intermediary of elemental nature spirits, was seen by Pfeiffer as one of contemporary humanity's preeminent tasks. Nature spirits received their nourishment from right thought and action of their neighbor humans, and Pfeiffer outlined a program for healing the split between humanity and Nature through the contemplation and cultivation of the elemental world. The first step was to foster among humans an awareness of the reciprocal relations between nature spirits and humanity, followed by educational efforts to "increase the sense and desire for beauty and harmony": "If this continent will be able to produce spiritual art, including all discipline and color and especially architecture, it will help raise the neglected elemental world to a higher level." The most critical task before order could be restored to the elemental world of America, according to Pfeiffer, was the formation of a new mystery center, on the order of the one founded by Rudolf Steiner at

Dornach. Pfeiffer's deepest sadness was that, in the wake of Steiner's death, disharmony and egotism had flourished under the Goetheanum's graceful dome. Threefold Farm was far from free of similar disharmony.[19]

By 1947, when Pfeiffer delivered this lecture, an ever-growing number of Americans were adopting some version of John Burroughs's "Gospel of Nature." An entire prewar generation of American nature writers effortlessly extended the Seer of Slabside's language of scientific Naturalism. Free of the old saccharine sentimentalism, writers like Aldo Leopold, Edwin Way Teale, and Joseph Wood Krutch evoked a feeling of awe for untrammeled Nature without having to invoke the name of God. Out of the primal past of Native America, D. H. Lawrence offered a gospel of pagan pantheism; from the Big Sur coast of California, Robinson Jeffers fashioned Naturalism into his own craggy philosophy, "Inhumanism."

Rudolf Steiner often stressed that those who sought to describe the spiritual world needed to do so with the exactness and specificity of naturalists describing the component creatures and myriad interrelations found in a meadow. As twentieth-century natural science grew ever more precise in its mapping of the sensible meadow, those who would forge a theology out of Nature grew ever foggier in their formulations of some supersensible meadow. The more facts that Bill Carr added to the nature trails at Harriman, the more his audience craved spokesmen like Burroughs who might reassure them that their Naturalism was enough. Across the Fault from Threefold Farm, Nature was known through its specificity—which plants grew in which habitats, which animals were found where within the park—down to the level of knowing where every individual beaver lived within the ten thousand acres. In Hungry Hollow, on the other hand, organisms seemed to float in some Platonic realm, for the most part devoid of such specific associations. Threefold Farm's thirty-two acres provided a very limited diversity in much modified habitats; the assemblage of flora and fauna was fairly meager in comparison to Harriman's biological bounty. Nature study at Threefold Farm constituted itself at a pole opposite that at Harriman Park. Though it lacked the SSI and Trailside Museum's imperial eye of surveillance—a satisfying cornucopia of natural history detail in the sensible meadow—in Virginia Birdsall's nature walks and Pfeiffer's talks, nature study at Threefold Farm aspired toward Steiner's challenge of a fuller ecology of the supersensible.

Ehrenfried Pfeiffer was well aware that the anthroposophical view of nature, even when communicated in such vernacular language as that of "nature spirits," had little chance of acceptance by the American scientific community. In a 1947 book published by Rodale Press, *The Earth's Face and Human Destiny*, Pfeiffer set out an exoteric version of the esoteric landscape offered to fellow anthroposophists at Threefold Farm. In its survey of American environmental problems and suggestions for solutions, the book resembled Paul Sears's *Deserts on the March* or the writings of Benton MacKaye, Lewis Mumford, and other regionalist authors. Pfeiffer used the terminology of mainstream ecological thought—the "law of the minimum," "symbiosis," and so on. In places, however, the book's tone was unmistakably esoteric. At first, a reader would probably have been unaware of the underlying heterodoxy of Pfeiffer's view of nature. When in the introduction Pfeiffer speaks of the character of a landscape emerging "from the interaction of the Greeks' four elements," uninitiated readers might assume this to be a metaphorical flourish. On the subject of the biological and atmospheric disequilibrium caused by stream channelization, Pfeiffer's statement that "the circulatory interaction of earth, water and air is interrupted, which leads to torpidity, and hardening or the formation of a spongy, swampy structure" could easily be read without knowledge of etheric theory. But at certain points Pfeiffer disavowed that his words were merely metaphorical. Ancient peoples' tales of "river gods" and their representation of rivers as "masculine" or "feminine" were not just fancy but "actual experiences of the life-activity of the body of the earth, dreamed or imagined in mythological pictures . . . although the age of romanticism has contributed much towards making symbols out of facts. . . . A heightening of our powers of observation and perception will lead us again, in time, to connect a deeper meaning with names which spring from the pure folk instincts, undimmed by the intellect."[20]

At times Pfeiffer's antimodern animus sounded just like Benton MacKaye's; he railed against metropolitan growth as "pathological," saying that the city "has acted as a vacuum sucking everything into itself." But Pfeiffer moderated his Arcadianism: "It would be absurd to follow a one-sided call 'back to Nature.' People would only swing the pendulum back to the other side. The cities in their development have full justification as centres of art, science, education, business and government. The questions that stand in the foreground are those of correct division, interpenetration, balance." *The Earth's Face* ultimately echoed the same message of reenchantment and redemption of Nature that Pfeiffer carried to the anthroposophical faithful at Threefold. Following a brief history of agriculture, Pfeiffer returned to the language of the supersensible beings standing behind visible nature: "To satisfy his egotistic, bodily needs, man interfered with the course of a god- and demon-guided Nature; claimed something not due to his own powers; for the interworkings of light, warmth, air, water and earth required the deeds of gods, with the results that the forces so used had to be withdrawn from the general course of cosmic earthly happenings and interwoven with human fate; and the whole process had come to symbolize man's fate." Whether reforesting ravaged slopes, crafting urban parks, or developing the etheric clairvoyance necessary once again to perceive nature as "god- and demon-guided," humanity must recognize that its fate was clearly to redeem Nature, not be redeemed by it.[21] Despite their commitment to reenchantment, the Threefold Farm anthroposophists, after two decades of research and teaching activity along Goethean lines, were often seized by a spirit of disenchantment, as America marched ever forward along the Naturalist path. By the 1950s, at every turn in the trail, new vistas of materialism presented themselves, and some of the most dramatic apotheoses of those vistas continued to be seen from the sublime summits of the Ramapo ridge.

CONCLUSION

The Unity of Knowledge

The Arden House Summit, 1954

One by one, on a Friday afternoon in late October 1954, dozens of limousines made the three-mile switchback climb from the gatehouse, pulled past the pair of huge lion statues into the circular drive before Arden House, and delivered their august occupants. Among those representing Nature were: Marston Bates, professor of zoology at the University of Michigan; Niels Bohr, from the Institute of Theoretical Physics; Theodosius Dobzhansky, professor of zoology at Columbia University; Harold Urey, professor of chemistry at the University of Chicago; B. F. Skinner, Harvard University psychologist; Gardner Murphy, director of research at the Menninger Foundation; and John von Neumann, of the Institute for Advanced Study in Princeton. Representing History were: Harvard sociologist Talcott Parsons; University of California anthropologist Alfred Kroeber; Margaret Mead of the American Museum of Natural History; Columbia University historians Jacques Barzun, Richard Hofstadter, and J. Bartlett Brebner; Harvard philosopher Willard Quine; and essayist Lionel Trilling. Two of the Arden House arrivals—the Jesuit paleontologist Pierre Teilhard de Chardin and British biologist Julian Huxley—clearly represented the summit organizers' hopes for a true unity of knowledge.

Those who had never made the pilgrimage to the former Harriman household at the top of the Ramapos were stunned by such sylvan beauty so close to Manhattan. Many passed small herds of grazing deer on the ride up through the oak woods, whose dun autumn shades were punctuated by the bright yellow foliage of tulip trees and black birch and the scarlet of sassafras and sweet gum. Each turn of the winding road brought into view massive outcrops or boulder fields of gray gneiss, the Precambrian primeval brought up along the Ramapo fault into full view. The solidity, the sense of permanence and natural beauty, continued once the guests entered the ridge-top chateau. Despite the European architecture of Arden House, the guests could not help but be struck by how American it was in its furnishings and fashions. The exterior was largely built from gneiss blasted out of the Ramapo ridge top, trimmed by limestone from Indiana, while the interior stone came from Utah. Slate for the roof came from Vermont quarries, as did the marble for the floors of the entrance foyer and the music room, where Mary Harriman had served high tea each Sunday during the summer. The eight ram's heads supporting the carved buttresses high up on the walls of the music room had been carved in 1910 by sculptor Carl Rumsey, shortly before he married the Harrimans' daughter, Mary ("Eugenia"). Rumsey had also executed the bas-relief over the music room's mantel, a portrait of Arden's chief architect, Thomas Hastings. In 1954, its pipe organ (the largest privately owned in America) no longer used for Sunday afternoon concerts, the room displayed trophy heads of an impressive array of American game animals.

On their way to their rooms, the cosmopolitan representatives of Nature and History passed Malvina Hoffman's white marble bust of Mrs. Harriman at the end of a long brick-tiled loggia whose north wall held an enormous mural by Barry Faulkner. Commissioned by Mrs. Harriman in 1907, Faulkner's fresco combined the Old World and the New. On the left stood the regal presences of Chevalier Bayard, the ideal of Renaissance chivalry, Tamerlane the Tatar conqueror, Leonidas the Spartan, Alexander the Great, Roland, defender of the Christians against the Saracens, David, the Hebrew shepherd and prophet, and Guatemozin, the last of the Aztec kings of Mexico. On the left stood Cornelia, Dante's Beatrice, Judith, the heroine of a book of the Apocrypha, Helen of Troy, Joan of Arc, the Queen of Sheba, and Pocahontas. Just behind Cornelia, Faulkner had painted Mrs. Harriman into the historic assemblage. The south wall of the corridor was all glass, looking onto a rectangular courtyard whose plantings included an "upside-down" American beech tree (created by grafting the limbs pointing down), presented to Mrs. Harriman by her Alaska Expedition friend John Muir. Close by stood James Earle Fraser's statue of a nude man with a turtle and mountain lion, symbolizing humanity's ability to live in unity with nature.

There was more American megafauna in the game room, including the bear shot by E. H. Harriman on the Alaska outing. Mounting the wide staircase, the guests passed tapestries (fabricated by the Harter Looms of New York City) depicting the construction of Arden House and then passed down a hall lined with Edward S. Curtis's Alaska Expedition photographs of American Indians. Just beyond, in the wing that housed Mary Harriman's office, where she had met many times with Charles Davenport and other leaders of the American eugenics movement, was a fresco by American artist Edward Deming of a group of Lenape Indians. They stood before a dugout canoe on the bank of what might have been the Ramapo River, with the Ramapo Mountain front forming the backdrop. After the guests had found their rooms, some made their way up to the tower room, which, on a clear day like that one in late October, offered a panoramic view some thirty or forty miles in every direction, easily taking in the Manhattan skyline.

After Mrs. Harriman died in 1932, her son, Averell, and his family lived at Arden until 1950, when they donated the house and grounds flanking Harriman Park to Columbia University. In the following years Arden hosted a number of international summits, as Columbia president Dwight Eisenhower had made Arden the home of the American Assembly. This 1954 summit, the "Unity of Knowledge Conference," was one of many events held in celebration of Columbia University's bicentennial, whose overall theme was "Man's Right to Knowledge and the Free Use Thereof." In his opening statement to the conference participants, Columbia University scholar Lewis Leary set the stage with a series of rhetorical questions suggesting the "two culture" problem—scientific versus humanistic knowledge—rather than a unity of knowledge:

> The Unity of Knowledge: Problem or Chimera? To what extent or in what manner can knowledge be said to be unified? What are the instruments, the skills, or the insights by which man can discover harmony amid the diversity which seems to surround him? Has science the answer, or philosophy, or any product of the reasoning power of man, or does one approach it more surely through the intuitive reachings of religion or the creative arts? To which of the disciplines or to what kind of cooperative enterprise among the disciplines must we look for unity?[1]

Despite the presence of a seemingly wide array of humanists, the deck was stacked in favor of the scientists, who, even in that decade of American skepticism about the limitations of science, possessed tremendous self-confidence that any future unity of knowledge would surely issue from their midst, not from the ranks of philosophy or history.

So wide-ranging a forum as this one cried out for some magisterial centering voice, one that could synthesize the diversity of contemporary *scientias*—from physics to philosophy—and also harmonize present and past. In 1954, despite the recent triumphs of subatomic physics, chemistry, and molecular biology, such a subject still called for a knowledge worker practiced in the art of thinking about whole organisms, not merely their organic or inorganic constituents. Though in the postwar decade systems theorists like Ludwig von Bertalanffy held out the hope of higher unities, their rhetoric rarely seemed satisfactory when they turned their gaze from mathematical systems to the realm of the human being.

Since the mid-nineteenth century the biological sciences had offered the promise of a unity of nature, and after some early-twentieth-century setbacks, the "modern synthesis" in biology—the marriage of natural selection theory to genetics—seemed to renew that promise. As the most enthusiastic interpreter of the modern synthesis to a wide audience, and especially given his ardent quest for an "evolutionary humanism," Julian Huxley was Columbia's natural choice for the keynote address at the summit. A lifelong eugenicist, Huxley was a spectacular specimen of good breeding, representing both sides of the two-culture divide: eldest grandson of "Darwin's bulldog," Thomas Henry Huxley, he was also descended from the historian Thomas Arnold, and his uncle was the poet and the essayist Matthew Arnold. Ever since his collaboration in 1929 with H. G. Wells on *The Science of Life*, Huxley had reached a wide audience with his view of biology, and in the decade before the 1954 conference, in his role as the first director-general of the United Nations Educational, Scientific, and Cultural Organization (UNESCO), Huxley had emerged as perhaps the premier international statesman for science.

"Man's Place and Role in Nature"—Julian Huxley's title echoed his grandfather's 1863 work, *Evidence as to Man's Place in Nature*—was certainly the conference's apotheosis, the moment when the eminence and eloquence of a speaker might best create a feeling of optimism for the future of science and the humanities, Nature and History. Huxley began by noting that the present age was the first to have a reasonably comprehensive, scientifically based picture of humanity's place and role in nature since the Darwinian "upheaval" had first put human beings *in* nature rather than above it. Though the late-nineteenth-century faith in humankind's achievements moderated this sense of the human being as "just another animal," the catastrophes of the twentieth century had shaken that faith. Huxley, however, was ever a believer in progress, whether biological or sociocultural, and looked forward to "future possibilities."[2]

The possibilities foreseen by Huxley lay outside the biological realm. He conjectured that sometime in the Pliocene, "the last possibilities of major improvement in the material and physiological properties of self-reproducing matter had been exhausted." Huxley maintained that humans had put a "cap" on evolution, that even if biological evolution had not effectively ended in the Pliocene, human beings now stood in the way of any major evolutionary developments. As "the only organism capable of further major transformation or evolutionary advance," humanity had taken on the role of creator, the "instrument" of evolutionary process. Borrowing from his friend and fellow conference member Teilhard de Chardin, Huxley acknowledged that evolution had passed out of the biosphere into the "noosphere."[3]

Modern biology had labored long and hard to rid itself of any metaphysical crutches in its quest to explain the nature of life, yet in Teilhardism—which Huxley shared with Dobzhansky—Bergsonian vitalism had resurfaced with a vengeance. Indeed, the presence at the Arden summit of Huxley, Dobzhansky, and Père Teilhard himself, and the absence of any vocal scientific critics of Teilhard's brand of "emergent evolutionism," suggested the degree to which the Unity of Knowledge Conference diverged from the unity of science movement of a generation earlier. In the late 1920s and 1930s, led by logical positivists of the Vienna Circle (of whose number only Willard Quine could be counted at Arden House in 1954), unification proponents had attacked emergent evolutionists like Huxley, seeing as pure mysticism any invocations of wholes that were more than the sum of their parts, no matter how devoid these attempts at holism were of truly religious sentiment.[4]

Huxley was as confident about the prospects for a unified knowledge of History as he was for a transcendental knowledge of Nature: "Our age is the first in history in which we have acquired a comprehensive knowledge of historical fact, from the present back to the Paleolithic, and therefore the first age in which it is possible to attempt a unified history." Huxley, the universal historian, pointed to his own UNESCO effort—the *Scientific and Cultural History of Mankind*—as an example. Huxley was perhaps being too modest in claiming such retrospective clarity only as far back as the Paleolithic, for in his audience was Harold Urey, whose "primal soup" experiment had recently convinced a wide array of scientists and humanists that the mystery of the origin of life had now been solved in the laboratory. And the work of another guest at Arden House that October weekend—*Walden Two* author (and John B. Watson disciple) B. F. Skinner—virtually obliterated the need for historical thinking about the human being. As a product of operant conditioning, the human mechanism required very limited historical acuity on the part of its observers.[5]

A Crack in the Wall

Despite the many philosophical, methodological, and epistemological differences that stood in the way of unification of the disciplines represented at Arden House, there was an overwhelming sense among the participants that they were headed in the right direction. If the scientists could just stay alert to the dangers of reductionism, if the humanists could watch their romanticism, all would eventually be well. But in 1954 there were small signs that the unified front, the magnificent wall of modern wisdom, was marred by a fissure or two. In the eyes of some unifiers, these cracks were temporary, easily reparable; more of them dismissed the cracks entirely, rationalizing them as hallucinations, illusions, atavistic reversions to obsolete noosystems.

Even at Arden House, at least a couple of individuals believed these cracks demanded serious consideration. Gardner Murphy had been a keen student of parapsychology for decades, publishing articles in nearly every issue of the *Journal of the American Society for Parapsychology* in the 1940s and 1950s. After leaving Columbia to head the research department at the Menninger Foundation, Murphy had encouraged studies of subliminal perception and autokinetic effects. Six weeks after the Arden conference, Murphy advocated research on extrasensory perception in a letter to *Science* magazine. Margaret Mead, who had encountered paranormal phenomena on a number of occasions in her anthropological fieldwork in traditional societies, was an outspoken defender of parapsychological research. Her efforts led the American Association for the Advancement of Science to permit the creation of a parapsychology branch.[6]

Julian Huxley was not unaware of the challenge to any "modern synthesis" posed by the violations of space and time represented by phenomena like precognition, retrocognition, telepathy, and other forms of clairvoyance. His brother Aldous in 1954 was coming face to face with the paranormal in his experiments with mescaline. Aldous Huxley's *Doors of Perception* was published in February, and in April he had attended a parapsychology conference with Eileen Garret, president of the American Society for Parapsychological Research. Julian Huxley thought that extrasensory perception might represent the "more ultimate state," the "Omega point" prophesied by Teilhard de Chardin.[7]

Fault Lines

The weakness of the modern materialistic world conception was made apparent on two fronts: its incapacity to manufacture even an abstract and artificial unity of knowledge; and its hesitant approach to paranormal phenomena. That the jargon-rich, poetic philosophy of the Jesuit paleontologist was the most promising alternative at Arden to full-blown scientific Naturalism testified to the fact that the fault line between materialist and nonmaterialist epistemologies had only grown more active. Twenty-one

years after the first summer conference at Threefold Farm, spiritual science remained an altogether alien terrain, restricted to its side of the
Ramapo Fault.

Earlier in 1954, in Switzerland, Hermann Poppelbaum had contributed one segment of a radio series on parapsychology. Though he admitted that dowsers, psychics, and producers of telekinetic phenomena
penetrated into "otherwise closed fields of Nature's existence," Poppelbaum
stressed that they did so in the absence of daylight consciousness. Most
instances of extrasensory perception did not offer glimpses of some
"higher" consciousness, but were actually lowerings of consciousness, mo-
mentary obliterations of the critical distance the Ego necessarily maintains
from its own experience and action. Unlike anthroposophy, which applied
its empirical attitude from a consciousness *above* paranormal phenomena,
parapsychology sought to understand the paranormal from the same level
as the phenomena themselves. Modern parapsychology lacked anthroposophy's critical concept of the etheric and astral bodies and thus was
riddled with error in its approach to the paranormal. "It is not the subject
dealt with, but the method of dealing with it, which decides whether something is science or not," Poppelbaum reminded his listeners.[8]

Poppelbaum took up the perennial problem of "so-called messages
from the dead," an issue that Rudolf Steiner had often attempted to clarify
during Spiritualism's heyday in the opening decades of the twentieth century. As had Steiner, Poppelbaum told his audience that the communications believed to be from the dead were actually produced by the discarded
astral sheaths of deceased persons. It took only three and a half days after
death for the etheric body to dissipate into the cosmic etheric formative
forces, but the astral body persisted for a period equal to one-third of the
dead individual's life span, leaving it available to contact by mediums and
others who flirted with diminished ego consciousness. The alleged messages of the departed were "nothing but echoes of a stratum that has grown
soul-less," advised Poppelbaum. Telekinetic phenomena of the sort that so
fascinated Gardner Murphy were seen to be effects of the will forces separated after death from the dead, and hence subject to manipulation by
discarnate beings, who frequently used these will forces to play "factual
physical tricks."[9]

In 1954, in an article for the *Anthroposophic News Sheet*, Poppelbaum
called for a spiritual scientific understanding of the supposedly beatific visions of Aldous Huxley. The mescaline intoxication Huxley described in
The Doors of Perception, instead of revealing a glimpse into "higher
worlds," actually strengthened the relation of his astral body to his physical organism so as to give him a magnified perception of his own physical

body. Along with the intensification of his sensory impressions, Huxley recorded his conviction that he had been given a taste of the transcendental, a vision of what lay *behind* the physical universe's semblance. This conviction, Poppelbaum held, was a result of the Ego's breaking away from the physical body as the astral seized hold of the body. "Undoubtedly, every word reported by Huxley is noteworthy—but not as a description of a genuine 'higher world,' but as the description of a state of mind in which above all the feeling of reality, the physical *and* the spiritual, has been *lost.*" Like the somnambulist seeker of the dead, Huxley failed to bring his daytime consciousness into his hallucinatory state.[10]

In the misinterpretation of the paranormal by parapsychology and in Huxley's unabashed call to unhinge the doors of perception, Poppelbaum saw serious missteps on the part of humanity. It pained him to think that as long ago as 1906, in *Knowledge of the Higher Worlds*, Rudolf Steiner had made an exact scientific description of how, just before the soul enters the supersensible realm, colors and forms detach themselves from the objects to which they ordinarily cling, just as Huxley described in *The Doors of Perception*. But whereas Steiner offered precise instructions for how then to stay awake on that threshold, so that truly scientific knowledge could be won from the encounter with the spiritual world, Huxley hovered in a state of blissful stupor, awash in a sea of bright colors falsely seen.

The year 1954 marked a time of real reflection on the part of anthroposophists regarding the degree to which they had accomplished certain goals. Ralph Courtney and Ehrenfried Pfeiffer were deeply disappointed in the failure of America and the world to take up the process of social threefolding; instead, the state increasingly impinged on the cultural and spiritual spheres of human life. Pfeiffer continued to remind his lecture audiences at Threefold Farm of Steiner's injunction that two things were needed for the Christ impulse truly to take hold in the future, so that humanity might properly receive etheric clairvoyance: threefolding in at least one place upon the earth; and implementation of Waldorf education, so that initiates could in the future incarnate into properly prepared physical bodies. America's fascination with the paranormal in the 1950s might have offered an opportunity to crack wide open the fortress wall of Naturalist reckoning of Nature and History. Two years after the Arden summit, the nation would be swept up in a craze for the ostensibly otherworldly pronouncements of Bridey Murphy, but America never heard a spiritual scientific explanation of the girl's deception in the dark. The fault line between materialist science and spiritual science was too steep to breach.

And what of Rudolf Steiner's prediction of an increased experience of etheric clairvoyance by midcentury? By 1954, America had thrilled to reports of many sensational "near-death experiences," in which individuals reported fleeting panoramic visions of their lives, followed by an encounter with a being of light whom many identified as Christ. While mainstream science dismissed the reports as trauma-induced wish fulfillment, spiritual science saw these experiences as the fulfillment of Rudolf Steiner's indication of the reappearance of Christ in the earth's etheric realm. To the anthroposophists at Threefold Farm, the fleeting panoramic vision was clearly the etheric "life review" precipitated by the etheric body's separation from the physical body, and the being of light was indeed the Christ, met in near-death, just as those who practiced anthroposophical meditation hoped to meet Him while still alive and in the body.[11]

In 1943, George Ritchie, a twenty-year-old recruit in basic training at Camp Barkeley, Texas, underwent a near-death experience and later told of it in *Return from Tomorrow*. Though lacking the language of spiritual science to make sense of his experience, Ritchie gave a faithful rendering of this deeply transformative event. On Easter Sunday in 1949, Ehrenfried Pfeiffer told his Threefold audience that the war had interfered with the recognition of experiences like Ritchie's: "The opposing forces become so strong that they try to hinder . . . [the recognition of] the coming of the Etheric Christ. Whoever may have this experience, it is necessary for many to prepare it. It should be the task of the Anthroposophical Society . . . to prepare the entire world for this event." The "demon" identified by Pfeiffer as opposing the rightful redemption of Nature and History was Naturalism.[12]

All through the 1950s, Pfeiffer spoke out about the dangers of materialist science, particularly its recent descent into subnature through the atom. Pfeiffer spoke of the atomic concept of matter in personal terms: "At the time when I went to school and university, in 1920, 1922, 1923, and 1924, we . . . were trained to look at nature in such a way that we wanted to dissect, to atomize, to split, to study the bombardment of atoms, and all such things." This training, Pfeiffer said, was a training to recognize death, and "this language of death is also a language of warfare. . . . If you approach nature with this state of mind, you will discover all that leads to destruction." The remedy for such diseased thought was the living Goethean approach to nature, leading to the freeing of the supersensible etheric thought forces, rather than a descent into imprisonment by the subsensible forces of subnature. Thinking of a photograph he had seen of a test explosion of the atomic bomb in Nevada, Pfeiffer concluded that humanity in the twentieth century, instead of receiving the life-giving power of the true Sun force of the etheric Christ, had accepted its "caricature," "the sun of death."[13]

Had Pfeiffer or Poppelbaum been invited to Arden House in October

1954 to sit at the long oak boardroom table given to Mrs. Harriman by J. P. Morgan, surrounded by the mid-twentieth century's greatest unifiers of knowledge, the Great Border Fault that split the twentieth century asunder would have been made manifest. A few months earlier, Poppelbaum had finished a course of lectures at the Goetheanum entitled "How Can Spiritual Science Deepen the Observation of Nature?" and a new German edition of his *Tierwesenskunde* had just appeared. Across the Ramapo Fault at Threefold, Pfeiffer was still pursuing his crystallization research, teaching farmers about biodynamic agriculture, and giving his Sunday lectures, which offered a much higher unity of knowledge than anything heard at the Arden House summit. Children in the Waldorf school that backed up to the same oak woods where audiences first heard Pfeiffer in 1933 went into those woods with Goethean eyes, fledged on stories of nature spirits and imbued with Poppelbaum's poetic language of animal metamorphoses.

None of these subterranean currents broke forth into the rarefied atmosphere of Arden House in October 1954. The complacency of that gathering was countered by the urgency felt among the anthroposophical community that the unification of fact and value, faith and knowledge sought within the scope of modern materialist thought continued to starve both man and the gods while nourishing the adversarial forces. Just a year before the Unity of Knowledge Conference, the ground under Arden House and Threefold Farm had been shaken by earthquake tremors along the Ramapo Fault. The quakes came in July and August of 1953, in the middle of a long heat wave and terrible drought that Ehrenfried Pfeiffer attributed to elemental spirits upset by American materialism. Indeed, the earthquakes themselves were understood by Pfeiffer and the Threefold anthroposophists as expressions of elemental imbalance, an imbalance that hung upon the cognitive efforts of human beings.[14]

From the Naturalist perspective, the earthquakes felt in the New York metropolitan area were a reminder of wholly physical forces active along the hidden Great Border Fault running the length of the Appalachians. From the anthroposophical point of view, the quakes called to mind supersensible forces along the great border fault of human consciousness at the twentieth-century turning point in time. In Hungry Hollow, the tremors seemed to signify that the battle for human consciousness was still being waged in earnest, that Ahriman ruled in America as at Arden. The absence of spiritual scientific perspectives at the Unity of Knowledge Conference reflected the negligible impact on American culture of the ideas nurtured for two decades at Threefold Farm.

This book also reflects the seeming incommensurability of the two worlds: the "back to Nature" impulse that early-twentieth-century Manhattan metropolitans stewarded at the Trailside Museum, the Station for the Study of Insects, and in eugenics fieldwork; and the anthroposophical impulse at Threefold Farm to redeem Nature through the human. The lack of narrative continuity between the first and second halves of this book—save for Percy MacKaye, no Arcadian set foot across the fault line—is perhaps a metaphor for the sort of process of historical "causation" implied by spiritual science. What for academic storytelling would be the formative events—the automobile, advertising, the Arcadian myth, and the power of the modern metropolis to shape our perceptions of nature—are but footnotes in this tale. The Threefold Farm Arcadians would likely argue that the real history is written somewhere unseen, in a script that we have not yet learned to read.

Reading that esoteric script still lies far outside the ability and inclination of contemporary historians, but we can at least assess the accuracy of the anthroposophists' prognostications by asking if the wall of Naturalism has either strengthened or weakened in the half century since 1954. In 1998 Harvard biologist Edward O. Wilson published *Consilience: The Unity of Knowledge*; though he makes no reference to the 1954 Arden House conference, his book can be seen as a status report on the hopes nurtured there. As Julian Huxley once did, Wilson communicates his authority by his seemingly magisterial command of both Nature and History. As he moves back and forth between the two domains, the sureness of his grasp of the biological realm lends credence to his relatively superficial knowledge of the historical realm. Unequivocally devoted, as Huxley was, to the "Ionian Enchantment" (historian of science Gerald Holton's phrase describing the quest for a unity of the sciences), Wilson believes that a "united system of knowledge is the surest means of identifying the still unexplored domains of reality. It provides a clear map of what is known, and it frames the most productive questions for future inquiry." Looking at the Romantic quest for a monism alternative to the Enlightenment's, Wilson disparages Goethe in classic Naturalist fashion: "The German Romantics, led by Goethe, Hegel, Herder and Schelling, set out to reinsert metaphysics into science and philosophy. The product, *Naturphilosophie*, was a hybrid of sentiment, mysticism, and quasi-scientific hypothesis. Johann Wolfgang von Goethe, preeminent among its expositors, wanted most of all to be a great scientist. . . . He would have grieved had he foreseen history's verdict: great poet, poor scientist. He failed in his synthesis through lack of what is today called the scientist's instinct. Not to mention the necessary technical skills. Calculus baffled him, and it is said he could not tell a lark from a sparrow."[15]

Few American scientists are seemingly more qualified to mock Goethe's abilities. E. O. Wilson, the world authority on ants and inventor of sociobiology, biodiversity, and the biophilia hypothesis, is America's consummate naturalist, a critical bridge, as Julian Huxley was in his time, between science and the public. As a good naturalist, and thus a good man, Wilson can dismiss Goethe and raise no public outcry, not even from historians of science. No public or academic dissent greeted Wilson's sweeping materialist formulations of human history and culture, either. When Wilson declared that "Gene-Culture evolution is, I believe, the underlying process by which the brain evolved and the arts originated," his words were read by a wide public who shared his Naturalism. This public took comfort in Wilson's confession that "Science is religion liberated and writ large. . . . Preferring a search for objective reality over revelation is another way of satisfying religious hunger."[16]

Where John Burroughs in 1920 had to wrestle with his own Naturalism, and his readers had to wrestle along with him, Wilson could assume that struggle to be over. Wilson's 1994 autobiography, *Naturalist*, paints the old religion in the same colors that historians reserve for William Jennings Bryan. *Naturalist* opens with scenes of the six-year-old Wilson in Sunday School class at Pensacola First Baptist Church, learning to sing "Onward Christian Soldiers," and the fourteen-year-old Wilson being baptized by a cynical cigar-smoking preacher. In 1947, as a college freshman, Wilson was introduced to the theory of evolution, and his naturalist instincts were given a Naturalist basis. Wilson admits no baptismal epiphany, claiming an inner conviction of the truth of Naturalism since boyhood: "From the beginning I never could accept that science and religion are separate domains, with fundamentally different questions and answers. Religion had to be explained as a material process, from the bottom up, atoms to genes to the human spirit. It had to be embraced by the single grand naturalistic image of man." The title *Naturalist* suggests no double entendre; *all* naturalists are Naturalists, or they are pretenders to the name. Used to identify a philosophical stance, the word *naturalist* appears nowhere in Wilson's autobiography. Invisible, transparent, *mythic*, Naturalism is the common coin of our time.[17]

Myth works its culturally cohesive power—for both good and ill— by virtue of its invisibility. It has taken nearly the entire century for America's Arcadian myth to come into full view, such that the paradoxical conjunction of individuals and events described in the first half of this book no longer seems surprising or unnerving: Harriman Park was as much a landscape of exclusion (of people seen by eugenicists as rural "degenerates") as it was a landscape of inclusion (of urban masses); the Appalachian Trail, initiated as an agent of communitarian social transformation, became a key corridor for individualistic seekers of authentic, therapeutic contact with Nature; the nation's first nature trail owes its origin as much to the artificial worlds of advertising and automobiles as to modern natural scientific knowledge. Such paradoxes help us to understand why the secular salvation sought by Arcadian enthusiasts in America during the twentieth century has proved as chimerical as the monist's quest for a unity of knowledge. Both searches have unfolded within the confines of a materialist, Naturalist episteme whose limitations have become most apparent at the margins of knowledge.

The knowledge of Nature and History developed by the anthroposophists at Threefold Farm has remained invisible because of America's pervasive modern myth of Naturalism. Naturalism's triumphal status has easily allowed it to label as "myth"—in its pejorative, truth-denying sense—the nonmaterialist monism that anthroposophical knowledge claims to be. The only way to discern a myth's truth value is to hold it up to the light, preferably alongside a competing myth. Like the two dramatically different geological terrains juxtaposed along the Ramapo Fault, this book brings the two myths in contact with one another; perhaps it can serve as a tentative trail map across the fault, to some new, as yet undiscovered, myth.

NOTES

Introduction: Back to (Which) Nature?

1. William Cronon, "The Trouble with Wilderness; or Getting Back to the Wrong Nature," *Environmental History* 1 (1990): 7–28, reprinted in William J. Cronon, ed., *Uncommon Ground: Toward Reinventing Nature* (New York: W. W. Norton, 1995). The *Environmental History* issue includes three critical commentaries on Cronon's essay and Cronon's response; for a more recent critique by conservation biologists of social scientific thought about nature, see Michael E. Soule and Gary Lease, eds., *Reinventing Nature: Responses to Postmodern Deconstruction* (Washington, D.C.: Island Press, 1995). For recent literature that treats the impact of humans upon the American landscape without using rhetoric shaped by a wilderness ethic and aesthetic, see: Richard White, *The Organic Machine: The Remaking of the Columbia River* (New York: Hill and Wang, 1995); Michael Pollan, *Second Nature: A Gardener's Education* (New York: Delta, 1991); William Cronon, *Nature's Metropolis: Chicago and the Great West* (New York: W. W. Norton, 1991).

2. William Cronon, *Changes in the Land: Indians, Colonists, and the Ecology of New England* (New York: Hill and Wang, 1983); Raymond Williams, "Ideas of Nature," in *Keywords: A Vocabulary of Culture and Society* (Oxford: Oxford University Press, 1983). In "Ecology, Objectivity, and Critique in Writings on Nature and Human Societies" (*Journal of Historical Geography* 20 [1994]: 22–37), David Demeritt argues that environmental history has not responded adequately to the challenges posed by revisions of ecological knowledge or to the linguistic turn in historical study and so clings to an outdated foundationalism. In defending his colleagues, William Cronon noted that even Donald Worster's *Nature's Economy: A History of Ecological Ideas* (Cambridge: Cambridge University Press, 1985), a pioneering work in environmental history self-consciously allied with the "Arcadian" stream of American thought, was not unaware of the theoretical debates within ecological science about its own models of natural order. Cronon, "Cutting Loose or Running Aground?" *Journal of Historical Geography* 20 (1994): 39. For the debate about "organismic" versus "individualistic" models of ecological change, see: Frank N. Egerton, "Changing Concepts in the Balance of Nature," *Quarterly Review of Biology* 48 (1973): 322–50; Donald Worster, "The Ecology of Order and Chaos," *Environmental History Review* 14 (1990): 1–18; Daniel B. Botkin, *Discordant Harmonies: A New Ecology for the Twenty-first Century* (New

York: Oxford University Press, 1990). Other self-evaluations by environmental historians on the issues of their professional epistemology can be found in Richard White, "Environmental History, Ecology, and Meaning," *Journal of American History* 76 (1990): 1111–16, and William Cronon, "A Place for Stories: Nature, History, and Narrative," *Journal of American History* 78 (1992): 1347–76.

Among early works in the history of ecology that show how ecological narratives are shaped by cultural, social, and political metaphors are Sharon Kingsland, *Modeling Nature: Episodes in the History of Population Ecology* (Chicago: University of Chicago Press, 1985), and Gregg Mitman, *The State of Nature: Ecology, Community, and American Social Thought, 1900–1950* (Chicago: University of Chicago Press, 1992).

3. Peter J. Schmitt, *Back to Nature: The Arcadian Myth in Urban America* (Oxford: Oxford University Press, 1969; Baltimore: Johns Hopkins University Press, 1990), xvii.

4. For example, in 1998 the University Press of New England initiated the "Middlebury College Series in Environmental Studies" to explore a bioregional approach to environmental studies. The call for manuscripts addresses itself explicitly to the new ethos of regionalism: "Natural and human history will accordingly be viewed as a continuum that is illuminated through closely focused attention on particular ecosystems. . . . The inclusiveness of bioregionalism is a natural outgrowth of the complex environmental history of New England and the Adirondacks. New, and healthy, irony can enter into environmental discourse through focusing on a turbulent history and such a surprising present." Advertisement in *Environmental History* 3 (1998): 425.

5. Ralph Lutts, *The Nature Fakers: Wildlife, Science, and Sentiment* (Golden, Colo.: Fulcrum Publishing, 1990).

6. On new models of scientific popularization, see Steve Shapin, "Science and the Public," in *Companion to the History of Modern Science*, ed. R. C. Olby et al. (New York: Routledge, 1990), and Terry Shinn and Richard Whitley, eds., *Expository Science: Forms and Functions of Popularization* (Dordrecht: D. Reidel, 1985). Among works examining the relationship between natural science and the public in the late nineteenth century, see: Lynn Barber, *The Heyday of Natural History, 1820–1870* (London: Jonathan Cape, 1981); Sally Gregory Kohlstedt, "The Nineteenth-Century Amateur Tradition: The Case of the Boston Society of Natural History," in *Science and Its Public*, ed. Gerald Holton and W. A. Blanpied (Dordrecht: D. Reidel, 1976); Kohlstedt, "From Learned Society to Public Museum: The Boston Society of Natural History," in *The Organization of Knowledge in Modern America, 1860–1920*, ed. Alexandra Oleson and John Voss (Baltimore: Johns Hopkins University Press, 1979); Toby A. Appel, "Science, Popular Culture, and Profit: Peale's Philadelphia Museum," *Journal for the Society for a Bibliography of Natural History* 9 (1980): 619–34; Kohlstedt, "Henry A. Ward: The Merchant Naturalist and American Museum Development," *Journal for the Society for a Bibliography of Natural History* 9 (1980): 647–61; Margaret W. Rossiter, "Benjamin Silliman and the Lowell Institute: The Popularization of Science in Nineteenth-Century America," *New England Quarterly* 44 (1971): 602–26. Studies dealing with the twentieth century include: Gregg Mitman, "Cinematic Nature: Hollywood Technology, Popular Culture, and the American Museum of Natural History," *Isis* 84 (1993): 637–61; Mitman, "When Nature Is the Zoo: Vision and Power in the Art and Science of Natural History," *Osiris* 11 (1996): 117–43; David Peterson de Mar, "'Our Animal Friends': Depictions of Animals in *Reader's Digest* during the 1950s, *Environmental History* 3 (1998): 25–44; Susan Davis, *Spectacular Nature: Corporate Culture and the Sea World Experience* (Berkeley: University of California Press, 1997); Jennifer Wolch and Jody

Emel, *Animal Geographies: Place, Politics, and Identity in the Nature-Culture Borderlands* (New York: Verso, 1998); Ralph Lutts, *The Wild Animal Story* (Philadelphia: Temple University Press, 1998).

7. Philip Pauly, "Essay Review: The Eugenics Industry—Growth or Restructuring?" *Journal of the History of Biology* 26 (1993): 131–45.

8. Mark Haller, *Eugenics: Hereditarian Attitudes in American Thought* (New Brunswick, N.J.: Rutgers University Press, 1963); Donald Pickens, *Eugenics and the Progressives* (Nashville: Vanderbilt University Press, 1968); Kenneth Ludmerer, *Genetics and American Society: A Historical Appraisal* (Baltimore: Johns Hopkins University Press, 1972); Daniel Kevles, *In the Name of Eugenics: Genetics and the Uses of Human Heredity* (Berkeley: University of California Press, 1985); Garland Allen, "The Eugenics Record Office at Cold Spring Harbor, 1910–1940: An Essay in Institutional History," *Osiris* 2 (1986): 225–64. Among recent regional studies of American eugenics, see: Edward J. Larson, *Sex, Race, and Science: Eugenics in the Deep South* (Baltimore: Johns Hopkins University Press, 1995); Steven Noll, *Feeble-Minded in Our Midst: Institutions for the Mentally Retarded in the South, 1900–1940* (Chapel Hill: University of North Carolina Press, 1995). Martin Pernick, *The Black Stork: Eugenics and the Death of Defective Babies in American Medicine and Motion Pictures since 1915* (Oxford: Oxford University Press, 1996), and Marouf A. Hasian Jr., *The Rhetoric of Eugenics in Anglo-American Thought* (Athens: University of Georgia Press, 1996), considerably expand the picture of how eugenic ideals were communicated to a wide audience.

9. Along with Philip Pauly's 1993 review (see above, note 7), see: Frank Dikotter, "Race Culture: Recent Perspectives on the History of Eugenics," *American Historical Review* 103 (1998): 467–78; Kathy J. Cooke, "The Limits of Heredity: Nature and Nurture in American Eugenics before 1915," *Journal of the History of Biology* 31 (1998): 263–78; Diane B. Paul, "Culpability and Compassion: Lessons from the History of Eugenics," *Journal of Politics and the Life Sciences* 15 (1996): 99–106; Robert A. Nye, "The Rise and Fall of the Eugenics Empire: Recent Perspectives on the Impact of Biomedical Thought in Modern Society," *Historical Journal* 36 (1993): 687–700.

10. Although provocative in its class analysis of "natural aristocracies," Gray Brechin's "Conserving the Race: Natural Aristocracies, Eugenics, and the U.S. Conservation Movement," *Antipode* 28 (1996): 229–45, is rather weak in contextualizing the suite of movements and characters he considers. Grant Rothwell considers the coincidence of eugenics and nature study in "Nature Enthusiasm, Social Planning and Eugenics in Australian State Schools, 1900–1920," *Journal of Educational Administration History* 29 (1997): 1–19.

11. Excellent source material for thinking about the landscape dimension of the eugenics movement can be found in Nicole Hahn Rafter, *White Trash: The Eugenic Family Studies, 1877–1919* (Boston: Northeastern University Press, 1988). I have described very briefly the landscape dimension of the eugenic movement in Vermont; see Kevin Dann, "From Degeneration to Regeneration: The Eugenics Survey of Vermont, 1925–1937," *Vermont History* 59, no. 1 (1991): 5–29. See also Samuel A. McReynolds, "Eugenics and Rural Development: The Vermont Commission on Country Life's Program for the Future," *Agricultural History* 71 (1997): 33–50.

12. Thomas Bewick, quoted on the title page of James L. Drummond, *Letters to a Young Naturalist: Study of Nature and Natural Theology* (London: Longman, 1831).

13. On the professionalization of the natural historical sciences, see Toby A. Appel, "Organizing Biology: The American Society of Naturalists and its 'Affiliated Societies,'

1883–1923," and Keith R. Benson, "From Museum Research to Laboratory Research: The Transformation of Natural History into Academic Biology," both in *The American Development of Biology*, ed. Ronald Rainger, Keith R. Benson, and Jane Maienschein (Philadelphia: University of Pennsylvania Press, 1988).

14. Thomas Henry Huxley, *Collected Essays*, vol. 1 (New York: Appleton, 1894), 51.

15. The *OED*'s definition of *naturalism* in its philosophical sense is: "A view of the world, and of man's relation to it, in which only the operation of natural (as opposed to supernatural or spiritual) laws and forces is admitted or assumed." Within vernacular usage, by the 1930s, *naturalism* most often connoted a literary style or method (*Oxford English Dictionary*, 2d ed., s.v. "naturalism"). As a term signifying a philosophical stance, it became largely restricted to theologians and other occasional critics of modern science. Twentieth-century shifts in the predominant meaning of the word have made its usage for scholars today somewhat problematic. The reasoning of Frank Miller Turner in *Between Science and Religion: The Reaction to Scientific Naturalism in Late Victorian England* (New Haven: Yale University Press, 1974) is helpful. Although Turner admits that "settling upon a label for a movement united more by common sentiment than by specific ideas or goals was a problem that plagued the participants as well as the historian" (10), he chooses "naturalism." Turner says "positivism" does not work because of T. H. Huxley's antipathy for English Positivists; "scientism" is a more modern term. "By the close of the nineteenth century, the words *naturalism* and *naturalistic* appear to be the terms employed most frequently to denote the movement associated with contemporary scientific men and ideas" (10). The *Encyclopedia Britannica* discontinued its entry for "naturalism" in 1970, suggesting that by then it had become de rigeur for *all* scientific thinking people.

16. Roy Wood Sellars, *Evolutionary Naturalism* (1922; rpt. New York: Russell and Russell, 1969), i, 4. Sellars, though an opponent of vitalist biological theory, recognized its utility to modern science: "The warfare between naturalist and antinaturalist has resembled that between mechanist and vitalist in biology. While vitalism has gained little headway as a doctrine, it has prevented scientists from falling too completely into dogmatic slumber" (5).

17. John Burroughs, *Accepting the Universe: Essays in Naturalism* (New York: Houghton Mifflin, 1920), 20–23.

18. Ibid., 45. In further declaring that "God is now little more than a name for that tendency or power in the universe which makes for righteousness, and which has brought evolution thus far on its course" (40), Burroughs demonstrated his reliance on Darwinian evolution as the ultimate arbiter of Nature.

19. Ibid., 96, 110–11, 200.

20. "The bogey of teleology frightens a good many scientific minds. To recognize anything akin to intelligence in nature, or to believe that a universal mind is immanent in, or a part of, the cosmos, is looked upon as disloyalty to the scientific spirit. . . . Is a biologist or evolutionist to be charged with mysticism because he refuses to admit that the development of species is all a matter of chance?" (ibid., 211–12). Another of Burroughs's statements has an eerily prophetic ring: "Many scientific men are so shy of teleology that they tend to the other extreme and land in a world of chance" (213).

21. Ibid., 247. Burroughs's equation of "consciousness" and "soul" reflected the triumph of Naturalism in psychology. G. T. W. Patrick commented on this in 1911: "The history of the soul appears to be the history of a vanishing quantity. It has indeed come now to have hardly more than an anthropological interest. In recent textbooks of psy-

chology the word 'soul' does not occur and the word 'mind' seldom or not at all. 'Psychology without a soul' is no longer a reproach but a truism. 'The soul,' as a prominent psychologist recently said, 'is as dead as the dodo.'" Patrick, "The Search for Soul in Contemporary Thought," *Popular Science Monthly* 78 (1911): 461. See also C. H. Judd, "Evolution and Consciousness," *Psychological Review* 17 (1910): 77–97.

22. In 1933 *Scientific American* published the results of a series of experimental tests on mental telepathy that it had commissioned after a decade of regular reporting upon psychical research. Among those earlier pieces, see, for example, the articles by William Franklin Prince: "Experiences Which I Cannot Explain Away," 131 (1924): 384–86; "Make-believe Telepathy," 136 (1927): 10–11; "Specimens from the Telepathic Mine," 137 (1927): 210–13; "Mr. Sinclair's Mental Radio," 146 (1932): 135–38; "Extra-Sensory Perception," 151 (1934): 5–7. Among the many reports in the popular periodical press dealing with science's reaction to psychical phenomena, the following are useful: C. L. Moore, "New Literature of the Occult," *Dial* 58 (1915): 405–8; C. Henderson, "Occultism and Practical Life," *Dial* 51 (1911): 289; G. S. Tytus, "Twilight of Experience," *Forum* 52 (1914): 100–108; J. A. Hill, "Attack of Modern Science on the Realm of Occultism," *Scientific American* 73 (1912): 34–35; A. Bruce, "Timidity of Modern Science in the Presence of the New Ghost," *Current Opinion* 57 (1914): 113.

23. Burroughs, *Accepting the Universe*, 248.

24. Ibid., 250.

25. Ibid., 248.

26. Linda Henderson, in *The Fourth Dimension and Non-Euclidean Geometry in Modern Art* (Princeton: Princeton University Press, 1983), suggests the richness of the interchange between occultism and a variety of intellectuals and artists in the early twentieth century. One of her subjects, the architect Claude Bragdon, offers a particularly intriguing example of a modern American explorer and celebrant of the physical world's lifelong attempt to work out an alternative philosophy to his generation's Naturalism. Among Bragdon's works, see: *The Beautiful Necessity: Seven Essays on Theosophy and Architecture* (New York: Knopf, 1922); *Architecture and Democracy* (New York: Knopf, 1926); *Projective Ornament* (New York: Knopf, 1927); *The Frozen Fountain; Being Essays on Architecture and the Art of Design in Space* (New York: Knopf, 1932); *The Secret Spring: An Autobiography* (London: Andrew Dakers, 1938); *More Lives Than One* (New York: Knopf, 1938).

27. Rudolf Steiner, *Nature and Our Ideals* (1880; rpt. Spring Valley, N.Y.: Mercury Press, 1983); A *Theory of Knowledge Based on Goethe's World Conception* (1888; rpt. New York: Anthroposophic Press, 1968); *Truth and Knowledge* (1892; rpt. Blauvelt, N.Y.: Rudolf Steiner Publications, 1981); *The Philosophy of Spiritual Activity* (1894; rpt. New York: Anthroposophic Press, 1986); *Mysticism at the Dawn of the Modern Age* (1901; rpt. Blauvelt, N.Y.: Rudolf Steiner Publications, 1980). *Conceptions of the World and of Life in the Nineteenth Century* became part one of *Riddles of Philosophy* (1914; rpt. New York: Anthroposophic Press, 1974). Steiner's publications in the authoritative Gesamtausgabe edition in German number 354 volumes; about 20 of these were written as books, and the rest are compilations of various lecture cycles.

28. *Occult Science: An Outline* (1909; rpt. London: Rudolf Steiner Press, 1969), 26–27.

29. Sharon Kingsland, "Essay Review: The History of Ecology," *Journal of the History of Biology* 27 (1994): 353.

CHAPTER 1   *Arcadia and Metropolis*

1. A. K. Lobeck, *The Physiography of the New York Region* (New York: Geographical Press, 1930). Dickinson provided the sketches to illustrate this work, and Erwin Raisz added his trademark physiographic block diagrams.

2. The biographical details are from an unpublished manuscript by George Barbour, "RLD: The Life of Robert Latou Dickinson, 1861–1950," Robert Latou Dickinson Papers, Countway Medical Library, Harvard University, Cambridge, Mass.

3. Raymond H. Torrey, Frank Place Jr., and Robert L. Dickinson, *New York Walk Book: Suggestions for excursions afoot within a radius of fifty to one hundred miles of the city and including Westchester County, the Highlands of the Hudson and the Ramapo, northern and central New Jersey and the New Jersey Pine Barrens, Long Island, the Shawangunk Range, the Catskills, and the Taconics* (New York: American Geographical Society, 1923), 62–63. This sketch, minus the Bear Mountain Bridge, does not bear the "Best Wild Up-and-Down Country" title; that sketch, which shows the same region of the Ramapos, is on page x. Dickinson added the bridge to his sketch for later editions of the book.

4. E. Stagg Whitin, "The Opening of Harriman Park," *Independent* 71 (1911): 182–85.

5. Edward H. Harriman to Governor Charles Hughes, June 9, 1909, Hughes Papers, New York State Archives, Albany.

6. "Panoramic View of a Section of the Vast Harriman Park, From the Abandoned Prison Site," *The Evening Mail*, June 4, 1910, 1.

7. Marjorie W. Brown, *Arden House: A Living Expression of the Harriman Family* (1976; rpt. n.p.: American Assembly, Columbia University, 1981), 66.

8. For a full discussion of the history of the aestheticization of the Highlands, see Raymond J. O'Brien, *American Sublime: Landscape and Scenery of the Lower Hudson River Valley* (New York: Columbia University Press, 1981).

9. American Scenic and Historic Preservation Society, *Twelfth Annual Report* (Albany, 1907), 60; *Thirteenth Annual Report* (1908), 72; E. L. Partridge, "A Highlands Park," *Outlook*, November 9, 1907. Also see Partridge, "A Forest Preserve Near the Metropolis," *Country Life in America* (September 1908): 456–59.

10. Frances F. Dunwell, *The Hudson River Highlands* (New York: Columbia University Press, 1991), 152–55.

11. Commissioners of the Palisades Interstate Park, *Annual Reports*, 1911–1920.

12. Robert Latou Dickinson, *Palisades Interstate Park* (New York: American Geographical Society, 1921). Upon publication of the *New York Walk Book*, the second volume in the Outing series, the American Geographical Society offered, along with the standard "Pocket Edition," a special limited edition that included fifteen photographs and a reprint of *Palisades Interstate Park* printed on high-grade paper with stiff, clothbound covers. See also Commissioners of the Palisades Interstate Park, *Annual Report* (1920), 19; Meade C. Dobson, "Interstate Park Commissioners' Map Opens Forest Roads for Motorists," *New York Post*, September 10, 1920.

13. Torrey et al., *New York Walk Book*, ix.

14. Ibid., 13.

15. "Near and Far Walks," *New York Times*, November 17, 1923; Torrey et al., *New York Walk Book*, x.

16. Torrey et al., *New York Walk Book*, 324. Despite its despoliation of country road walking and its tendency to make trail walking seem a more Arcadian pleasure, the automobile in the early twentieth century was itself experienced as an adventurous,

"strenuous" form of recreation, in comparison to more traditional forms of touring, via the railroad, for example. For background on the early years of automobile touring, see Warren J. Belasco, *Americans on the Road: From Autocamp to Motel, 1910–1945* (Cambridge, Mass.: MIT Press, 1979).

17. Torrey et al., *New York Walk Book*, 182, 69.

18. Ibid., 202.

19. Ibid., 208, 207.

20. Scene and last line drawn from Benton MacKaye, "The Battle of Doodletown: A Skirmish with Civilization" (typescript), Box 166, MacKaye Family Papers, Baker Library, Dartmouth College, Hanover, N.H.

21. Diary of Benton MacKaye, 1921, Box 183, MacKaye Family Papers. Also see: MacKaye, "Some Early AT History," *Potomac Appalachian Trail Club Bulletin* (October–December 1957); Lewis Mumford's introduction to the 1962 edition of MacKaye, *The New Exploration: A Philosophy of Regional Planning* (1928; rpt. Urbana: University of Illinois Press, 1962); MacKaye, "An Appalachian Trail: A Project in Regional Planning," *Journal of the American Institute of Architects* 9 (1921): 325–30.

22. MacKaye, "An Appalachian Trail," 328, 329.

23. Ibid., ix. On the relationship between Lewis Mumford and Benton MacKaye, see John L. Thomas, "Lewis Mumford, Benton MacKaye, and the Regional Vision," in *Lewis Mumford: Public Intellectual*, ed. Thomas P. Hughes and Agatha C. Hughes (New York: Oxford University Press: New York, 1990). For examples of MacKaye's ideas during these years, see his *Employment and Natural Resources: A Report to the Department of Labor* (Washington, D.C.: Department of Labor, 1919); "Labor and the War: The Soldier, the Worker, and the Land's Resources," *Monthly Labor Review* (January 1918); "Making New Opportunities for Employment," *Monthly Labor Review* (April 1919); "A Plan for Cooperation Between Farmer and Consumer," *Monthly Labor Review* (August 1920).

24. MacKaye, "An Appalachian Trail," 330. MacKaye's teacher William M. Davis also mixed drama with "geotechnics," MacKaye's name for the sort of environmental visualization they practiced. He had a vivid memory of his first day in Davis's "Geography A." Davis stood motionless on the platform of a lecture hall in the Agassiz Museum, then suddenly held up a globe and, giving it a spin, declared: "Gentlemen, here is the subject of our study—this planet, its lands, waters, atmosphere, and life; the abode of plant, animal and man—*the earth as a sustainable globe*." Paul T. Bryant, *The Quality of the Day: The Achievement of Benton MacKaye* (Ann Arbor, Mich.: University Microfilms International, 1965), quoted in Thomas, "Mumford, MacKaye, and the Regional Vision," 70.

25. "Landscaping of the Perkins Memorial Drive in Bear Mountain Park" (press release), April 29, 1937, Trailside Museum Archives, Palisades Interstate Park Commission, Bear Mountain, N.Y.; Raymond Torrey to Frank Lutz, December 6, 1926, Central Archives, American Museum of Natural History, New York.

26. On the beaver introduction program, see Commissioners of the Palisades Interstate Park, *Annual Report* (1922), 22.

27. MacKaye, *The New Exploration*, 58, 208, 209.

28. Ibid., 138, 131. The earliest version of his central idea was stated in Benton MacKaye, "The New Exploration: Charting the Industrial Wilderness," *The Survey Graphic* 13 (1925): 153–57. On Patten, see Gregg Mitman, "Evolution as Gospel: William Patten, the Language of Democracy, and the Great War," *Isis* 81 (1990): 446–63.

29. MacKaye, *The New Exploration*, 1–3, 126.

30. Benton MacKaye, "Outdoor Culture—The Philosophy of Through-Trails," *Landscape Architecture* (April 1927). Shortly after giving his talk, MacKaye received an invitation from Joseph Leventhal, editor of *The Knapsack: The Magazine for Hikers*, to write an article about his ideas for a "barbarian invasion." Leventhal signed his letter "Fellow Barbarian." Lewis Mumford, Ray Torrey, and others took to using the term for themselves. Leventhal to MacKaye, January 29, 1927, MacKaye Family Papers.

31. Interview with Christy MacKaye Barnes, May 28, 1997. Also see Bryant, *Quality of the Day*.

32. MacKaye, *The New Exploration*, 10, 14, 16–17.

33. Spengler, quoted in ibid., 23; Percy MacKaye to Lewis Mumford, April 4, 1927, Box 111, MacKaye Family Papers.

34. Benton to Percy MacKaye, March 15, 1920, Box 111, MacKaye Family Papers; Lewis Mumford quoting Benton MacKaye in MacKaye, *The New Exploration*, viii.

35. Benton MacKaye, "The Appalachian Trail: A Guide to the Study of Nature," *Scientific Monthly* 32 (1932): 330–42; MacKaye, "The Appalachian Trail as a Primeval Influence" (draft manuscript), Box 184, MacKaye Family Papers.

36. Benton MacKaye, "The Trail as a Dramatizer of Nature" (draft lecture, 1927), Box 184; "The Appalachian Revolution: A Detective Story of Nature Told by the AT" (manuscript, August 11, 1932), Box 184, MacKaye Family Papers. Around the time that MacKaye was drafting his guide, he came up with a proposal for a "Nature Guide Service" consisting of a series of nature trails, a travelers' service, and a series of publications. "A Nature Guide Service for the AT" (memo, August 20, 1932), Box 184, MacKaye Family Papers.

37. MacKaye, "The Appalachian Trail," 339. A generation later, MacKaye still held this view of the close intertwining of the social and the biological. In a note to himself in 1952 about the *Scientific Monthly* piece, he recommitted himself to Davis's riverine landscape successional model, but added that, were he rewriting the piece for a contemporary audience, he would substitute biotic succession instead for climatic succession because it would far better illustrate the forest as a "natural society." Memo attached to reprint of "The Appalachian Trail," Box 166, MacKaye Family Papers.

38. Benton MacKaye, "The Drama of Conservation: A Geographic Allegory" (manuscript, 1918), Box 181, MacKaye Family Papers; Percy MacKaye, *Sanctuary: A Bird Masque* (New York: Frederick A. Stokes, 1913), x.

39. Percy MacKaye, *Sanctuary*, 5.

40. Percy MacKaye, "The Drama and Conservation" (undated typescript), Box 66, MacKaye Family Papers. For an excellent survey of American historical pageantry, and particularly the role of Percy MacKaye, see David Glassberg, *American Historical Pageantry: The Uses of Tradition in the Early Twentieth Century* (Chapel Hill: University of North Carolina Press, 1990).

41. On MacKaye's conception of "geotechnics," see Benton MacKaye, *From Geography to Geotechnics* (Urbana: University of Illinois Press, 1968). Percy MacKaye, inundated with requests from conservation and civic groups for permission to perform *Sanctuary*, turned over the rights and management of the drama to Baynes, whose promotion of the "Meriden Idea" led to the founding of more than two hundred bird clubs between 1912 and 1916. Among the promotional materials developed by Baynes was a permanent window display at Manhattan's Hotel McAlpin, maintained by the Rutherford, New Jersey, Bird Club. See Box 66, MacKaye Family Papers.

42. David Glassberg points out that in the vicinity of the Pine Mountain School where he resided, Percy MacKaye encountered a more genteel than authentic version of mountain culture; Glassberg, *American Historical Pageantry*, 138.

43. Benton MacKaye, "The 'Open Door' in America: Manifest Destiny for Appalachia, not Manchuria" (manuscript, 1932), Box 166, MacKaye Family Papers; Percy MacKaye to Mary and Marette Longley, summer 1895, quoted in Arvia MacKaye Ege, *The Power of the Impossible: The Life Story of Percy and Marion MacKaye* (Falmouth, Me.: Kennebec River Press, 1992), 34–35.

    It is interesting to note that, aside from his contact with Shaler and his lifelong conversations with Benton about nature, Percy MacKaye had his own early passion for natural history. He kept entomological notebooks as a teenager. A letter from his father in 1890 captures an earlier generation's surer sense of the spiritual world's immanence in nature: "Try to write for me a story of the romance of an entomologist's life. Tell how, pursuing a bug, he found beauty—and trying to catch an insect, caught God himself—and felt Him ever after glorifying his every glimpse of this poor world." Steele to Percy MacKaye, September 19, 1890, quoted in Ege, *The Power of the Impossible*, 24.

CHAPTER 2   *On Nature's Trail: Nature Study at Harriman Park*

1. Peter J. Schmitt, *Back to Nature: The Arcadian Myth in Urban America* (Oxford: Oxford University Press, 1969; Baltimore: Johns Hopkins University Press, 1990), pioneered the history of American nature study; see chapters 7–10. Tyree G. Minton, "The History of the Nature-Study Movement and Its Role in the Development of Environmental Education" (Ph.D. diss., University of Massachusetts, 1980), and Richard R. Olmsted, "The Nature-Study Movement in American Education" (Ed.D. diss., Indiana University, 1967), survey nature study as the antecedent to environmental education. For a comparative study of the American and Australian nature-study movements, see Sally Gregory Kohlstedt, "Nature Study in North America and Australasia, 1890–1945: International Connections and Local Implementations," *Historical Records of Australian Science* 11 (1997): 439–54.

2. Arthur Platts Abbott, *The Greatest Park in the World: Palisades Interstate Park, Its Purpose, History and Achievements* (New York: Historian Press, 1914), 62.

3. The chronology for the following narrative is based upon the one given by Hyde in "P. I. P.," a manuscript history of nature-study work in Harriman Park, Benjamin T. B. Hyde Papers, Trailside Museum Archives, Palisades Interstate Park Commission, Bear Mountain, N.Y. Other biographical information on Hyde can be found in William H. Carr, "Bear Mountain Trail Blazers," *The Conservationist* 29 (1974–1975): 7–11, and Jack Focht, "Uncle Bennie, Founder of Nature Education in the Palisades Interstate Park, 1920," *Trailside Museum and Zoo Historical Papers*, Historical Series, no. 34 (1990).

4. "Brotherhood of the Backwoods" was a phrase coined by Sir Ernest Baden Powell, founder of the English Boy Scouts. On the clash of Arcadian ideals and institutional realities in the Scouts and other "backwoods brotherhoods," see Schmitt, *Back to Nature*, chap. 10.

5. For an overview of the pedagogical objectives of the Boy Scouts, see David I. MacLeod, *Building Character in the American Boy: The Boy Scouts, YMCA, and Their Forerunners, 1870–1920* (Madison: University of Wisconsin Press, 1983).

6. Brochure for "Nature Leader's Training Course" (1921), Hyde Papers. Hyde's fixation

244   Notes to Pages 55–63

on fear extended to girls: "The girl of today is the woman of tomorrow. The knowledge and understanding, also the complete lack of fear in the mother, radiates its influence to her children and household and gives her the opportunity to cooperate with her family in meeting and overcoming 'fear' problems." "Biography of Leadership" (undated course of lectures given to the Manhattan Girl Scouts' "Nature Troop"), Hyde Papers.

7. "Conquering the Fear of Snakes," Hyde Papers. Hyde was himself once bitten by a rattlesnake he was handling and was rushed to the Tuxedo Park hospital.

8. When G. Stanley Hall wrote an introduction to his protégé Clifton F. Hodge's "portable" nature-study curriculum, developed from Hodge's experience with the Worcester, Massachusetts, school system, he lamented the "effeminization" projected by much modern nature-study literature; Hodge, *Nature Study and Life* (Boston: Ginn and Company, 1902), xv. On the martial ideal as a symptom of antimodernist protest against the loss of a sense of male selfhood, see T. J. Jackson Lears, *No Place of Grace: Antimodernism and the Transformation of American Culture, 1880–1920* (New York: Pantheon, 1981).

   Hyde's voluntary forsaking of a life of luxury seems to have added to his stature among his peers. At a ceremony at Kanawauke Lakes dedicating a plaque to Hyde after his death in 1933, "nature lore" promoter William Gould Vinal stressed Hyde's "roughing it" when he could have been "enjoying feather beds in Brooklyn"; flyer for Hyde memorial dedication, August 5, 1934, Hyde Papers.

9. Clark Wissler, "Pueblo Bonito as Made Known by the Hyde Expedition," *Natural History* 22 (1922): 343–54.

10. On the soap industry and its participation in the rise of national advertising, see: Vincent Vinikas, *Soft Soap, Hard Sell: American Hygiene in an Age of Advertisement* (Ames: Iowa State University Press, 1992); "Leadership Among Boys in Nature," Hyde Papers.

11. For G. Stanley Hall's theories of child development, see his *Adolescence* (New York: Appleton, 1904). Schmitt, *Back to Nature*, 77–80, discusses Hall's theories in relation to nature study; see also Dorothy Ross, *G. Stanley Hall: The Psychologist as Prophet* (Chicago: University of Chicago Press, 1972). Hyde's remarks are from the 1922 museum staff report and a 1923 report by Hyde to the Boy Scouts of America, Hyde Papers.

12. Hyde, "Biography of Leadership"; "Fieldbook for Nature Leaders" (no date), Hyde Papers.

13. George Sherwood to Henry Fairfield Osborn, February 4, 1920; Hyde to Osborn, June 9, 1921; Osborn to Hyde, July 6, 1922, May 31, 1918, Hyde Papers.

14. Annual reports of camp museums, 1921–1927, Hyde Papers.

15. Frank Lutz to Henry Fairfield Osborn, October 16, 1924, Folder 765, Central Archives, American Museum of Natural History, New York.

16. Henry Fairfield Osborn to Frank Lutz, October 22, 1924, Folder 765, Central Archives; Lutz to Osborn, October 28, 1924 (with enclosed "Memorandum Concerning a Station for the Study of Insects"), Frank E. Lutz Papers, American Museum of Natural History, New York.

17. For a provocative discussion of the symbiotic relationship between genteel summer resorts and field biological research, see Philip J. Pauly, "Summer Resort and Scientific Discipline: Woods Hole and the Structure of American Biology, 1882–1925," in *The American Development of Biology*, ed. Ronald Rainger, Keith R. Benson, and Jane Maienschein (Philadelphia: University of Pennsylvania Press, 1988). Pauly makes the important point that such locales, though "close to nature," were sheltered from nature's

unpleasantries, making them amenable not only to the life scientists but also to their children and spouses. On Tuxedo, see Cleveland Amory, *The Last Resorts* (New York: Harper and Brothers, 1948), 90. Tuxedo's residents traveled not on spectacular yachts but arrived by chauffeured limousine or, for its most privileged few, like Edward Harriman or Mrs. William Pierson Hamilton, daughter of the elder J. P. Morgan, via private railroad car. (Both Harriman and Mrs. Hamilton even had their own stations on the Erie Railroad, Mrs. Hamilton's Sterlington just to the south of Tuxedo and Harriman's Arden station stop immediately north of town.) Less prosperous members of the Tuxedo elite needed only to show their badge of Tuxedo membership—a solid gold oak leaf pin—to an Erie conductor and the train, even if it was scheduled to stop only for the principal stations, would be halted at the little Tudor station house at Tuxedo.

18. Frank Lutz to Henry Fairfield Osborn, October 28, 1924, Lutz Papers.
19. Frank Lutz to Hermon Bumpus, October 6, 1930; Lutz to George Sherwood, October 1, 1931, October 25, 1932, Central Archives.
20. George Sherwood to Frank Lutz, September 24, 1924; Department of Entomology Staff Meeting Report, January 27, 1925; Lutz to Sherwood, March 18, 1933, Central Archives.
21. Frank Lutz to Henry Fairfield Osborn, October 28, 1924; Osborn to Lutz, November 21, 1924; Osborn to E. L Partridge, December 15, 1924; Lutz to George Sherwood, December 17, 1924, Lutz Papers.
22. Henry Fairfield Osborn to Frank Lutz, December 23, 1924 (memo on the status of the field station plan); George Pindar to Osborn, November 27, 1924, Central Archives; Lutz to E. L. Partridge, December 27, 1924; Lutz to William Welch, April 25, 1925; Paul S. Tichenor to Palisades Interstate Park Commissioners, April 7, 1925, Lutz Papers.
23. Frank Lutz to William Welch, May 16, 1925; Lutz Diary, May 2, 5, 9, 1925, Lutz Papers.
24. Frank Lutz, "Nature Trails: An Experiment in Out-door Education," *Miscellaneous Publications of the American Museum of Natural History*, no. 21 (1931); "Taking Nature Lore to the Public," Natural History 26 (1926): 111–13; and *A Lot of Insects: Entomology in a Suburban Garden* (New York: G. P. Putnam, 1941), 280–85.
25. Anne Lutz, "The Station for the Study of Insects and the First Nature Trail," *Trailside Museum and Zoo Historical Papers*, Historial Series, no. 2 (1989); Albert C. Redmond, "My SSI Days," *Trailside Museum and Zoo Historical Papers*, Historical Series, no. 2 (1991).
26. Lutz, *A Lot of Insects*, 282–83.
27. Hank Childs to Palisades camp directors, July 8, 1925; Frank Lutz to George Sherwood, July 8, 1925, July 28, 1925; Lutz to William H. Welch, June 18, 1925; Welch to Lutz, June 16, 1925, July 11, 1925, Central Archives.
28. Frank Lutz to William H. Welch, October 19, 1925; Welch to Lutz, January 14, 1925, Central Archives; Ida St John Oye and Wilhelmine S. Oetjen to Lutz, August 21, 1925, Lutz Papers. A "downstate-upstate" battle for priority for the nature trail idea has been waged for years between Harriman Park devotees, who maintain that Lutz's was the first, and loyalists of Allegheny State Park, who maintain that there, as early as 1921, the Buffalo Society of Natural Sciences operated a camp where a path was cut and labeled with natural history materials. W. P. Alexander, field naturalist and director of extension work for the Buffalo group, developed the trail as an extension of a nature museum at the Roosevelt Field Camp. Issues of priority aside, it is worth noting that developers of the Alleghany State Park nature trail similarly saw it as a response to the problem of guiding large numbers of people through fields and woods while keeping them in as natural a condition as possible. They also emphasized its time-saving features,

supporting historical interpretations of the importance of efficiency during this phase of American nature-study pedagogy. The fact that Alexander's initiative seems not to have sparked the explosion of imitators fostered by Lutz's SSI trail may have been due to any one of a number of factors, including Alleghany's less metropolitan location and the possibility that Alexander's label text was less appealing than Lutz's. Perhaps the difference of four years of rising popular familiarity with billboards holds the key. See I. C. Robertson, ed., *75 Years: A History of the Buffalo Society of Natural Science, 1861–1936* (Buffalo: Buffalo Museum of Science Press, 1939), 152, and Sherman C. Bishop, "An Early Experiment in Natural History Trails," *School and Society* 27 (1928): 541–43.

29. George Sherwood to Grace Stone, April 9, 1926 (Sherwood had first sent Stone's letter to Lutz, who penciled in the margin: "They shd make their own"); Frank Lutz to Henry Fairfield Osborn, September 3, 1925; Lutz to Sherwood, October 19, 1926, Central Archives; "Blazing the First Nature Trail In NYC" (flyer, June 7, 1927), Lutz Papers

30. Frank Lutz to Hermon Bumpus, October 11, 1925, Lutz Papers.

31. Frank Lutz Jr. to Anne Lutz, February 11, 1985, Lutz Papers. Outdoor signage is so much a part of twentieth-century American culture that to suggest it had an influence on the development of the nature trail may seem preposterous. A useful way to gain a better perspective on that development might be through a comparative historical approach. As far as I am aware, nature trails, where they exist outside the United States, have been directly inspired by American exemplars. More fundamentally, the ubiquity of what historical geographer Wilbur Zelinsky calls "nonessential" signs in America, and their relative paucity outside America, seem to suggest that Americans expect and take "direction" via outdoor signage more readily than other cultures. Scholarship on the relative abundance of and the peculiar rhetoric of both outdoor advertising and of nature trail interpretive signage is needed to further triangulate whether nature trails are peculiarly American and the ways in which they have changed during the twentieth century. Zelinsky attributes the "superabundance" of American road signage to the fact that Americans "remain strangers in this strange and wonderful land, restless, eager strangers yearning to establish, or re-establish, connections and community." Wilbur Zelinsky, "On the Superabundance of Signs in Our Landscape," *Landscape* 31, no. 3 (1992): 38.

32. Frank Lutz to Hermon Bumpus, August 18, 1925, Lutz Papers; Lutz, *A Lot of Insects*, 280.

33. Lutz, *A Lot of Insects*, 283; Frank Lutz to Hermon Bumpus, August 18, 1925, Lutz Papers. On the nature-faking controversy, see Ralph Lutts, *The Nature Fakers: Wildlife, Science, and Sentiment* (Golden, Colo.: Fulcrum Publishing, 1990). For an alternative interpretation consistent with the theme of this chapter—the triumph of naturalistic philosophy—see Matt Cartmill, *A View to a Death in the Morning: Hunting and Nature through History* (Cambridge, Mass.: Harvard University Press, 1993), 150–56.

34. Frank Lutz to Hermon Bumpus, August 18, 1925, Lutz Papers. On the history of outdoor advertising in America, see James Fraser, *The American Billboard: 100 Years* (New York: Harry Abrams, 1991).

35. Frank Lutz to Hermon Bumpus, August 18, 1925, Lutz Papers. Lutz promoted this idea of a natural history–informed populace of motorists in "The Still-open Road," *Natural History* 27 (1927): 373–82.

36. *Cornell Rural School Leaflet* 23, no. 1 (1929): 40.

37. Fraser, *The American Billboard*, 52.
38. Frank Lutz to Hermon Bumpus, October 11, 1925; Bumpus to Lutz, October 15, 1925, Lutz Papers.
39. C. J. Hamlin to William A. Welch, October 5, 1926, Lutz Papers. The Laura Spelman Rockefeller Memorial Fund, which in 1924 had granted $70,000 for the association's plan for a nature museum in Yosemite National Park, made $15,000 available to be shared by the Harriman Park project and an outdoor museum planned for Grand Canyon National Park. The fund also gave a half million dollars to the Palisades Interstate Park to purchase two steamboats to transport New Yorkers of limited means up the Hudson for Arcadian regeneration at Bear Mountain. On the AAM's role in developing natural history museums in state and national parks, see Ralph H. Lewis, *Museum Curatorship in the National Park Service, 1904–1982* (Washington, D.C.: Department of the Interior, National Park Service, Cultural Services Division, 1993).
40. William Carr, *Pebbles in Your Shoes* (Tuscon: Arizona-Sonora Desert Museum, 1982), 6–7.
41. William Carr to Clyde Fisher, May 2, 5, 1927; Fisher to Carr, May 6, 1927; Carr to George Sherwood, May 7, 23, 1927, Trailside Museum Archives.
42. William Carr to Clyde Fisher, May 31, 1927; Carr to George Sherwood, May 31, 1927, Trailside Museum Archives.
43. William Carr to George Sherwood, December 31, 1927, Trailside Museum Archives; William Carr, "Signs Along the Trail." *American Museum of Natural History School Service Series* 1 (1927). "Signs Along the Trail" proved as popular as Lutz's earlier promotional pamphlet; within a year, more than 12,000 copies of the pamphlet were distributed. Raymond Torrey, "Insect Life as a Subject for Field Museums" (press release, 1928), Trailside Museum Archives.
44. William Carr, "Labels Along the Bear Mountain Nature Trail" (manuscript, 1927), William Carr Papers, Trailside Museum Archives.
45. Hyde, "How to Tell a Story" (undated lecture manuscript), Hyde Papers. Opposite the title page of Carr's second pamphlet detailing the nature trails at Bear Mountain is a photograph of gray birch trees; according to the caption, the trees "offer opportunities for telling inspirational as well as informational stories." William Carr, "Blazing Nature's Trail," American Museum of Natural History School Service Series 2/3 (1928).
46. William Carr, "Blazing Nature's Trail," 6, 11.
47. Ibid., 10. Other examples of Carr's making sport out of the public's natural history ignorance can be found in "Trailside Unnatural History," *Natural History* 34, no. 3 (1934): 287–96, and "A Trailside Convert," *Natural History* 33, no. 3 (1933): 278–86.
48. William Carr, "Trailside Conversations," *American Museum of Natural History School Service Series* 4 (1930): 13–14.
49. Ibid., 19; William Carr, "Trailside Family," *American Museum of Natural History School Service Series* 7 (1932): 20; "Handbook of Nature Trails and Trailside Museums" (manuscript), Carr Papers, p. 105.
50. William Carr, "Trailside Actions and Reactions," *American Museum of Natural History School Service Series* 5 (1931): 13, 8.
51. Ibid., 32, 6.
52. *New York Times* and *Atlantic* reviews quoted in Kerry W. Buckley, *Mechanical Man: John Broadus Watson and the Beginnings of Behaviorism* (New York: Guilford Press, 1989), 98. Robert Richards notes that between 1927 and 1958, entries in *Psychological Abstracts* for "instinct" rapidly declined from 68 percent to 8 percent of total key-

word entries; the terms "drive," "reinforcement," and "motivation" replaced it. Richards, *Darwin and the Emergence of Evolutionary Theories of Mind and Behavior* (Chicago: University of Chicago Press, 1987), 504.

53. William H. Carr, "Two Thousand Miles Along the Crest of the Atlantic Highlands," *Natural History* 33 (1933): 405.

54. William Carr, "Trailside Interdependence: Being an Account of the Building of a Trailside Museum Exhibit to Show That a State of True Independence Does Not Exist in the World of Nature," *American Museum of Natural History School Service Series* 8 (1933): 6.

55. On the 1899 Harriman Alaska Expedition, see William H. Goetzmann and Kay Sloan, *Looking Far North: The Harriman Expedition to Alaska, 1899* (New York: Viking Press, 1982).

56. John Burroughs, "The Gospel of Nature," *Century* 84 (1912): 199, 202; Burroughs, *Accepting the Universe: Essays in Naturalism* (Boston and New York: Houghton Mifflin Company, 1920), 103.

57. Burroughs, "The Gospel of Nature," 202–3.

58. Burroughs, *Accepting the Universe*, 103.

59. Just how closely allied Burroughs was with Whitman is tellingly demonstrated in *Accepting the Universe*, which closes with an essay about "The Poet of the Cosmos." At the end of a long volume debunking any philosophies that regard human beings as other than material creatures produced by natural selection, Burroughs champions Whitman as the representative of a new "cosmic consciousness." In doing so, Burroughs invokes Whitman's "naturalism"—his natural history knowledge—to celebrate Whitman's philosophical alliance with himself: "Our modern nature poets are holiday flower-gatherers beside this inspired astronomer, geologist, and biologist, all in one, sauntering the streets, loitering on the beach, roaming the mountains, or rapt and silent under the midnight skies" (324).

60. Jo Davidson, *Between Sittings* (New York: Dial Press, 1951), 294–95; Averell Harriman to Percy MacKaye, May 17, 1938; Percy to Benton MacKaye, February 28, 1939, MacKaye Family Papers.

61. Pamphlet from November 17, 1940, ceremony of Walt Whitman statue installation commemorating Mary Harriman's gift of park lands, Trailside Museum Archives. Addresses were also given by two men who had come to shape the face of the Manhattan hinterland in a direction that, rather than implementing Benton MacKaye's vision of maintaining the hinterland against the power of the metropolis, gave it over to the metropolis. Myron Avery, chairman of the Appalachian Trail Club, noted the birth of the Appalachian Trail at the point where the statue stood. Robert Moses, whose parkways provided Manhattanites easy automobile access to Arcadia, noted that he had wanted to put the statue near Whitman's birthplace, now conveniently accessible along the new Northern Parkway in Suffolk County.

62. Interview with Henry and Christy MacKaye Barnes, Harlemville, N.Y., May 28, 1997.

CHAPTER 3   *Science and the Sensible*

1. Garland Allen originally formulated the "naturalist-experimentalist" distinction in *Life Science in the Twentieth Century* (Cambridge: Cambridge University Press, 1975). Subsequent scholarship in the history of biology has refined this distinction; see, for example, Jane Maienschein, Ronald Rainger, and Keith Benson, "Introduction: Were

American Morphologists in Revolt?" *Journal of the History of Biology* 14 (1981): 83–87, and Joel Hagen, "Experimentalists and Naturalists in Twentieth-Century Botany: Experimental Taxonomy, 1920–1950," *Journal of the History of Biology* 17 (1984): 249–70.

2. John Burroughs, *Accepting the Universe: Essays in Naturalism* (Boston and New York: Houghton Mifflin, 1920), 51.

3. Raymond Torrey, "Insect Life as a Subject for Field Museums" (press release, 1928), Trailside Museum Archives, Palisades Interstate Park Commission, Bear Mountain, N.Y. Torrey's article also emphasized the special role of insects in natural history instruction with respect to the growing concern for protection of wildlife: "Collection of insects either for life exhibits or for mounted specimens does not involve such disturbance of the balance of life in a region devoted to conservation such as the Harriman Park, as does the collection of plants, snakes, turtles, birds or mammals, which has to be restricted in order that rare species may not be too severely drawn upon for study in camp museums . . . boys or girls might collect all the insects they could find without affecting the population."

4. Frank Lutz to William Welch, February 4, 1927; Lutz to George Sherwood, October 19, 1926, Frank E. Lutz Papers, Trailside Museum Archives, Palisades Interstate Park Commission. Although Steele did not return to SSI, he did publish one paper from his 1926 research; Brandt Steele, "Notes on the Feeding Habits of Carrion Beetles," *Journal of the New York Entomological Society* 35 (1927): 1–27. Steele wished to spend the summer closer to his father, who had become ill, so he was thinking of taking a summer position with the Indiana State Parks department. He also thought that he might turn from entomology to medicine. Though Lutz wrote Steele a sympathetic letter of support, he also told Steele that he might, especially with the prospect of improved lab facilities at SSI, pursue research in line with both medicine and entomology. Steele to Lutz, January 22, 1927; Lutz to Steele, January 26, 1927, Lutz Papers.

5. F. M. Brown, "Descriptions of New Bacteria Found in Insects," *American Museum Novitates* 251 (1927); Frank E. Lutz and F. M. Brown, "A New Species of Bacteria and the Gall of an Aphid," *American Museum Novitates* 305 (1928); Lutz, *A Lot of Insects: Entomology in a Suburban Garden* (New York: G. P. Putnam, 1941), 52–53.

6. W. S. Creighton, "The Slave-Raids of *Harpagoxenus americanus*," *Psyche* 34, no. 1 (1927): 16–24; Lutz, *A Lot of Insects*, 130–32.

7. Lutz, *Field Book of Insects* (New York: G. P. Putnam's Sons, 1918), 131, 135.

8. Lutz, "Apparently Non-Selective Characters and Combinations of Characters, Including a Study of Ultraviolet in Relation to the Flower-Visiting Habits of Inseects," *Annals of the New York Academy of Science* 29 (1924): 233–83; Lutz and F. K. Richtmyer, "The Reaction of *Drosophila* to Ultraviolet," *Science* 55 (1922): 519; Lutz, "Flowers and Their Insect Visitors," *Natural History* 23 (1923): 125–34; Lutz, *A Lot of Insects*, 100–101. When Lutz went on to continue recording the ultraviolet reflectivity of flowers in his Ramsey yard and at SSI, he could not afford a UV filter, so he substituted a piece of black cardboard with a pinhole in place of the lens and made very long exposures.

9. Frank Lutz to George Sherwood, September 12, 1927, Central Archives, American Museum of Natural History, New York.

10. Frank Lutz to George Sherwood, September 14, 1926, Central Archives; Luis W. Alvarez, "Alfred Lee Loomis," *Biographical Memoirs of the National Academy of Sciences* 51 (1980): 309–41.

11. Frank Lutz, "Experiments with 'Wonder Creatures,'" *Natural History* 29 (1929): 160–68.

12. Alfred L. Loomis and R. W. Wood, "The Physical and Biological Effects of High-Frequency Sound-Waves of Great Intensity," *Philosophical Magazine* 4 (1927): 417–36; William Seabrook, *Doctor Wood, Modern Wizard of the Laboratory; The Story of an American Small Boy Who Became the Most Daring and Original Experimental Physicist of Our Day—But Never Grew Up* (1941; rpt. New York: Harcourt, Brace, 1983), 214–16; Frank Lutz, "A Much-Abused But Still Cheerful Cricket," *Journal of the New York Entomological Society* 35 (1927): 307–8.

13. Lutz, "Apparently Non-Selective Characters," 272–73.

14. Lutz, "Apparently Non-Selective Characters," 279; Lutz, "'Invisible' Colors of Flowers and Butterflies," *Natural History* 33 (1933): 565–76. Lutz had raised doubts about the operation of natural selection in patterns of butterfly mimicry as early as 1911; see Lutz, "Mimicry," *American Naturalist* 45 (1911): 190–92.

15. Lutz, "Apparently Non-Selective Characters," 278, 275, 280, 281. Dr. Brown's research also showed that it was the odor of yeast growing on rotting fruit, not the fruit itself, that attracted *Drosophila*; Frank Lutz to George Sherwood, October 17, 1927, Central Archives.

16. On anti-Darwinian theories in the early twentieth century, see Peter J. Bowler, *The Eclipse of Darwinism: Anti-Darwinian Evolutionary Theories in the Decades around 1900* (Baltimore: Johns Hopkins University Press, 1983).

17. Lutz, "Apparently Non-Selective Characters," 279–82; Lutz to Henry F. Osborn, April 27, 1925, Central Archives. On Osborn's ideas about evolution, see Ronald Rainger, *An Agenda for Antiquity: Henry Fairfield Osborn and Vertebrate Paleontology at the American Museum of Natural History, 1890–1935* (Tuscaloosa: University of Alabama Press, 1991). The limits of the adaptationist explanation of biological form continues to be an issue of considerable contention; see R. N. Brandon, *Adaptation and Environment* (Princeton: Princeton University Press, 1990).

18. For press coverage of the Scopes trial and a discussion of the absence at the time of any consideration of the nature of knowledge, see Edward Caudill, *Darwinism in the Press: The Evolution of an Idea* (Hillsdale, N.Y.: Lawrence Erlbaum Associates, 1989), 94–113.

19. Summary sheet of correspondence to Education Department for 1926, Central Archives; Frank E. Lutz, "The New Insect Groups in the American Museum," *Natural History* 25 (1925): 126–35. On the Hall of the Age of Man, see Rainger, *Agenda for Antiquity*, 169–81, and also Charlotte Porter, "The Rise of Parnassus: Henry Fairfield Osborn and the Hall of the Age of Man," *Museum Studies Journal* 1 (1983): 26–34. For a sense of the sort of criticism that Osborn and the museum received from antievolutionists, see John Roach Straton, "The Fancies of the Evolutionists," *Forum* 75 (1926): 245–51.

20. Philip Pauly notes that evolutionary theory was absent from the official biology syllabus in New York State before 1925 and that it was much less prominent in biology texts than in pre-1910 books on botany, zoology, or geology. What helped to marginalize evolution, he says, was primarily its historical character, which was not amenable to the current emphasis on observation and experiment in high school biology. Pauly, "The Development of High School Biology, New York City, 1900–1925," *Isis* 82 (1991): 662–88. On the Scopes trial, see Ray Ginger, *Six Days or Forever? Tennessee vs. John Thomas Scopes* (Boston: Beacon Press, 1958), and Edward J. Larson, *Summer for the Gods: The Scopes Trial and America's Continuing Debate over Science and Religion* (Cambridge, Mass.: Harvard University Press, 1997).

21. Frank Lutz to George Sherwood, October 4, 1928, Central Archives; Chauncey Hamlin to Lutz, January 28, 1927, Lutz Papers; H. F. Osborn, "How to Teach Evolution in the Schools," *School and Society* 23 (1926): 28.

22. Osborn, "How to Teach Evolution in the Schools," 27.

23. Henry F. Osborn to Mary Harriman, February 3, 1926, Central Archives; Frank Lutz to Hermon C. Bumpus, March 28, 1927, Lutz Papers. Despite this unprecedented solicitation of Mrs. Harriman, the degree of Osborn's real knowledge of and interest in SSI is suggested by his reference to it as the "Summer Museum and Nature Trail Station."

24. Frank Lutz to George Sherwood, October 4, 1928, Lutz Papers. Beginning in the early 1930s, Rockefeller made nearly annual donations to the Entomological Fund that Lutz had created to augment the museum's limited research budget for his department.

25. Frank Lutz to William H. Welch, October 29, 1928; Lutz to George Sherwood, March 15, 1928; Ruby Jollife to Welch, April 7, 1932, Lutz Papers.

26. C. H. Curran, "Report on the Diptera Collected at the SSI, HSP, NY," *Bulletin of the American Museum of Natural History* 61 (1931): 21–115.

27. Edgar Mearns, "A Study of the Vertebrate Fauna of the Hudson Highlands," *Bulletin of the American Museum of Natural History* 10 (1898): 303–52. Mearns's reports on the avifauna of the Highlands appeared from 1878 to 1881 in the *Bulletin of the Essex Institute*. For further information about Mearns's scientific career, see M. J. Brodhead, "Of Mice and Mastodons: Contributions to the Literature of Mammalogy by Officers and Men of the United States Army in the Nineteenth Century," *Archives of Natural History* 18 (1991): 363–74, and R. H. Baker, "A Watcher of Birds," *Michigan History* 66 (1982): 40–45. Among early-twentieth-century foresters and botanists, there was a controversy over the nature of the Highlands forest and the degree to which it had been disturbed by humans. William L. Bray and many others believed that the Highlands had been a more mesic forest in precontact times and had been driven toward its present xerophytic character by widespread timber cutting in the eighteenth and nineteenth centuries. See Bray, *The Development of the Vegetation of New York State* (Syracuse: New York State College of Forestry, 1915), and Hugh Raup, *Botanical Studies in the Black Rock Forest* (Cornwall-on-Hudson, N.Y.: Black Rock Forest, 1931).

28. Mearns, "A Study of the Vertebrate Fauna of the Hudson Highlands," 1–77, 34. The Highlands, and the Ramapos in particular, are conspicuous in the relative abundance of albino vertebrates that have been reported in the scientific literature. Considering that the human population of the Ramapo region has long been thought to have the highest rate of albinism in the United States, it is odd that more research has not been conducted on this striking coincidence. In his published reports of his research on the heredity of albinism among humans in the Ramapo area (see chap. 4), Charles Davenport never mentions the incidence of albinism in the regional fauna.

29. Charles C. Adams, "An Ecological Survey of the Palisades Interstate Park," *Empire Forester* 5 (1919): 12–18. G. S. Myers also made use of Boy Scout labor in his 1923 herpetological inventory of the park; see Myers, "Amphibians and Reptiles Observed in the Palisades Interstate Park," *Copeia* 173 (1930): 99–103.

30. William Carr to William Welch, May 9, 1930, November 1, 1931, Trailside Museum Archives.

31. On the ECW program, see R. Gerald Wright, *Wildlife Research and Management in the National Parks* (Urbana: University of Illinois Press, 1992), and J. C. Paige, *The Civilian Conservation Corps and the National Park Service: An Administrative History* (Washington, D.C.: National Park Service, 1985).

32. William Carr to William Welch, January 21, 1935; Carr to Conrad Wirth, January 9, 1935, Trailside Museum Archives.

33. "Survey by 'E.C.W.' Wildlife Technicians in the Bear Mtn-Harriman Section of the Palisades Interstate Park" (manuscript report), 3 vols., Trailside Museum Archives.

34. Raymond Torrey, "Assaying Forest Associations by their Autumn Coloring" (press release, October 19, 1936); Torrey, "Natural Forest Types in the Highlands of the Hudson," February 6, 1937, Trailside Museum Archives.

35. Raymond Torrey, "Rare Birds in Palisades Interstate Park," August 27, 1936; "Ancient Life Equilibrium Returns in Palisades Interstate Park," May 13, 1937; "Garden Clubs Approve Conservation in Palisades Interstate Park," June 24, 1936; "Bronze Elk Head Dedicated in Bear Mountain Park," May 7, 1936, Trailside Museum Archives.

36. William Carr to Clyde Fisher, June 2, 1933; Palisades Interstate Park Commission, Annual Report to the Legislature, 1944; Carr to Fairfield Osborn, December 26, 1944, Trailside Museum Archives.

    On the use of motion pictures as a tool in natural science, see Gregg Mitman, *Reel Nature: America's Romance with Wildlife on Film* (Cambridge, Mass.: Harvard University Press, 1999).

37. William Carr, "Seeing What You Are Looking At," undated manuscript lecture; "Disconnected Thoughts on The Clarity of Vision," manuscript lecture, March 1, 1925, Carr Papers, American Heritage Center, American Heritage Center, Laramie, Wyo.

38. W. H. Carr, "The Modern Nature-Faker," *Natural History* 44 (1944): 22–30; Carr, "Telling the Beaver Story," *Natural History* 31 (1931): 640–50; Carr, "Indian Beaver Legends," *Natural History* 31 (1931): 81–92. After the Roosevelt-Seton-Burroughs episode at the turn of the century, periodic eruptions of "nature-faking" accusations also occurred in the 1920s; see, for example: H. G. Evarts, "Bugaboo Natural History," *Saturday Evening Post*, November 10, 1923, 62; W. J. Maddox, "Insect Stories and Nature Fakes," *Hygeia* 4 (1926): 689–91; S. F. Aaron, "Nature Faking: Popular Fallacies Have Grown Out of Pseudo-Scientific Nature Lore," *Scientific American* 134 (1926): 322–23.

39. W. H. Carr, "A Manual of Bird Study: A Description of Twenty-five Local Birds with Study Outlines," *American Museum of Natural History School Service Series* 1 (1934): 1–77; Carr, "Seeing What You Are Looking At," 6, 7.

40. Carr, *The Stir of Nature: A Book for Young American Naturalists* (New York: Oxford University Press, 1930), 23–24.

41. Ibid., 176–78.

42. The "founding texts" of American Theosophy, Helena P. Blavatsky's *Isis Unveiled: The Master Key to the Mysteries of Ancient and Modern Science and Theology* (New York: J. W. Bouton, 1877) and *The Secret Doctrine: The Synthesis of Science, Religion, and Philosophy* (London: Theosophical Publishing Company, 1888), were filled with explicit criticism of the theory of natural selection as originally proposed by Darwin and expounded upon by Thomas H. Huxley, Ernst Haeckel, and others. In a sense, all Theosophical literature was directed at "accelerating" human evolution and thus frequently made reference to orthodox evolutionary theory; see, for example: Hereward Carrington, *The Coming Science* (New York: American Universities Publishing, 1920); Richard Ingalese and Isabella Inglaese, *Occult Philosophy* (New York: Dodd, Mead, 1920); Rudolf Steiner, *Occult Science: An Outline* (1909; rpt. New York: Anthroposophic Press, 1997); Arthur Edward Waite, *The Occult Sciences: A Compendium of Transcendental Doctrine and Experiment* (New York: Dutton, 1923).

43. Wildlife manager and conservationist Aldo Leopold, though typical of other American natural scientists in his enthusiasm for the animate view of nature offered by nature writers like Burroughs, John Muir, and Liberty Hyde Bailey, also read and appreci-

ated the occult writer P. D. Ouspensky. See Curt Meine, *Aldo Leopold: His Life and Work* (Madison: University of Wisconsin Press, 1988), 214–15. In 1924 Lewis Mumford met Alfred R. Orage, editor of the English *New Age*, when Orage was in New York on a lecture tour, and Mumford wrote to his mentor, Patrick Geddes, fairly approvingly of Orage's enthusiasm for the teachings of George I. Gurdjieff. But Mumford was attracted more by the self-improvement potential of Gurdjieff's doctrines and had little patience for any "cryptic and unmentionable theosophic hocus pocus." Mumford to Geddes, January 9, 1924, *Lewis Mumford and Patrick Geddes: The Correspondence*, ed. Frank Novak (New York: Routledge, 1995), 191–92.

44. For Ouspensky's theories of biological mimicry, see P. D. Ouspensky, *A New Model of the Universe: Principles of the Psychological Method in its Applications to Problems of Science, Religion, and Art* (New York: Knopf, 1931), 41–46.

45. Opal Whiteley, "Journal of an Understanding Heart," *Atlantic Monthly* 126 (1920): 125, 293; Ellery Sedgwick, *The Happy Profession* (Boston: Little, Brown, 1946), 252–66. On the controversy over the authenticity of the diary, see: "Child of Seven Is Hailed as a Great Writer," *Current Opinion* 69 (1920): 692–94; "Quarrel Over Opal," *Literary Digest* 67 (1920): 34–35; "Who Is Opal Whiteley?" *Bookman* 53 (1921): 137–40. The Opal Whiteley story continues to generate discussion about the limits of modern understanding of nature; see Benjamin Hoff, *The Singing Creek Where the Willows Grow: The Rediscovered Diary of Opal Whiteley* (New York: Ticknor and Fields, 1986). For a survey of American "nature mysticism" in the 1920s, see H. E. M. Stutfield, "Nature Mysticism," *Living Age* 323 (1924): 261–66.

46. Joel Morrow, "The Mystery of Opal Whiteley," *Biodynamics* 164 (1987): 44–56.

47. Sedgwick, *The Happy Profession*, 264–66.

48. On the Cottingley fairy incident, see: Arthur Conan Doyle, *The Coming of the Fairies* (New York: Hodder and Stoughton, 1922); Edward L. Gardner, *Fairies: The Cottingley Photographs* (1922; rpt. Wheaton, Ill.: Theosophical Publishing Company, 1966); Peter Tompkins, *The Secret Life of Nature: Living in Harmony with the Hidden World of Nature Spirits from Faeries to Quarks* (San Francisco: Harper Collins, 1997).

CHAPTER 4   *Caught between Nature and History*

1. Elizabeth Kite, "The Jackson-Whites: A Study in Racial Degeneracy," Elizabeth Kite Papers, Alexander Library, Rutgers University, pp. 40–41. Although this manuscript is attributed to Elizabeth Kite, the bulk of the text was written by Jane Griffiths in 1913. The introduction, conclusion, and significant editorial amendments were added by Kite in 1917.

2. Jane Griffiths to Henry H. Goddard, May 13, 1911; Griffiths to Miss Bell, November 4, 1911, Henry H. Goddard Papers, Archives of the History of American Psychology, University of Akron, Akron, Ohio.

3. Kite, "The Jackson-Whites," 42, 43.

4. Ibid., 70, 71.

5. Charles B. Davenport, "Heredity of Skin-Pigment in Man," *American Naturalist* 44 (1910): 42–72, 305–31 (also see "Degeneration, Albinism, and Inbreeding," *Science* 28 [1908]: 454–55); Sumner Meringham to Davenport, March 24, April 5, 1909; Davenport to Henry H. Goddard, March 18, 1909, January 3, 1912; Goddard to Davenport, March 15, 1909, December 26, 1911, January 8, 1912, Charles B. Davenport Papers, American Philosophical Society, Philadelphia.

6. Charles B. Davenport, Diary, February 16, 1910; Mary Harriman to Davenport, August 10, 1910, Davenport Papers.

7. Charles B. Davenport to Edward H. Harriman, June 28, July 10, 1907, November 4, 1908; Harriman to Davenport, July 8, 1907, Davenport Papers.

8. Mary Harriman to Charles B. Davenport, July 8, 1910; Davenport to Harriman, May 23, June 24, 1910; David Starr Jordan to Harriman, July 22, 1910, Davenport Papers.

9. Charles B. Davenport, "The Attitude of Field Workers Toward the Work," Davenport Papers. The early correspondence between Davenport and Goddard also reflects their anxiety about the way that eugenics fieldwork would be portrayed in the press. See Henry H. Goddard to Davenport, April 13, 1910; Davenport to Goddard, April 15, January 3, 1910, Davenport Papers.

10. Davenport, "Attitude of Field Workers."

11. Charles B. Davenport to Mary Harriman, July 20, 1910, Davenport Papers.

12. On the interaction of geography and ecology at the University of Chicago, see Gregg Mitman, *The State of Nature: Ecology, Community, and American Social Thought, 1900–1950* (Chicago: University of Chicago Press, 1992), 10–20.

13. Both Goddard and Grant had suggested to Davenport that fruitful areas for eugenic study could be found near Bar Harbor (Henry H. Goddard to Charles B. Davenport, January 17, 1912, Davenport Papers). Philip J. Pauly documents a parallel geographic link between summer resorts and biological research stations in America in "Summer Resort and Scientific Disipline: Woods Hole and the Structure of American Biology, 1882–1925," in *The American Development of Biology*, ed. Ronald Rainger, Keith R. Benson, and Jane Maienschein (Philadelphia: University of Pennsylvania Press, 1988).

   As coastal Maine was colonized by metropolitan areas further south, native residents who remained on offshore islands and isolated peninsulas were routinely set adrift by their fellow townsfolk, who by act of legislature declared these areas "no man's land" so as not to have to pay for their less-well-off neighbors. By 1908 Maine had even established a school for the feebleminded, to remove the "poor unfortunates" from public view. In 1912 the state went so far as to evict forcibly the forty-five mixed-race residents of Malaga Island, not long after local newspaper items speculated on how Malaga would be a perfect spot for more summer homes. The newspaper headline in the wake of the incident read: "Cleaning Up Malaga Island: No Longer a Reproach to the Good Name of the State." See William David Barry, "The Shameful Story of Malaga Island," *Down East* (November 1980): 53–56, 83–86.

14. On the development of the myth of "the menace of the feeble-minded" in America between 1910 and 1920, see Robert W. Trent, *Inventing the Feeble-Mind: A History of Mental Retardation in the United States* (Berkeley: University of California Press, 1994). For a discussion of the descriptive terminology of "mental deficiency" in the late nineteenth and early twentieth centuries, see Steven Noll, *Feeble-Minded in Our Midst: Institutions for the Mentally Retarded in the South, 1900–1940* (Chapel Hill: University of North Carolina Press, 1995), 1–5. Noll and a number of the other recent investigators of institutions for the feebleminded fail to note that a substantial percentage of the individuals labeled feebleminded by eugenicists were not in any way mentally retarded.

15. Harry H. Laughlin to Charles. B. Davenport, November 15, 1920, Davenport Papers; "David Starr Jordan's Claim to 'The First Car Ride,'" *Literary Digest*, September 26, 1925, 62–66.

16. Charles B. Davenport, "Directions for the Guidance of Field Workers," Davenport Papers.

17. Arthur H. Estabrook to Charles B. Davenport, May 5, 1912, Davenport Papers.

18. In Garland Allen's "naturalist-experimentalist" typology, Davenport is considered to belong to the "experimentalist" group. Yet his enthusiasm for eugenics fieldwork would seem to give evidence of his equal commitment to the "naturalist" tradition in biology. See Garland Allen, "Naturalists and Experimentalists: The Genotype and the Phenotype," *Studies in the History of Biology* 3 (1979): 179–209. Although Allen's thesis has been revised to acknowledge considerable overlap in the two traditions, instead of a sharply defined break at the end of the nineteenth century, one could suggest a similar "break" in the evolution of eugenics. Faithful to the "naturalist" model, the family study genre, which made up the bulk of eugenics research at ERO and other principal eugenics research institutions, had given way by 1920 to more experimental eugenics work (in part because Mary Harriman's financial support ended in 1918). Still, family studies continued to be pursued and published as late as the 1930s in more rural places like Vermont; see Kevin Dann, "From Degeneration to Regeneration: The Eugenics Survey of Vermont, 1925–1937," *Vermont History* 59, no. 1 (1991): 5–27. Even at ERO, especially with Davenport and Laughlin on staff, there remained plenty of enthusiasm for fieldwork. Laughlin was conducting a very traditional eugenics survey in Connecticut during the 1930s, up to the point when ERO was closed down by the Carnegie Institute of Washington.

19. Charles B. Davenport to Mary Harriman, January 5, 25, May 22, July 11, 1911; Harriman to Davenport, May 29, November 24, 1911; C. C. Tegethoff to Davenport, June 6, 7, 1911, Davenport Papers.

20. State of New York Department of Mental Hygiene, *Twenty-fourth Annual Report of the Board of Visitors of Letchworth Village* (Utica: State Hospitals Press, 1933), 101; Mary Harriman to Charles B. Davenport, October 8, 1912; Davenport to Harriman, January 25, 1911, Davenport Papers; Persia Crawford Campbell, *Mary Williamson Harriman* (New York: Columbia University Press, 1960).

21. Report of Florence Smith, March 27, 1914, Eugenics Record Office Papers, American Philosophical Society, Philadelphia (microfilm reel 1769819), pp. 28, 137.

22. Report of Florence Smith, 260, 264, 413.

23. Report of Florence Smith, 353, 349, 350.

24. Report of Ethel Thayer, September 1914, ERO Papers (microfilm reel 1822182), p. 46. For a sampling of family study narratives, along with an excellent interpretive history, see Nicole Hahn Rafter, *White Trash: The Eugenic Family Studies, 1877–1919* (Boston: Northeastern University Press, 1988).

25. Report of Ethel Thayer, 1, 3.

26. William James Dobbin, "Wild Men Within Commuting Distance," *New York Tribune*, June 12, 1921; "A Community of Outcasts," *Appleton's Journal of Literature, Science and Art*, March 23, 1872, 325.

27. "A Community of Outcasts," 326.

28. Kite, "The Jackson-Whites," 30, 154, 27, 156.

29. Ibid., 15, 21–22.

30. E. Carleton MacDowell, "Charles Benedict Davenport, 1866–1944: A Study of Conflicting Influences," *Bios* 17 (1946): 4.

31. Alexander Graham Bell to Charles B. Davenport, December 27, 1910, Davenport Papers; Percy MacKaye, Scrapbooks "Tomorrow I and II," Box 90, MacKaye Family Papers, Baker Library, Dartmouth College, Hanover, N.H.

32. Percy MacKaye, *To-Morrow: A Play in Three Acts* (New York: Frederick A. Stokes, 1912), iii, viii.

33. Luther Burbank, *The Training of the Human Plant* (New York: Century, 1907), 82, 90; Percy to Marion MacKaye, August 11, 1910, MacKaye Family Papers.

34. MacKaye, *To-Morrow*, 9–17. On Burbank, see Peter Dreyer, *A Gardener Touched with Genius: The Life of Luther Burbank* (Berkeley: University of California Press, 1985). MacKaye had been in California earlier, visiting writers George Sterling, Jack London, and Herman Whittaker. At one point, with poet Harry Lafler, MacKaye bought a Big Sur ranch and planned to make a home there, but he was called back east to supervise the production of one of his plays.

35. MacKaye, *To-Morrow*, 18, 22, 34.

36. Ibid., 131, 163.

37. *New York Times*, March 10, 1912; Willard H. Wright, "MacKaye Indulges in Impeccable Eugenics," *Los Angeles Times*, April 9, 1912; Winthrop Ames to Percy MacKaye, August 6, 1912; Irving Fisher to MacKaye, April 8, 1912; Mary Harriman to MacKaye, May 1, 1912; Theodore Roosevelt to MacKaye, December 24, 1912; John D. Rockefeller Jr. to MacKaye, March 1, 1912; Luther Burbank to MacKaye, March 4, 1912, MacKaye Family Papers.

38. Charles B. Davenport to Percy MacKaye, June 10, July 1, 1912, MacKaye Family Papers; E. O. Grover, ed., *Annals of an Era, Percy MacKaye and the MacKaye Family 1826–1932: A Record of Biography and History* (Washington, D.C.: Pioneer Press, 1932).

39. Advertising prospectus for *Annals of an Era*, Annals folder, MacKaye Family Papers.

40. Percy MacKaye to Charles B. Davenport, December 11, 1927; Davenport to MacKaye, September 9, December 22, 1932, Davenport Papers.

41. Descriptions of exhibits at the American Museum are drawn from Henry F. Perkins, ed., *A Decade of Progress in Eugenics: Scientific Papers of the Third International Congress of Eugenics* (Baltimore: Williams and Wilkins, 1934).

42. Henry Fairfield Osborne, "Birth Selection versus Birth Control," in Perkins, ed., *A Decade of Progress*, 40. On the differences between Osborne's and King's paleoanthropology, see Rainger, *Agenda for Antiquity*, 228–39.

43. Charles B. Davenport to Henry F. Osborne, September 26, 1932, Davenport Papers.

44. Charles B. Davenport to Board of Overseers, July 18, 1913, Davenport Papers.

45. New York State Department of Mental Hygiene, *Survey of Methods of Care, Treatment and Training of the Feeble-Minded, Together with a Program for the Future* (Utica: State Hospitals Press, 1937), 18.

46. *Survey of Methods of Care*, 2; Lura Beam to George Barbour, November 18, 1960, Robert Latou Dickinson Papers, Countway Medical Library, Harvard University, Cambridge, Mass. For excellent examples of Dickinson's anatomical drawings, see Robert Latou Dickinson and Clarence Gamble, *Human Sterilization: Techniques of Permanent Conception Control* (Baltimore: Waverly Press, 1950), and Dickinson, *Human Sex Anatomy: A Topographical Hand Atlas* (Baltimore: Williams and Wilkins, 1933).

47. George Barbour, "RLD: The Life of Robert Latou Dickinson, 1861–1950," Dickinson Papers.

48. Dickinson and Gamble, *Human Sterilization*, 6, 31. Dickinson's and Gamble's 1936 source—Karl Heinrich Bauer and F. von Mikulicz-Radecki, *Praxis der Sterilizierungs-Operationen* (Leipzig: Barth, 1936)—was the standard textbook of surgical sexual sterilization for the Nazi racial hygiene program. The American military government later made Bauer the first postwar president of the University of Heidelberg; Götz Aly, Peter Chroust, and Christian Pross, *Cleansing the Fatherland: Nazi Medicine and Racial Hygiene* (Baltimore: Johns Hopkins University Press, 1994), 19. See also Stefan Kuhl,

The Nazi Connection: Eugenics, American Racism, and German National Socialism (New York: Oxford University Press, 1994).

49. Eleanor Larson to Dorothy Barbour, November 1, 1960; prayer card in Dickinson Diary, 1930–1936, Dickinson Papers.

50. Robert L. Dickinson to Edith Hamilton, draft letter, no date; Dickinson to Mr. Gill of Williams and Wilkins Publishing Co., February 23, 1941, Dickinson Papers.

51. Robert L. Dickinson, "A Gospel Too Simple," 1924, Dickinson Papers.

52. William Carlos Williams, *The Collected Poems of William Carlos Williams, 1909–1939* (New York: New Directions, 1938).

53. For an analysis of the co-opting of MacKaye's social vision for the Appalachian Trail by the forces of modernity, see Ronald Foresta, "Transformation of the Appalachian Trail," *Geographical Review* 77 (1987): 76–85.

Chapter 5 ***Not an Earthly Service***

1. Constance Ling, manuscript lecture on the history of Threefold Farm given to Rudolf Steiner Institute students, September 16, 1974, Threefold Farm Papers, Threefold Educational Foundation, Spring Valley, N.Y.

2. Charlotte Parker, "A Short History of the Threefold Community, Spring Valley, NY, 1922–1972" (undated pamphlet), Threefold Farm Papers; Frederick C. Heckel, "Words Spoken at the Funeral of RC, July 4, 1965," *Newsletter of the Anthroposophical Society in America* 3, no. 4 (1965): 1.

3. Ralph Courtney, "Recollections," *Newsletter of the Anthroposophical Society in America* (winter 1981–82). On the threefold social order, see Rudolf Steiner, *The Threefold Commonwealth* (1922; rpt. New York: Anthroposophic Press, 1943). This book has also been published under the titles *The Threefold Social Order* (New York: Anthroposophic Press, 1966) and *Towards Social Renewal: Basic Issues of the Social Question* (London: Rudolf Steiner Press, 1977). Steiner's ideas about the operation of the economic sphere are given in *World Economy: The Formation of a Science of World Economics* (1922; rpt. New York: Anthroposophic Press, 1944). Individual lectures on the threefold order can be found in *The Inner Aspect of the Social Question* (London: Anthroposophic Publishing Company, 1950).

4. Alla Selawry, *Ehrenfried Pfeiffer, a Pioneer in Spiritual Research and Practice: A Contribution to His Biography* (Spring Valley, N.Y.: Mercury Press, 1992), 9–10.

5. As with contemporaneous speculative thought about the nature of the "fourth dimension," the key to successful employment of the etheric forces as a concept required the supercession of the tendency to think of them in physical-spatial terms. Rudolf Steiner only suggested the solution in calling for mathematical formulation of what he termed *Gegenraum* (counterspace). George Adams pioneered the investigation of counterspace and its application to plant morphology and physiology; see Adams, "Physical and Ethereal Spaces," *Anthroposophical Quarterly* 8 (1933), and Adams and Olive Whicher, *The Plant Between Sun and Earth* (1952; rpt. Boulder, Colo.: Shambhala, 1982).

6. Rudolf Steiner, *Occult Science: An Outline* (1909; rpt. New York: Anthroposophic Press, 1997), chap. 2. Innumerable references to the etheric realm are found throughout Steiner's lectures and books; a collection of excerpts can be found in *World Ether-Elemental Beings-Kingdoms of Nature*, ed. Ernst Hageman (Spring Valley, N.Y.: Mercury Press, 1992).

The most important works following from Steiner's initial indications are: Guenther

Wachsmuth, *The Etheric Formative Forces in Cosmos, Earth and Man: A Path of Investigation into the World of the Living* (1924; rpt. New York: Anthroposophic Press, 1932); Wachsmuth, *Die ätherische Welt in Wissenschaft, Kunst und Religion* (Dornach: Philosophisch-Anthroposophischer Verlag am Goetheanum, 1927); Wachsmuth, *The Evolution of Mankind: Cosmic Evolution, Incarnation on the Earth, the Great Migrations, Spiritual History* (1953; rpt. Dornach: Philosophic-Anthroposophic Press, 1961); Hermann Poppelbaum, *Der Bildekräfteleib der Lebewesen als Gegenstand wissenschaftlicher Erfahrung* (Stuttgart: Kommende Tag Verlag, 1924); Jochen Bockemühl, *Toward a Phenomenology of the Etheric World: Investigations into the Life of Nature and Man* (Spring Valley, N.Y.: Anthroposophic Press, 1985); Otto Wolff, *The Etheric Body* (Spring Valley, N.Y.: Mercury Press, 1990).

In the twentieth century, a variety of "field" concepts proposed by neo-vitalist thinkers share a superficial resemblance to the concept of the etheric body; Hermann Poppelbaum addressed the inadequacy of the field concept in *The Etheric Body in Idea and Action* (London: Anthroposophic Publishing Company, 1955), 10.

7. For one anthroposophically informed interpretation of aspects of twentieth-century cultural history as marking the advent of the consciousness soul, see Richard Leviton, *The Imagination of Pentecost: Rudolf Steiner and Contemporary Spirituality* (Hudson, N.Y.: Anthroposophic Press, 1994).

8. Selawry, *Ehrenfried Pfeiffer*, 47–49. A number of anthroposophists who knew Pfeiffer recall an additional story about the inspiration for the crystallization work. Pfeiffer was said to have been passing a bakery on a winter day, and he noticed that the frost crystal patterns on the windows had different patterns. This led him to question whether crystallization patterns might serve as a form of biochemical analysis. Interview with Sally Burns, May 26, 1997; interview with John and Nancy Root, August 20, 1997.

9. Selawry, *Ehrenfried Pfeiffer*, 52

10. Descriptions of the 1933 Anthroposophical Summer School Conference at Threefold Farm are drawn from numerous documents in the archives of the Threefold Educational Foundation. The description of Pfeiffer's early involvement in the demonstration of the etheric formative forces is related in Ehrenfried Pfeiffer, *Autobiographie* (Basel: Perseus Verlag, 1996). Pfeiffer tells the story of Steiner's Bosch factory lecture in *The Spiritual Leadership of Mankind* (Spring Valley, N.Y.: Mercury Press, 1985), 1–2.

11. For Rudolf Steiner's theories about eurythmy, see *Eurythmy as Visible Music* and *Eurythmy as Visible Speech*, both published by Anthroposophic Press in 1956.

12. The focal character in all of the plays, Benedictus, seems to stand at a level of spiritual development above that of his pupils, and yet his destiny is inextricable from that of the rest of his group. At the Threefold performances of the mystery dramas, Ralph Courtney took the role of Benedictus. On the mystery dramas, see: Eileen Hutchins, *Introduction to the Mystery Plays of Rudolf Steiner* (London: Rudolf Steiner Press, 1984); Hans Pusch, *Working Together on Rudolf Steiner's Mystery Dramas* (New York: Anthroposophic Press, 1980); Harry Collison, *Commentary on Rudolf Steiner's Four Mystery Plays* (London: Rudolf Steiner Publishing Co., 1949).

13. Interview with Sally Burns, May 26, 1997; interview with John and Nancy Root, August 20, 1997.

14. Interview with Sally Burns, May 26, 1997; interview with Henry and Christy Barnes, May 28, 1997.

15. Rudolf Steiner, "The Meaning of Art in Ancient Times and Today," *Anthroposophical Review* 4, no. 29 (1927): 227. On the esoteric aspects of the Goetheanum design, see

David Adams, "The Goetheanum as White Magic, or Why Is Anthroposophical Archi-tecture So Important?" *Journal of Anthroposophy* 64 (1997): 13–46. For a survey of architecture inspired by the Goetheanum, see Hagen Biesantz and Arne Klingborg, *The Goetheanum: Rudolf Steiner's Architectural Impulse* (London: Rudolf Steiner Press, 1979).

16. Rev. J. Alson Smith, "The Fringe Religions," *American Mercury* (April 1950): 53–58. Smith went on to say that anthroposophy "is so complicated as to be almost inexpli-cable in fewer than several thousand words, representing, as it does, an extraordinary synthesis of Theosophy, fresh occult intuitions, and certain motifs of nineteenth-century German thought. . . . [Anthroposophy] has never caught on in either the United States or Great Britain, but it is the fastest growing cult in post-war Germany, where its popu-larity rivals that of Existentialism in France. Many students, writers, and artists are af-filiated with it" (56). For a response to Smith's characterization of anthroposophy, see Stewart Easton, "Are Religions Fair Game for the Social Scientists?" *Proteus Quar-terly* 1 (1950): 23–30.

17. Ernst Lehrs, *Man or Matter: Introduction to a Spiritual Understanding of Nature on the Basis of Goethe's Method of Training, Observation, and Thought* (New York: Harper, 1950), 19–24.

18. Ibid., 39–41.

19. Both Theosophy and Anthroposophy acknowledged 1899 as marking the end of the Kali Yuga, but it is important to note that they held radically different interpretations of the historical significance of Christ. It was Steiner's rejection of the Theosophical Society's proclamation of Krishnamurti as the reincarnation of Christ that led to his break with Theosophy and his formation of the Anthroposophical Society. For anthroposophists, the end of the Kali Yuga and the advent of the Satya Yuga in the year 1899 were consequences of the cosmic inscription of Christ's deeds; see Robert Powell, *Chronicle of the Living Christ* (Hudson, N.Y.: Anthroposophic Press, 1996), 418.

20. Steiner described his experience of witnessing Christ's resurrection in his *Autobiogra-phy: Chapters in the Course of My Life* (1925; rpt. Hudson, N.Y.: Anthroposophic Press, 1977), 319. For an explanation of how Steiner was able to experience Christ's etheric return in advance of 1933, see Powell, *Chronicle of the Living Christ*, 417–19, and also Powell, *Hermetic Astrology*, vol. 1, *Astrology and Reincarnation* (Kinsau, West Ger-many: Hermetica, 1987).

21. Steiner, *Esoteric Christianity and the Mission of Christian Rosenkreuz* (London: Rudolf Steiner Press, 1984), 112. For an exposition of the timing of Christ's reappearance in the earth's etheric realm, see the afterword in Powell, *Chronicle of the Living Christ*, and also Powell's *The Sophia Mystery and the Christ Mystery* (forthcoming). An ex-cellent exposition of the Second Coming that brings Rudolf Steiner's teachings to bear on the Gospels can be found in Edward Reaugh Smith, *The Burning Bush* (Hudson, N.Y.: Anthroposophic Press, 1997), 213–43. A full discussion of Steiner's lectures on Christ's etheric return, along with the dates and titles of lectures between 1909 and 1920, can be found in subsection 2 of Sergei Prokofieff, *The Cycle of the Year as a Path of Initiation* (London: Temple Lodge Press, 1991).

22. Rudolf Steiner, *The Reappearance of Christ in the Etheric* (Hudson, N.Y.: Anthroposophic Press, 1983), 82.

23. For an exploration of the six basic exercises and the *Rückschau* as constituting the "new yoga of the senses," see Dennis Klocek, *Seeking Spirit Vision: Essays on Developing Imagination* (Fair Oaks, Calif.: Rudolf Steiner College Press, 1998), 255–63.

24. For Steiner's fundamental formulation of the stages of world evolution, see *Occult Science: An Outline* (1909; rpt. Hudson, N.Y.: Anthroposophic Press, 1997). Edward Smith, *The Burning Bush*, 550–54, offers an excellent summary of anthroposophic concepts of cosmic and earth history, with helpful chronological charts.

25. Steiner's introductory elaboration of the human etheric organs (known variously as "lotus flowers," "wheels," or "chakras" in Theosophical and other esoteric writings) can be found in *The Way of Initiation, or How to Attain Knowledge of the Higher Worlds* (London: Theosophical Publishing Society, 1908), chap. 6. Dennis Klocek extends Steiner's and Pfeiffer's work in occult physiology, particularly regarding the interaction of the pineal gland and the heart, in *Seeking Spirit Vision*, 123–41.

26. See Steiner, "The Etherization of the Blood," in *The Reappearance of Christ in the Etheric*; lectures 8 and 9 in *Wonders of the World, Ordeals of the Soul, Revelations of the Spirit* (London: Rudolf Steiner Press, 1963); and lecture 4 in *An Occult Physiology* (1951; rpt. London: Rudolf Steiner Press, 1983).

27. Robert Powell links the chronology of Nazification to parallel events in the first century C.E.; see *Chronicle of the Living Christ*, 418–22. Powell demonstrates how the rhythmically recurring "etheric remembrance" of the last three and one-half years of Jesus' life—the period between the baptism in the Jordan and the Crucifixion and Resurrection—is a time of particularly strong benevolent influence of Christ upon humanity, and how during these periods there are renewed attacks to counter this influence. In the twentieth century he points to the periods June 29, 1929–January 8, 1933, October 27, 1962–May 9, 1966, and February 24, 1996–September 6, 1999. In the first period, during which Christ was working to effect an awakening among humanity to the inner power of the etheric body, opposition arose in the form of the false outer power of the Führer. In the second period, when Christ awakened humanity to impulses of brotherhood and community, opposition arose in the form of the drug culture. Powell sees the last period, in which we now live, as the time when the most important impulse of the Second Coming should be awakened—the knowledge of the living being of Nature. Powell sees the global environmental movement as a manifestation of this impulse; he finds its opposition in the widespread fascination with virtual reality, the substitution of lifeless images for living reality. Powell interprets these three historical oppositions during the twentieth century as repetitions of Christ's temptations in the desert as described in the Gospel of Matthew: period 1, "If you will fall down and worship me" (Matt. 4:9) (the temptations of the will to power); period 2, "casting oneself down from the pinnacle of the temple" (Matt. 4:5) (hedonistic surrender to instinctual urges that dim the faculty of reason); period 3, "turn[ing] stones into bread," (Matt. 4:3) (the embrace of ersatz life, that is, "stones").

28. See, for example, the lecture of April 17, 1949, "The Healing Forces of Christ," in Ehrenfried Pfeiffer, *Notes and Lectures: Compendium I* (Spring Valley, N.Y.: Mercury Press, 1991), 112.

29. Waldemar Kaempffert, "Can the Stock Be Improved by Weeding Out Non-Aryans?" *New York Times*, July 25, 1933, p. 9, col. 1. The Hereditary Health Law was based on the same model legislation enacted in a number of states; this model bill was drafted by Harry H. Laughlin, Charles. B. Davenport's lieutenant at the Eugenics Record Office. On the relationship of the American eugenics movement to eugenics under the National Socialists, see Stefan Kuhl, *The Nazi Connection: Eugenics, American Racism, and German National Socialism* (New York: Oxford University Press, 1994).

30. Steiner, "Changes in Humanity's Spiritual Make-Up," in *Fall of the Spirits of Dark-*

ness (Bristol, England: Rudolf Steiner Press, 1993), 81. Steiner made a number of remarks critical of Francis Galton's work; see, for example, lecture 2 in *Karmic Relationships: Esoteric Studies*, vol. 1 (Bristol, England: Rudolf Steiner Press, 1972).

31. Steiner, *The Wrong and Right Use of Esoteric Knowledge, or Secret Brotherhoods* (Bristol, England: Rudolf Steiner Press, 1966), 52–53.

32. Steiner even ascribed the creation of human races to this Atlantean period of "eugenic" activity: "Then there really were laws which enabled people to determine size, growth, and all kinds of things by cross-breeding and the like. It was a science that was widespread in Atlantean times—and . . . sorely misused. Atlantean science worked on the basis of physical relationships and it was known that if such a man was brought together with such a woman—differences between men and women were much greater at the time—the result would be such and such a creature, and then a different variety could be produced—just as plant breeders do today. The Mysteries brought order into this cross-breeding, where related and different elements were brought together. They established groups and withdrew anything which had to be withdrawn from humanity. The blackest of black magic was practiced in Atlantean times, and order was created by establishing classes and taking these matters out of human control. This was one of the factors which led to the nations and races of today. The issue of the nation as an entity is coming up again in our present time; it is an echo of the soulless brain from Atlantean times." Steiner, *Fall of the Spirits of Darkness*, 81–82.

Because of their use of the term "Aryan" in their conceptions of human evolution, both Theosophy and Anthroposophy have often been seen as racist, a perception reinforced by the occult activity of certain National Socialist leaders. For a response by an anthroposophist to these charges, see Douglas Sloan, "Reflections on the Evolution of Consciousness," *Research Bulletin of the Waldorf Education Research Institute* 1 (1996): 9–15. Steiner spoke often of the obsolescence of racial ideas, and indeed, his life's work can be characterized as an attempt to bring forth the "universal human." See, for example, lecture 9 in *The Influence of Spiritual Beings Upon Man* (New York: Anthroposophic Press, 1961). For Steiner's conceptions of "material occultism"—mechanical, eugenic, and hygienic—see lecture 3, "The Mechanistic, Eugenic, and Hygienic Aspects of the Future," in *In the Changed Conditions of the Times* (New York: Anthroposophic Press, 1941).

33. Steiner described this experience in his *Autobiography*.

34. For Steiner's lectures at the Sonnenhof, see *Curative Education* (Bristol, England: Rudolf Steiner Press, 1993).

35. In 1936 the Hales began an anthroposophical endeavor in Vanceboro, Maine. See Judson Hale, *The Education of a Yankee: An American Memoir* (New York: Harper and Row, 1987).

36. Steiner, *Destiny or Karma* (London: Harry Collison, 1931), 5–6, 7; Steiner, *Curative Education*, 44. For a compilation of Steiner's teaching on karma and reincarnation, with a helpful commentary, see *A Western Approach to Reincarnation and Karma: Selected Lectures and Writings by Rudolf Steiner*, ed. René Querido (Hudson, N.Y.: Anthroposophic Press, 1997), and also Pietro Archiati, *Reincarnation in Modern Life: Towards a New Christian Awareness* (London: Temple Lodge Publishing, 1996).

37. Interview with Ruth Barnett Pusch, May 27, 1997; notebook of personal reminiscences of Gladys Barnett Hahn, provided by Ruth Pusch.

38. Interview with Henry and Christy Barnes, May 28, 1997; Henry Barnes, *A Life for the*

Spirit: Rudolf Steiner in the Crosscurrents of Our Time (Hudson, N.Y.: Anthroposophic Press, 1997), 1–2.

39. Robin MacKaye, undated (1918?) manuscript biographical reflections in "Miscellaneous Writings," MacKaye Family Papers, Baker Library, Dartmouth College, Hanover, N.H.

40. Robin MacKaye, "A Spray of Butternut Leaves," in "Miscellaneous Writings," MacKaye Family Papers; Robert Keith MacKaye, "Brackish Water," in *Beginnings* (New Haven: Yale University Press, 1927).

41. Robert Keith MacKaye, *Wings for Hands: Grist for a Crow Play in the Theatre of Evolution* (Chapel Hill, N.C.: Milton A. Abernethy, 1934).

42. Robin MacKaye, "A Spray of Butternut Leaves."

43. Interview with Henry and Christy Barnes, May 28, 1997. Robin MacKaye improved greatly at Wiesnick; he continued to write poetry and completed a translation of Friedrich Husemann's *Goethe and the Art of Healing: A Commentary on the Crisis in Medicine* (New York: Anthroposophic Press, 1938).

44. On Percy MacKaye's response to Steffen's *Peace Tragedy*, see Arvia MacKaye Ege, *The Power of the Impossible: The Life Story of Percy and Marion MacKaye* (Falmouth, Me.: Kennebec River Press, 1992), 422–35.

45. Percy MacKaye, "First Meeting," in Albert Steffen and Percy MacKaye, *In Another Land* (Dornach: Verlag für Schöne Wissenschaften, 1937).

46. Percy MacKaye, "Metamorphosis," in Steffen and MacKaye, *In Another Land*. On Percy MacKaye's friendship with Albert Steffen, see Ege, *Power of the Impossible*, 435–47.

47. Percy to Benton MacKaye, September 29, 1938, February 28, 1939, MacKaye Family Papers.

48. Percy to Benton MacKaye, December 14, 1939, MacKaye Family Papers.

49. Ehrenfried Pfeiffer, *The Spiritual Leadership of Mankind* (Spring Valley, N.Y.: Mercury Press, 1985), 32. Recently, anthroposophical authors have relaxed earlier self-imposed restrictions upon speaking about the prior incarnations of the founder of anthroposophy. The most extensive account can be found in a book available only to members of the Anthroposophical Society: Margarete Kirchner-Bockholt, *Rudolf Steiner's Mission and Ita Wegman* (London: Rudolf Steiner Press, 1977). Subsequent books have taken for granted the remarkable sequence of incarnations outlined in that work. See, for example, Sergei Prokofieff, *Rudolf Steiner and the Founding of the New Mysteries* (New York: Anthroposophic Press, 1986), 135–59 (although the entire work is devoted to the question voiced on its opening page: "Who was Rudolf Steiner?"), and Smith, *The Burning Bush*, 540–44.

50. Ehrenfried Pfeiffer, "Christ as the Fulfillment of the Mysteries," in *Notes and Lectures*, 45–49; unpublished notes from June 1984 lecture by Paul Scharff, made available to the author by Scharff.

51. Pfeiffer, "Christ as the Fulfillment of the Mysteries," 28.

52. Ehrenfried Pfeiffer, "Chart of Spiritual History," Threefold Foundation Archives.

53. Ibid., 15.

CHAPTER 6   *Spiritual Science and the Redemption of the Senses*

1. On the diversification of American zoology in the early twentieth century, see Toby A. Appel, "Organizing Biology: The American Society of Naturalists and its 'Affiliated Societies,' 1883–1923," in *The American Development of Biology*, ed. Ronald Rainger, Keith R. Benson, and Jane Maienschein (Philadelphia: University of Pennsylvania Press, 1988).

2. Hermann Poppelbaum, *A New Zoology* (Dornach: Philosophic-Anthroposophic Press, 1961), 56. My imagination of this scene is drawn primarily from that text, which incorporates much of the material from his ten-lecture course at the 1939 summer conference.

3. Biographical information comes from Hermann Poppelbaum, *The Battle for the New Consciousness* (Spring Valley, N.Y.: Mercury Press, 1993), i; Hermann Poppelbaum, *Man and Animal: Their Essential Difference* (1931; rpt. London: Anthroposophical Publishing, 1960), viii.

4. Poppelbaum, *A New Zoology*, 20.

5. Ibid., 22.

6. Ibid., 24.

7. This terminology of earth history is not original with Rudolf Steiner. Helena Blavatsky, E. P. Sinnett, and other authors of occult works introduced it to a wide public in the 1870s and 1880s.

8. Poppelbaum, *A New Zoology*, 24–27.

9. Ibid., 27–29.

10. Poppelbaum, *Man and Animal*, 109–10.

11. Ibid., 114.

12. Poppelbaum, *A New Zoology*, 76; 77.

13. Ibid., 80.

14. Ibid., 84, 88, 90.

15. Interview with Ruth Pusch, Spring Valley, N.Y., May 18, 1997.

16. Poppelbaum, *A New Zoology*, 93.

17. Ibid., 94, 95. Although Hermann Poppelbaum's zoological work stands alone in its completeness of formulation and its artfulness of expression, a number of other authors have taken up his approach. See, for example, Wolfgang Schad, *Man and Mammals: Toward a Biology of Form* (Garden City, N.Y.: Waldorf Press, 1977), and Mark Riegner, "Horns, Hooves, Spots and Stripes," *Orion Nature Quarterly* 4 (1985): 22–35. A revised version of Riegner's article appears in *Goethe's Way of Science: A Phenomenology of Nature*, ed. David Seamon and Arthur Zajonc (Albany: SUNY Press, 1998).

18. Poppelbaum, *A New Zoology*, 14; Poppelbaum, *Man's Eternal Biography: Three Essays on Life and Death* (New York: Adonis Press, 1945), 77.

19. Ehrenfried Pfeiffer, "In Memory of Goethe" (lecture at Threefold Farm, June 1, 1947), in *Notes and Lectures: Compendium I* (Spring Valley, N.Y.: Mercury Press, 1991), 65–67. In this same lecture Pfeiffer noted how Steiner frequently pointed to the study of plant metamorphosis as the ideal training for understanding the metamorphosis of the human ego, that is, reincarnation. Guenther Wachsmuth's *Reincarnation as a Phenomenon of Metamorphosis* (New York: Anthroposophic Press, 1937) systematically elaborates this extension of Goethean thought to the human individuality.

20. Within the scholarly literature on the history of science, aside from some recent sympathetic flirtations (cf. Robert J. Richards, *Darwin and the Emergence of Evolutionary Theories of Mind and Behavior* [Chicago: University of Chicago Press, 1987]), the overwhelming majority of historians treat *Naturphilosophie* as if it were an aberrant derailment on the inevitable path to Darwinian evolutionary theory. For a recent example of this sort of treatment, see Michael Ruse, *Monad to Man: The Concept of Progress in Evolutionary Biology* (Cambridge, Mass.: Harvard University Press, 1996). Although the disdain for Goethe, thanks to his polemics against Newton's color theory, is more pronounced among physical scientists and historians of the physical sciences, Goethe also routinely comes in for caricature by biologists; see for example Edward O. Wilson,

Consilience: The Unity of Knowledge (New York: Knopf, 1998), 88. Ruse is equally dismissive: "To this day, as he was in that day, Goethe is taken as a paradigm of a poet meddling beyond his ken or ability" (82).

21. Hermann Poppelbaum, "Ways and Byways to Spiritual Perception—Goethe and Oken," in *Battle for the New Consciousness*.

22. Poppelbaum, *Man and Animal*, 122. The first person to grasp the significance of Goethean epistemology was undoubtedly Rudolf Steiner, who developed a close knowledge of Goethe's scientific work in the years 1883–1897, when he was serving as editor of Goethe's scientific publications for Kürschner's *Deutsche National Literatur*. Although Steiner discussed Goethe's scientific method in scores of lectures and books, two works are critical: *A Theory of Knowledge Based on Goethe's World Conception* (1886; rpt. New York: Anthroposophic Press, 1968) and *Goethean Science* (1883–1897; Spring Valley, N.Y.: Mercury Press, 1968) (originally published as introductions to Goethe's natural scientific works, edited by Steiner). Among subsequent anthroposophical authors, a seminal work is Ernst Lehrs, *Man or Matter: Introduction to a Spiritual Understanding of Nature on the Basis of Goethe's Method of Training, Observation, and Thought* (New York: Harper, 1950). In more recent years, exceptional explorations of Goethean epistemology have appeared: Henri Bortoft, *The Wholeness of Nature: Goethe's Way Toward a Science of Conscious Participation in Nature* (Hudson, N.Y.: Lindisfarne Press, 1996); *Goethe and the Sciences: A Reappraisal*, ed. Frederick Amrine, Francis J. Zucker, and Harvey Wheeler (Dordrecht: D. Reidel, 1987); Frederick Amrine, "The Metamorphosis of the Scientist," Walter Heitler, "Goethean Science," Herbert Hensel, "Goethe, Science, and Sensory Experience," and Ronald H. Brady, "The Idea in Nature: Rereading Goethe's Organics," all in *Goethe's Way of Science*. For an exhaustive bibliographical record of literature on Goethe's science and Goethean science, see the multivolume work by Frederick Amrine, *Goethe in the History of Science*, 2 vols. (New York: Peter Lang, 1996–97).

23. Goethe, "From Makaria's Archive," in *Wilhelm Meister's Wanderjahre, Hamburger Ausgabe*, 8:473, translated by and quoted in Amrine, "The Metamorphosis of the Scientist," 37–38. Goethe was unsparing in his criticism of Newtonian science's need for sensory proxies. The sentence that follows his affirmation of human senses as the "most precise scientific instrument"—"this is the greatest disservice of modern science; that it has divorced the experiment from the human being, and wants to know nature only through that which is shown by instruments"—sounds particularly prescient from the vantage of the late twentieth century, when science gets much of its sensory "data" in digital form from computer screens.

24. Rudolf Steiner, *The Karma of Human Vocation in Connection with the Life of Goethe* (1916; rpt. New York: Anthroposophic Press, 1944), 34, 36. Mainstream science, lacking the concept of the etheric, still cannot explain many of the phenomena produced by the loosening of the etheric body. High fevers are one of the most common producers of temporary, spontaneous etheric cognition; Steiner's statement that Goethe's initial experience of etheric cognition coincided with his illness makes sense in light of this. For other manifestations of the loosened etheric body, see Kevin Dann, *Bright Colors Falsely Seen: Synaesthesia and the Search for Transcendental Knowledge* (New Haven: Yale University Press, 1998).

25. On the development of the natural history film in American culture, and particularly its role in promoting spectatorship over sensory engagement with wildlife, see Gregg Mitman, *Reel Nature: America's Romance with Wildlife on Film* (Cambridge, Mass.: Harvard University Press, 1999).

26. Poppelbaum, "The Dimming of Consciousness by Technology—in Particular by Motion Pictures," in *Battle for the New Consciousness*, 29.
27. Ibid., 29, 30, 31. In this same lecture, Poppelbaum noted that Rudolf Steiner had said earlier in the century that a veritable "schooling in dishonesty" is created by cursory, superficial reading, the "reporter-like attitude to the world that is afflicting us all" (34). The convergence of advertising, journalistic facticity, and spectatorship on the nature trails at the Trailside Museum suggests that nature study, the "solution" to urban artificiality, was merely another symptom of modernity's failure to overcome onlooker consciousness.
28. Ibid., 34, 35, 36. Poppelbaum believed this to be true also of educational films, including those used for biological instruction: "Of course we should be able to look at instructional films of plant life, but we should then always shift our observation back to the reality of this life, because it is just from this return to the real world that the cinema would like to distract us" (36).
29. Hermann Poppelbaum, "The Arabian Element Within Darwinism," in *Battle for the New Consciousness*, 98–99.
30. Ibid., 100–101. Though Poppelbaum did not specifically identify by name Darwin's previous eighth-century incarnation, Rudolf Steiner had; see Steiner, *Karmic Relationships: Esoteric Studies*, vol. 5 (1924; rpt. London: Rudolf Steiner Press, 1966), 44–51.
31. Poppelbaum, "The Arabian Element Within Darwinism," 103, 104, 108.
32. Ibid., 106, 107.

Chapter 7 *Reenchanting Nature: Anthroposophical Nature Study*

1. This imagined scene is drawn from Virginia Field Birdsall's translation of Gerbert Grohmann, *The Living World of Plants: A Book for Children and Students of Nature*, originally published by the Waldorf Institute for Liberal Education, Adelphi University, and later reissued by the Association of Waldorf Schools of North America (Great Barrington, Mass., n.d.), and from a lecture by Rudolf Steiner, "The Nature of Butterflies," October 8, 1923 (manuscript translation from Rudolf Steiner Library, Ghent, N.Y.).
2. Grohmann, *The Living World of Plants*, trans. Birdsall, 67.
3. Rudolf Steiner, *A Modern Art of Education* (1928; rpt. London: Rudolf Steiner Press, 1972), 11.
4. Ibid., 144–45.
5. Steiner, "The Nature of Butterflies," 10.
6. Steiner, "How Old Is History," Part 3, *Anthroposophic News Sheet* 2, no. 51/2 (1934): 31, 33. This is the text of a lecture given at Dornach on October 21, 1917.
7. Virginia Birdsall and Margaret Peckham, *Nature Stories Leading to Geography* (privately printed, n.d.), 19.
8. Rudolf Steiner, "Elemental Beings of Earth and Water," lecture of April 3, 1912, in *Nature Spirits* (London: Rudolf Steiner Press, 1992), 22. In the discussion that follows, it is to be understood that all perception of elementary beings, such as the Hierarchies and other supersensible phenomena, is not *physical* but spiritual perception. Certain Theosophical writers, particularly in the wake of Sir Arthur Conan Doyle's publication in 1922 of photographs of fairies taken by two young girls, have attempted to explain how fairies can occasionally marshal enough "etheric substance" to become visible to normal sight, and hence to photographic film. See, for example, Edward L. Gardner,

Fairies: The Cottingley Photographs (1922; rpt. Wheaton, Ill.: Theosophical Publishing Company, 1966).

9. Steiner, *Nature Spirits*, 31; Steiner, *The Influence of Spiritual Beings Upon Man* (New York: Anthroposophic Press, 1961), 156, 126 (from lectures given in 1908).

10. Steiner, *Influence of Spiritual Beings Upon Man*, 140.

11. Ibid., 135, 138.

12. The debate about the pedagogical value of fairy tales began in the 1910s and continued into the early 1930s; see, for example: F. Ricklin, "Wish Fulfillment and Symbolism in Fairy Tales," *Nation* 103 (1916): 12–13; G. L. Brown, "Case Against Myths, Folklore and Fairy Stories as Basal Reading for Children," *Education* 42 (1921): 159–65, 400–407; "Crusade Against Fairy Tales," *Current Opinion* 72 (1922): 87–88; "Killing the Fairies," *Literary Digest* 76 (1923): 31; W. L. Bailey, "Fairy Tales as Character Builders," *Libraries* 31 (1926): 44–46; C. H. Seelig, "Defense of Fairies," *Hygeia* 6 (1928): 636–37; H. E. Wheeler, "Psychological Case Against the Fairy Tale," *Elementary School* 29 (1929): 754–55; P. Beard, "Why Banish the Fairy Tale?" *Libraries* 34 (1929): 457–59; A. E. Moore, "Shall We Banish the Fairies?" *Parents* 6 (1931): 29.

I am unaware of any historical study of the twentieth-century pedagogical debate, but there are a number of recent works that explore the role of fairy tales in modern popular culture: Jack Zipes, *Fairy Tale as Myth: Myth as Fairy Tale* (Lexington: University Press of Kentucky, 1994); Charles Solomon, *Enchanted Drawings: The History of Animation* (New York: Knopf, 1989). Solomon describes how magic lantern shows, magicians' tricks, shadow theaters, animation devices, and sequential photography all contributed to the early development of the motion picture. All of these genres, as well as early film, frequently drew upon fairy motifs. For a scholarly work that approaches fairies through the esoteric framework of the "subtle body," see Peter M. Rojcewicz, "Between One Eye Blink and the Next: Fairies, UFOs, and Problems of Knowledge," in *The Good People: New Fairylore Essays*, ed. Peter Narvaez (New York: Garland, 1991).

13. In the fall of 1956, when his friend and fellow crystallization researcher Alla Selawry was visiting Pfeiffer in Spring Valley, they drove to Pfeiffer's former farm in Chester, New York, and Pfeiffer showed the drainage system and stone bridge he had built himself. Selawry remembered, "At various spots he remembered encounters with elementals—gnomes, undines, sylphs and salamanders. He had a perceptive organ for them. . . . He understood their language and was able to communicate with them." Selawry, *Ehrenfried Pfeiffer, a Pioneer of Spiritual Research and Practice: A Contribution to His Biography* (1987; rpt. Spring Valley, N.Y.: Mercury Press, 1992), 103–4. For other affirmations of Pfeiffer's ability to perceive elementary beings, see Hans Heinze, "Ehrenfried Pfeiffer and the Bio-Dynamic Agricultural Movement," in "Ehrenfried Pfeiffer, Feb 19, 1899–Nov 30, 1961," Special Supplement to *Anthroposophical Society in America Newsletter* (January 1962): 4–5, and Paul Scharff, "Ehrenfried Pfeiffer" manuscript lecture of June 1984.

14. Ehrenfried Pfeiffer, untitled Threefold Farm lecture, October 10, 1948, in *Notes and Lectures: Compendium I* (Spring Valley, N.Y.: Mercury Press, 1991), 92.

15. Ehrenfried Pfeiffer, "Elemental Beings in the Spiritual World," lecture at Threefold Farm, June 1941, in *Notes and Lectures*, 5–9.

16. Ibid., 6. Pfeiffer's exact words were: "It is not necessary to mention whether this disturbance was accidental or was rather what has been intended. But it seems that the lack of understanding between the larger groups of humanity was a main factor which helped to increase the disturbance" (6).

17. Ibid., 7. Pfeiffer even said that the European elementary beings who had accompanied

the colonial emigrants were more delicate and gentle, compared to the coarser, wilder, and more violent ones in America. According to Pfeiffer, the European elementals had to suffer a great deal under their local counterparts and sought refuge in human religious activities and meditation. Selawry, *Ehrenfried Pfeiffer*, 103–4. There are striking parallels between Pfeiffer's descriptions of American elementary beings and so-called "aliens." For commentary upon this parallel from an anthroposophical point of view, see Richard Leviton, *The Imagination of Pentecost: Rudolf Steiner and Contemporary Spirituality* (Hudson, N.Y.: Anthroposophic Press, 1994).

18. Pfeiffer, "Elemental Beings in the Spiritual World," 7, 8, 5; Pfeiffer, untitled lecture, October 10, 1948, in *Notes and Lectures*, 93.

19. Pfeiffer, "Elemental Beings in the Spiritual World," 8.

20. Ehrenfried Pfeiffer, *The Earth's Face and Human Destiny* (Emmaus, Pa.: Rodale Press, 1947), 23, 61, 62.

21. Ibid., 95, 102.

Conclusion: The Unity of Knowledge

1. *The Unity of Knowledge*, ed. Lewis Leary (Garden City, N.Y.: Doubleday, 1955), 5.

2. Huxley, "Man's Place and Role in Nature" in *The Unity of Knowledge*, 82. On Julian Huxley's belief in progress, see Michael Ruse, *Monad to Man: The Concept of Progress in Evolutionary Biology* (Cambridge, Mass.: Harvard University Press, 1996), 328–38.

3. Huxley, "Man's Place and Role in Nature," 85, 86.

4. On the effort to unify the biological sciences, see V. Betty Smocovitis, "Unifying Biology: The Evolutionary Synthesis and Evolutionary Biology," *Journal of the History of Biology* 25, no. 1 (1992): 1–65. Michael Ruse notes Huxley's and Dobzhansky's interest in Teilhardism in *Monad to Man*, 336–38, 396–400.

5. Huxley, "Man's Place and Role in Nature," 93. Ehrenfried Pfeiffer said about the Miller-Urey experiment: "You can imagine that scientists might think that they have here the first step towards the synthetic production of life. This is an error, yet it is irritating for a bio-dynamist or an Anthroposophist to have a product heretofore considered as an expression of life obtained in a test tube experiment. It is actually what Goethe in his *Faust* called Homunculus, the shadow form of a living man. Actually these experiments are interesting because they indicate the borderline between living and dead substances. They also show that an organic substance like an amino-acid or a protein might some day be produced. But this would still have nothing to do with life. It is still a product of energies and forces that are strictly in the mineral physical realm. It is important for us to understand this." Pfeiffer, "Life's Resources," lecture at Threefold Farm Summer Conference, 1958, in Pfeiffer, *Life's Resources and Esoteric Streams of Christianity* (New York: Anthroposophic Press, 1963), 15–16.

6. Gardner Murphy, letter to the editor, *Science* 120 (December 17, 1954): 1041. On Murphy's interest in parapsychology, see Lois Barclay Murphy, *Gardner Murphy: Integrating, Expanding, and Humanizing Psychology* (Jefferson, N.C.: McFarland, 1990).

7. Julian Huxley, "Introduction" in Pierre Teilhard de Chardin, *The Phenomenon of Man* (New York: Harper and Row, 1959), 18.

8. Hermann Poppelbaum, "Some Problems Connected with Parapsychology," *Anthroposophic News Sheet* 22 (1954): 43–45. American interest in the paranormal during the 1950s included a fascination with dowsing, which received great public attention in 1951 with Kenneth Roberts's *Henry Gross and His Dowsing Rod* (Garden City, N.Y.: Doubleday, 1951).

9. Poppelbaum, "Some Problems Connected with Parapsychology," 44, 45.

10. Hermann Poppelbaum, "Aldous Huxley Takes a Dose of Mescaline," *Anthroposophic News Sheet* 22 (1954): 67–68.

11. For an overview of the near-death experience from an anthroposophical perspective, see Calvert Roszell, *The Near-Death Experience in the Light of Scientific Research and the Spiritual Science of Rudolf Steiner* (Hudson, N.Y.: Anthroposophic Press, 1988).

12. Pfeiffer, *Notes and Lectures: Compendium I* (Spring Valley, N.Y.: Mercury Press, 1991), 112. Rudolf Steiner, referring to the possibility that Christ's etheric return might not be recognized in the future, put it this way: "If these faculties do not become apparent in the middle of the twentieth century, it will be proof that the human being is not so endowed but will only prove that human beings have crushed under foot the budding young shoots." Steiner, *The Reappearance of Christ in the Etheric* (Hudson, N.Y.: Anthroposophic Press, 1983), 83.

13. Ehrenfried Pfeiffer, "Rosicrucian Striving," lecture at Threefold Farm, August 24, 1952, in *Notes and Lectures*, 124–125, 130.

14. On the 1953 earthquakes in the region, see the *New York Times* reports on July 16 and 17 and August 28.

15. Edward O. Wilson, *Consilience: The Unity of Knowledge* (New York: Knopf, 1998), 298, 36.

16. Wilson, *Consilience*, 218, 6.

17. Edward O. Wilson, *Naturalist* (Washington, D.C.: Island Press, 1994), 45. A recent book by David Takacs, *The Idea of Biodiversity: Philosophies of Paradise* (Baltimore: Johns Hopkins University Press, 1996), chillingly suggests that Naturalism in America is currently undergoing a transformation from civic religion to religion. For all of his faint rhetorical nods acknowledging the social construction of nature, Takacs's book is nothing if not a deliberate essentializing of nature, as understood by contemporary conservation biologists. The lack of a narrative may lull the casual reader into believing that Takacs succeeds in avoiding environmental history's oppositional tendencies, but from the outset, Takacs's language is implicitly oppositional. People "fight," "mine," "exploit" nature. The book's third paragraph begins: "At places distant from where you are, but also uncomfortably close, a holocaust is under way. People are slashing, hacking, bulldozing, burning, poisoning, and otherwise destroying huge swaths of life on Earth at a furious pace." Takacs understands human labor not as so much sinew and bone knowing nature in a particular way due to the forces of industrial capitalism (à la Richard White's *The Organic Machine: The Remaking of the Columbia River* [New York: Hill and Wang, 1995]), but as the enemy. Takacs's conservation biologists, on the other hand, are "scientists who love" nature, just as he himself does. In a series of interviews with leading conservation biologists, prominent among them E. O. Wilson, Takacs presents these "biophilic" exemplars as the priests of the new Naturalist religion.

BIBLIOGRAPHY

Manuscript Collections

American Museum of Natural History. Central Archives, New York.

Carr, William. Papers. American Heritage Center, Laramie, Wyo.

Carr, William. Papers. Arizona-Sonora Desert Museum, Tucson, Ariz.

Carr, William. Papers. Trailside Museum Archives, Palisades Interstate Park Commission, Bear Mountain, N.Y.

Davenport, Charles B. Papers. American Philosophical Society Library, Philadelphia.

Dickinson, Robert Latou. Papers. Special Collections, Countway Medical Library, Harvard University, Cambridge, Ma.

Eugenics Record Office. Papers, American Philosophical Society Library, Philadelphia.

Goddard, Henry H. Papers. Archives of the History of American Psychology, University of Akron, Akron, Ohio.

Hyde, Benjamin T. B. Papers. Trailside Museum Archives, Palisades Interstate Park Commission, Bear Mountain, N.Y.

Kite, Elizabeth. "The Jackson-Whites: A Study in Racial Degeneracy." Elizabeth Kite Papers, Alexander Library, Rutgers University, New Brunswick, N.J.

Lutz, Frank E. Papers. American Museum of Natural History, New York.

Lutz, Frank E. Papers. Trailside Museum Archives, Palisades Interstate Park Commission, Bear Mountain N.Y.

MacKaye Family Papers. Rauner Special Collections, Baker Library, Dartmouth College, Hanover, N.H.

Threefold Farm. Papers, Threefold Educational Foundation, Spring Valley, N.Y.

Works Cited

Aaron, S. F. "Nature Faking: Popular Fallacies Have Grown Out of Pseudo-Scientific Nature Lore." *Scientific American* 134 (1926): 322–23.

Abbott, Arthur Platts. *The Greatest Park in the World: Palisades Interstate Park, Its Purpose, History and Achievements.* New York: Historian Press, 1914.

Adams, Charles C. "An Ecological Survey of the Palisades Interstate Park." *Empire Forester* 5 (1919): 12–18.

Adams, David. "The Goetheanum as White Magic, or Why Is Anthroposophical Architecture So Important?" *Journal of Anthroposophy* 64 (1997): 13–46.

Adams, George. "Physical and Ethereal Spaces." *Anthroposophical Quarterly* 8 (1933): 2–6.

———, and Olive Whicher. *The Plant Between Sun and Earth*. 1952. Reprint, Boulder, Colo.: Shambhala, 1982.

Allen, Garland. "The Eugenics Record Office at Cold Spring Harbor, 1910–1940: An Essay in Institutional History." *Osiris* 2 (1986): 225–64.

———. *Life Science in the Twentieth Century*. Cambridge: Cambridge University Press, 1975.

———. "Naturalists and Experimentalists: The Genotype and the Phenotype." *Studies in the History of Biology* 3 (1979): 179–209.

Alvarez, Luis W. "Alfred Lee Loomis." *Biographical Memoirs of the National Academy of Sciences* 51 (1980): 309–41.

Amory, Cleveland. *The Last Resorts*. New York: Harper and Brothers, 1948.

Amrine, Frederick. *Goethe in the History of Science*. 2 vols. New York: Peter Lang, 1996–97.

———, Francis J. Zucker, and Harvey Wheeler, eds. *Goethe and the Sciences: A Reappraisal*. Dordrecht: D. Reidel, 1987.

Appel, Toby A. "Organizing Biology: The American Society of Naturalists and Its 'Affiliated Societies,' 1883–1923." In *The American Development of Biology*, edited by Ronald Rainger, Keith R. Benson, and Jane Maienschein. Philadelphia: University of Pennsylvania Press, 1988.

———. "Science, Popular Culture, and Profit: Peale's Philadelphia Museum." *Journal for the Society for a Bibliography of Natural History* 9 (1980): 619–34.

Archiati, Pietro. *Reincarnation in Modern Life: Towards a New Christian Awareness*. London: Temple Lodge Publishing, 1996.

Bailey, W. L. "Fairy Tales as Character Builders." *Libraries* 31 (1926): 44–46.

Baker, R. H. "A Watcher of Birds." *Michigan History* 66 (1982): 40–45.

Barber, Lynn. *The Heyday of Natural History, 1820–1870*. London: Jonathan Cape, 1981.

Barnes, Henry. *A Life for the Spirit: Rudolf Steiner in the Crosscurrents of Our Time*. Hudson, N.Y.: Anthroposophic Press, 1997.

Barry, William David. "The Shameful Story of Malaga Island." *Down East,* November 1980, 53–56, 83–86.

Bauer, Karl Heinrich, and F. von Mikulicz-Radecki. *Praxis der Sterilizierungs-Operationen*. Leipzig: Barth, 1936.

Beard, P. "Why Banish the Fairy Tale?" *Libraries* 34 (1929): 457–59.

Belasco, Warren J. *Americans on the Road: From Autocamp to Motel, 1910–1945*. Cambridge, Mass.: MIT Press, 1979.

Benson, Keith R. "From Museum Research to Laboratory Research: The Transformation of Natural History into Academic Biology." In *The American Development of Biology*, edited by Ronald Rainger, Keith R. Benson, and Jane Maienschein. Philadelphia: University of Pennsylvania Press, 1988.

Biesantz, Hagen, and Arne Klingborg. *The Goetheanum: Rudolf Steiner's Architectural Impulse*. London: Rudolf Steiner Press, 1979.

Birdsall, Virginia, and Margaret Peckham. *Nature Stories Leading to Geography*. Privately printed, n.d.

Bishop, Sherman C. "An Early Experiment in Natural History Trails." *School and Society* 27 (1928): 541–43.

Blavatsky, Helena Petrovna. *Isis Unveiled: The Master Key to the Mysteries of Ancient and Modern Science and Theology*. New York: J. W. Bouton, 1877.

———. *The Secret Doctrine: The Synthesis of Science, Religion, and Philosophy*. London: Theosophical Publishing Company, 1888.

Bockemühl, Jochen. *Toward a Phenomenology of the Etheric World: Investigations into the Life of Nature and Man*. Spring Valley, N.Y.: Anthroposophic Press, 1985.

Bortoft, Henri. *The Wholeness of Nature: Goethe's Way toward a Science of Conscious Participation in Nature*. Hudson, N.Y.: Lindisfarne Press, 1996.

Botkin, Daniel B. *Discordant Harmonies: A New Ecology for the Twenty-first Century*. New York: Oxford University Press, 1990.

Bowler, Peter J. *The Eclipse of Darwinism: Anti-Darwinian Evolutionary Theories in the Decades around 1900*. Baltimore: Johns Hopkins University Press, 1983.

Bragdon, Claude. *Architecture and Democracy*. New York: Knopf, 1926.

———. *The Beautiful Necessity: Seven Essays on Theosophy and Architecture*. New York: Knopf, 1922.

———. *The Frozen Fountain; Being Essays on Architecture and the Art of Design in Space*. New York: Knopf, 1932.

———. *More Lives Than One*. New York: Knopf, 1938.

———. *Projective Ornament*. New York: Knopf, 1927.

———. *The Secret Spring: An Autobiography*. London: Andrew Dakers, 1938.

Brandon, R. N. *Adaptation and Environment*. Princeton: Princeton University Press, 1990).

Bray, William L. *The Development of the Vegetation of New York State*. Syracuse: New York State College of Forestry, 1915.

Brechin, Gray. "Conserving the Race: Natural Aristocracies, Eugenics, and the U.S. Conservation Movement." *Antipode* 28 (1996): 229–45.

Brodhead, M. J. "Of Mice and Mastodons: Contributions to the Literature of Mammalogy by Officers and Men of the United States Army in the Nineteenth Century." *Archives of Natural History* 18 (1991): 363–74.

Brown, F. M. "Descriptions of New Bacteria Found in Insects." *American Museum Novitates* 251 (1927).

Brown, G. L. "Case Against Myths, Folklore and Fairy Stories as Basal Reading for Children." *Education* 42 (1921): 159–65, 400–407.

Brown, Marjorie W. *Arden House: A Living Expression of the Harriman Family*. 1976. Reprint, n.p.: American Assembly, Columbia University, 1981.

Bruce, A. "Timidity of Modern Science in the Presence of the New Ghost." *Current Opinion* 57 (1914): 113.

Bryant, Paul T. *The Quality of the Day: The Achievement of Benton MacKaye*. Ann Arbor, Mich.: University Microfilms International, 1965.

Buckley, Kerry W. *Mechanical Man: John Broadus Watson and the Beginnings of Behaviorism*. New York: Guilford Press, 1989.

Burbank, Luther. *The Training of the Human Plant*. New York: Century, 1907.

Burroughs, John. *Accepting the Universe: Essays in Naturalism*. Boston and New York: Houghton Mifflin, 1920.

———. "The Gospel of Nature." *Century* 84 (1912): 195–204.

Campbell, Persia Crawford. *Mary Williamson Harriman*. New York: Columbia University Press, 1960.

Carr, William H. "Bear Mountain Trail Blazers." *The Conservationist* 29 (1974/5): 7–11.

———. "Blazing Nature's Trail." *American Museum of Natural History School Service Series* 2/3 (1928).

———. "Indian Beaver Legends." *Natural History* 31 (1931): 81–92.

————. "A Manual of Bird Study: A Description of Twenty-five Local Birds with Study Outlines." *American Museum of Natural History School Service Series* 1 (1934).

————. "The Modern Nature-Faker." *Natural History* 44 (1944): 22–30.

————. *Pebbles in Your Shoes*. Tucson: Arizona-Sonora Desert Museum, 1982.

————. "Signs Along the Trail." *American Museum of Natural History School Service Series* 1 (1927).

————. *The Stir of Nature: A Book for Young American Naturalists*. New York: Oxford University Press, 1930.

————. "Telling the Beaver Story." *Natural History* 31 (1931): 640–50.

————. "Trailside Actions and Reactions." *American Museum of Natural History School Service Series* 5 (1931).

————. "Trailside Conversations." *American Museum of Natural History School Service Series* 4 (1930).

————. "A Trailside Convert." *Natural History* 33 (1933): 278–86.

————. "Trailside Family." *American Museum of Natural History School Service Series* 7 (1932).

————. "Trailside Interdependence: Being an Account of the Building of a Trailside Museum Exhibit to Show That a State of True Independence Does Not Exist in the World of Nature." *American Museum of Natural History School Service Series* 8 (1933).

————. "Trailside Unnatural History," *Natural History* 34 (1934): 287–96.

————. "Two Thousand Miles Along the Crest of the Atlantic Highlands." *Natural History* 33 (1933): 395–406.

Carrington, Hereward. *The Coming Science*. New York: American Universities Publishing, 1920.

Cartmill, Matt. *A View to a Death in the Morning: Hunting and Nature through History*. Cambridge, Mass.: Harvard University Press, 1993.

Caudill, Edward. *Darwinism in the Press: The Evolution of an Idea*. Hillsdale, N.Y.: Lawrence Erlbaum Associates, 1989.

Chardin, Pierre Teilhard de. *The Phenomenon of Man*. New York: Harper and Row, 1959.

"Child of Seven Is Hailed as a Great Writer." *Current Opinion* 69 (1920): 692–94.

Collison, Harry. *Commentary on Rudolf Steiner's Four Mystery Plays*. London: Rudolf Steiner Publishing Co., 1949.

"A Community of Outcasts." *Appleton's Journal of Literature, Science and Art*, March 23, 1872, 324–29.

Cooke, Kathy J. "The Limits of Heredity: Nature and Nurture in American Eugenics before 1915." *Journal of the History of Biology* 31 (1998): 263–78.

Courtney, Ralph. "Recollections." *Newsletter of the Anthroposophical Society in America*, winter 1981/82.

Creighton, W. S. "The Slave-Raids of *Harpagoxenus americanus*." *Psyche* 34 (1927): 16–24.

Cronon, William J. *Changes in the Land: Indians, Colonists, and the Ecology of New England*. New York: Hill and Wang, 1983.

————. "Cutting Loose or Running Aground?" *Journal of Historical Geography* 20 (1994): 38–43.

————. "A Place for Stories: Nature, History, and Narrative," *Journal of American History* 78 (1992): 1347–76.

————. *Nature's Metropolis: Chicago and the Great West*. New York: W. W. Norton, 1991.

————. "The Trouble with Wilderness; or Getting Back to the Wrong Nature." *Environmental History* 1 (1990): 7–28.

————, ed. *Uncommon Ground: Toward Reinventing Nature*. New York: W. W. Norton, 1995.

"Crusade Against Fairy Tales." *Current Opinion* 72 (1922): 87–88.

Curran, C. H. "Report on the Diptera Collected at the SSI, HSP, NY." *Bulletin of the American Museum of Natural History* 61 (1931): 21–115.

Dann, Kevin. *Bright Colors Falsely Seen: Synaesthesia and the Search for Transcendental Knowledge*. New Haven: Yale University Press, 1998.

————. "From Degeneration to Regeneration: The Eugenics Survey of Vermont, 1925–1937." *Vermont History* 59 (1991): 5–29.

Davenport, Charles Benedict. "Degeneration, Albinism, and Inbreeding." *Science* 28 (1908): 454–55.

————. "Heredity of Skin-Pigment in Man." *American Naturalist* 44 (1910): 42–72, 305–31.

"David Starr Jordan's Claim to 'The First Car Ride.'" *Literary Digest*, September 26, 1925, 62–66.

Davidson, Jo. *Between Sittings*. New York: Dial Press, 1951.

Davis, Susan. *Spectacular Nature: Corporate Culture and the Sea World Experience*. Berkeley: University of California Press, 1997.

de Mar, David Peterson. "'Our Animal Friends': Depictions of Animals in *Reader's Digest* during the 1950s." *Environmental History* 3 (1998): 25–44.

Demeritt, David. "Ecology, Objectivity, and Critique in Writings on Nature and Human Societies." *Journal of Historical Geography* 20 (1994): 22–37.

Dickinson, Robert Latou. *Human Sex Anatomy: A Topographical Hand Atlas*. Baltimore: Williams and Wilkins, 1933.

————. *Palisades Interstate Park*. New York: American Geographical Society, 1921.

————, and Clarence Gamble. *Human Sterilization: Techniques of Permanent Conception Control*. Baltimore: Waverly Press, 1950.

Dikotter, Frank. "Race Culture: Recent Perspectives on the History of Eugenics." *American Historical Review* 103 (1998): 467–78.

Dobbin, William James. "Wild Men Within Commuting Distance." *New York Tribune*, June 12, 1921.

Dobson, Meade C. "Interstate Park Commissioners' Map Opens Forest Roads for Motorists." *New York Post*, September 10, 1920.

Doyle, Arthur Conan. *The Coming of the Fairies*. New York: Hodder and Stoughton, 1922.

Dreyer, Peter. *A Gardener Touched with Genius: The Life of Luther Burbank*. Berkeley: University of California Press, 1985.

Drummond, James L. *Letters to a Young Naturalist: Study of Nature and Natural Theology*. London: Longman, 1831.

Dunwell, Frances F. *The Hudson River Highlands*. New York: Columbia University Press, 1991.

Easton, Stewart. "Are Religions Fair Game for the Social Scientists?" *Proteus Quarterly* 1 (1950): 23–30.

Ege, Arvia MacKaye. *The Power of the Impossible: The Life Story of Percy and Marion MacKaye*. Falmouth, Me.: Kennebec River Press, 1992.

Egerton, Frank N. "Changing Concepts in the Balance of Nature." *Quarterly Review of Biology* 48 (1973): 322–50.

Evarts, H. G. "Bugaboo Natural History." *Saturday Evening Post*, November 10, 1923.

Focht, Jack. "Uncle Bennie, Founder of Nature Education in the Palisades Interstate Park, 1920." *Trailside Museum and Zoo Historical Papers*, Historical Series, no. 34 (1990).

Foresta, Ronald. "Transformation of the Appalachian Trail." *Geographical Review* 77 (1987): 76–85.

Fraser, James. *The American Billboard: 100 Years*. New York: Harry Abrams, 1991.

Gardner, Edward L. *Fairies: The Cottingley Photographs and Their Sequel*. 1922. Reprint, Wheaton, Ill.: Theosophical Publishing House, 1966.

Ginger, Ray. *Six Days or Forever? Tennessee vs. John Thomas Scopes*. Boston: Beacon Press, 1958.

Glassberg, David. *American Historical Pageantry: The Uses of Tradition in the Early Twentieth Century*. Chapel Hill: University of North Carolina Press, 1990.

Goetzmann, William H., and Kay Sloan, *Looking Far North: The Harriman Expedition to Alaska, 1899*. New York: Viking Press, 1982.

Gotz, Aly, Peter Chroust, and Christian Pross. *Cleansing the Fatherland: Nazi Medicine and Racial Hygiene*. Baltimore: Johns Hopkins University Press, 1994.

Grohmann, Gerbert. *The Living World of Plants: A Book for Children and Students of Nature*. Great Barrington, Mass: Waldorf Institute for Liberal Educationn, n.d.

Grover, E. O., ed. *Annals of an Era: Percy MacKaye and the MacKaye Family 1826–1932: A Record of Biography and History*. Washington, D.C.: Pioneer Press, 1932.

Hagen, Joel. "Experimentalists and Naturalists in Twentieth-Century Botany: Experimental Taxonomy, 1920–1950." *Journal of the History of Biology* 17 (1984): 249–70.

Hale, Judson. *The Education of a Yankee: An American Memoir*. New York: Harper and Row, 1987.

Hall, G. Stanley. *Adolescence*. New York: Appleton, 1904.

Haller, Mark. *Eugenics: Hereditarian Attitudes in American Thought*. New Brunswick, N.J.: Rutgers University Press, 1963.

Hasian, Marouf A., Jr. *The Rhetoric of Eugenics in Anglo-American Thought*. Athens: University of Georgia Press, 1996.

Heckel, Frederick C. "Words Spoken at the Funeral of RC, July 4, 1965." *Newsletter of the Anthroposophical Society in America* 3 (1965): 1.

Heinze, Hans. "Ehrenfried Pfeiffer and the Bio-Dynamic Agricultural Movement." In "Ehrenfried Pfeiffer, Feb 19, 1899–Nov 30, 1961," Special Supplement to *Anthroposophical Society in America Newsletter* (January 1962): 4–5.

Henderson, C. "Occultism and Practical Life." *Dial* 51 (1911): 289.

Henderson, Linda. *The Fourth Dimension and Non-Euclidean Geometry in Modern Art*. Princeton: Princeton University Press, 1983.

Hill, J. A. "Attack of Modern Science on the Realm of Occultism." *Scientific American* 73 (1912): 34–35.

Hodge, Clifton F. *Nature Study and Life*. Boston: Ginn and Company, 1902.

Hoff, Benajmin. *The Singing Creek Where the Willows Grow: The Rediscovered Diary of Opal Whiteley*. New York: Ticknor and Fields, 1986.

Holton, Gerald, and W. A. Blanpied, eds. *Science and Its Public*. Dordrecht: D. Reidel, 1976.

Hughes, Thomas P., and Agatha C. Hughes, eds. *Lewis Mumford: Public Intellectual*. New York: Oxford University Press, 1990.

Husemann, Friedrich. *Goethe and the Art of Healing: A Commentary on the Crisis in Medicine*. New York: Anthroposophic Press, 1938.

Hutchins, Eileen. *Introduction to the Mystery Plays of Rudolf Steiner*. London: Rudolf Steiner Press, 1984.

Huxley, Thomas Henry. *Collected Essays*. New York: Appleton, 1894.

Ingalese, Richard, and Isabella Ingalese. *Occult Philosophy*. New York: Dodd, Mead, 1920.

Judd, C. H. "Evolution and Consciousness." *Psychological Review* 17 (1910): 77–97.

Kaempffert, Waldemar. "Can the Stock Be Improved by Weeding Out Non-Aryans?" *New York Times*, July 25, 1933.

Kevles, Daniel. *In the Name of Eugenics: Genetics and the Uses of Human Heredity*. Berkeley: University of California Press, 1985.

"Killing the Fairies." *Literary Digest* 76 (1923): 31.

Kingsland, Sharon. "Essay Review: The History of Ecology." *Journal of the History of Biology* 27 (1994): 349–57.

———. *Modeling Nature: Episodes in the History of Population Ecology*. Chicago: University of Chicago Press, 1995.

Kirchner-Bockholt, Margarete. *Rudolf Steiner's Mission and Ita Wegman*. London: Rudolf Steiner Press, 1977.

Klocek, Dennis. *Seeking Spirit Vision: Essays on Developing Imagination*. Fair Oaks, Calif.: Rudolf Steiner College Press, 1998.

Kohler, Robert. *Lords of the Fly: Drosophila, Genetics, and the Experimental Life*. Chicago: University of Chicago Press, 1994.

Kohlstedt, Sally Gregory. "From Learned Society to Public Museum: The Boston Society of Natural History." In *The Organization of Knowledge in Modern America, 1860–1920*, edited by Alexandra Oleson and John Voss. Baltimore: Johns Hopkins University Press, 1979.

———. "Henry A. Ward: The Merchant Naturalist and American Museum Development." *Journal for the Society for a Bibliography of Natural History* 9 (1980): 647–61.

———. "Nature Study in North America and Australasia, 1890–1945: International Connections and Local Implementations." *Historical Records of Australian Science* 11 (1997): 439–54.

———. "The Nineteenth-Century Amateur Tradition: The Case of the Boston Society of Natural History." In *Science and Its Public*, edited by Gerald Holton and W. A. Blanpied. Dordrecht: D. Reidel, 1976.

Kuhl, Stefan. *The Nazi Connection: Eugenics, American Racism, and German National Socialism*. New York: Oxford University Press, 1994.

Larson, Edward J. *Sex, Race, and Science: Eugenics in the Deep South*. Baltimore: Johns Hopkins University Press, 1995.

———. *Summer for the Gods: The Scopes Trial and America's Continuing Debate over Science and Religion*. Cambridge, Mass.: Harvard University Press, 1997.

Lears, T. J. Jackson. *Fables of Abundance: A Cultural History of American Advertising*. New York: Basic Books, 1994.

———. *No Place of Grace: Antimodernism and the Transformation of American Culture, 1880–1920*. New York: Pantheon, 1981.

Leary, Lewis, ed. *The Unity of Knowledge*. Garden City, N.Y.: Doubleday, 1955.

Lehrs, Ernst. *Man or Matter: Introduction to a Spiritual Understanding of Nature on the Basis of Goethe's Method of Training, Observation, and Thought*. New York: Harper, 1950.

Leviton, Richard. *The Imagination of Pentecost: Rudolf Steiner and Contemporary Spirituality*. Hudson, N.Y.: Anthroposophic Press, 1994.

Lewis, Ralph H. *Museum Curatorship in the National Park Service, 1904–1982*. Washington, D.C.: Department of the Interior, National Park Service, Cultural Services Division, 1993.

Lobeck, A. K. *The Physiography of the New York Region*. New York: Geographical Press, 1930.

Loomis, Alfred L., and R. W. Wood. "The Physical and Biological Effects of High-Frequency Sound-Waves of Great Intensity." *Philsophical Magazine* 4 (1927): 417–36.

Ludmerer, Kenneth. *Genetics and American Society: A Historical Appraisal.* Baltimore: Johns Hopkins University Press, 1972.

Lutts, Ralph. *The Nature Fakers: Wildlife, Science, and Sentiment.* Golden, Colo.: Fulcrum Publishing, 1990.

———. *The Wild Animal Story.* Philadelphia: Temple University Press, 1998.

Lutz, Anne. "The Station for the Study of Insects and the First Nature Trail." *Trailside Museum and Zoo Historical Papers*, Historical Series, no. 2 (1989).

Lutz, Frank Eugene. "An Analysis by Movie-tone of a Cricket's Chirp (*Gryllus assimilis*)." *American Museum Novitates* no. 420 (1924).

———. "Apparently Non-Selective Characters and Combinations of Characters, Including a Study of Ultraviolet in Relation to the Flower-Visiting Habits of Insects." *Annals of the New York Academy of Science* 29 (1924): 181–283.

———. "Combinations of Alternative and Blending Inheritance." *Science* 28 (1908): 317.

———. "Experiments with 'Wonder Creatures,'" *Natural History* 29 (1929): 160–68.

———. *Field Book of Insects.* New York: G. P. Putnam's Sons, 1918.

———. "Flowers and Their Insect Visitors." *Natural History* 23 (1923): 125–34.

———. "How Bees Make Honey." *The Woodcraft Totem Board* 4, no. 8 (1921): 7.

———. "How Crickets Chirp." *The Woodcraft Totem Board* 4, no. 4 (1920): 3.

———. "How Moths and Butterflies Spend the Winter." *The Woodcraft Totem Board* 4, no. 6 (1920): 3.

———. "How to Collect Insects." *The Woodcraft Totem Board* 4, no. 10 (1921): 3.

———. "How to Preserve Insects." *The Woodcraft Totem Board* 4, no. 11 (1921): 3.

———. "'Invisible' Colors of Flowers and Butterflies." *Natural History* 33 (1933): 565–76.

———. *A Lot of Insects: Entomology in a Suburban Garden.* New York: G. P. Putnam, 1941.

———. "Mimicry." *American Naturalist* 45 (1911): 190–92.

———. "A Much-Abused But Still Cheerful Cricket." *Journal of the New York Entomological Society* 35 (1927): 307–8.

———. "Nature Trails: An Experiment in Out-door Education." *Miscellaneous Publications of the American Museum of Natural History*, no. 21 (1931).

———. "The New Insect Groups in the American Museum." *Natural History* 25 (1925): 126–35.

———. "The Still-open Road." *Natural History* 27 (1927): 373–82.

———. "String Figures from the Patomana Indians of British Guiana." *Anthropological Papers of the American Museum of Natural History* 12 (1912): 1–14.

———. "A Study in the Variations in the Number of Grooves Upon the Shells of *Pecten irradians*." *Science* 12 (1900): 373.

———. "Taking Nature Lore to the Public." *Natural History* 26 (1926): 111–13.

———. "The Variations and Correlations of Certain Taxonomic Characters of *Gryllus*." *Carnegie Institute of Washington Publication* no. 101 (1905).

———, and F. M. Brown. "A New Species of Bacteria and the Gall of an Aphid." *American Museum Novitates* 305 (1928).

———, and F. K. Richtmyer. "The Reaction of *Drosophila* to Ultraviolet." *Science* 55 (1922): 519.

MacDowell, E. Carleton. "Charles Benedict Davenport, 1866–1944: A Study of Conflicting Influences." *Bios* 17 (1946): 3–50.

MacKaye, Benton. "The Appalachian Trail: A Guide to the Study of Nature." *Scientific Monthly* 32 (1932): 330–42.

————. "An Appalachian Trail: A Project in Regional Planning." *Journal of the American Institute of Architects* 9 (1921): 325–30.

————. *Employment and Natural Resources*: A Report to the Department of Labor. Washington, D.C.: Department of Labor, 1919.

————. "Labor and the War: The Soldier, the Worker, and the Land's Resources." *Monthly Labor Review* (January 1918).

————. "Making New Opportunities for Employment." *Monthly Labor Review* (April 1919).

————. *The New Exploration: A Philosophy of Regional Planning*. 1928. Reprint, Urbana: University of Illinois Press, 1962.

————. "The New Exploration: Charting the Industrial Wilderness." *The Survey Graphic* 13 (1925): 153–57.

————. "Outdoor Culture—The Philosophy of Through-Trails." *Landscape Architecture* (April 1927).

————. "A Plan for Cooperation Between Farmer and Consumer." *Monthly Labor Review* (August 1920).

————. "Some Early AT History." *Potomac Appalachian Trail Club Bulletin* (October/December 1957).

MacKaye, Percy. *Sanctuary: A Bird Masque*. New York: Frederick A. Stokes Co, 1913.

————. *To-Morrow: A Play in Three Acts*. New York: Frederick A. Stokes Co., 1912.

MacKaye, Robert Keith. *Beginnings*. New Haven: Yale University Press, 1927.

————. *Wings for Hands: Grist for a Crow Play in the Theatre of Evolution*. Chapel Hill, N.C.: Milton A. Abernethy, 1934.

MacLeod, David I. *Building Character in the American Boy: The Boy Scouts, YMCA, and Their Forerunners, 1870–1920*. Madison: University of Wisconsin Press, 1983.

Maddox, W. J. "Insect Stories and Nature Fakes." *Hygeia* 4 (1926): 689–91.

Maienschein, Jane, Ronald Rainger, and Keith Benson. "Introduction: Were American Morphologists in Revolt?" *Journal of the History of Biology* 14 (1981): 83–87.

McReynolds, Samuel A. "Eugenics and Rural Development: The Vermont Commission on Country Life's Program for the Future." *Agricultural History* 71 (1997): 33–50.

Mearns, Edgar. "A Study of the Vertebrate Fauna of the Hudson Highlands." *Bulletin of the American Museum of Natural History* 10 (1898): 303–52.

Meine, Curt. *Aldo Leopold: His Life and Work*. Madison: University of Wisconsin Press, 1988.

Minton, Tyree G. "The History of the Nature-Study Movement and Its Role in the Development of Environmental Education." Ph.D. diss., University of Massachusetts, 1980.

Mitman, Gregg. "Cinematic Nature: Hollywood Technology, Popular Culture, and the American Museum of Natural History." *Isis* 84 (1993): 637–61.

————. "Evolution as Gospel: William Patten, the Language of Democracy, and the Great War." *Isis* 81 (1990): 446–63.

————. *Reel Nature: America's Romance with Wildlife on Film*. Cambridge, Mass.: Harvard University Press, 1999.

————. *The State of Nature: Ecology, Community, and American Social Thought, 1900–1950*. Chicago: University of Chicago Press, 1992.

————. "When Nature Is the Zoo: Vision and Power in the Art and Science of Natural History." *Osiris* 11 (1996): 117–43.

Moore, C. L. "New Literature of the Occult." *Dial* 58 (1915): 405–8.

Moore, E. "Shall We Banish the Fairies?" *Parents* 6 (1931): 29.

Morrow, Joel. "The Mystery of Opal Whiteley." *Biodynamics* 164 (1987): 44–56.

Murphy, Gardner. Letter to editor. *Science*, December 17, 1954.

Murphy, Lois Barclay. *Gardner Murphy: Integrating, Expanding, and Humanizing Psychology*. Jefferson, N.C.: McFarland, 1990.

Myers, G. S. "Amphibians and Reptiles Observed in the Palisades Interstate Park." *Copeia* 173 (1930): 99–103.

Narvaez, Peter, ed. *The Good People: New Fairylore Essays* New York: Garland, 1991.

Nash, Roderick. *Wilderness and the American Mind*. New Haven: Yale University Press, 1973.

"Near and Far Walks." *New York Times*, November 17, 1923.

Noll, Steven. *Feeble-Minded in Our Midst: Institutions for the Mentally Retarded in the South, 1900–1940*. Chapel Hill: University of North Carolina Press, 1995.

Novak, Frank, ed. *Lewis Mumford and Patrick Geddes: The Correspondence*. New York: Routledge, 1995.

Nye, Robert A. "The Rise and Fall of the Eugenics Empire: Recent Perspectives on the Impact of Biomedical Thought in Modern Society." *Historical Journal* 36 (1993): 687–700.

O'Brien, Raymond J. *American Sublime: Landscape and Scenery of the Lower Hudson River Valley*. New York: Columbia University Press, 1981.

Oelschlager, Max. *The Idea of Wilderness: From Prehistory to the Age of Ecology*. New Haven: Yale University Press, 1991.

Olby, R. C., et al., eds. *Companion to the History of Modern Science*. New York: Routledge, 1990.

Oleson, Alexandra, and John Voss, eds. *The Organization of Knowledge in Modern America, 1860–1920*. Baltimore: Johns Hopkins University Press, 1979.

Olmsted, Richard R. "The Nature-Study Movement in American Education." Ed.D. diss., Indiana University, 1967.

Osborn, Henry Fairfield. "How to Teach Evolution in the Schools." *School and Society* 23 (1926): 25–31.

Ouspensky, P. D. *A New Model of the Universe: Principles of the Psychological Method in Its Applications to Problems of Science, Religion, and Art*. New York: Knopf, 1931.

Paige, J. C. *The Civilian Conservation Corps and the National Park Service: An Administrative History*. Washington, D.C.: National Park Service, 1985.

"Panoramic View of a Section of the Vast Harriman Park, From the Abandoned Prison Site." *Evening Mail*, June 4, 1910.

Partridge, E. L. "A Forest Preserve Near the Metropolis." *Country Life in America* (September 1908): 456–59.

———. "A Highlands Park." *Outlook*, November 9, 1907.

Patrick, G. T. W. "The Search for Soul in Contemporary Thought." *Popular Science Monthly* 78 (1911): 460–68.

Paul, Diane B. "Culpability and Compassion: Lessons from the History of Eugenics." *Journal of Politics and the Life Sciences* 15 (1996): 99–106.

Pauly, Philip J. "The Development of High School Biology, New York City, 1900–1925." *Isis* 82 (1991): 662–88.

———. "Essay Review: The Eugenics Industry—Growth or Restructuring?" *Journal of the History of Biology* 26 (1993): 131–45.

———. "Summer Resort and Scientific Disipline: Woods Hole and the Structure of American Biology, 1882–1925." In *The American Development of Biology*, edited by Ronald Rainger, Keith R. Benson, and Jane Maienschein. Philadelphia: University of Pennsylvania Press, 1988.

Perkins, Henry F., ed. *A Decade of Progress in Eugenics: Scientific Papers of the Third International Congress of Eugenics*. Baltimore: Williams and Wilkins Co., 1934.

Pernick, Martin. *The Black Stork: Eugenics and the Death of Defective Babies in American Medicine and Motion Pictures since 1915*. Oxford: Oxford University Press, 1996.

Pfeiffer, Ehrenfried. *Autobiographie*. Basel: Perseus Verlag, 1996.

———. *The Earth's Face and Human Destiny*. Emmaus, Pa.: Rodale Press, 1947.

———. *Life's Resources and Esoteric Streams of Christianity*. New York: Anthroposophic Press, 1963.

———. *Notes and Lectures: Compendium I*. Spring Valley, N.Y.: Mercury Press, 1991.

———. *The Spiritual Leadership of Mankind*. Spring Valley, N.Y.: Mercury Press, 1985.

Pickens, Donald. *Eugenics and the Progressives*. Nashville: Vanderbilt University Press, 1968.

Pollan, Michael. *Second Nature: A Gardener's Education*. New York: Delta, 1991.

Poppelbaum, Hermann. "Aldous Huxley Takes a Dose of Mescaline." *Anthroposophic News Sheet* 22 (1954): 67–68.

———. *The Battle for the New Consciousness*. Spring Valley, N.Y.: Mercury Press, 1993.

———. *Der Bildekräfteleib der Lebewesen als Gegenstand wissenschaftlicher Erfahrung*. Stuttgart: Kommende Tag Verlag, 1924.

———. *The Etheric Body in Idea and Action*. London: Anthroposophic Publishing Company, 1955.

———. *Man and Animal: Their Essential Difference*. 1931. Reprint, London: Anthroposophical Publishing, 1960.

———. *Man's Eternal Biography: Three Essays on Life and Death*. New York: Adonis Press, 1945.

———. *A New Zoology*. Dornach, Switzerland: Philosophic-Anthroposophic Press, 1961.

———. "Some Problems Connected with Parapsychology." *Anthroposophic News Sheet* 22 (1954): 43–45.

Porter, Charlotte. "The Rise of Parnassus: Henry Fairfield Osborn and the Hall of the Age of Man." *Museum Studies Journal* 1 (1983): 26–34.

Powell, Robert. *Chronicle of the Living Christ*. Hudson, N.Y.: Anthroposophic Press, 1996.

———. *Hermetic Astrology*. Vol. 1, *Astrology and Reincarnation*. Kinsau, Germany: Hermetica, 1987.

Prince, William Franklin. "Experiences Which I Cannot Explain Away." *Scientific American* 131 (1924): 384–86.

———. "Extra-Sensory Perception." *Scientific American* 151 (1934): 5–7.

———. "Make-believe Telepathy." *Scientific American* 136 (1927): 10–11.

———. "Mr. Sinclair's Mental Radio." *Scientific American* 146 (1932): 135–38.

———. "Specimens from the Telepathic Mine." *Scientific American* 137 (1927): 210–13.

Prokofieff, Sergei. *The Cycle of the Year as a Path of Initiation*. London: Temple Lodge Press, 1991.

———. *Rudolf Steiner and the Founding of the New Mysteries*. New York: Anthroposophic Press, 1986.

Pusch, Hans. *Working Together on Rudolf Steiner's Mystery Dramas*. New York: Anthroposophic Press, 1980.

"Quarrel Over Opal." *Literary Digest* 67 (1920): 34–35.

Rafter, Nicole Hahn. *White Trash: The Eugenic Family Studies, 1877–1919*. Boston: Northeastern University Press, 1988.

Rainger, Ronald. *An Agenda for Antiquity: Henry Fairfield Osborn and Vertebrate Paleon-*

tology at the American Museum of Natural History, 1890–1935. Tuscaloosa: University of Alabama Press, 1991.

Redmond, Albert C. "My SSI Days." *Trailside Museum and Zoo Historical Papers*, Historical Series, no. 2 (1991).

Richards, Robert J. *Darwin and the Emergence of Evolutionary Theories of Mind and Behavior*. Chicago: University of Chicago Press, 1987.

Ricklin, F. "Wish Fulfillment and Symbolism in Fairy Tales." *Nation* 103 (1916): 12–13.

Riegner, Mark. "Horns, Hooves, Spots and Stripes." *Orion Nature Quarterly* 4 (1985): 22–35.

Roberts, Kenneth. *Henry Gross and His Dowsing Rod*. Garden City, N.Y.: Doubleday, 1951.

Robertson, I. C., ed. *75 Years: A History of the Buffalo Society of Natural Science, 1861–1936*. Buffalo: Buffalo Museum of Science Press, 1939.

Rojcewicz, Peter M. "Between One Eye Blink and the Next: Fairies, UFOs, and Problems of Knowledge." In *The Good People: New Fairylore Essays*, edited by Peter Narvaez. New York: Garland, 1991.

Ross, Dorothy. *G. Stanley Hall: The Psychologist as Prophet*. Chicago: University of Chicago Press, 1972.

Rossiter, Margaret W. "Benjamin Silliman and the Lowell Institute: The Popularization of Science in Nineteenth-Century America." *New England Quarterly* 44 (1971): 602–26.

Roszell, Calvert. *The Near-Death Experience in the Light of Scientific Research and the Spiritual Science of Rudolf Steiner*. Hudson, N.Y.: Anthroposophic Press, 1988.

Rothwell, Grant. "Nature Enthusiasm, Social Planning and Eugenics in Australian State Schools, 1900–1920." *Journal of Educational Administration History* 29 (1997): 1–19.

Ruse, Michael. *Monad to Man: The Concept of Progress in Evolutionary Biology*. Cambridge, Mass.: Harvard University Press, 1996.

Schad, Wolfgang. *Man and Mammals: Toward a Biology of Form*. Garden City, N.Y.: Waldorf Press, 1977.

Schmitt, Peter J. *Back to Nature: The Arcadian Myth in Urban America*. Oxford: Oxford University Press, 1969; Baltimore: Johns Hopkins University Press, 1990.

Seabrook, William. *Doctor Wood, Modern Wizard of the Laboratory; The Story of an American Small Boy Who Became the Most Daring and Original Experimental Physicist of Our Day—But Never Grew Up*. 1941. Reprint, New York: Harcourt, Brace, 1983.

Seamon, David, and Arthur Zajonc, eds. *Goethe's Way of Science: A Phenomenology of Nature*. Albany: SUNY Press, 1998.

Sedgwick, Ellery. *The Happy Profession*. Boston: Little, Brown, 1946.

Seelig, C. H. "Defense of Fairies." *Hygeia* 6 (1928): 636–37.

Selawry, Alla. *Ehrenfried Pfeiffer, a Pioneer of Spiritual Research and Practice: A Contribution to His Biography*. 1987. Reprint, Spring Valley, N.Y.: Mercury Press, 1992).

Sellars, Roy Wood. *Evolutionary Naturalism*. 1922. Reprint, New York: Russell and Russell, 1969.

Shapin, Steve. "Science and the Public." In *Companion to the History of Modern Science*, edited by R. C. Olby et al. New York: Routledge, 1990.

Shinn, Terry, and Richard Whitley, eds. *Expository Science: Forms and Functions of Popularization*. Dordrecht: D. Reidel, 1985.

Sloan, Douglas. "Reflections on the Evolution of Consciousness." *Research Bulletin of the Waldorf Education Research Institute* 1 (1996): 9–15.

Smith, Edward Reaugh. *The Burning Bush*. Hudson, N.Y.: Anthroposophic Press, 1997.

Smith, J. Alson "The Fringe Religions." *American Mercury*, April 1950, 53–58.

Smocovitis, V. Betty. "Unifying Biology: The Evolutionary Synthesis and Evolutionary Biology." *Journal of the History of Biology* 25 (1992): 1–65.

Solomon, Charles. *Enchanted Drawings: The History of Animation.* New York: Knopf, 1989.

Soule, Michael E. "The Social Siege of Nature." In *Reinventing Nature: Responses to Postmodern Deconstruction,* edited by Michael E. Soule and Gary Lease. Washington, D.C.: Island Press, 1995.

———, and Gary Lease, eds. *Reinventing Nature: Responses to Postmodern Deconstruction.* Washington, D.C.: Island Press, 1995.

Steele, Brandt. "Notes on the Feeding Habits of Carrion Beetles." *Journal of the New York Entomological Society* 35 (1927): 1–27.

Steffen, Albert, and Percy MacKaye. *In Another Land.* Dornach, Switzerland: Verlag für Schöne Wissenschaften, 1937.

Steiner, Rudolf. *An Autobiography.* 1925. Reprint, Blauvelt, N.Y.: Garber Communications, 1977 [latest reissue, 1999].

———. "Changes in Humanity's Spiritual Make-Up," in *Fall of the Spirits of Darkness.* Bristol, England: Rudolf Steiner Press, 1993.

———. *The Course of My Life.* Hudson, N.Y.: Anthroposophic Press, 1986.

———. *Curative Education.* Bristol, England: Rudolf Steiner Press, 1993.

———. *Destiny or Karma.* London: Harry Collison, 1931.

———. *Esoteric Christianity and the Mission of Christian Rosenkreuz.* London: Rudolf Steiner Press, 1984.

———. *Eurythmy as Visible Music.* New York: Anthroposophic Press, 1956.

———. *Eurythmy as Visible Speech.* New York: Anthroposophic Press, 1956.

———. *Goethean Science.* 1883–1897. Reprint, Spring Valley, N.Y.: Mercury Press, 1988.

———. "How Old Is History," pt. 3. *Anthroposophic News Sheet* 2, no. 51/2 (1934): 31, 33. Text of a lecture given October, 21, 1917, in Dornach, Switzerland.

———. *The Influence of Spiritual Beings Upon Man.* New York: Anthroposophic Press, 1961.

———. *The Inner Aspect of the Social Question.* London: Anthroposophic Publishing Company, 1950.

———. *In the Changed Conditions of the Times.* New York: Anthroposophic Press, 1941.

———. *The Karma of Human Vocation in Connection with the Life of Goethe.* 1916. Reprint, New York: Anthroposophic Press, 1944.

———. *Karmic Relationships: Esoteric Studies.* Vol. 1. Bristol, England: Rudolf Steiner Press, 1972.

———. *Karmic Relationships: Esoteric Studies.* Vol. 5. 1924. Reprint, London: Rudolf Steiner Press, 1966.

———. "The Meaning of Art in Ancient Times and Today." *Anthroposophical Review* 4, no. 29 (1927): 227–29.

———. *A Modern Art of Education.* 1928. Reprint, London: Rudolf Steiner Press, 1972.

———. *Mysticism at the Dawn of the Modern Age.* 1901. Reprint, Blauvelt, N.Y.: Rudolf Steiner Publications, 1980.

———. *Nature and Our Ideals.* 1880. Reprint, Spring Valley, N.Y.: Mercury Press, 1983.

———. "The Nature of Butterflies" (October 8, 1923). Manuscript translation from Rudolf Steiner Library, Ghent, N.Y.

———. *Nature Spirits.* London: Rudolf Steiner Press, 1992.

———. *An Occult Physiology.* 1951. Reprint, London: Rudolf Steiner Press, 1983.

———. *Occult Science: An Outline.* 1909. Reprint, New York: Anthroposophic Press, 1997.

————. *The Philosophy of Spiritual Activity*. 1894. Reprint, New York: Anthroposophic Press, 1986.

————. *The Reappearance of Christ in the Etheric*. New York: Anthroposophic Press, 1983.

————. *Riddles of Philosophy*. 1914. Reprint, New York: Anthroposophic Press, 1974.

————. *A Theory of Knowledge Based on Goethe's World Conception*. 1886. Reprint, New York: Anthroposophic Press, 1968.

————. *The Threefold Commonwealth*. 1922. Reprint, New York: Anthroposophic Press, 1943.

————. *The Threefold Social Order*. New York: Anthroposophic Press, 1966.

————. *Towards Social Renewal: Basic Issues of the Social Question*. London: Rudolf Steiner Press, 1977.

————. *Truth and Knowledge*. 1892. Reprint, Blauvelt, N.Y.: Rudolf Steiner Publications, 1981.

————. *The Way of Initiation, or How to Attain Knowledge of the Higher Worlds*. London: Theosophical Publishing Society, 1908.

————. *A Western Approach to Reincarnation and Karma: Selected Lectures and Writings by Rudolf Steiner*. Edited by René Querido. Hudson, N.Y.: Anthroposophic Press, 1997.

————. *Wonders of the World, Ordeals of the Soul, Revelations of the Spirit*. London: Rudolf Steiner Press, 1963.

————. *World Economy: The Formation of a Science of World Economics*. 1922. Reprint, New York: Anthroposophic Press, 1944.

————. *World Ether-Elemental Beings-Kingdoms of Nature*. Edited by Ernst Hagemann. Spring Valley, N.Y.: Mercury Press, 1992.

————. *The Wrong and Right Use of Esoteric Knowledge, or Secret Brotherhoods*. Bristol, England: Rudolf Steiner Press, 1966.

Straton, John Roach. "The Fancies of the Evolutionists." *Forum* 75 (1926): 245–51.

Stutfield, H. E. M. "Nature Mysticism." *Living Age* 323 (1924): 261–66.

Takacs, David. *The Idea of Biodiversity: Philosophies of Paradise*. Baltimore: Johns Hopkins University Press, 1996.

Thomas, John L. "Lewis Mumford, Benton MacKaye, and the Regional Vision." In *Lewis Mumford: Public Intellectual*, edited by Thomas P. Hughes and Agatha C. Hughes. New York: Oxford University Press, 1990.

Tompkins, Peter. *The Secret Life of Nature: Living in Harmony with the Hidden World of Nature Spirits from Faeries to Quarks*. San Francisco: HarperCollins, 1997.

Torrey, Raymond H., Frank Place Jr., and Robert L. Dickinson. *New York Walk Book: Suggestions for excursions afoot within a radius of fifty to one hundred miles of the city and including Westchester County, the Highlands of the Hudson and the Ramapo, northern and central New Jersey and the New Jersey Pine Barrens, Long Island, the Shawangunk Range, the Catskills, and the Taconics*. New York: American Geographical Society, 1923.

Trent, Robert W. *Inventing the Feeble-Mind: A History of Mental Retardation in the United States*. Berkeley: University of California Press, 1994.

Turner, Frank Miller. *Between Science and Religion: The Reaction to Scientific Naturalism in Late Victorian England*. New Haven: Yale University Press, 1974.

Tytus, G. S. "Twilight of Experience." *Forum* 52 (1914): 100–108.

Valentine, Kenneth F. "My Memories of SSI." *Trailside Museum and Zoo Historical Papers*, Historical Series, no. 9 (1991).

Vinikas, Vincent. *Soft Soap, Hard Sell: American Hygiene in an Age of Advertisement*. Ames: Iowa State University Press, 1992.

Wachsmuth, Guenther. *Die ätherische Welt in Wissenschaft, Kunst und Religion*. Dornach, Switzerland: Philosophisch-Anthroposophischer Verlag am Goetheanum, 1927.

―――. *The Etheric Formative Forces in Cosmos, Earth and Man: A Path of Investigation into the World of the Living*. 1924. Reprint, New York: Anthroposophic Press, 1932.

―――. *The Evolution of Mankind: Cosmic Evolution, Incarnation on the Earth, the Great Migrations, Spiritual History*. 1953, Reprint, Dornach, Switzerland: Philosophic-Anthroposophic Press, 1961.

―――. *Reincarnation as a Phenomenon of Metamorphosis*. New York: Anthroposophic Press, 1937.

Waite, Arthur Edward. *The Occult Sciences: A Compendium of Transcendental Doctrine and Experiment*. New York: Dutton, 1923.

Wheeler, H. E. "Psychological Case Against the Fairy Tale." *Elementary School* 29 (1929): 754–55.

White, Richard. *The Organic Machine: The Remaking of the Columbia River*. New York: Hill and Wang, 1995.

―――. "Environmental History, Ecology, and Meaning." *Journal of American History* 76 (1990): 1111–16.

Whiteley, Opal. "Journal of an Understanding Heart." *Atlantic Monthly* 125 (1920): 289–98, 445–55, 639–50, 772–82; 126 (1921): 56–67, 201–3.

Whitin, E. Stagg. "The Opening of Harriman Park," *Independent* 71 (1911): 182–85.

"Who Is Opal Whiteley?" *Bookman* 53 (1921): 137–40.

Williams, Raymond. *Keywords: A Vocabulary of Culture and Society*. Oxford: Oxford University Press, 1983.

Williams, William Carlos. *The Collected Poems of William Carlos Williams, 1909–1939*. New York: New Directions, 1938.

Wilson, Edward O. *Consilience: The Unity of Knowledge*. New York: Knopf, 1998.

―――. *Naturalist*. Washington, D.C.: Island Press, 1994.

Wissler, Clark. "Pueblo Bonito as Made Known by the Hyde Expedition." *Natural History* 22 (1922): 343–54.

Wolch, Jennifer, and Jody Emel. *Animal Geographies: Place, Politics, and Identity in the Nature-Culture Borderlands*. New York: Verso, 1998.

Wolff, Otto. *The Etheric Body*. Spring Valley, N.Y.: Mercury Press, 1990.

Worster, Donald. "The Ecology of Order and Chaos." *Environmental History Review* 14 (1990): 1–18.

―――. *Nature's Economy: A History of Ecological Ideas*. Cambridge: Cambridge University Press, 1985.

Wright, R. Gerald. *Wildlife Research and Management in the National Parks*. Urbana: University of Illinois Press, 1992.

Wright, Willard H. "MacKaye Indulges in Impeccable Eugenics." *Los Angeles Times*, April 9, 1912.

Zelinsky, Wilbur. "On the Superabundance of Signs in Our Landscape." *Landscape* 31, no. 3 (1992): 30–38.

Zipes, Jack. *Fairy Tale as Myth: Myth as Fairy Tale*. Lexington: University Press of Kentucky, 1994.

INDEX

Abbe, Cleveland, 54

Adams, Charles C.: and Ecological Society of America, 5; at Trailside Museum, 75; plans for ecological survey of Palisades Interstate Park, 101

Alden, Coolidge, 97

Alexander, Samuel, 8

advertising: and nature study, 56–57; and John B. Watson, 80; influence on nature trail, 70–73

Agassiz, Louis, 120

Ahriman, 214, 215; and earth history, 181; as inspirer of eugenics, 139

Akashic Record, 212

albinism: in Ramapo region, 113–114

America: etheric geography of, 180–181

American Museum of Natural History, 48, 192, 195, 204; and Trailside Museum, 74–78; Naturalist philosophy at, 144; nature study program at, 52–56, 59, 61; Third International Congress of Eugenics at, 133–136

American Pageantry Association, 48

American Scenic and Historic Preservation Society, 26

Ames, Winthrop, 131–132

anthroposophy: and natural historical science, 12, 159–160; and nature study, 205–220; as knowledge system, 160–161; Percy MacKaye's encounter with, 173–176; theory of evolution of, 190–

191; theory of history of, 162–164, 165–166

anthroposophists: attitude toward natural science, 161

antimodernism: and anthroposophy, 162; of Percy MacKaye, 175–176

Appalachian Trail, 4, 47, 232–233; as dramatizer of nature, 38, 45; as exemplar of 'primeval,' 35–44; Benton MacKaye's ideal for, 42–47, 142–143; creation of, 35–40; Walt Whitman statue on, 85–86

Arcadian myth, 2–3, 4, 5–6, 14–15; and eugenics, 118–119; and nature study, 51–87; anthroposophical community's view of, 181–182; convergence with Naturalism, 143–144; Ehrenfried Pfeiffer's critique of, 219; replaces Christian faith, 49–50, 83–84

Arden House, 85, 115, 122, 124, 136, 137; Unity of Knowledge conference at, 221–226

Arden, New York: Parrott property at, 24–25

astral body: and animal form, 184, 186, 188–189, 192; and hallucinogenic drugs, 227–228; of snakes, 195; relationship to etheric body, 154; social insects and, 185

Atlantean epoch, 167–168; 177; equivalent to Cenozoic, 191

Kevin Dann has taught at Rutgers University and the University of Vermont and is the director of LandMarks Historical Research and Consulting in Woodstock, Vermont. He is the author of *Traces on the Appalachians: A Natural History of Serpentine in Eastern North America* and *30 Walks in New Jersey*, both available from Rutgers University Press, and *Bright Colors Falsely Seen: Synaesthesia and the Search for Transcendental Knowledge* (Yale University Press, 1998).